So you really want to learn

Science

Book 2

By W. R Pickering B.Sc., Ph.D., M.I.Biol., C.Biol., F.L.S.

Edited by Louise Martine B.Sc. (Lon)

ISEB
Independent Schools
Examinations Board

www.galorepark.co.uk

GALORE PARK

Published by ISEB Publications, an imprint of Galore Park Publishing Ltd,
19/21 Sayers Lane, Tenterden, Kent TN30 6BW
www.galorepark.co.uk

Text copyright © W. R. Pickering 2004
Illustrations copyright © Galore Park 2004
Illustrations by Graham Edwards
Cartoons by Ian Douglass

Typography and layout by Typetechnique, London W1
Printed and bound by Charlesworth Press, Wakefield
Cover design by GKA Design, London WC2H

ISBN: 978 1 902984 37 7

First published 2004
Reprinted 2005, 2006, 2007, 2008, 2009, 2010, 2010, revised reprint 2011,
2012, 2013

Details of other Galore Park publications are available at
www.galorepark.co.uk

ISEB Revision Guides, publications and examination papers may also be
obtained from Galore Park.

Photograph **p.211** © Dr D.A. Hodgson; Photograph **p.286** © Paul Battley

b = bottom, *m* = middle, *t* = top, *r* = right, *l* = left

Photographs also supplied by the Science Photo Library: **p.14***r* Claude Nuridsany & Marie Perennou;
p.14/ Dr Gopal Murti; **p.57***r* CNRI; **p.57/** D. Phillips; **p.88***r* Barbara Strnadova; **p.88/** Lawrence Lawry;
p.123, **p.384** Science Photo Library; **p.197***tl*, **p.131** Charles D. Winters; **p.194** Novosti; **p.197***tm* Alfred
Pasieka; **p.197***tr* Russ Lappa; **p.197***bl*, **p.197***br*, **p.159**, **p.235** Andrew Lambert; **p.197***bm* Martyn F.
Chillmaid; **p.202** Francoise Sauze; **p.212** Sidney Moulds; **p.428** Kent Wood; **p.317***t* Geoff Tompkinson;
p.317*b* Alex Bartel; **p.353**, **p.356** NASA; **p.359** George Post; **p.361** Jerry Shad; **p211**, **p.241** John Mead.

All other photographs are © W.R. Pickering

Acknowledgements

I should like to acknowledge the ideas for illustrations given to me by Zoe Panayi, Jenny Bowen, Jacquie Blundell and Amy Warburton – where would I be without ladies to organise my life! The production of the book was made immeasurably more straightforward by the editing skills of Louise Martine and the drawing talents of Graham Edwards. I should like to dedicate this volume to Barbara and Bill, my Mum and Dad – without them none of this would have been possible (see page 31 for further explanation).

W. R. Pickering
August 2004

The publishers would like to thank David Penter, Richard Balding and Sue Hunter for their invaluable comments during the production of this book. They would also like to thank Charlie Grover for his outstanding attention to detail in proof-reading this book.

New 2010 Common Entrance Syllabus

This edition incorporates the changes to the 2008 syllabus, for first examination in 2011/12.

Important Note for Teachers: Update in Energy Terminology

The syllabus for 2008 refers to 'internal thermal energy'. It is no longer desirable to use 'heat' as a noun or adjective as in the term 'heat energy'. Strictly, the energy that an object has due to its temperature should be called its 'internal energy'. When an object is heated, 'thermal energy' flows into it thus increasing its 'internal energy'. So the **flow** of what used to be called 'heat energy' should be called 'thermal energy' and how much it actually has should be called its 'internal energy'. However, we consider this distinction between internal and thermal energy an unnecessary complication at this level. In *So you really want to learn Science Book 2* the term 'internal/thermal energy' has been used to indicate that either adjective is acceptable. This has been shortened to 'thermal energy' where the use of the full term would be awkward (in labelling some diagrams and where the term is used several times in a paragraph).

The energy stored by an object that has been bent, stretched or compressed has been described as 'elastic/strain (potential) energy' as either 'elastic' or 'strain' is acceptable and 'potential' is optional.

Tom Adams (Team Leader, ISEB Physics Panel)

Preface

I hope that Science Book 1 started you on the many adventures that make up the study of science. The book will have provided some of the basic factual content essential for scientists (it is important that you know some science). In addition, it should have explained to you the scientific way of thinking about experiments and results and, we hope, will have stimulated your imagination and enthusiasm so that you will want to find out more.

Science Book 2 will take both your knowledge and your understanding further. You will find out more about the structure of the body, and how cells carry out the life processes (this will help you to appreciate what scientists mean when they talk about stem cells). You will gain more insight into energy, and how the management of energy resources is one of the biggest challenges facing scientists and industry in the modern world. There is more information on the basic structure of matter (did you know that there are more molecules in a glass of water than there are humans on the Earth?), and about our place in the Universe. When your Year 9 studies are complete, you should be able to explain just how a satellite is important in transferring information from a football game in Brazil to a TV set in your living room, and how the electrical energy generated in a power station is made available to the same TV set.

All of these illustrations are examples of what is meant by **How Science Works**. How Science Works is now included as part of all science specifications, including the Common Entrance Syllabus, and we have addressed this throughout Science Book 2. How Science Works includes sections on

- **Scientific thinking**: using ideas to explain observations and to generate theories, and analysing evidence from experiments in a critical way. This includes a sub-section known as **critical understanding of evidence**, although this has a wider meaning as it includes the techniques of searching for information from both primary and secondary sources (with particular regard to 'searching' using ICT).

- **Applications and implications of science**: understanding how our knowledge of science can affect the way people think and behave, and considering the moral and ethical implications of science.

- **Cultural understanding**: realising that there are different approaches to scientific practice, and that our scientific knowledge includes contributions from different societies and cultures.

- **Practical and enquiry skills**: particularly the ability to plan and carry out valid experimental work, and to collect meaningful and reliable information.

- **Collaboration and communication**: the ability to share information with different branches of knowledge, and to use appropriate methods (including ICT) to communicate scientific information to groups of people, including non-scientists.

To help you with this important part of your scientific education, Science Book 2 identifies the examples of How Science Works with a clear 'mark' alongside the text in the appropriate sections in the book.

Science Book 2 also includes some new factual material. There are a few very tiny changes (for example, you will have to know a little more about where energy is released in cells), and there is a quite lengthy 'extra' section on the Exploration of Space. This extra section will not be examined in your CE papers, but it is so exciting that I knew you wouldn't want to miss it! You will be able to appreciate how not much more than half a century of scientific work has provided us with so much information and understanding about our Solar System and the rest of the Universe. Surely there will be days (actually, more likely that it will be nights – think why!) when you will look out into the sky and let your imagination go to work … one day, I could be there, you might think.

You make hundreds of decisions every day. You decide what to wear for exercise, what to eat, what type of battery to use in a portable appliance, how to work safely in a challenging environment, how your actions affect other members of your community and other living things in the environment you share with them, and how you can maintain a healthy lifestyle, for example. Studying science with Science Book 2 (paying particular attention to How Science Works) will help you to make more of these decisions in a more sensible way. I also strongly believe that you will continue to believe that science is fun and worth your time – you are the scientists of the future, and we're depending on you!

W. R. Pickering
April 2011

Contents

Materials and their properties

Energy, forces and space

Introduction

About this book

So you really want to learn Science Book 2 completes the syllabus for science at Key Stage 3 and is the second stage of an ISEB-approved course leading to Common Entrance at 13.

It covers all three sciences:

- **Life processes and living things:** Here you will continue your exploration and investigations into the lives of plants and animals. You will learn something about the ways in which different living organisms, including ourselves, all depend on one another for survival; and about how different organisms get their differences, and how they are passed on from generation to generation. You will also from time to time meet Felix the Helix, an interesting biological character who will help you to unravel some of the mysteries of life.

- **Materials and their properties:** This is where you will find out about the properties of different materials. You will see that many of these properties are explained by the fact that materials are made of tiny particles. Hydrogena Peroxide (Gena) understands much about the properties of materials, and is very good at explaining how different materials can react with one another.

- **Energy, forces and space:** Freddie Force the Biker Boy is really keen on this section. He is always trying to find out about the physical processes that affect his everyday life. He will do his best to explain about forces, electricity and magnetism, and the properties of light rays and sound waves.

Of course, scientists from the different areas of science work together so don't be surprised if any one of these characters turns up when you might not expect him to!

What is science?

As we go through this book we will continue to build on the scientific knowledge we have already gained. Remember that asking questions about the world around us is the first step to becoming a scientist. Carrying out experiments is a good way for scientists to start finding things out and to begin to answer some of the more challenging questions we have. You will already have got to grips with the idea of conducting fair tests when carrying out experiments and in this book we will give you the opportunity to do many more. You will also see some of the things we have found out from the results of experiments carried out by other scientists.

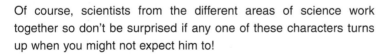

Investigations in science

Before we launch into this book it is worth pausing and taking some time to go over some of the rules we need to stick to in order that we can carry out experiments in a reliable way. This section will show you:

- why scientists carry out experiments;
- what we mean by a variable;
- what we mean by a fair test;
- how we measure variables;
- how we can record and display our results;
- how we can spot a pattern in our results; and
- how we draw a conclusion from our results.

What is an experiment?

Every day we make hundreds of observations; for example 'it's raining again', 'that car is moving faster than the other one', 'that tree looks bigger today' or 'some of the pet mice are bigger than the others'. When we think like a scientist we might try to give some sort of *explanation* for what we observe. We might think that some mice are bigger than others because of what they eat. An **experiment** is a way of collecting information to check out our explanations. Before a scientist begins an experiment, he or she will have a definite **purpose** or **aim**. The aim of an experiment is a way of stating carefully what you are trying to find out.

The aim of an experiment

I'm going to do an experiment.

My aim is to investigate the effect of protein on the growth of mice.

Say **exactly** what you will do, not just: "studying mice" or "changing the diet for mice."
The aim should say **why** you are doing the experiment.

What about variables?

An experiment has the aim of investigating the effect of one factor (protein in the diet, for example) on another factor (weight, for example). These factors can have different values, and so are called **variables**. In our experiment we can change the **values** of these variables, so we might give one group of mice more protein than we give another group. Anything that we can measure is a variable.

The experiment must be a fair test

An experiment will not be a **fair test** if you change more than one variable at a time. So **only change one variable** at a time. Here are the steps you should follow before conducting an experiment.

Step 1:   Identify the variables. Variables are factors that might affect the results.

Step 2:   Choose which variable you will change. This is called the **input variable**.

Step 3:   Choose the variable that you think will be affected by changing the input variable. This is called the **outcome variable**.

Step 4:   Decide what equipment you will need to measure any changes. Then go ahead and carry out your experiment.

For example in Felix's experiment on the weight of mice, he must make sure it is a fair test by **only changing one variable at a time**. The weight of the mice might be affected by:

- how old they are;
- how much water they drink;
- other foods they eat; and
- how big their cage is.

If he wants to investigate how protein affects the weight of mice, all these other variables **must stay the same**.

Finally remember to **work safely**:

- always wash your hands after touching plants or animals;
- carry equipment carefully;
- don't run in the laboratory; and
- wear suitable clothing.

How we measure variables

During an experiment a scientist will change one variable. This is called the **independent (input) variable**. The scientist will want to find out if the change in this variable causes a change in another variable. This second variable is called the **dependent (outcome) variable**. To make sure that the experiment is a fair test, the scientist will also want to check that none of the other possible variables is changing. Scientists like you need special equipment to measure any changes in these variables. Some of these pieces of equipment, and what you would use them for, have already been described in *Science* Book 1. The table on the next page will give you a quick reminder:

Table 1: Measuring equipment for use in Science

Equipment	What it measures	Units (Symbol)
Forcemeter	force	newtons (N)
Balance	weight	grams (g)
Stopwatch	time	seconds (s)
Measuring cylinder	volume	millilitres (ml) and litres (dm³)
Ruler/tape measure	length	millimetres (mm) and metres (m)
Thermometer	temperature	degrees Celsius (°C)

Making a record of our results

Results (or **observations**) are a record of the measurements you have taken during an experiment. There are certain rules about the way you should show these results. They should be recorded in a table, like the one shown below:

Making a table of results

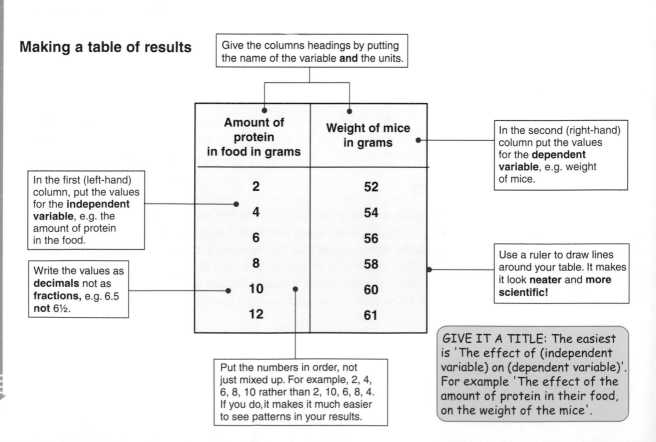

Give the columns headings by putting the name of the variable **and** the units.

Amount of protein in food in grams	Weight of mice in grams
2	52
4	54
6	56
8	58
10	60
12	61

In the first (left-hand) column, put the values for the **independent variable**, e.g. the amount of protein in the food.

Write the values as **decimals** not as **fractions,** e.g. 6.5 **not** 6½.

In the second (right-hand) column put the values for the **dependent variable**, e.g. weight of mice.

Use a ruler to draw lines around your table. It makes it look **neater** and **more scientific!**

Put the numbers in order, not just mixed up. For example, 2, 4, 6, 8, 10 rather than 2, 10, 6, 8, 4. If you do, it makes it much easier to see patterns in your results.

GIVE IT A TITLE: The easiest is 'The effect of (independent variable) on (dependent variable)'. For example 'The effect of the amount of protein in their food, on the weight of the mice'.

When you look at your results, you may see a certain pattern. It might seem that the more protein a mouse gets in its diet, for example, the faster it grows.

● Your results will be more reliable if you carry out each test more than once, and then take an **average** of the results. Why? (I hear you ask). Just think about it. If you happen to get the greediest mouse this side of Timbuctoo, your results might be unusual. If you do the experiment with ten mice and work out the average weight, the results will be more reliable.

● If one or two of the results don't fit the pattern, the first thing to do is check your measurement. If your measurement was accurate, and you have the time, you can **repeat** the test to check the 'odd' result.

Displaying your results

Sometimes you can see a pattern in your results from the table you have made. It isn't always easy to spot a pattern directly from a table, and it may be better to look at them in another way. **Charts** and **graphs** display your results like pictures and they can make it very easy to see patterns, but only if they are drawn in the correct way. There are rules for drawing graphs and charts, just as there are rules for putting results into tables.

● First of all, look at the variables you measured. If both of the variables have numbers as their values, you should draw (sometimes we say 'plot') a **line graph**. If one of the variables isn't measured in numbers, you should choose a **bar chart**.

● You should always put the **independent variable** on the **horizontal** axis and the **dependent variable** on the **vertical** axis. If you don't do this, you can easily mix up the patterns between the two variables.

Make sure before you read on that you know how to draw a bar chart and a line graph. Hopefully you've had a lot of practice, not only in your science lessons but in your maths lessons too.

Using graphs

A graph can let you see a pattern between two variables. For example, as protein in their diet increases, so does the weight of mice. The graph can also let you make **predictions** if it shows an obvious pattern. So, you might be able to predict how much a mouse would weigh if it were fed on a diet containing a certain amount of protein.

Just before we look at how to do this using a graph, it is worth making an important point about predictions. It is in fact very useful indeed to make some of your own predictions even **before** you get started on your experiment. If you do this, it can help you to plan much better experiments. If we take the example of looking at the effect protein has on the weight of the mice eating it, we can make a pretty good guess (a prediction) that the more we feed them the heavier they are likely to become. We can also start to plan what apparatus we will need and so on.

Right, now you know this you can have a look on the next page to see how we can use graphs to help make predictions. You may remember doing this in Book 1.

Using a graph to make a prediction

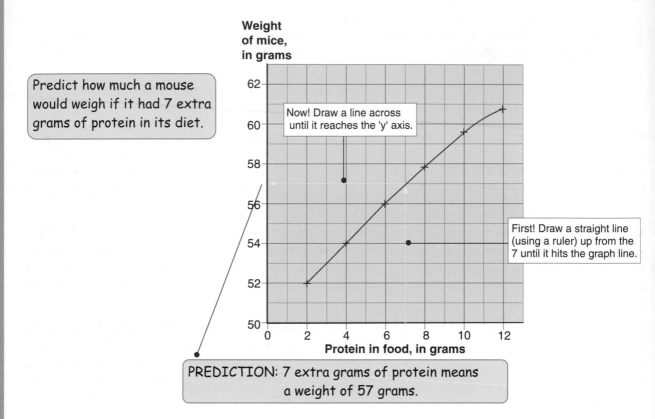

Predict how much a mouse would weigh if it had 7 extra grams of protein in its diet.

Now! Draw a line across until it reaches the 'y' axis.

First! Draw a straight line (using a ruler) up from the 7 until it hits the graph line.

PREDICTION: 7 extra grams of protein means a weight of 57 grams.

Making conclusions

Once you have collected all of your results into a table, and perhaps drawn a graph or chart, you need to sum up what you have found out. This summing up is called a **conclusion**, and here are some tips:

- **Your conclusion should be related to the aim of your experiment.**
  If your aim was to investigate the effect of light intensity on plant growth and you saw a clear pattern, then your conclusion might be that 'the higher the light intensity the taller the plant'.

- **Try to write your conclusion simply** (one sentence is often enough) but make sure it explains how the input variable affects the outcome variable for your experiment.

- **Don't just describe your results.**
  For example, in the experiment on mouse growth the statement 'a lot of protein in the diet makes a mouse heavy' is really giving only one of your results. A much better conclusion would be 'the greater the amount of protein in the diet, the heavier the mouse becomes'.

Chapter 1
Biology is the study of life and living organisms

Scientists believe that the Earth was formed from an enormous cloud of gases about 5 000 000 000 (5 billion) years ago. Conditions were harsh – there was no oxygen gas and the environment was very unstable. It is thought that there might have been rainstorms which lasted for hundreds of years, erupting volcanoes that could have caused tremendous temperature changes in some areas and certainly would have released great clouds of suffocating gases. Conditions were clearly very unsuitable for life as we know it!

Many scientists also believe that the first and simplest living organisms appeared on the Earth about 2 800 000 000 years ago. These simple organisms probably fed themselves from chemicals present in a sort of 'soup' (sometimes called the **primordial soup**) which made up some of the shallow seas on the Earth at that time. Scientists, philosophers and leaders of the world's religions ask the question: "What is the difference between these first living organisms and the molecules in the primordial soup?"

Everyone has some ideas about what living things do. Birds fly, horses run, fish swim and plants bend towards light. Most living things get taller, heavier and wider. They all seem to produce seeds or eggs, or give birth to live young. On the other hand, bricks, steel girders, car tyres and pieces of furniture don't do any of these things and so we say that they are non-living. It is not so easy to be definite about some other 'structures'. For example, is a dried-out seed or a virus particle living or non-living? To try to answer this type of question it is useful to make a list of characteristics which we might expect living organisms to have.

Characteristics of living organisms

All living organisms carry out these seven life processes:

- respiration;
- sensitivity (they respond to their environment);
- movement;
- nutrition (they nourish themselves);
- growth (they grow and develop);
- excretion; and
- reproduction.

The seven processes: The characteristics of life

Important!

Without **ENERGY** a living organism cannot carry out its life processes. When scientists check Moon dust for signs of life, they look to see if there's anything there that can carry out the process of **RESPIRATION**.

RESPIRATION: This is the process which releases energy from food. Plants and animals need energy for movement, growth and repair. Respiration usually needs oxygen (see page 45).

glucose + oxygen ⟶ carbon dioxide + water + energy

MOVEMENT: Animals use energy to move around in search of food, water, warmth and safety. Most plants are fixed by their roots. They move towards light, water and nutrients by growth. This is much slower than animal **locomotion** (see page 28).

GROWTH: Plants and animals grow from a single cell until they are adults. Animals usually stop growing at this stage but trees and other plants can keep growing until they cannot get enough nutrients from their surroundings (see Chapter 7).

EXCRETION: Nutrition and other processes produce waste material that cannot be used. Animals get rid of waste gases from their lungs. The kidneys keep the body free from impurities, they remove excess water from the blood and create a waste liquid called urine. Animals also excrete dissolved waste in sweat. Unused solid material is removed (**egested**) as faeces. Plants accumulate waste products in their leaves. These are excreted when the leaves fall from the plant.

NUTRITION: Plants and animals need food for energy and growth. Green plants make their own food from carbon dioxide and water by photosynthesis. Animals cannot make their own food so they eat organic food made by plants (see page 20).

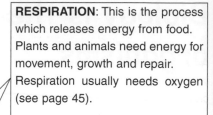

SENSITIVITY: All living things can sense and react to changes in the the environment. Animals react to temperature, light, sound, smell, taste and physical stimuli, e.g. being jabbed with a pin. Plants react by growing towards light, away from gravity. Some carnivorous plants react quickly when touched by an insect (see page 183).

REPRODUCTION: All living things can make new organisms like themselves. Simple organisms, such as bacteria, do this by splitting in half (**asexual reproduction**). Complex plants and animals reproduce **sexually** to produce fertilised eggs or seeds (see page 31).

Living organisms are made of cells

●   Living organisms have certain recognisable characteristics called life processes.

●   Living organisms depend on a supply of energy to keep their life processes going.

A living organism is made up of many different chemicals. Even the simplest organisms have the chemicals arranged into units called **cells**. Although cells may take on very specialised functions, they have certain common features which can be recognised in almost all of them. Each cell, whether it comes from a plant or an animal, has:

●   a **cell surface membrane** which surrounds the cell and separates it from its environment;

●   **cytoplasm** which provides the environment for most of the work of the cell, including respiration in mitochondria; and

●   a **nucleus** which contains the information to control the activities of the cell.

In **addition, plant cells**:

●   are surrounded by a **cellulose cell wall**;

●   often contain a fluid-filled **vacuole**; and

●   may have **chloroplasts** within the cytoplasm.

The *common features* of plant and animal cells allow these cells to carry out the basic processes necessary to remain alive. For example, within the cytoplasm there are small structures which can release energy from food, and within the nucleus the DNA is arranged in a way which allows the cell to control its own activities. The *differences* between plant and animal cells are due to the differences in lifestyle between animals and plants, especially in their different methods of nutrition. The diagram below shows a comparison of typical animal and plant cells.

Animal cell

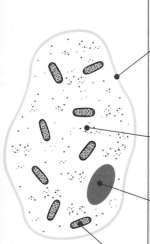

Plant and **animal cells** have **common features** which relate to carrying out life processes.

The CELL SURFACE MEMBRANE surrounds the cytoplasm. It controls the entry and exit of dissolved substances and is responsible for separating the cell's contents from its surroundings.

The CYTOPLASM contains water and dissolved chemicals. Most of the chemical reactions, such as respiration, go on in the cytoplasm.

The NUCLEUS contains the genetic material called DNA which makes up genes and chromosomes. The DNA carries the coded instructions controlling the activities and characteristics of the cell.

The MITOCHONDRIA are structures which carry out the release of energy, by respiration, from glucose and oxygen.

Plant cell

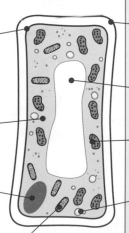

Special plant cell features often relate to **photosynthesis**.

The CELLULOSE CELL WALL is rigid (stiff) enough to support the cell but lets water and gasses pass through.

The LARGE VACUOLE helps to support the cell and can be used as a store for chemicals.

The CHLOROPLASTS contain the chlorophyll needed to absorb light energy for photosynthesis (see page 68).

The STARCH STORAGE GRANULES show that photosynthesis has been going on (see page 70).

The size of cells

Most animals' cells are quite small. In fact you could fit 40 to 50 of them into a 1 mm circle. Plant cells are bigger. You could only fit about 10 of them into a 1 mm circle. Both types of cell (plant and animal) are too small to be seen with your unaided eye. You need to use a microscope to see them (see page 14).

Large organisms are always **multicellular**; that is, they are made up of many cells. Different types of cell develop to carry out different tasks and functions – they have become *specialised*. Some examples of **specialised cells**, and the jobs which they carry out, are shown below:

Specialised cells are adapted to carry out one task very efficiently

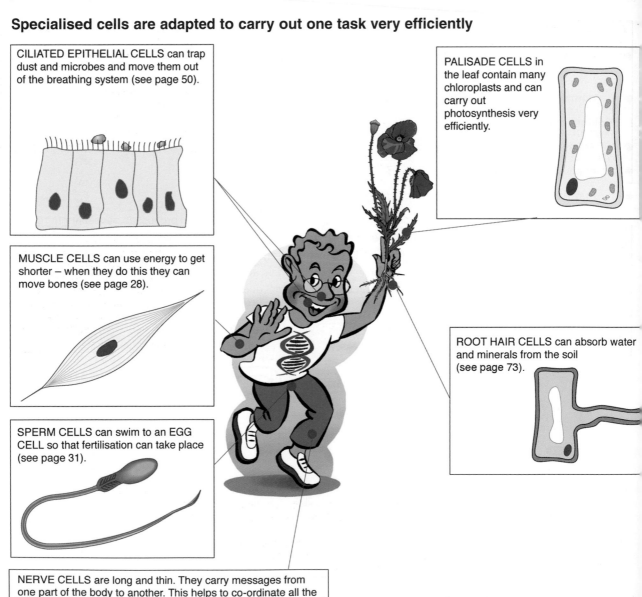

CILIATED EPITHELIAL CELLS can trap dust and microbes and move them out of the breathing system (see page 50).

PALISADE CELLS in the leaf contain many chloroplasts and can carry out photosynthesis very efficiently.

MUSCLE CELLS can use energy to get shorter – when they do this they can move bones (see page 28).

ROOT HAIR CELLS can absorb water and minerals from the soil (see page 73).

SPERM CELLS can swim to an EGG CELL so that fertilisation can take place (see page 31).

NERVE CELLS are long and thin. They carry messages from one part of the body to another. This helps to co-ordinate all the different activities around the body.

Cells which have similar structure and function are joined together into **tissues**, and several tissues may be combined to form an **organ**. An organ is a complex structure with a particular function. When the different jobs needed to keep a whole organism alive are separated into different cells, tissues and organs, we say that there is **division of labour**.

Cells, tissues and organ systems

Multicellular plants and animals contain many different types of cell. Each type of cell is designed for a particular function. Cells are organised to form tissues, organs and organ systems. In a **healthy** organism all systems work together.

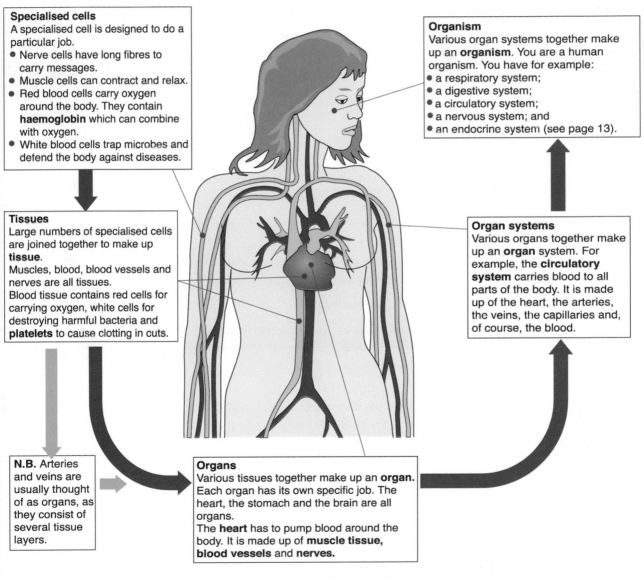

Specialised cells
A specialised cell is designed to do a particular job.
- Nerve cells have long fibres to carry messages.
- Muscle cells can contract and relax.
- Red blood cells carry oxygen around the body. They contain **haemoglobin** which can combine with oxygen.
- White blood cells trap microbes and defend the body against diseases.

Organism
Various organ systems together make up an **organism**. You are a human organism. You have for example:
- a respiratory system;
- a digestive system;
- a circulatory system;
- a nervous system; and
- an endocrine system (see page 13).

Tissues
Large numbers of specialised cells are joined together to make up **tissue**.
Muscles, blood, blood vessels and nerves are all tissues.
Blood tissue contains red cells for carrying oxygen, white cells for destroying harmful bacteria and **platelets** to cause clotting in cuts.

Organ systems
Various organs together make up an **organ** system. For example, the **circulatory system** carries blood to all parts of the body. It is made up of the heart, the arteries, the veins, the capillaries and, of course, the blood.

N.B. Arteries and veins are usually thought of as organs, as they consist of several tissue layers.

Organs
Various tissues together make up an **organ**. Each organ has its own specific job. The heart, the stomach and the brain are all organs.
The **heart** has to pump blood around the body. It is made up of **muscle tissue**, **blood vessels** and **nerves.**

In the most complex organisms certain tasks may be carried out by several different organs working together. These organs all belong to a particular **system**.

Even though there is **division of labour** between different parts of the body, the efficient working of a complete living organism means that each part must be aware of what the other parts is doing and all their activities must be co-ordinated.

Where do all the cells come from?

You began life as a single cell. This single cell is called a **zygote** (fertilised egg cell – see page 38). You are now made up of millions and millions of cells and the amazing thing is that every one of them came from that original zygote. The zygote was copied by a process called **cell division**.

Growth depends on cell division

A fertilised egg cell divides to make two **daughter** cells which are identical.

These divide to make **four** identical cells which divide again and again to make a ball of cells.

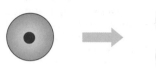    

HOW MANY DIVISIONS? Because every division doubles the number of cells, it only takes about 35 divisions to go from a fertilised egg to a whole organism.

WHAT CAN GO WRONG?

Once there are enough cells to carry out life processes, cell division should stop. CANCER can result if the cell division continues out of control. This can be due to:

- a mistake in the genes inside the nucleus; or

- something in the environment, such as tar in cigarette smoke.

At the same time as the cells were dividing to provide more 'building blocks' for your body, different groups of cells were taking on the special functions described in the diagram on page 10. So it is a combination of **cell division** and **cell specialisation** that made that original fertilised egg into the complete organism known as 'you'.

Development of a whole organism needs cell division and specialisation

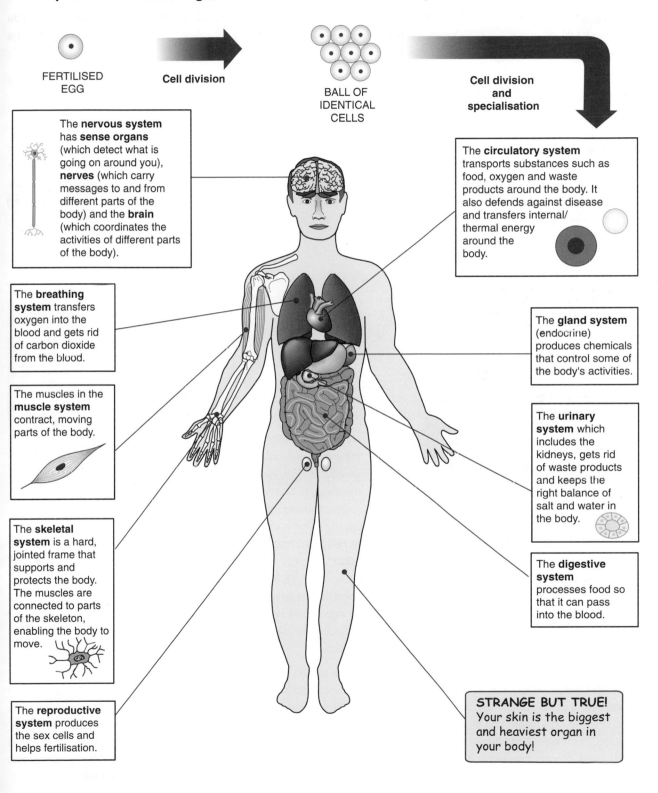

FERTILISED EGG

Cell division

BALL OF IDENTICAL CELLS

Cell division and specialisation

The **nervous system** has **sense organs** (which detect what is going on around you), **nerves** (which carry messages to and from different parts of the body) and the **brain** (which coordinates the activities of different parts of the body).

The **circulatory system** transports substances such as food, oxygen and waste products around the body. It also defends against disease and transfers internal/ thermal energy around the body.

The **breathing system** transfers oxygen into the blood and gets rid of carbon dioxide from the blood.

The **gland system** (endocrine) produces chemicals that control some of the body's activities.

The muscles in the **muscle system** contract, moving parts of the body.

The **urinary system** which includes the kidneys, gets rid of waste products and keeps the right balance of salt and water in the body.

The **skeletal system** is a hard, jointed frame that supports and protects the body. The muscles are connected to parts of the skeleton, enabling the body to move.

The **digestive system** processes food so that it can pass into the blood.

The **reproductive system** produces the sex cells and helps fertilisation.

STRANGE BUT TRUE! Your skin is the biggest and heaviest organ in your body!

It's a question of scale!

A human body consists of between 50 and 100 million million cells. Each of these cells is too small even to see with the unaided naked eye, so to *study* them clearly requires help. The instrument which is used to study cells is called a **microscope**.

- A microscope uses visible light to shine through a suitable **specimen**. A series of **lenses** then magnifies the image which is formed (see below).

- The specimen, such as a sample of cells, is very thin, so it needs to be supported on a thin glass **slide**.

- The slide and specimen are transparent and allow the visible light to pass through to the magnifying lenses. The contrast of the image can be improved by using dyes or stains to pick out certain structures in the cell. The nucleus of an animal cell, for example, shows up particularly well when stained with a dye called **methylene blue**. A typical light microscope can give a useful magnification of about 400 times, which means the image the viewer sees is actually 400 times larger than the specimen.

A light microscope

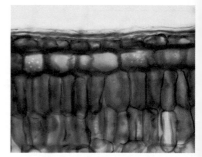

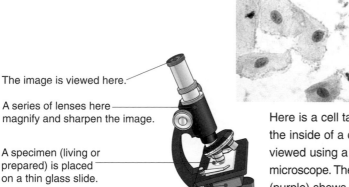

The image is viewed here.

A series of lenses here magnify and sharpen the image.

A specimen (living or prepared) is placed on a thin glass slide.

A source of visible light.

Here is a cell taken from the inside of a cheek, viewed using a light microscope. The nucleus (purple) shows up clearly using a stain. (It has been magnified 1000 times.)

Palisade cells in a holly leaf. These are the column-like cells beneath the top layer. Viewed using a light microscope. (It has been magnified 240 times.) A stain has been used on this sample.

In the late 1930s a new kind of microscope was invented. This used a beam of electrons rather than visible light and was therefore called an **electron microscope**. The image shows up on a fluorescent screen. It is much more powerful than a light microscope and can give a useful magnification of *around half a million times!* Enlarged to this extent, a single cell would cover an area the size of a football pitch.

Since we need a microscope to see a cell, we might ask ourselves how big a cell actually is. If you look at the edge of a typical school ruler, it is likely that you will see it divided into millimetres (mm) – a person with good eyesight can quite easily see an object which is one-tenth of a millimetre in length, but still cannot see an animal cell. A typical animal cell is about one-fiftieth of a millimetre in diameter, and a typical plant cell is about one-tenth of a millimetre in diameter. Tenths, twentieths and fiftieths are rather clumsy terms to use, so scientists more commonly use a system which deals with units of one thousand: one metre (m) contains one thousand millimetres (mm), one millimetre contains one thousand micrometres (μm or just μ). Thus a typical animal cell is about 20 μ (i.e. 1000/50) in diameter.

Key words

Cell – a building block of a living organism.

Tissue – a collection of cells that look the same and carry out the same function.

Organ – several tissues working together.

Multicellular – made up of many cells.

Microscope – an instrument that can be used to magnify very small objects, such as cells.

System – several organs that are connected to one another, so that one job can be carried out very efficiently.

Specialisation – how cells change their structure, so that they can carry out particular functions.

Exercise 1.1: Cells and tissues

1. This diagram shows a small group of cells from the stem of a plant.

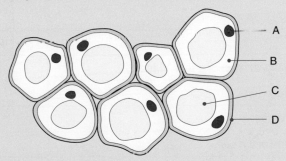

   (a) Identify the parts labelled A, B, C and D.

   (b) What do we call a group of similar cells with the same function?

   (c) Your teacher gives you a very thin slice of a stem. How would you get it ready for viewing under a microscope?

   (d) Suggest two ways in which these cells are different from typical animal cells.

   (e) Suggest one way in which these cells are different from typical leaf cells.

2. Organs can carry out their functions because of the special cells they have. Rearrange these lists to match up the correct cell with its function and process. Write out your answer as a table, with the three headings Cell, Function, Process.

Cell:	white blood cell	leaf cell	cell in the intestine	red blood cell
Function:	absorbs light	transports oxygen	traps microbes	produces enzymes
Process:	to prevent disease	to digest food	for photosynthesis	for respiration

3. The diagram below shows a plant cell.

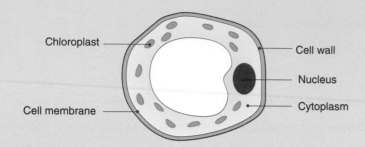

Chloroplast

Cell wall

Nucleus

Cytoplasm

Cell membrane

(a) The cell is a leaf cell. Give the name of the part which is present in this leaf but not present in root cells.

(b) Give two parts of the cell, labelled on the diagram, which are not present in animal cells.

(c) The five parts of the cell labelled on the diagram have different functions. Copy the table below and write the name of the correct part of the cell next to its function. The first has been done for you.

Function	Part of the cell
A place where many chemical reactions take place.	Cytoplasm
Photosynthesis takes place here.	
It controls the cell's activities.	
It helps to keep the shape of the cell.	
It controls substances entering and leaving the cell.	

Chapter 2
Nutrition: A balanced diet

All living organisms require **food** to carry out the processes essential for life. They need this food to supply:

- the **substances** which will be the raw materials for growth and for repair of damaged parts of the body;

- a **source of energy** to build these raw materials into cells and body parts; and

- **elements** and **compounds** which are needed for the raw materials and energy to be used efficiently.

All living organisms have these requirements. Some organisms, the green plants for example, can make their own food substances by combining carbon dioxide gas from the air with water and nutrients from the soil (see page 74). Other organisms *cannot* make their own food and must take in foods from their surroundings. Humans, like all other animals, are totally dependent on other organisms for their supply of food substances.

The total of all of these food substances or **nutrients** is called the **diet**. A healthy diet provides a human with the *balanced* selection of nutrients which it needs to carry out its life processes.

A balanced diet should contain the following seven ingredients:

- **Carbohydrates** should supply most of the energy we need. They include **starches** and **sugars**, such as **glucose**. Starches are usually better than sugars because: the body breaks them down more slowly, so we feel full for longer; and they don't cause problems such as tooth decay.

  Carbohydrates should make up about 70% of the solid part of our diet. No more than 25% of this should be sugars. One chocolate bar and a single fizzy drink could easily contain all of the sugar you need for a day. (Examples: bread, pasta, cereals, rice, biscuits, cakes, sweets.)

- **Proteins** are needed for the growth and repair of cells. We need proteins particularly while we're growing, or when we are getting over an illness or injury. Pregnant women need to eat enough protein for themselves *and* for their growing baby. (Examples: fish, meat, milk, eggs, beans.)

- **Fats** supply energy. We can store lots of fat beneath our skin, where it can act as padding and help to keep us warm. Fats contain more energy than carbohydrates and we need to be careful that we don't eat too many fatty foods. These might make us put on too much weight and can cause damage to the heart and the circulation. There's too much fat in chips and crisps and even lean meat has a lot of hidden fat. Full cream milk, milk chocolate and ice cream also contain fat. (Examples: milk, cheese, butter, cooking oil, meat.)

- **Minerals** are substances that usually combine with another food to form parts of the body. For example, we need **calcium** (found in milk) to make strong teeth and bones and **iron** for producing the red blood cells. They are usually taken in with other foods, especially meats. (Examples: meat such as liver, milk, vegetables.)

- **Vitamins** are substances which are needed in very small amounts, but are crucial for the body to be able to use other nutrients efficiently. There are many of them and they are usually taken in with other foods, especially dairy products. One of the most important is **vitamin C**. Citrus fruits such as oranges and lemons provide vitamin C. Without this vitamin we get bleeding gums and loose teeth and are more likely to catch a cold. (Examples: fruit, vegetables.)

- **Water** forms about 70% of the human body. Two-thirds of this water is in the cells, the other third is in blood. Humans lose about 1.5 litres of water each day, in urine, faeces, exhaled air and sweat. This lost water must be replaced by water in the diet. We replace this water in two main ways: as a drink and in food, especially in salad foods like tomato and lettuce.

- **Dietary fibre** is the indigestible component of the food which comes largely from plant cell walls. It provides bulk for the faeces. As a result the muscles of the intestines are stretched and can push the food along. A shortage of fibre can cause constipation and may be a factor in the development of bowel cancer. (Examples: whole grain bread, cereals, fruit, vegetables.)

If the diet does not provide all the nutrients in the correct proportions, the person may suffer from **malnutrition**. The diagram below shows a food pyramid. It can help you to achieve a **balanced diet** by showing us the amounts of different foods we should choose to eat each day.

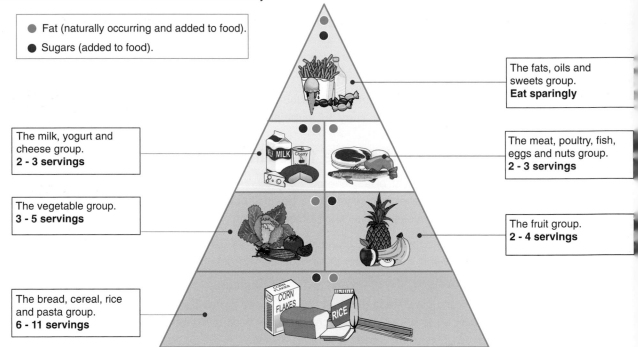

- Fat (naturally occurring and added to food).
- Sugars (added to food).

The fats, oils and sweets group.
Eat sparingly

The milk, yogurt and cheese group.
2 - 3 servings

The meat, poultry, fish, eggs and nuts group.
2 - 3 servings

The vegetable group.
3 - 5 servings

The fruit group.
2 - 4 servings

The bread, cereal, rice and pasta group.
6 - 11 servings

Testing foods for starch

Starch is an important food source for humans. There is a simple test that can be used to tell us whether a certain food contains starch or not. This test uses **iodine solution**. The iodine solution gives a dark blue-black colour when it is mixed with a food containing starch.

Iodine test for starch

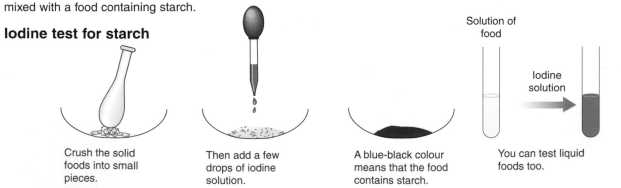

Solution of food

Iodine solution

Crush the solid foods into small pieces.

Then add a few drops of iodine solution.

A blue-black colour means that the food contains starch.

You can test liquid foods too.

Key words

Diet – all the nutrients supplied to the body.

Starch – a large carbohydrate molecule and the food store in many plant tissues.

Iodine – a chemical that reacts with starch to give a blue-black colour.

Malnutrition – the result of not receiving the correct balance of foods.

Exercise 2.1: A balanced diet

1. A balanced diet consists of water and six other substances. What are these six other substances?

2. Match up the words in the first list with the functions in the second. Choose the *best* match in each case.

    List 1 : fish; butter; spaghetti; milk; wholemeal bread; lettuce.

    List 2 : can provide a lot of our water needs; a good food for body-builders; a main source of energy; dairy product that can supply energy and some vitamins; helps prevent constipation; excellent source of vitamins and minerals – an ideal baby food.

3. The table below shows the mass of water, fat, fibre and vitamin C in 100g of potato. The potatoes have been cooked in three different ways.

	Water in grams	Fat in grams	Fibre in grams	Vitamin C in milligrams
100 g of chips	57	7	2	9
100 g of boiled, peeled potatoes	80	hardly any	1	6
100 g of potato baked in its skin	63	hardly any	3	14

    (a) Use this information to help you fill in the gaps in the following sentences.

        (i)   Chips are crisper than boiled potato because chips contain **less** ....

        (ii) Most of the fibre in a potato is in the .... of the potato.

    (b) Use the information in the table to work out how much vitamin C there is in:

        200 g of chips: .... mg.

        200 g of potato baked in its skin: .... mg.

    (c) People do **not** always eat a balanced diet. Match the facts about a person's diet to the organ(s) it harms.

Fact about the diet	Organ harmed
Not enough calcium	Heart
Not enough fibre	Intestine
Too much fat	Lung
	Bones

Nutrition provides a supply of usable food molecules

Nutrition involves a sequence of processes

Food molecules are obtained from the environment. Often these molecules are not in the form needed by a living organism to carry out its life processes. The processes of nutrition must change these food molecules into the sort of molecules that can be used by the living organism. This transformation process takes place in a specialised region of the body called the **alimentary canal** or sometimes simply referred to as the **gut**. The alimentary canal is really a tube, which runs from the front end of the animal (its **mouth**) to the rear end (its **anus**). While the food is still inside the tube it is not actually available to the body tissues. The food molecules must be changed, so that they can cross the gut wall and then be transported to the places where they will be used or stored. The processes which make up nutrition are described below.

There are several stages in nutrition

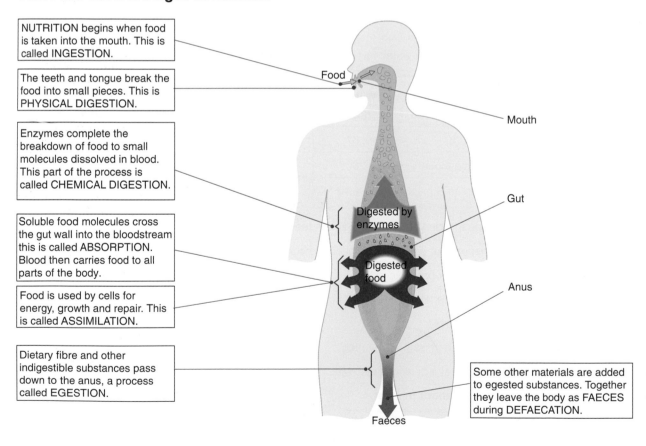

NUTRITION begins when food is taken into the mouth. This is called INGESTION.

The teeth and tongue break the food into small pieces. This is PHYSICAL DIGESTION.

Enzymes complete the breakdown of food to small molecules dissolved in blood. This part of the process is called CHEMICAL DIGESTION.

Soluble food molecules cross the gut wall into the bloodstream this is called ABSORPTION. Blood then carries food to all parts of the body.

Food is used by cells for energy, growth and repair. This is called ASSIMILATION.

Dietary fibre and other indigestible substances pass down to the anus, a process called EGESTION.

Some other materials are added to egested substances. Together they leave the body as FAECES during DEFAECATION.

Food

Mouth

Gut

Digested by enzymes

Digested food

Anus

Faeces

Although the alimentary canal is really just a tube running from the mouth to the anus, it has become very specialised in humans. These specialisations mean that the food molecules can be changed to a useable form in a very clear sequence. Each part of the gut is adapted to carry out particular functions. The layout of the alimentary canal, and of the important organs that work with it, is shown below.

The human gut

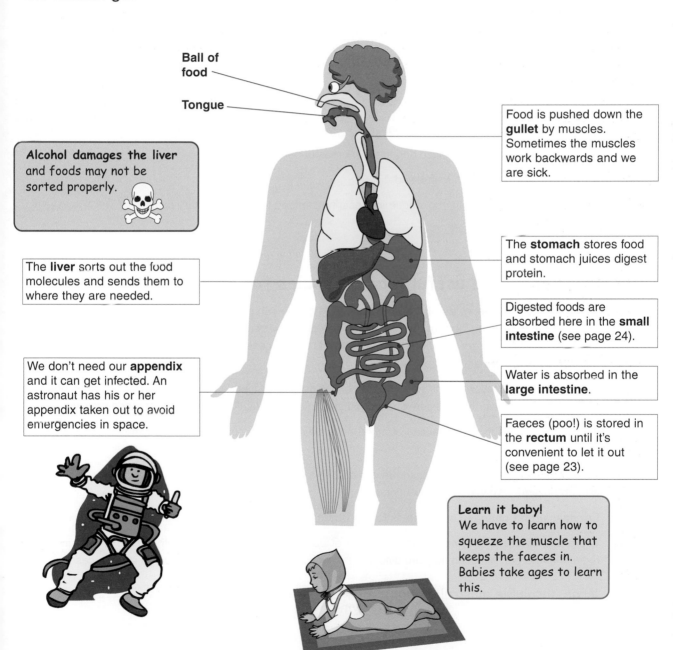

Ball of food

Tongue

Food is pushed down the **gullet** by muscles. Sometimes the muscles work backwards and we are sick.

Alcohol damages the liver and foods may not be sorted properly.

The **liver** sorts out the food molecules and sends them to where they are needed.

The **stomach** stores food and stomach juices digest protein.

Digested foods are absorbed here in the **small intestine** (see page 24).

We don't need our **appendix** and it can get infected. An astronaut has his or her appendix taken out to avoid emergencies in space.

Water is absorbed in the **large intestine**.

Faeces (poo!) is stored in the **rectum** until it's convenient to let it out (see page 23).

Learn it baby!
We have to learn how to squeeze the muscle that keeps the faeces in. Babies take ages to learn this.

Ingestion provides food for the gut to work on

Food molecules must be taken into the gut before they can be fully processed for use by the organism. Once the food has been caught or collected, and perhaps cooked or processed in some other way, it is placed in the mouth. Here it is cut up by the **teeth** and the pieces are mixed with **saliva** by the **tongue**. This **chewing** produces a ball of food which can then be swallowed and so passed on to further parts of the gut. It is clear that the teeth play an important role in this chewing process. Remember:

● The structure of a tooth is closely related to its function.

● There are different types of teeth to deal properly with all types of food. Test yourself to see if you can remember the names of the different teeth, their design and the function they perform.
(See **Science** Book 1 chapter 2)

Before we move on to the next stage in nutrition, just make sure you have mastered and understood the following:

● the several stages that take place during the process of nutrition;

● the basic layout of the human gut; and

● the part played by the teeth and tongue in preparing the food for the alimentary canal.

Digestion prepares useful food molecules for absorption

A healthy diet contains three types of food molecule in large amounts – carbohydrates, proteins and fats. These molecules are often in an unsuitable form when they are eaten. They may be too large to cross the gut wall and often they won't dissolve in the watery blood plasma. **Digestion** is the process which converts these ingested foods into a form which *can* be absorbed and transported.

As we have just seen, digestion begins with the teeth chopping the food into smaller pieces. This is sometimes called **physical digestion** because the foods aren't changed into anything else; the pieces are just made smaller.

Complete digestion depends on the action of other molecules called **enzymes**. These enzymes are really amazing molecules:

● They can really **speed up** the breakdown of foods. This breakdown can be more than ten thousand times faster with an enzyme involved than without one.

● Enzymes **aren't changed** by the breakdown process, so they can be used over and over again.

● There are **different** enzymes for the digestion of each food type and each of them works best in different regions of the gut. Although they are different, the basic digestive process is the same in each case:

large, insoluble molecule + water $\xrightarrow{\text{enzyme}}$ small, soluble molecule

For example,

starch + water $\xrightarrow{\text{amylase}}$ simple sugars

How enzymes work in digestion

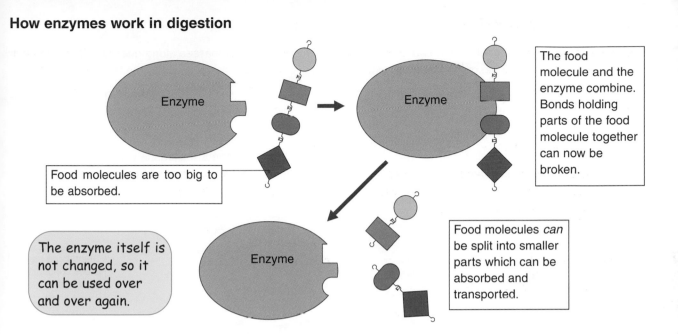

Food molecules are too big to be absorbed.

The food molecule and the enzyme combine. Bonds holding parts of the food molecule together can now be broken.

The enzyme itself is not changed, so it can be used over and over again.

Food molecules *can* be split into smaller parts which can be absorbed and transported.

Egestion removes undigested food

The ingested food may contain some molecules which cannot be digested by the enzymes of the human gut. Usually these are molecules in plant foods, such as the cellulose in cell walls and the woody parts in stems and roots (see page 73). Once the water has been absorbed from the soupy material remaining in the gut, this indigestible food must be expelled. This process is called **egestion**. Some excreted materials, such as the remains of some worn-out blood cells, may be added to these indigestible foods to form the **faeces**. The faeces are stored for a short time in the rectum. Eventually the full rectum sets off a reflex action which causes the muscles of this part of the gut to contract and squeeze the faeces out of the anus. Humans have a ring of muscle called a sphincter at the anus which can prevent this defaecation occurring at an inconvenient time. The control of this sphincter has to be learned. Babies simply fill their nappies when the rectum is full.

Remember these important points:

- Digestion converts large insoluble molecules into smaller, soluble molecules ready for absorption.

- Enzymes speed up the breakdown of food.

- Undigested food must be passed out of the gut.

Absorption transfers food molecules to the blood

Enzymes act on foods and provide molecules that can dissolve in the watery blood plasma. These soluble molecules can now cross the lining of the gut into the bloodstream. This process is called **absorption**. Once absorption has taken place, the food molecules can be carried in the blood to the parts of the body where they are needed. Most absorption occurs from the small intestine (alcohol, and possibly a small amount of glucose, can be absorbed from the stomach). The small intestine is very well adapted to carry out this job.

The small intestine

- **It is very long**, about 6m in an adult human, which means that food passes along quite slowly and there is adequate time for absorption to occur.

- The main adaptation, however, is that the inside lining of the small intestine is **very folded**. This means that the surface area for absorption is increased hugely compared to what it would be if the intestine were just a simple tube.

- On the folds, the small intestine has hundreds of thousands of tiny 'fingers', called the **villi**, which stick out into the liquid digested food.

The whole structure is thus adapted to increase absorption.

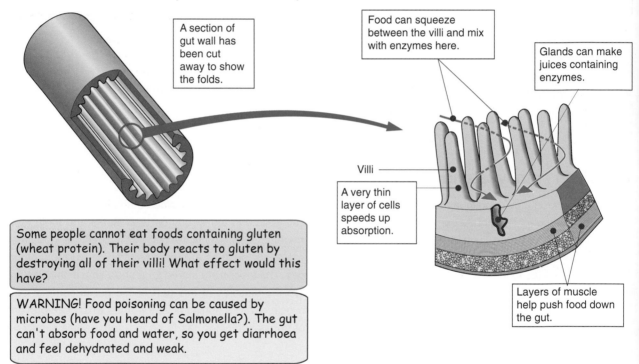

A section of gut wall has been cut away to show the folds.

Food can squeeze between the villi and mix with enzymes here.

Glands can make juices containing enzymes.

Villi

A very thin layer of cells speeds up absorption.

Layers of muscle help push food down the gut.

Some people cannot eat foods containing gluten (wheat protein). Their body reacts to gluten by destroying all of their villi! What effect would this have?

WARNING! Food poisoning can be caused by microbes (have you heard of Salmonella?). The gut can't absorb food and water, so you get diarrhoea and feel dehydrated and weak.

The contents of the gut are now not much more than a soup of water and indigestible matter. Most of the water is reabsorbed into the bloodstream from the large intestine. Some minerals and vitamins are also absorbed from the large intestine.

The liver and assimilation

Digested food is absorbed into the bloodstream. Each type of absorbed food has a particular function in the body, so it is important that food molecules of the right type are available at the right time in the right place. The **liver** plays the main part in 'sorting out' food molecules – all foods absorbed into the capillaries of the villi are sent to the liver before they go anywhere else.

The cells in the liver can carry out more than 500 different reactions. As a result of these activities the liver is able to provide ideal concentrations of food molecules for the working of the body tissues. Each type of tissue will use food molecules for different purposes. For example, muscle cells will manufacture muscle protein; bone cells will take up calcium to make bone and all cells will use glucose to release energy by respiration (see page 46). The processes of using up food molecules in these various ways are together called **assimilation**.

Key words

Alimentary canal – the long tube that runs from mouth to anus.

Ingestion – the taking of food into the alimentary canal through the mouth.

Digestion – the breaking down of large insoluble molecules into small soluble molecules.

Enzyme – a biological molecule that can speed up a reaction such as digestion.

Absorption – the transfer of digested foods across the wall of the gut into the blood.

Assimilation – the use of foods in the body.

Exercise 2.2: Digestion

1. Match up the words in the first column with the definitions in the second column.

Enzyme	The process of taking food into the gut.
Ingestion	Transferring digested food into the bloodstream.
Digestion	Removing indigestible materials from the gut.
Absorption	A molecule that speeds up the digestion of foods.
Egestion	Breaking food down into small, soluble particles (molecules).

2. Felix wanted to find out the effects of temperature on the action of an enzyme. He measured how long it took for an enzyme to digest a certain type of food, at different temperatures. This table contains the results of his experiment:

Temperature in °C	Time taken for reaction to occur in seconds
20	450
30	200
35	75
40	105
45	320
50	420

   (a) How would he check the temperatures in the different parts of the experiment?

   (b) Plot the results as a graph. Join the points with a curve and not with a straight line.

   (c) Which is the best temperature for the enzyme-controlled reaction to occur?

   (d) What is human body temperature? Use your graph to predict how long the reaction would take at human body temperature.

   (e) Predict how long the reaction would take to occur at 60 °C

   (f) Explain how Felix would have made sure that this experiment was a fair test.

Extension question

3. Felix and Gena got together to try to make a model gut. They used a cellulose tube, as shown in the diagram. The tube contained a mixture of saliva and starch.

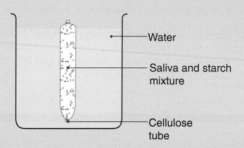

Water

Saliva and starch mixture

Cellulose tube

(a) How could they prove that starch was present at the start of the experiment?

(b) They believed that the saliva contained an enzyme that could break down starch. What would be the best temperature to keep the mixture, while this breakdown was going on?

(c) After twenty minutes they tested the contents of the model gut for starch. They got a negative result. Gena thought that this was because the starch had crossed the wall of the gut into the water. How could Felix try to prove that this wasn't the explanation?

(d) Felix and Gena eventually agreed that starch could not cross the wall of their model gut. Why can't starch cross in this way?

(e) In the body, what is represented by the water in the beaker?

Chapter 3
The functions of the skeleton

Humans are **vertebrates** which means they have a backbone and a bony skeleton. Bone is a hard tissue and cannot be compressed (squashed). This hardness is important in the functions of bone.

The **skeleton of any vertebrate** has certain important functions:

- **To provide support**: This is probably the most obvious of the skeleton's jobs. Air does not support soft tissues like muscle and so hard, incompressible bone must do this.

- **Protection of delicate tissues**: Vital tissues and organs can be protected from physical damage by a covering of bone. For example, the brain is protected from shock inside the skull and the heart and lungs are protected inside the ribcage.

- **To provide movement and locomotion**: Bone provides the levers operated by muscles. For this to happen there must be **joints** in the rigid skeleton.

The skeleton also has two other functions that don't depend on the hardness of bone:

- storage of calcium and some other minerals are stored in the bone; and

- production of blood cells takes place in the marrow inside some of the bones.

The functions of the human skeleton

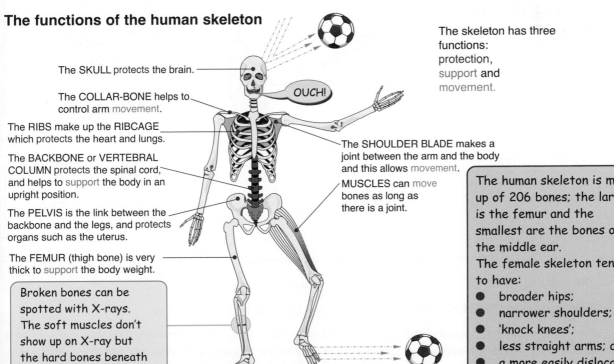

The SKULL protects the brain.

The COLLAR-BONE helps to control arm movement.

The RIBS make up the RIBCAGE which protects the heart and lungs.

The BACKBONE or VERTEBRAL COLUMN protects the spinal cord, and helps to support the body in an upright position.

The PELVIS is the link between the backbone and the legs, and protects organs such as the uterus.

The FEMUR (thigh bone) is very thick to support the body weight.

OUCH!

The SHOULDER BLADE makes a joint between the arm and the body and this allows movement.

MUSCLES can move bones as long as there is a joint.

The skeleton has three functions: protection, support and movement.

Broken bones can be spotted with X-rays. The soft muscles don't show up on X-ray but the hard bones beneath them do show up.

The human skeleton is made up of 206 bones; the largest is the femur and the smallest are the bones of the middle ear.
The female skeleton tends to have:
- broader hips;
- narrower shoulders;
- 'knock knees';
- less straight arms; and
- a more easily dislocated lower jaw compared to the male.

This should give you some idea of just how important the skeleton is. The skeleton is not simply a dead framework for the body. In the next section we consider one part of the skeleton in more detail and go on to show how it performs the function of movement.

Muscles, bones and movement

The hardness of the skeleton is ideal for support and protection, but for movement it is important that the different bones in the skeleton should not be completely locked in one place. The flexibility required is made possible by a series of **joints**. A joint is a part of the skeleton where two bones meet. There are several types of joint in the body. The joint that allows the greatest amount of movement is called the **synovial joint**. In this type of joint, the point where the two bones meet is protected by **cartilage** and the whole joint is wrapped up in a sac. This sac contains **fluid** which cushions the joint and feeds the tissues there.

A synovial joint allows free movement between bones

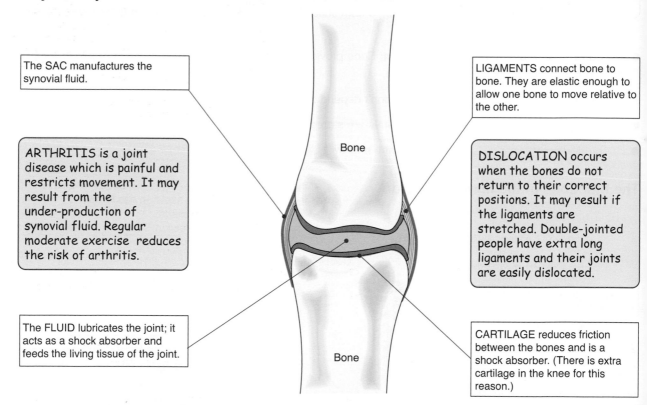

The SAC manufactures the synovial fluid.

LIGAMENTS connect bone to bone. They are elastic enough to allow one bone to move relative to the other.

Bone

ARTHRITIS is a joint disease which is painful and restricts movement. It may result from the under-production of synovial fluid. Regular moderate exercise reduces the risk of arthritis.

DISLOCATION occurs when the bones do not return to their correct positions. It may result if the ligaments are stretched. Double-jointed people have extra long ligaments and their joints are easily dislocated.

The FLUID lubricates the joint; it acts as a shock absorber and feeds the living tissue of the joint.

Bone

CARTILAGE reduces friction between the bones and is a shock absorber. (There is extra cartilage in the knee for this reason.)

The type and amount of movement possible at a synovial joint depends on:

● the shape of the bones at the point where they articulate (come together); and

● how much movement is allowed by the ligaments that bind the two bones together.

One of the most important features of these joints is that they largely look after themselves. The fluid that acts as a lubricant is usually secreted in exactly the correct amount to keep the joint operating smoothly and efficiently. Despite this, things can go wrong, as a result of an accident, disease, overweight or simply due to old age.

Muscle-bone machines

Movement, whether of the whole body, a single limb or even of an organ, involves **work**. A **machine** is a device for doing work and in a mammal muscles and bones work together as machines.

Muscles can only cause movement by **contracting** (shortening) – they cannot actively relax or push. Because of this, muscles must be arranged in pairs which have opposite actions – these are called **antagonistic pairs**. The diagram below shows the action of antagonistic muscles in the movement of a human forearm.

Muscles work in antagonistic pairs

TAKE NOTE! For muscles and bones to work as a machine the two opposite ends of **the muscle must be attached to different bones**. At the end of the muscle where the movement takes place **the tendon must always go across the joint.**

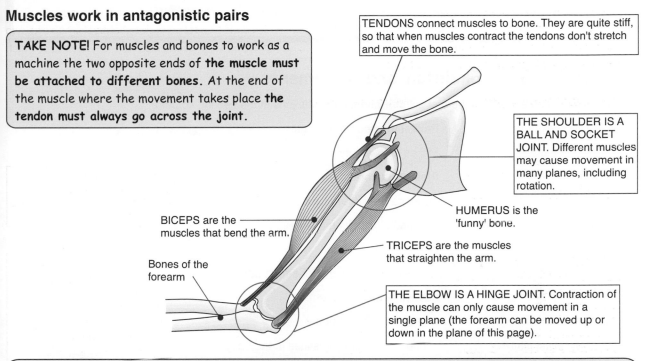

TENDONS connect muscles to bone. They are quite stiff, so that when muscles contract the tendons don't stretch and move the bone.

THE SHOULDER IS A BALL AND SOCKET JOINT. Different muscles may cause movement in many planes, including rotation.

HUMERUS is the 'funny' bone.

BICEPS are the muscles that bend the arm.

Bones of the forearm

TRICEPS are the muscles that straighten the arm.

THE ELBOW IS A HINGE JOINT. Contraction of the muscle can only cause movement in a single plane (the forearm can be moved up or down in the plane of this page).

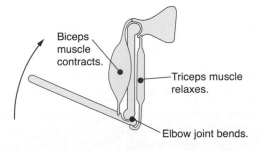 CRAZY BUT TRUE. The cheetah is the fastest animal on Earth. It runs so fast because it can take really big strides. It can do this by dislocating its shoulder joint with every stride. OUCH!

Antagonistic pairs of muscles are necessary for controlled movement at a joint. Muscles can only exert a force by **contraction**. The reversal of a muscular movement therefore requires contraction of an opposing (antagonistic) muscle.

A. Action of the biceps muscle bending

Biceps muscle contracts.

Triceps muscle relaxes.

Elbow joint bends.

B. Action of the triceps muscle

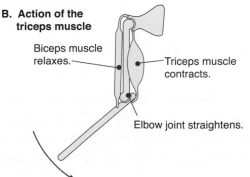

Biceps muscle relaxes.

Triceps muscle contracts.

Elbow joint straightens.

The biceps is a **flexor** and the triceps is the **extensor** of the elbow joint; together biceps and triceps make up an **antagonistic pair**.

Key words

Locomotion – the movement of the whole body from one place to another.

Arthritis – a disease of the joints.

Antagonistic pair – two muscles that have different effects on a joint – one contracts to bend the joint and the other contracts to straighten the joint.

Muscle – a tissue that can contract (shorten).

Exercise 3.1: Skeleton and movement

1. Match up the words in the first column with the descriptions in the second column.

The skeleton	Protect the heart and lungs.
Blood cells	Makes its own lubricating fluid.
Bone	Protects the brain.
Ligaments	Supports the softer tissues of the body.
Calcium	Are made inside some bones.
Tendons	Connect bone to bone.
The skeleton	Is an essential mineral for strong bones.
The skull	Has joints for movement.
The ribs	Connect muscle to bone.
A synovial joint	Is one of the hardest tissues in the body.
Cartilage	Reduces friction between the bones.

2. Explain the following:

    (a) The leg bones are stronger than the arm bones in humans.

    (b) Pregnant women should drink a lot of milk.

    (c) X-rays can be used to check for broken bones.

    (d) Scooter riders have to wear crash helmets by law.

    (e) Cartilage is essential in the knee joints.

3. Look back at the diagrams of the arm on page 29. Complete this paragraph by choosing the correct alternative word to fill in the gaps in the description of what happens when you bend your arm at the elbow.

    The biceps (CONTRACTS / RELAXES), thus becoming (LONGER AND THINNER / SHORTER AND FATTER). The triceps muscle is the (ANTAGONISTIC / SUPPORTING) muscle to the biceps and so it (CONTRACTS / RELAXES) and becomes (LONGER AND THINNER / SHORTER AND FATTER). If you straighten your arm, the (OPPOSITE / SAME) happens.

Chapter 4
Reproduction

No organism lives for ever. In order for species not to die out, individual organisms must be replaced. Living organisms use the process of **reproduction** to produce new members of their species. Humans, like all other mammals, only use **sexual reproduction**. Sexual reproduction involves the contribution of genetic information from two parents to produce a new individual.

Sexual reproduction involves a number of stages and, unless each of the stages is completed, sexual reproduction will be unsuccessful. The stages are:

Step 1. The development of the body, so that it can produce specialised sex cells, called **gametes** (**sperm** in the male, **ova** in the female).

Step 2. The development of sex organs, so that the gametes can be delivered by the male and received by the female.

Step 3. The joining together of the gametes at **fertilisation**, to produce a fertilised egg or **zygote**.

Step 4. The development of a place for the safe growth of the zygote into an **embryo**, a **fetus** and, eventually, a baby.

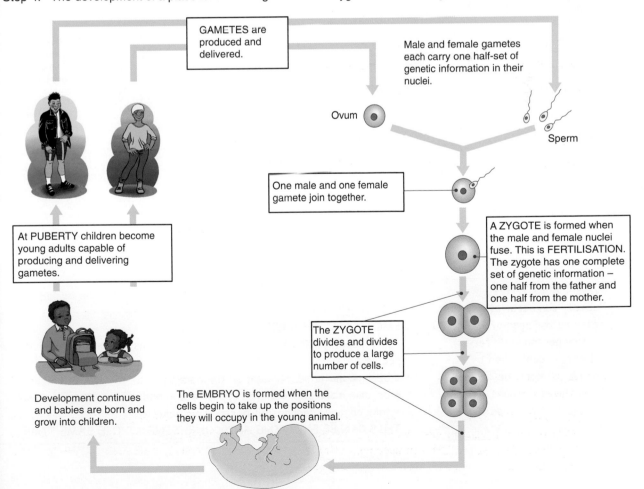

GAMETES are produced and delivered.

Male and female gametes each carry one half-set of genetic information in their nuclei.

Ovum

Sperm

One male and one female gamete join together.

At PUBERTY children become young adults capable of producing and delivering gametes.

A ZYGOTE is formed when the male and female nuclei fuse. This is FERTILISATION. The zygote has one complete set of genetic information – one half from the father and one half from the mother.

The ZYGOTE divides and divides to produce a large number of cells.

Development continues and babies are born and grow into children.

The EMBRYO is formed when the cells begin to take up the positions they will occupy in the young animal.

When a young human grows, he or she passes through a stage of development called **puberty**. At puberty, the body develops a reproductive system that can complete the stages of sexual reproduction. The changes at puberty are controlled by **sex hormones**. The signs that puberty has taken place are shown below.

Puberty is a time of change

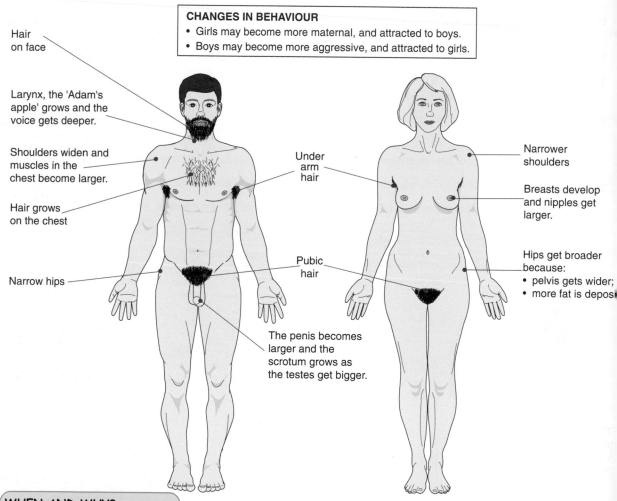

CHANGES IN BEHAVIOUR
• Girls may become more maternal, and attracted to boys.
• Boys may become more aggressive, and attracted to girls.

Hair on face

Larynx, the 'Adam's apple' grows and the voice gets deeper.

Shoulders widen and muscles in the chest become larger.

Hair grows on the chest

Narrow hips

Under arm hair

Pubic hair

The penis becomes larger and the scrotum grows as the testes get bigger.

Narrower shoulders

Breasts develop and nipples get larger.

Hips get broader because:
• pelvis gets wider;
• more fat is deposi

WHEN AND WHY?
Puberty can occur at any time between the ages of 10 and 20 – every person is different. Puberty is controlled by chemicals from the brain and from the sex organs. These chemicals are the **sex hormones**.

EMOTIONAL CHANGES
After puberty the period of **adolescence** begins. During this period young people:
● become more independent of their parents;
● become more aware of the opposite sex; and
● take on more responsibility for their behaviour.
THIS CAN BE EXCITING AND CONFUSING AT THE SAME TIME.

The male reproductive system

The male reproductive system is simpler than the female reproductive system. It really has only two functions – firstly, to make the male gametes and, secondly, to deliver them to the site of fertilisation. The male gametes, called spermatozoa or **sperm** for short, are made in the **testes**. These structures are enclosed inside a sac of skin called the **scrotum**, which hangs between the legs outside the body. In this position the testes are protected from physical damage, but more importantly are kept at a temperature 2 – 3 °C below body temperature. This lower temperature is ideal for development of the sperm. As well as making the sperm, the testes also produce the male sex hormone **testosterone**. This hormone is necessary for the action of the male sex organs and for controlling male sexual behaviour. Once the sperm have been made, they can be delivered to the site of fertilisation through the **penis**. To help their release and increase the chances of fertilisation, the sperm are released in a fluid, the **semen**.

The structure of the **male reproductive system** is illustrated below.

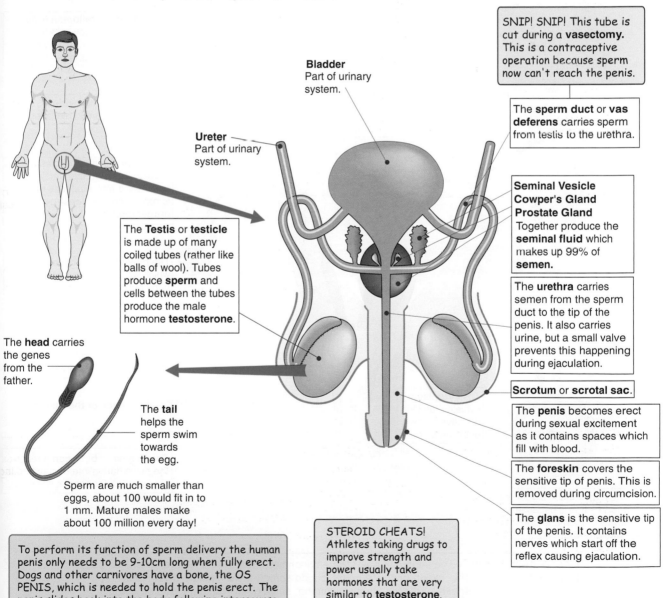

SNIP! SNIP! This tube is cut during a **vasectomy**. This is a contraceptive operation because sperm now can't reach the penis.

Bladder
Part of urinary system.

Ureter
Part of urinary system.

The **sperm duct** or **vas deferens** carries sperm from testis to the urethra.

Seminal Vesicle
Cowper's Gland
Prostate Gland
Together produce the **seminal fluid** which makes up 99% of **semen.**

The **Testis** or **testicle** is made up of many coiled tubes (rather like balls of wool). Tubes produce **sperm** and cells between the tubes produce the male hormone **testosterone**.

The **urethra** carries semen from the sperm duct to the tip of the penis. It also carries urine, but a small valve prevents this happening during ejaculation.

The **head** carries the genes from the father.

Scrotum or **scrotal sac**.

The **tail** helps the sperm swim towards the egg.

The **penis** becomes erect during sexual excitement as it contains spaces which fill with blood.

The **foreskin** covers the sensitive tip of penis. This is removed during circumcision.

Sperm are much smaller than eggs, about 100 would fit in to 1 mm. Mature males make about 100 million every day!

The **glans** is the sensitive tip of the penis. It contains nerves which start off the reflex causing ejaculation.

To perform its function of sperm delivery the human penis only needs to be 9-10cm long when fully erect. Dogs and other carnivores have a bone, the OS PENIS, which is needed to hold the penis erect. The penis slides back into the body following intercourse.

STEROID CHEATS! Athletes taking drugs to improve strength and power usually take hormones that are very similar to **testosterone**.

The female reproductive system

The reproductive system of the female is more complicated than that of the male. As well as producing female gametes, the female system must also receive male gametes and provide a site for fertilisation and for the development of the zygote. The gametes, called **ova**, are produced in the two **ovaries**. The gametes travel towards the uterus in the fallopian tubes or **oviducts**. This is where fertilisation occurs, and it is in the uterus that the development of the zygote into a new baby takes place. The **vagina** has a dual function. Firstly it receives the penis and secondly it acts as a birth canal for the eventual delivery of the baby from its mother's body. The **female reproductive system** is illustrated below.

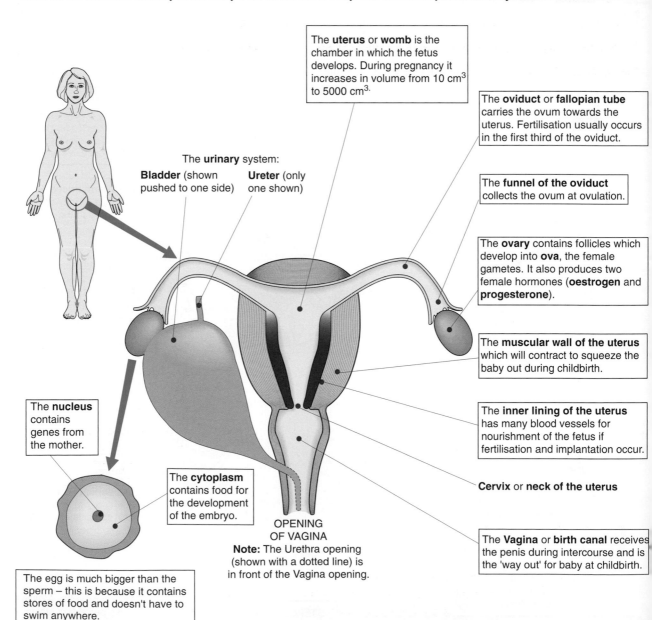

The **uterus** or **womb** is the chamber in which the fetus develops. During pregnancy it increases in volume from 10 cm^3 to 5000 cm$^{3.}$

The **oviduct** or **fallopian tube** carries the ovum towards the uterus. Fertilisation usually occurs in the first third of the oviduct.

The **urinary** system:
Bladder (shown pushed to one side)   **Ureter** (only one shown)

The **funnel of the oviduct** collects the ovum at ovulation.

The **ovary** contains follicles which develop into **ova**, the female gametes. It also produces two female hormones (**oestrogen** and **progesterone**).

The **muscular wall of the uterus** which will contract to squeeze the baby out during childbirth.

The **nucleus** contains genes from the mother.

The **inner lining of the uterus** has many blood vessels for nourishment of the fetus if fertilisation and implantation occur.

The **cytoplasm** contains food for the development of the embryo.

Cervix or **neck of the uterus**

OPENING OF VAGINA
Note: The Urethra opening (shown with a dotted line) is in front of the Vagina opening.

The **Vagina** or **birth canal** receives the penis during intercourse and is the 'way out' for baby at childbirth.

The egg is much bigger than the sperm – this is because it contains stores of food and doesn't have to swim anywhere.

ACID AND ALKALI! The vagina is a hostile environment for sperm! Bacteria which live on the wall of the vagina produce acids. So do some of the female's own cells. These acids harm sperm and stop them swimming, so seminal fluids include an alkali to neutralise the secretions of the vagina and allow some sperm to survive.

Key words

Sexual reproduction – the production of new individuals with a combination of features from two parents.

Gametes – special sex cells, the sperm and the egg.

Zygote – the organism formed when a sperm and an egg combine.

Fertilisation – the joining together of sperm and egg.

Puberty – a stage of human development at which the person becomes able to reproduce.

Sex hormones – chemicals that control the physical and mental changes at puberty.

Exercise 4.1: The reproductive systems

1. Look at this diagram.
   Identify each of the structures A – G.

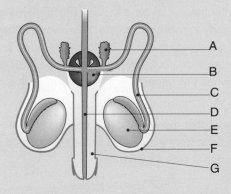

2. Look at this diagram.
   Identify each of the structures A – F

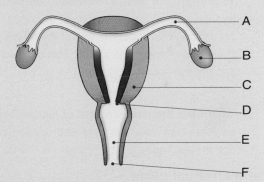

3. Match the words in list 1 with the descriptions in list 2.

   List 1:   Testes, Sperm, Semen, Scrotum, Sperm duct, Penis, Prostate gland

   List 2:   Produces a fluid for sperm to swim in; Carries sperm from testes to the penis; Delivers sperm in semen to the vagina; Produce the sperm and the male sex hormone; Hold the testes outside the body; A fluid for the sperm to swim in; The male gamete.

4. Match the words in list A with the descriptions in List B.

   List A: Ovaries, Egg, Oviducts, Vagina, Womb, Cervix

   List B   The place where the baby develops; Carry eggs from ovaries to uterus; The birth canal; Where the sperm are released when the male ejaculates; The female gamete; Produce the female gametes.

5. Explain why the egg and sperm are different from each other. Give one important way in which they are the same as each other.

The menstrual cycle

- Boys and girls go through a stage of development called puberty.

- Puberty prepares the body for sexual reproduction.

- Following puberty, girls can produce ova in their ovaries.

Both the testes and the ovaries produce sex cells or gametes. However, they differ in how often they work and in the number of gametes they produce. The male continues to produce sperm at the rate of about 100 000 000 per day from puberty to old age. Females, however, produce their gametes, called ova or eggs, at the rate of only one per month. In fact each ovary takes about two months (56 days) to produce a mature ovum. The two ovaries are a month out-of-phase with one another so that the female reproductive system actually releases one egg every 28 days. The cycle of producing and releasing mature ova is called the **menstrual cycle** (this comes from the Latin word *menstruus*, meaning 'monthly').

This important process is very carefully co-ordinated by a number of hormones. These hormones have two functions:

- **To prepare the uterus to receive any fertilised eggs:** During the menstrual cycle the wall of the uterus goes through several stages which get the inner lining of the uterus ready to receive a zygote. This involves growing extra blood vessels in the wall of the uterus. If no fertilised egg, is present this inner lining breaks down and is passed out through the vagina. This is called **menstruation**. Menstruation marks the end of one menstrual cycle and the start of the next one. The girl will notice a loss of blood when this happens – this is known as 'having a period'.

- **To control the development of mature ova**: The same hormones that make the uterus wall ready to receive a zygote also make certain that properly-developed ova are released from the ovaries at the correct time. The egg is released half-way through the menstrual cycle – this process is called **ovulation**.

The menstrual cycle

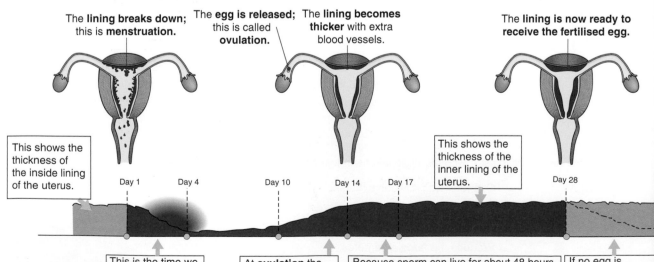

The **lining breaks down;** this is **menstruation.**

The **egg is released;** this is called **ovulation.**

The **lining becomes thicker** with extra blood vessels.

The **lining is now ready to receive the fertilised egg.**

This shows the thickness of the inside lining of the uterus.

This shows the thickness of the inner lining of the uterus.

Day 1   Day 4   Day 10   Day 14   Day 17   Day 28

This is the time we call **having a period**. It lasts for 3 – 5 days.

At **ovulation** the girl's body temperature rises by about 0.6 °C.

Because sperm can live for about 48 hours, and an egg can live for several days, a woman can become pregnant any time from day 12 to day 17 of her menstrual cycle.

If no egg is fertilised, the lining breaks down and the cycle starts again.

Fertilisation and conception

Conception takes place when an ovum is fertilised by a sperm and the resulting zygote becomes implanted in the wall of the uterus. Before this can happen, the ovum and the sperm must meet and this is the purpose of **copulation** or **sexual intercourse**.

Ovulation provides a female gamete

As we have seen, an ovum or egg is released each month from one of the ovaries. Following this process of ovulation, the ovum moves slowly along the oviduct towards the uterus. This movement is helped by:

● 　　contractions of muscles in the wall of the oviduct that squeeze the ovum towards the uterus; and

● 　　fine hairs on the lining of the oviduct that sweep the ovum in the right direction.

It takes about 4 – 7 days for the ovum to reach the uterus. During this time in the oviduct fertilisation may take place.

Copulation delivers male gametes

Before intercourse, sexual stimulation causes blood to flow into the man's penis. The penis becomes hard and erect enough to enter the woman's vagina (helped by lubricating fluids released by the walls of the vagina). The rubbing of the tip of the penis (the glans) against the wall of the vagina sets off a nervous reflex that releases sperm from storage in the testes, and squeezes them along the sperm ducts and the urethra. As the sperm pass along these tubes, fluid is added to them so that the complete semen is ejaculated in spurts from the tip of the penis. There is usually about 3 or 4 cm^3 of semen ejaculated which contains about 300 000 000 sperm. The diagram below illustrates how the male and female gametes arrive at the same place.

Copulation: Sexual intercourse brings gametes together

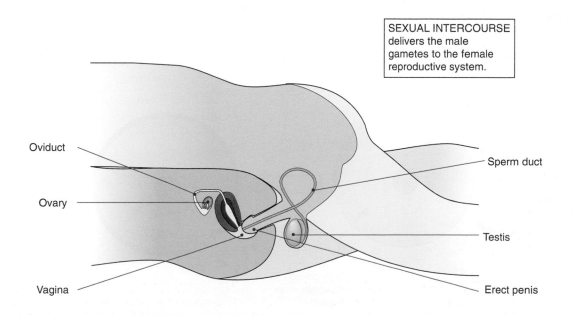

SEXUAL INTERCOURSE delivers the male gametes to the female reproductive system.

Oviduct

Ovary

Vagina

Sperm duct

Testis

Erect penis

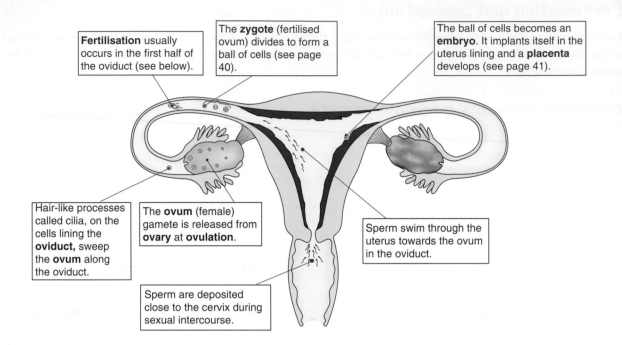

The **zygote** (fertilised ovum) divides to form a ball of cells (see page 40).

Fertilisation usually occurs in the first half of the oviduct (see below).

The ball of cells becomes an **embryo**. It implants itself in the uterus lining and a **placenta** develops (see page 41).

Hair-like processes called cilia, on the cells lining the **oviduct,** sweep the **ovum** along the oviduct.

The **ovum** (female) gamete is released from **ovary** at **ovulation**.

Sperm swim through the uterus towards the ovum in the oviduct.

Sperm are deposited close to the cervix during sexual intercourse.

Fertilisation involves the fusion of egg and sperm

Fertilisation is the joining together or **fusion** of an egg and a sperm. This process allows a set of genes from the mother and a set from the father to be mixed together. Fertilisation takes place in the oviduct and, although several hundred sperm may reach the egg, only one will penetrate the membrane that surrounds it. Once the sperm has penetrated the membrane, the fertilised egg – the **zygote** – now starts to divide, first into two cells, then into four and so on. The ball of cells then continues to move towards the uterus.

The events of fertilisation are summarised below:

Fertilisation

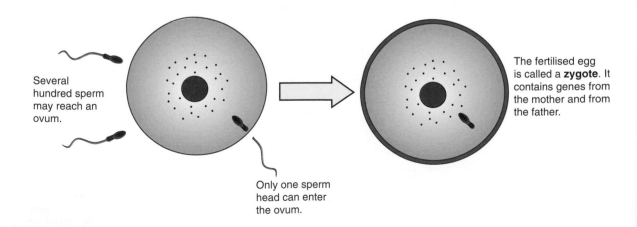

Several hundred sperm may reach an ovum.

The fertilised egg is called a **zygote**. It contains genes from the mother and from the father.

Only one sperm head can enter the ovum.

Conception is the implantation of the ball of cells

About six days after fertilisation, the ball of cells – now called an **embryo** – becomes embedded in the thickened wall of the uterus. Many fertilised eggs probably do not complete this process. In fact, conception, the beginning of the development of a new individual, has not taken place until this implantation has been successfully completed. Once the embryo is attached to the wall of the uterus, some of its outer cells combine with some of the mother's cells and a placenta begins to develop. The importance of the placenta in the development of the new individual is described on page 41.

Key words

Fertilisation – the joining together of sperm and egg.

Conception – the beginning of the development of a new individual.

Copulation – sexual intercourse – the time when the sperm from the male are delivered to the female's reproductive system.

Embryo – a stage of development when the ball of cells begins to rearrange itself so that some organs can be seen.

Menstruation – the release of the bloody lining of the uterus if no fertilisation has taken place.

Exercise 4.2: Menstruation and fertilisation

1. Match up the processes named in the first column with the descriptions in the second column.

Ovulation	Sexual intercourse.
Ejaculation	Egg and sperm joining together.
Menstruation	The release of a mature female gamete.
Fertilisation	The time when a fertilized egg sticks to the wall of the uterus.
Conception	The release of sperm in the semen.
Copulation	The breakdown and release of the inner wall of the uterus.

Pregnancy: The role of the placenta

- A fertilised egg (zygote) contains genes from both mother and father.

- The fertilised egg becomes attached to the wall of the uterus at conception.

From the time of conception it takes about nine months, or forty weeks, for a fertilised egg to become a fully formed baby. The production of the new baby involves two linked processes:

- **Growth**: The original zygote has to divide to provide the many cells that make up the baby.

- **Development**: The organisation of the many cells into different tissues and organs.

The growth stages involve the division of the zygote into many identical copies. One zygote at conception becomes thirty million million cells at birth. As the cells are produced, each one takes up its correct position in the embryo. As they become organised into particular tissues (see page 13), they begin to take on special functions. For example, quite early on during pregnancy it is possible to recognise nerve cells and skin cells. These first steps in the development of a human baby, from the **growth and development of a zygote**, are outlined below.

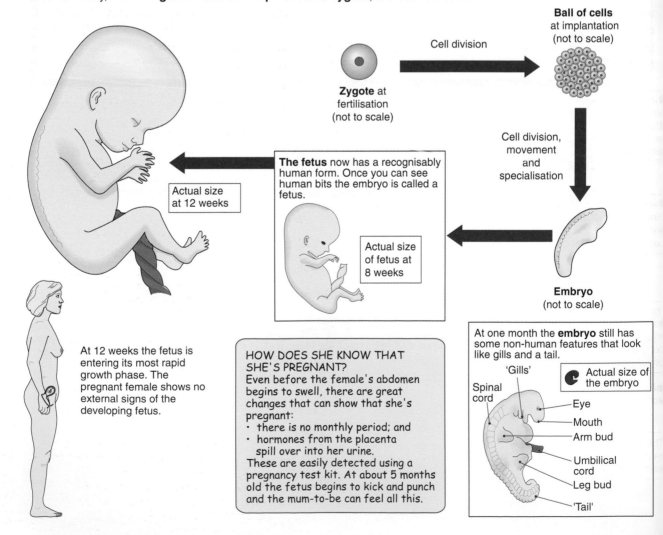

Ball of cells at implantation (not to scale)

Cell division

Zygote at fertilisation (not to scale)

Cell division, movement and specialisation

The fetus now has a recognisably human form. Once you can see human bits the embryo is called a fetus.

Actual size at 12 weeks

Actual size of fetus at 8 weeks

Embryo (not to scale)

At 12 weeks the fetus is entering its most rapid growth phase. The pregnant female shows no external signs of the developing fetus.

HOW DOES SHE KNOW THAT SHE'S PREGNANT?
Even before the female's abdomen begins to swell, there are great changes that can show that she's pregnant:
· there is no monthly period; and
· hormones from the placenta spill over into her urine.
These are easily detected using a pregnancy test kit. At about 5 months old the fetus begins to kick and punch and the mum-to-be can feel all this.

At one month the **embryo** still has some non-human features that look like gills and a tail.

'Gills'

Spinal cord

Actual size of the embryo

Eye
Mouth
Arm bud
Umbilical cord
Leg bud
'Tail'

The time taken for the development of a baby from an implanted zygote is called the **gestation period**. We say that the mother is **pregnant** during this period. During this time the mother provides a stable environment for the developing fetus. The mother controls the important factors of the fetus' environment:

● the supply of soluble foods, such as glucose and minerals, for the growth of new cells;

● the removal of waste materials, such as carbon dioxide which could be poisonous to the fetus;

● the supply of oxygen which is necessary for the release of energy in aerobic respiration. Cell division actually requires a great deal of energy;

● keeping a constant body temperature;

● protection from the risk of infection by microbes in the outside environment; and

● protection from physical shock or damage. The developing nervous system is especially fragile.

All these vital functions are carried out by a structure called the **placenta**. The placenta is formed partly from the lining of the uterus and partly from the outside cells of the developing embryo. The fetus is attached to the placenta by the **umbilical cord** and is surrounded by a sac. This sac is called the **amniotic sac** and is filled with a fluid called the **amniotic fluid**. The placenta begins to develop as soon as the embryo has become implanted in the wall of the uterus and after about 12 weeks it is a thick, saucer-shaped structure that grows deep into the wall of the uterus. The placenta continues to grow to keep pace with the developing fetus and is about 15 cm across and weighs about 500 g at the time of birth. After the baby has been born (see page 42), the placenta, amniotic sac and umbilical cord are expelled from the uterus as the **afterbirth**. The structure of the placenta and some of its functions are shown below.

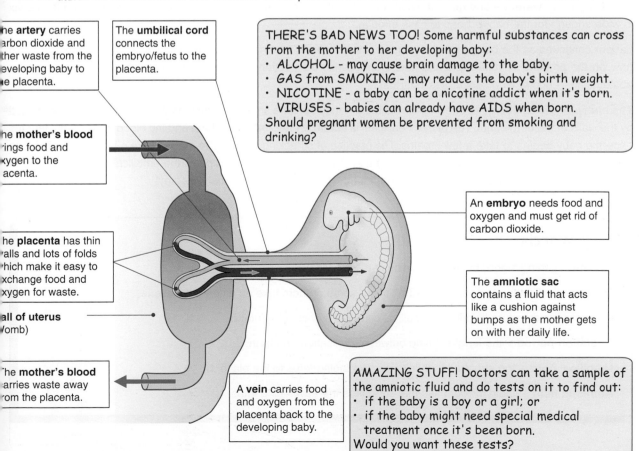

The **artery** carries carbon dioxide and other waste from the developing baby to the placenta.

The **umbilical cord** connects the embryo/fetus to the placenta.

The **mother's blood** brings food and oxygen to the placenta.

THERE'S BAD NEWS TOO! Some harmful substances can cross from the mother to her developing baby:
· ALCOHOL - may cause brain damage to the baby.
· GAS from SMOKING - may reduce the baby's birth weight.
· NICOTINE - a baby can be a nicotine addict when it's born.
· VIRUSES - babies can already have AIDS when born.
Should pregnant women be prevented from smoking and drinking?

The **placenta** has thin walls and lots of folds which make it easy to exchange food and oxygen for waste.

wall of uterus (Womb)

An **embryo** needs food and oxygen and must get rid of carbon dioxide.

The **amniotic sac** contains a fluid that acts like a cushion against bumps as the mother gets on with her daily life.

The **mother's blood** carries waste away from the placenta.

A **vein** carries food and oxygen from the placenta back to the developing baby.

AMAZING STUFF! Doctors can take a sample of the amniotic fluid and do tests on it to find out:
· if the baby is a boy or a girl; or
· if the baby might need special medical treatment once it's been born.
Would you want these tests?

Exchange of materials across the placenta

The placenta is the contact between the fetus and its mother's blood system. It has a number of adaptations that make sure the correct materials cross quickly enough to keep a safe and stable environment for the fetus.

- It has a large surface area which allows more molecules to cross the placenta in any unit of time.

- The blood of the mother is always separated from the blood of the fetus by membranes that control which molecules cross from mother to fetus. The blood of the mother and her developing baby do not mix.

- The fetus has arteries inside the umbilical cord that deliver blood to the placenta and a vein that returns from the placenta, carrying absorbed substances.

Birth

By the end of pregnancy the baby normally lies in the womb with its head close to the cervix. A doctor or midwife can tell that birth is near when the baby has dropped into this position. The birth can be separated into a number of stages. Together these stages are called **labour**. Labour may last from one hour to 12 hours (or even longer).

Labour begins with the first **contractions** of the muscle of the uterus. These contractions are controlled by hormones. Some of these chemical messages come from the mother and some come from the baby.

At first the contractions come every 20 minutes or so but as birth approaches they happen more often and with more power. The contractions break the **amniotic membrane** and release the **amniotic fluid** – this is known as the **breaking of the waters** – and make the cervix dilate (get wider). The first stage of labour is complete when the cervix is wide enough for the baby's head to pass through.

Labour continues as the baby's head is pushed past the cervix into the vagina which now acts as a birth canal. From now on the process is quite rapid and needs only gentle contractions by the mother, helped by the midwife or the obstetrician (a doctor who specialises in births).

The birth process can be quite stressful for the baby. It may become short of oxygen as the umbilical cord is squeezed by the walls of the birth canal. The baby's heartbeat is carefully checked during birth and the blood soon re-oxygenates once the baby begins to take a few breaths. The practice of smacking the baby to make it take a big lungful of air has now been stopped. Once the doctor is satisfied that the baby is breathing properly, the umbilical cord is clamped to prevent bleeding and cut. The mother and child are now two separate individuals. Hooray!

Key words

Growth – getting bigger by the production of more cells.

Development – the changes of cells that mean some of them take on different functions.

Placenta – a structure linking the umbilical cord to the wall of the uterus.

Gestation period – the length of time between fertilisation and birth.

Umbilical cord – the structure that links the developing fetus to the placenta.

Amniotic fluid – liquid inside a sac that surrounds the developing fetus.

Exercise 4.3: Placenta and birth

1. Complete the following paragraphs about the birth of a human baby. Use words from this list:

uterus	amniotic sac	umbilical	oxygen
cervix	placenta	afterbirth	vagina

    (a) An expectant mother knows when she is about to give birth because her .... begins to experience waves of contraction. Eventually the contractions are so powerful that the .... dilates, the .... bursts and the waters are released.

    (b) Further powerful contractions push the baby through the .... or birth canal. Once the baby has been delivered, it is important that it takes deep breaths because it may have been deprived of .... as the .... cord is compressed during delivery. This cord is clamped and cut, and gentle contractions of the uterus cause the .... to come away from the wall of the uterus and pass out of the vagina as the ....

2. Look at these two diagrams. Use words from this list to identify the structures that are labelled A – H on the two diagrams. Words may be used more than once.

embryo	fetus	placenta	amniotic sac
amniotic fluid	umbilical cord	cervix	wall of uterus

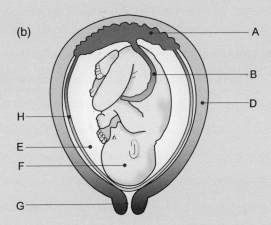

(a)

(b)

An embryo in the uterus about 4 weeks old.

A fetus in the uterus just before birth.

Extension question

3. **Gestation period**

The table below provides information about a range of mammals, including the gestation period (time between fertilisation and birth).

Species	Mass of adult in kilograms	Gestation period in days	Number of litters per year	Number of young per litter
Cat	4	60	2	3 to 5
Chimpanzee	75	270	1	1
Elephant	7000	640	$\frac{1}{2}$ (1 per 2 years)	1
Horse	1300	335	1	1
Mouse	0.025	21	5	4 to 8
Pig	300	115	2	6 to 16
Rabbit	1.5	30	3	4 to 10
Rat	0.5	22	2 to 6	5 to 15

(a) A scatter diagram is a type of graph used to show if there is any correlation between two groups of information. Use a scatter diagram to see if there is any correlation between the mass of an adult animal and its gestation period. Plot mass on the x axis, gestation period on the y axis.

(b) Using information from the table, explain whether there is evidence to support the hypotheses that:

(i) The lighter the mammal, the more young there are in a year.

(ii) The number of young per year varies according to the length of the gestation period.

(c) Estimate the approximate gestation period of the following mammals:

(i) A hedgehog (mass 0.8 kg) has 1 or 2 litters per year with 3 to 6 young in each one.

(ii) A hare (mass 5 kg) has 2 to 3 litters per year with 2 to 5 young in each one.

(iii) A tiger (mass 300 kg) has 1 litter per year with 2 to 4 young in it.

Chapter 5
Respiration

Remember that living organisms need to carry out certain processes to remain alive. The most important of these life processes is respiration. This process provides the energy needed to carry out the other life processes.

What is respiration?

Respiration is a special kind of chemical reaction:

●   It goes on in **every living cell** of every living organism. Remember living organisms include microbes and plants.

●   Glucose and oxygen react together to release energy in the mitochondria (see page 9), although some of this energy is wasted as thermal energy.

●   It produces two important chemical waste products – carbon dioxide and water.

●   For animals with lungs, it depends on breathing, but is not the same as this process (see page 49).

Respiration, like other chemical reactions, can be represented by a word equation.

$$\text{glucose + oxygen} \longrightarrow \text{carbon dioxide + water + energy}$$

         (Reactants)   **(Products)**

Because **oxygen** is required, this process is called **aerobic** respiration.

he reactants for respiration must be delivered to the cells in the bloodstream. The blood also takes away the waste products of this process. The supply of oxygen and the removal of carbon dioxide are made possible by the lungs which give an enormous surface area for these gases to move into or out of the blood (see page 51).

Checking on respiration

Because respiration produces carbon dioxide, water and energy, we can show that respiration is occurring if the amount of any of these products increases. The most reliable sign that respiration is taking place is the production of carbon dioxide.

Testing for respiration

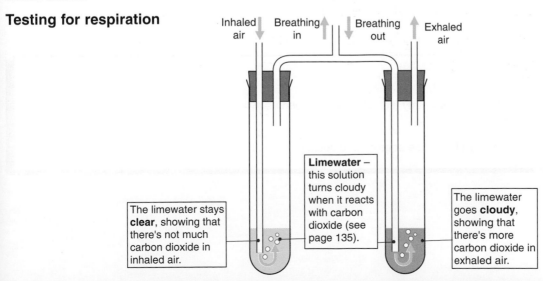

Inhaled air   Breathing in   Breathing out   Exhaled air

Limewater – this solution turns cloudy when it reacts with carbon dioxide (see page 135).

The limewater stays **clear**, showing that there's not much carbon dioxide in inhaled air.

The limewater goes **cloudy**, showing that there's more carbon dioxide in exhaled air.

Energy is used for life processes

Respiration is a sort of link process. The reaction links together a supply of food and oxygen with all the life processes which need energy to continue. Here are some of these processes.

Respiration provides energy for life processes

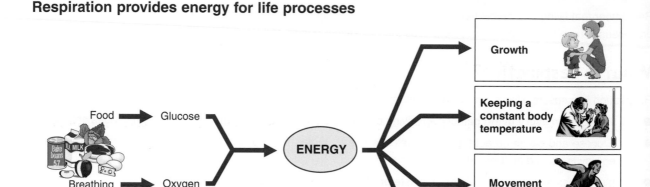

Respiration is such an important process that it must be carefully controlled. The process is controlled and speeded up by special **enzymes** that are present in every living cell.

Energy is supplied in food

Food supplies energy as well as the raw materials for growth (see page 17). The foods that have most energy in them are carbohydrates (including sugars like glucose) and fats. Each food can be tested for its energy content. Food packets must always show how much energy is present in the food. The amount of energy in a food is given in Joules or kilojoules (see page 341).

Key words

Limewater – solution that turns cloudy (sometimes described as milky/chalky) when carbon dioxide is bubbled through it.

Joule – the unit of energy (1 kilojoule equals 1000 Joules).

Exercise 5.1: Respiration

1. The drawing shows what happens to most of the energy that comes from the food that a hen eats in one day.

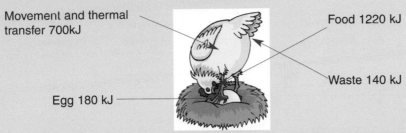

Movement and thermal transfer 700kJ

Food 1220 kJ

Waste 140 kJ

Egg 180 kJ

(a) In the cells of the hen's body, energy is released from food by respiration. Complete the word equation for this process.

glucose + ... ➡ .... + ... + ...

(b) (i) Calculate the total energy which remains in the body of the hen.

   (ii) What is the energy used for?

2. Felix burns a piece of crispbread to find out how much energy is stored in it. Energy from the burning crispbread raises the temperature of the water in the test tube.

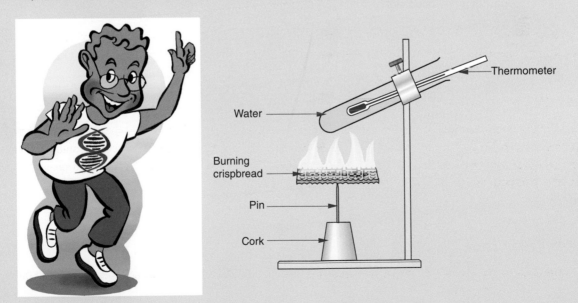

Thermometer

Water

Burning crispbread

Pin

Cork

(a) How should Felix arrange the apparatus so that he is working safely?

(b) Felix wants to find out if potato crisps contain as much energy as crispbread. He does the experiment again using a piece of potato crisp. Suggest two things he must do to make the experiment a fair test.

(c) The table below shows some of the nutritional information from a packet of crispbread and a packet of potato crisps.

	Energy in kilojoules	Protein in grams	Carbohydrate in grams	Fat in grams	Fibre in grams
100 g of crispbread	1455	11.6	58.1	7.3	14.7
100 g of potato crisps	2072	5.8	57.9	28.7	4.3

Using the same apparatus as shown on page 47, Felix burns 1.0 g of potato crisps. Which one of the results (i) to (iv) below will he get when he burns the potato crisps? Explain your choice.

    (i)   The change in the temperature of the water will be greater.

    (ii)   The change in the temperature of the water will be the same.

    (iii) The change in the temperature of the water will be smaller.

    (iv) There will be no change in the temperature of the water.

(d) (i)   Fibre contains energy. Explain why this energy cannot be used by the human body.

    (ii) Use the table in part (b) to give two reasons for choosing crispbread rather than potato crisps as part of a balanced diet.

Respiration and breathing

Remember

● Aerobic respiration uses oxygen to 'burn' (**oxidise**) food and so releases the **energy** which cells need to stay alive (see page 8).

● Aerobic respiration produces **carbon dioxide** and **water vapour** as waste products:

glucose + oxygen ⟶ carbon dioxide + water + energy

Living organisms must be able to take oxygen from the air and get rid of carbon dioxide to the air. Swapping oxygen for carbon dioxide in this way is called **gas exchange**. This gas exchange takes place through a thin membrane at a gas exchange (or respiratory) surface.

A gas exchange surface allows respiration to go on in cells

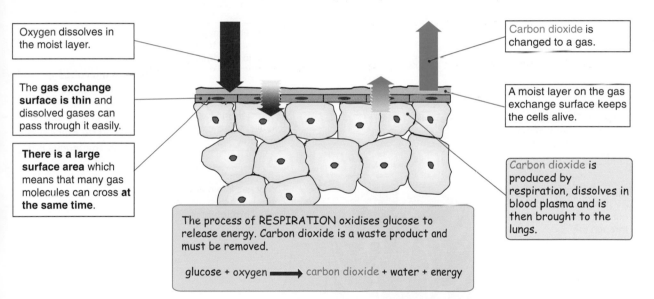

Oxygen dissolves in the moist layer.

The **gas exchange surface is thin** and dissolved gases can pass through it easily.

There is a **large surface area** which means that many gas molecules can cross **at the same time**.

Carbon dioxide is changed to a gas.

A moist layer on the gas exchange surface keeps the cells alive.

Carbon dioxide is produced by respiration, dissolves in blood plasma and is then brought to the lungs.

The process of RESPIRATION oxidises glucose to release energy. Carbon dioxide is a waste product and must be removed.

glucose + oxygen ⟶ carbon dioxide + water + energy

Gas exchange is much more efficient if there is a method for delivering fresh supplies of air to this gas exchange surface. This method is called BREATHING. It is very important to remember the difference between breathing and respiration.

Breathing is the process that **moves air in and out of the lungs.**

Respiration is the process that **releases energy from food.**

It can be hard to remember this difference, since breathing is only needed because respiration takes place.

Gas exchange in humans

Humans are mammals and like all other mammals they are active and keep a constant body temperature. Keeping a constant body temperature uses up a great deal of energy. The release of energy from respiration means that mammals must be able to gain oxygen and lose carbon dioxide. They must have a very efficient gas exchange system.

The gas exchange system in humans is called the **lungs**. Lungs are made up of:

● A surface for exchanging oxygen and carbon dioxide, i.e. the membranes lining the air sacs in the lungs.

● A set of tubes to allow outside air to reach the respiratory surface. This set of tubes has many branches, and is sometimes called the bronchial tree.

● A blood supply (a special artery and vein) to carry dissolved gases to and from the respiratory surface.

● A ventilation system (the rib muscles and the diaphragm) to keep a good flow of air over the respiratory surface.

The illustration below shows the arrangement of the parts of the human gas exchange system.

The structure of the lungs

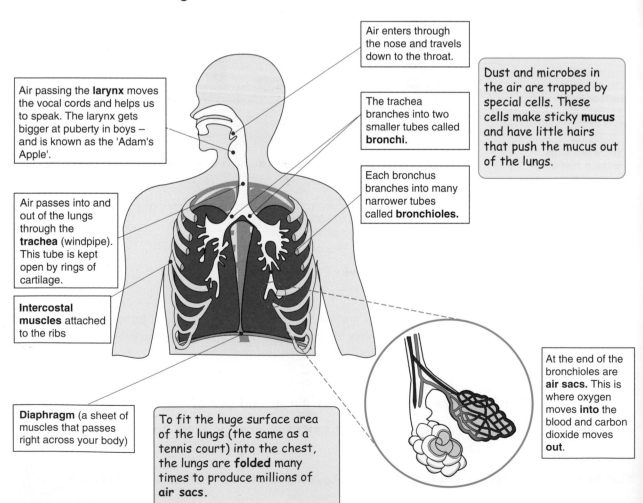

Air enters through the nose and travels down to the throat.

Dust and microbes in the air are trapped by special cells. These cells make sticky **mucus** and have little hairs that push the mucus out of the lungs.

Air passing the **larynx** moves the vocal cords and helps us to speak. The larynx gets bigger at puberty in boys – and is known as the 'Adam's Apple'.

The trachea branches into two smaller tubes called **bronchi.**

Each bronchus branches into many narrower tubes called **bronchioles.**

Air passes into and out of the lungs through the **trachea** (windpipe). This tube is kept open by rings of cartilage.

Intercostal muscles attached to the ribs

At the end of the bronchioles are **air sacs.** This is where oxygen moves **into** the blood and carbon dioxide moves **out**.

Diaphragm (a sheet of muscles that passes right across your body)

To fit the huge surface area of the lungs (the same as a tennis court) into the chest, the lungs are **folded** many times to produce millions of **air sacs.**

Breathing ventilates the lungs

Take a deep breath and remember that:

● Living organisms must obtain oxygen from their environment, and they must release carbon dioxide to their environment.

● An ideal gas exchange surface is thin, moist and with a large surface area.

● The human gaseous exchange system is made up of the lungs and the muscles that move them.

Breathing is the set of muscular movements which keep the respiratory surface well supplied with oxygen (and, of course, remove carbon dioxide).

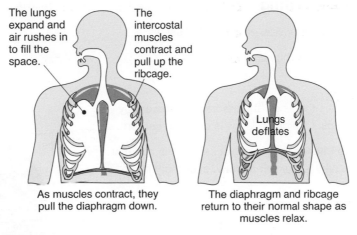

The lungs expand and air rushes in to fill the space.

The intercostal muscles contract and pull up the ribcage.

As muscles contract, they pull the diaphragm down.

Lungs deflates

The diaphragm and ribcage return to their normal shape as muscles relax.

What's the point?

All this breathing in and out makes sure that oxygen can enter the blood and carbon dioxide can be made to leave. If these changes didn't take place, there would be two unwanted results:

● Our cells wouldn't get enough oxygen which means they wouldn't get enough energy from respiration and we would die.

● We wouldn't be able to get rid of the waste carbon dioxide and we would poison ourselves. Carbon dioxide can turn our blood and other bodily fluids into a weak acid. This is another reason why we would die.

This diagram shows how the lungs are able to **exchange these two gases between the air and the blood**.

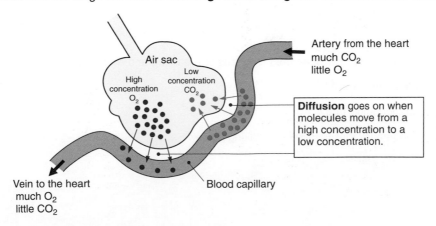

Air sac

High concentration O_2

Low concentration CO_2

Artery from the heart much CO_2 little O_2

Diffusion goes on when molecules move from a high concentration to a low concentration.

Vein to the heart much O_2 little CO_2

Blood capillary

Key words

Respiration – the release of energy from food molecules.

Breathing – the movements that bring air in and out of the lungs.

Intercostal muscles – muscles between the ribs that contract to lift up the ribcage during breathing.

Diaphragm – muscle that contracts to help the chest get bigger during breathing in.

Exercise 5.2: Breathing

1. Put the following list in order of size, with the smallest first.

   trachea, air sac, bronchiole, bronchus

2. (a) This diagram shows the lungs and the trachea, the airway leading to the lungs. One of the lungs is drawn in section.

      In the wall of the trachea there are pieces of a stiff material called cartilage. Why is this stiff material necessary in the wall of the trachea?

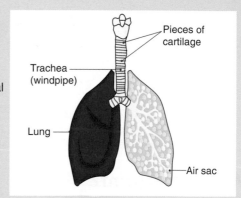

   (b) This diagram below shows one air sac and its blood supply.

      (i) Gas A enters the air sac from the blood. Gas B leaves the air sac and enters the blood. What are the names of gases A and B?

      (ii) Give one reason why it is easy for gases to pass across the wall of an air sac.

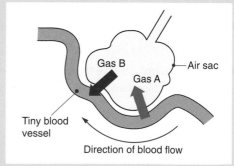

3. (a) Describe the differences between the processes of breathing and respiration.

   (b) Why is breathing important?

   (c) Why is respiration important?

   (d) How would you check that respiration is taking place?

4. Felix was trying to find out how much air he breathed out in one breath. He poured water into a bell-jar and placed it upside down in a trough of water. The bell-jar had a scale marked in cm^3.

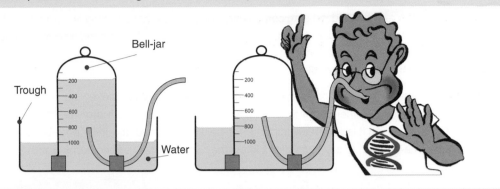

(a) How much air did Felix breathe out?

(b) Air contains carbon dioxide, nitrogen, noble gases, oxygen and water vapour. Give three differences between the composition of the air Felix breathed in and the air he breathed out.

(c) Which three items are contained in the air Felix breathed out?

Extension question

5. Two schoolboys were asked to take part in an investigation into the effect of exercise on breathing. The number of breaths they took in each half minute was measured and recorded, first of all while sitting still, then when recovering from two minutes of hard exercise. The results are shown in the table.

Time in minutes	Activity	Number of breaths in each half minute	
		Tom	Alan
0.5	Sitting still	7	8
1.0	Sitting still	7	8
1.5	Sitting still	7	8
2.0	Exercise (step ups)	7	8
2.5	Exercise (step ups)		
3.0	Exercise (step ups)		
3.5	Exercise (step ups)		
4.0	Recovery (sitting)	25	25
4.5	Recovery (sitting)	24	24
5.0	Recovery (sitting)	23	17
5.5	Recovery (sitting)	18	13
6.0	Recovery (sitting)	15	10
6.5	Recovery (sitting)	12	10
7.0	Recovery (sitting)	12	9
7.5	Recovery (sitting)	10	8
8.0	Recovery (sitting)	8	8
8.5	Recovery (sitting)	8	8
9.0	Recovery (sitting)	7	8

(a) Draw a graph to show the changes in breathing rate over the time period of this investigation. Plot both lines on the same axes.

(b) Which boy appears to be fitter? Explain your answer.

Smoking and disease

There have been many health authority advertising campaigns which stress that smoking is harmful. At the same time the manufacturers of cigarettes try to reduce the impact of these campaigns by emphasising the glamorous side to smoking. However, the manufacturers try to reduce the impact of negative advertising. They have to include, by law, a statement which points out 'smoking can seriously damage your health'.

Companies involved in sales of life insurance policies now routinely ask 'Do you smoke?' because they are aware of the effects of smoking on health. Whether or not to take up smoking is possibly **the major health decision** that many of us will ever make. For this reason it is extremely important to be well-informed about the possible effects of smoking. Nobody should really be in a position to say 'but I didn't know the risks' when she is confronted with the effects of her smoking habit.

How is smoking harmful?

Smoking involves inhaling smoke from burning tobacco and paper. This smoke can harm the lungs and respiratory passages for a number of reasons:

- it is hot;

- it is dry; and

- it contains many harmful chemicals.

Here is one simple experiment that can help to show the nasty chemicals in burning tobacco :

The dangers of tobacco smoke

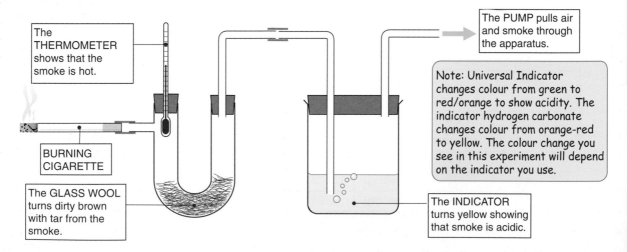

The THERMOMETER shows that the smoke is hot.

The PUMP pulls air and smoke through the apparatus.

Note: Universal Indicator changes colour from green to red/orange to show acidity. The indicator hydrogen carbonate changes colour from orange-red to yellow. The colour change you see in this experiment will depend on the indicator you use.

BURNING CIGARETTE

The GLASS WOOL turns dirty brown with tar from the smoke.

The INDICATOR turns yellow showing that smoke is acidic.

The heat and dryness caused by smoking irritates the lungs, but the main dangers of smoking relate to the chemicals in the burning tobacco. There are over 1000 known chemicals present in tobacco smoke. The most dangerous are tar, carbon monoxide and nicotine but there are even small quantities of arsenic and plutonium.

When doctors have to treat lung disease with medicine, the molecules of the medicine are always delivered in a spray form. Doctors know that the droplets of water can carry the helpful medicines right down through all of the respiratory tubes and deep into the lungs where they can carry out their useful work. Burning tobacco produces tiny droplets of water too, and these carry the harmful chemicals deep into the lungs in just the same way as medicines are delivered. It would be hard to find a more efficient way of delivering harmful chemicals to the lungs than smoking. Some of these dangerous chemicals, and the effects which they have on the body, are shown below:

The dangers of tobacco smoke

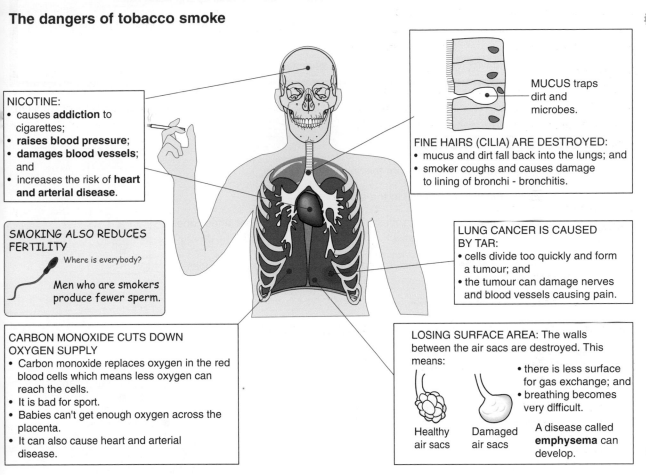

NICOTINE:
- causes **addiction** to cigarettes;
- **raises blood pressure**;
- **damages blood vessels**; and
- increases the risk of **heart and arterial disease**.

MUCUS traps dirt and microbes.

FINE HAIRS (CILIA) ARE DESTROYED:
- mucus and dirt fall back into the lungs; and
- smoker coughs and causes damage to lining of bronchi - bronchitis.

SMOKING ALSO REDUCES FERTILITY
Where is everybody?
Men who are smokers produce fewer sperm.

LUNG CANCER IS CAUSED BY TAR:
- cells divide too quickly and form a tumour; and
- the tumour can damage nerves and blood vessels causing pain.

CARBON MONOXIDE CUTS DOWN OXYGEN SUPPLY
- Carbon monoxide replaces oxygen in the red blood cells which means less oxygen can reach the cells.
- It is bad for sport.
- Babies can't get enough oxygen across the placenta.
- It can also cause heart and arterial disease.

LOSING SURFACE AREA: The walls between the air sacs are destroyed. This means:
- there is less surface for gas exchange; and
- breathing becomes very difficult.

Healthy air sacs   Damaged air sacs

A disease called **emphysema** can develop.

Cigarettes also affect the heart and circulation

Nicotine in tobacco smoke is very quickly absorbed into the bloodstream. It is thought of as the most dangerous chemical present in tobacco smoke. The nicotine reaches the brain and gives smokers the pleasurable feeling that they crave. The nicotine also closes down some blood vessels, including the important arteries that supply the heart muscle with oxygen and glucose. This means that smokers are much more likely to have a heart attack than non-smokers.

Burning tobacco and paper give off a gas called **carbon monoxide**. This gas locks onto the oxygen-carrying chemical in your red blood cells. This means that your blood can't carry as much oxygen as it should, and you will lack energy, as well as seriously straining your heart! Pregnant women who smoke make it more difficult for their developing babies to get oxygen across the placenta. The babies grow more slowly, and are lower in weight when they are born.

So don't forget!

- Smoking tobacco is harmful to the lungs and the circulation.

- There are many harmful components of tobacco smoke, but it is nicotine that causes addiction.

- It is very difficult to give up smoking, so it is better not to start in the first place!

Key words

Nicotine – the substance in tobacco that causes addiction – it also speeds up the heart rate.

Addiction – the body's dependence on a drug to such an extent that it can no longer function properly without it.

Cancer – a disease in which cells begin to divide out of control and harm normal body tissues.

Exercise 5.3 Smoking

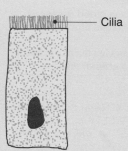
Cilia

1. This diagram shows a ciliated cell from the lining of the airway.

    (a) What is the function of this cell in the airway?

    (b) This cell is affected by substances in cigarette smoke. What effect does cigarette smoke have on the cilia?

    (c) Give the name of the substance, in cigarette smoke, which causes addiction to smoking.

2. The graph below shows the number of deaths from lung cancer and from tuberculosis of the lungs, in England and Wales, between 1920 and 1960.

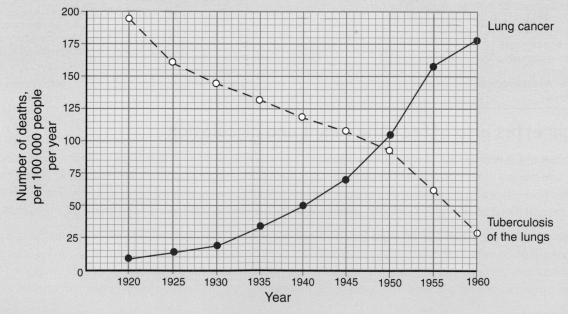

    (a) Between which two dates on the graph did the number of deaths from lung cancer rise fastest?

    (b) Lung cancer may be caused by cigarette smoking. Which substance in cigarette smoke causes lung cancer?

    (c) What effect does smoking have on the chances of developing heart disease?

Extension question

3. This table shows the causes of death of cigarette smokers in Great Britain.

Cause of death	Percentage of deaths
Lung cancer	8
Bronchitis and emphysema	17
Circulatory diseases	20
Other causes (not related to smoking)	55

(a) What percentage of smokers die from smoking-related diseases?

(b) Present the data in the form of a bar chart or a pie chart. Decide which is the best way to display the results. Explain your choice.

(c) Emphysema is a disease caused by smoking. The photograph on the left shows normal lung tissue and the photo on the right shows lung tissue from a person with emphysema.

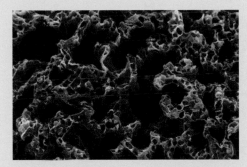

Air sacs (alveoli) in human lung tissue.

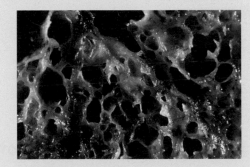

A section of lung affected by emphysema.

    (i) Describe two differences between the normal lung tissue and lung tissue from a person with emphysema.

    (ii) How will these differences affect the supply of oxygen to the blood in the person with emphysema?

    (iii) Name two other diseases caused by smoking, and say what the symptoms would be (i.e. how the patient would be affected).

Chapter 6
Healthy living

Starting points

- A living organism needs a supply of food and oxygen. These are required to provide the energy required to keep cells alive and to carry out life processes.

- The heart acts as a pump to move blood around the body. The blood can collect food from the gut and oxygen from the lungs and then take both the food and oxygen to the cells.

The human body is very good at carrying out life processes and a human can stay alive despite many problems. However, for a human to stay fit and keep healthy she/he should:

- eat a balanced diet (see page 17);

- take a regular amount of exercise; and

- take no unnecessary health risks.

Exercise is good for you

Remember that the heart is made of muscle. Because exercise makes the heart beat faster, it trains the heart muscle. This means that regular exercise gives you a fitter heart. You are much less likely to suffer a heart attack if you have taken regular exercise.

Exercise benefits the health in other ways too

- It reduces obesity because it uses up food reserves and reduces the chance of becoming overweight. **Obesity** (which is defined as being so overweight that your health is affected) can be very harmful. For example, the extra weight can cause damage to your joints and make it difficult to breathe freely. Obese people are also more likely to develop diabetes.

- It increases **stamina** because it trains the heart and lungs to deliver more oxygen to the working muscle cells. This means that a fit person can work for longer periods without causing damage to the body.

- It increases **strength** because the muscles are being trained. Different types of exercise can provide extra strength in different muscles. Lifting weights and swimming is good for the arms, whereas running is more likely to benefit the legs.

Most people who exercise regularly (3 times a week) will notice a difference in strength and stamina after just 4 weeks. Exercise also releases chemicals in the brain. These natural drugs make you feel much better after exercise.

Taking health risks can seriously damage the body and the brain

Humans are not all identical to one another. The differences between them could have been inherited from their parents (see page 80). Some differences could be the result of their environment. Some may lead to an obvious disease, although others may just make us less healthy. We can do nothing about the differences we inherit from our parents but we *can* be careful about our lifestyle. Some of these lifestyle risks are described below:

CIGARETTES: Smoking cigarettes can make breathing very difficult. If smoking continues for a long time, there is a high risk of heart disease and lung cancer (see page 55). The nicotine in tobacco smoke is very addictive.

SOLVENTS and AEROSOLS: These are abused by sniffing and breathing in fumes. Glues and paint can damage the brain, and aerosols can cause a person to choke and suffocate.

DRUGS: Any chemical that affects the way the body works is a drug. Some drugs (such as painkillers like paracetamol) are useful, but even they can be dangerous if they are over-used. Many others are just dangerous. Some, like LSD and ecstasy, can damage the brain. Some can make the heart beat dangerously fast. Many drugs sold by dealers are not pure, and the impurities can make people very ill.

ALCOHOL: Alcohol is a very dangerous drug if consumed in large quantities. Even in small amounts it slows down your reactions, and may cause you to lose a lot of your body heat. In larger amounts, alcohol damages the liver, stomach and the heart. It can make people put on weight and can damage their sex organs. Alcohol makes cigarette smoke more likely to cause cancer of the tongue or voice-box.

WHAT IS ADDICTION? Many people become addicted to drugs. This means that they can't carry on their normal lives without the drug. It may mean that drug addicts will steal from their friends, and may go without food to buy drugs. Drug addicts who use needles can also catch blood diseases from needles they share with other drug addicts, for example AIDS.

Don't forget that even without these health risks you will need to eat a balanced diet and to take regular exercise.

The most important point about these health risks is that **you have control over them**. You can make a choice about your lifestyle – remember that you have probably only lived one-seventh of your lifespan. It is possible that even a few uses of drugs can make you become addicted, and eating habits that you start when young can cause problems later in life. What you choose to do now could affect the rest of your life and the lives of your friends and relatives.

Key words

Obesity – where the body is so overweight that disease is more likely to occur.

Drug – any chemical that alters the activities of the body.

Fitness – the ability to deliver oxygen to working muscles efficiently.

Exercise 6.1: Healthy living

1. Make a list of the three requirements for a healthy lifestyle.

2. Why is it so difficult to give up smoking?

3. Give three benefits of regular exercise.

4. Match up the following features of lifestyle with the problems they cause:

Smoking	Weakness of muscles
Excessive use of alcohol	Damage to the liver
Addiction to drugs	Obesity
Over-eating of fatty foods	Choking to death
Too little exercise	Poor brain development
Breathing aerosols	Lung cancer

Extension questions

5. A pupil agreed to have his heart rate (pulse rate) measured every five minutes for a period of an hour. The results are shown in this table:

Time in minutes	0	5	10	15	20	25	30	35	40	45	50	55	60
Pulse rate in beats per minute	72	72	75	90	107	124	127	111	90	76	72	72	72

   (a) Plot a graph of the results. Put **time** on the horizontal axis (i.e. along the bottom) and **pulse rate** on the vertical axis (i.e. up the side). Put a suitable title on your graph.

   (b) From the graph give:

   (i)   The resting heart rate.

   (ii) When the pupil began to take exercise.

   (iii) When the pupil stopped exercising.

   (iv) How long the pupil's pulse took to return to normal.

   (c) Explain why the pulse rate increased during exercise.

6. Use the Internet or your library to find out more about the health problems caused by the overuse of alcohol.

Microbes and disease

Many of the life processes in the human body are under a sort of automatic control. These controls keep factors such as body temperature and the concentration of food molecules in the blood very close to the levels needed to keep an organism alive. Sometimes these controls can't keep up with changes in the body. A person in this situation will show certain **signs** (such as a raised body temperature) and will experience certain **symptoms** (such as feeling very tired). We would now say that the person is **diseased**.

Classification of diseases

At the simplest level diseases can be classified into two categories – **non-infectious** and **infectious**.

- **Non-infectious diseases** are not caught from another individual. These diseases may be the result of a number of causes *but do not normally result from the actions of another organism*. Good examples of non-infectious diseases are **heart disease** caused by a very fatty diet (see page 17), or **lung cancer** caused by smoking (see page 55).

- **Infectious diseases** are those which can be caught, or passed on from one individual to another. These diseases are caused by some other living organism, usually a microorganism. Examples of infectious diseases are **influenza** and **tuberculosis**.

Microorganisms are living organisms that are too small to be seen without help. Scientists have discovered many different types of microorganism (or **microbe**) by using an instrument called a **microscope** (see page 14). A good microscope can **magnify** a microbe, to make it look bigger, as well as making its structure look clearer. These microbes live in the environment but can invade our bodies. Pause for a moment and just discuss the ways microbes could enter our bodies.

Microbes cause disease when they interfere with the way the body works. Bacteria and viruses are microbes that can cause this kind of problem. The diagram below shows how they can cause disease.

Viruses (e.g. influenza and the common cold)

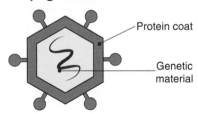
Protein coat
Genetic material

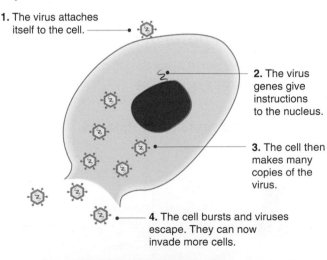
1. The virus attaches itself to the cell.
2. The virus genes give instructions to the nucleus.
3. The cell then makes many copies of the virus.
4. The cell bursts and viruses escape. They can now invade more cells.

- Viruses are very small microbes that only come *alive* when they enter the body.

- They have a simple structure, with just a few genes wrapped in a protein coat.

- They take over the cells of the host (you!) and use your cells to make hundreds of copies of themselves.

- The damaged cells can make you feel really ill.

- Viruses cannot be controlled by antibiotics.

We sneeze because broken bits of cells irritate the lining of the nose.

Bacteria (e.g. tuberculosis, tetanus and food poisoning)

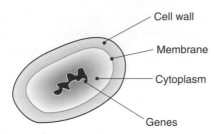

Cell wall

Membrane

Cytoplasm

Genes

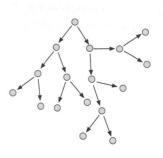

- Bacteria are smaller than cells but bigger than viruses.
- They have a membrane, cell wall, cytoplasm and genes, but no nucleus.
- They can live inside the body or on the skin.
- They divide very quickly, even as often as every 30 minutes.
- When they divide they use up foods that the body cells need. The bacteria can release **toxins** (poisons) that can make you feel very ill.
- Bacteria can be killed by:
  - **Antibiotics** inside the body.
  - **Antiseptics** on the skin.
  - **Disinfectants** on work surfaces and in toilets.

> **CRAZY BUT TRUE!**
> In 24 hours one bacterium can divide so many times that the colony would weigh more than 10 kg.

Defence against disease: how the work of scientists and doctors helps to keep us healthy

The body has several natural defences against disease:

- The **skin** helps to keep microbes away from the body's tissues.
- **Blood clots** stop microbes from entering the body through wounds.
- **White blood cells** engulf (eat) invading microbes, or produce antibodies to destroy microbes.

The skin is a natural barrier

The **skin** acts as a barrier to infection by microbes. Even if there are natural gaps in the skin, for example the eyes and ears, the body produces chemicals that help to defend these gaps. The part played by this first line of defence is shown below.

The skin is the first line of defence

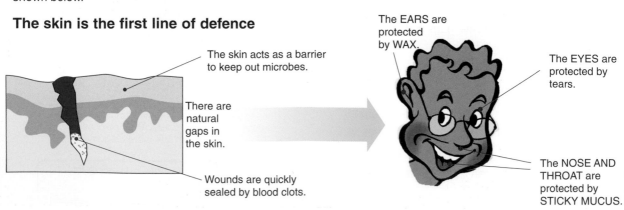

The skin acts as a barrier to keep out microbes.

There are natural gaps in the skin.

Wounds are quickly sealed by blood clots.

The EARS are protected by WAX.

The EYES are protected by tears.

The NOSE AND THROAT are protected by STICKY MUCUS.

Blood clotting protects open wounds

A blood clot forms when a wound is made in the skin. The clot is started by small pieces of blood cell called **platelets** and completed when red blood cells become trapped by a network of fibres. The blood dries out to form a scab. The scab falls off once the skin beneath it has been repaired. Sometimes a large scab will leave a **scar** when it falls off.

White blood cells help in two different ways

One group of white blood cells – called **phagocytes** – can find microbes and destroy them directly by eating and digesting them. Sometimes this kills the white blood cells themselves and in fact the **pus** that sometimes collects near a wound is formed of dead white blood cells. Another type of white blood cell – called a **lymphocyte** – can recognise microbes and can produce special proteins called **antibodies** to fight them. Your body can make a different antibody for every bacterium or virus it meets, and can remember any microbes that have been met in the past. A few of these memory lymphocytes are kept for each microbe that has ever infected the body so that if the same microbe infects you again, the antibodies are made much more quickly. A second infection by the same microbe will hardly cause any disease at all. When this happens, scientists say that the body has developed **immunity** to this microbe. The part played by white blood cells in defence against disease is shown here.

White blood cells are the second line of defence

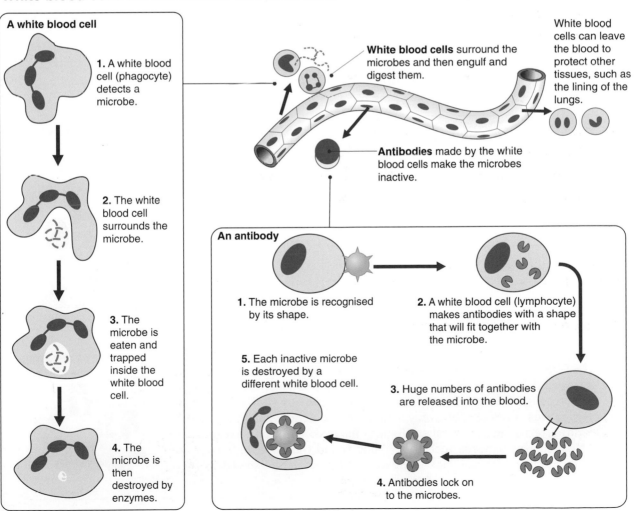

You can find white blood cells and bacteria inside spots on your skin.

Helping the body to fight disease

The immune system might not be able to work quickly enough to protect the body if it becomes infected by a really dangerous microbe. Doctors have developed a method for preparing the immune system for attack by this kind of microbe. This kind of protection is called **immunisation** or **vaccination**.

Weakened microbes can give us artificial immunity

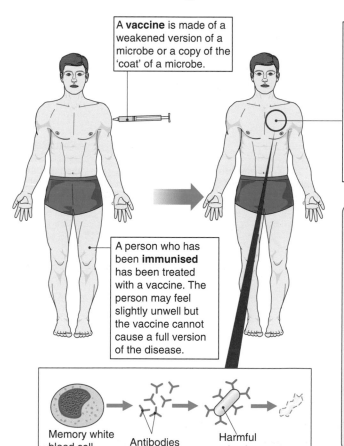

A **vaccine** is made of a weakened version of a microbe or a copy of the 'coat' of a microbe.

A person who has been **immunised** has been treated with a vaccine. The person may feel slightly unwell but the vaccine cannot cause a full version of the disease.

Memory white blood cell → Antibodies → Harmful microbe →

- The immunised person now has white blood cells that have been *tricked*. They have made antibodies that can recognise the real microbe and **not** just the weakened version.

- Some of these cells are **memory** cells and will be able to make antibodies if the **real** microbe infects the body.

- Sometimes a person needs **booster** injections to keep up the number of memory cells.

MUM CAN HELP TOO!

- A pregnant woman passes antibodies across the placenta. The new-born baby is already **naturally immunised** to some common illnesses!

- The first breast milk made by mother is made up of antibodies. The baby's immune system is topped up for the first few days.

HISTORY! The process is sometimes called vaccination because the Latin word for 'cow' is 'vacca'. This process was first tried out by a doctor called Edward Jenner in 1796. He found out that the disease cowpox was harmless, but very similar to the deadly smallpox.
He injected a small boy called James Phipps with cowpox microbes (he called this process vaccination) and found that it gave him protection against smallpox. Why wouldn't Jenner be allowed to try this out nowadays?

Sometimes a disease cannot be prevented. A person may become ill and need help to recover. It is important to know whether a particular disease is caused by a virus or a bacterium, because this information can help to decide the method of treatment. For example, **antibiotics** only work against bacteria and don't have any effect on diseases caused by viruses. Sometimes a patient can be helped to deal with an illness with **painkillers** such as aspirin or paracetamol. These drugs reduce the body temperature and make the person feel better and this can help them during a period of illness.

Key words

Signs – what a doctor looks for in a patient with a disease.

Symptoms – what a patient feels like when he has a disease.

Infectious – can be passed on to another person.

Phagocyte – a type of white blood cell that can engulf and digest microbes.

Antibody – a protein made by some white blood cells that can defend the body against microbes.

Immunity – when the body has antibodies ready to fight off an infection by a microbe.

Exercise 6.2: Microbes and disease

1. Name one disease that:

   (a) is caused by a virus.

   (b) is infectious.

   (c) could be caused by a poor diet.

   (d) is caused by bacteria.

   (e) can result from an unhealthy lifestyle.

2. My mother did not study science. She used to tell me that my body was protected by 'red and white soldiers'. What do you think she meant? Was she correct?

3. Write down two differences between bacteria and viruses.

4. What is an antibiotic? What is the difference between an antibiotic, an antiseptic and a disinfectant?

Extension question

5. Read this description of Jenner's discovery of vaccination.

   Edward Jenner worked in a country town. He noticed that girls who milked cows caught a disease called cowpox – they had spots on their hands but otherwise weren't ill at all. They never caught smallpox, a much more serious disease. Jenner collected the pus from one of the spots on a milkmaid's hand and scratched the pus into the arm of his nephew (an eight year-old boy called James Phipps). The boy caught cowpox and felt slightly unwell for a few days but soon recovered. Edward Jenner then transferred pus from a person with smallpox into the arm of James Phipps. James did not catch smallpox and showed no signs of the disease.

   Answer these questions:

   (a) What would have happened to James Phipps if Jenner's experiment hadn't worked?

   (b) Use a diagram to explain why James Phipps did not catch smallpox.

   (c) Use your library or the Internet to find out why people are no longer vaccinated against smallpox.

Individuals and the community can fight disease together

It is important to understand that the fight against disease involves several levels of responsibility.

●   The **personal** level – for example, each individual can take responsibility for his or her own social habits.

●   The **community** level – for example, local health services must be correctly managed and financed.

●   The **world-wide** level – for example, many nations could accept responsibility for setting up and carrying out vaccination programmes (see page 64).

The **individual** can reduce his or her chances of contracting some diseases by caring about the following:

●   Personal hygiene, such as washing, and cleaning teeth.

●   Balanced diet (see page 17).

●   Regular exercise (see page 58).

●   Sufficient rest, since the main production of chemicals controlling growth takes place during sleep, and a rested person is less likely to suffer from an accident.

●   Not smoking (see page 54).

●   Controlling alcohol intake (see page 21).

Because we often live close together in towns and cities, we share many facilities which affect our health. For these reasons we must accept **community responsibilities**. These responsibilities include:

●   Providing a supply of safe drinking water.

●   Removal of sewage and refuse.

●   Providing medical care for the unwell.

●   Keeping a check on standards of health and hygiene, especially in the preparation of food.

At the **world-wide** level the largest and most important group is the **World Health Organisation (WHO)**. This group aims at raising the level of health of all the citizens of the world so that they can lead socially productive lives.

The WHO has had some successes:

●   **Reduction of the infant death** rate, by providing a better diet for mothers and their infants.

●   **Elimination of smallpox**, by a well-coordinated vaccination programme.

●   **Reduction in malaria**, which affects more than 2 million people a year, by a variety of methods, including the draining of swampy areas.

●   **Improved supplies of safe water**, by the construction of water-treatment plants.

These combined efforts help to **fight disease**.

Fighting disease

PERSONAL HYGIENE

WASHING HAIR can help to keep bacteria and nits out of your hair.

WASHING UNDER ARMS stops bacteria feeding on body fluids and creating B.O. (body odour).

WASHING HANDS, especially after using the loo, reduces the risk of spreading food poisoning.

BRUSHING TEETH can help to fight tooth decay.

WASHING and DRYING FEET stops smells and can also stop athlete's foot.

REGULAR HEALTH CHECKS HELP!
Doctors can spot disease early and treat it very effectively. For example, eye and teeth check ups.

COMMUNITY HEALTH

REMOVE RUBBISH to stop smells or infestations with flies or rats.

PROVIDE SAFE CLEAN WATER to reduce the risk of diseases like cholera and dysentery.

GET RID OF SEWAGE to reduce unpleasant smells and stop risk of passing on harmful bacteria and viruses

WORLD HEALTH
- co-ordinate vaccination programmes;
- provide drugs to poor countries;
- develop wells for clean water;
- help to redistribute food to poor countries.

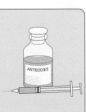

Chapter 7
Green plants as organisms: Photosynthesis

Remember

- Plants are living organisms and can carry out the life processes.
- Plants must be able to make foods. The foods provide raw materials for growth as well as energy.
- Plants do not move very much, so they must be able to feed without moving.

Green plants make food using sunlight

Very few plants can trap or catch ready-made food. Instead they must make their own food. They make their food by combining **carbon dioxide gas** from the air with **water** from the soil. They need **energy** to do this and as you will remember, this energy comes from **sunlight**. The energy in sunlight is trapped by a green pigment, called **chlorophyll**, in the cells of the leaves of the plant.

The method plants use to feed themselves is called **photosynthesis**. The name gives you a clue about what happens during this process. *Photo* means 'using light' and *synthesis* means 'putting together'.

Photosynthesis is summarised by the word equation:

$$\text{carbon dioxide} + \text{water} \xrightarrow[\text{chlorophyll}]{\text{light energy}} \text{glucose} + \text{oxygen}$$

(and the glucose is usually converted into starch, see page 70).

The process of photosynthesis provides **food** for the plant. This food can be used to provide energy which can be stored as starch or used for the growth of the plant. The food that the plant keeps inside its body is called **biomass**. This biomass eventually provides food for many animals (see page 99).

Photosynthesis and food

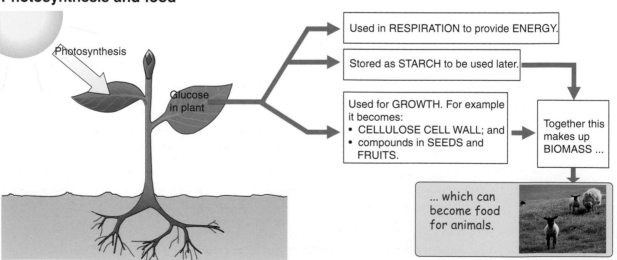

Photosynthesis also gives out the gas **oxygen**. All living cells need oxygen to release the maximum amount of energy from food. This is respiration (see page 45).

The processes of respiration and photosynthesis must be balanced against one another to keep a constant composition of the atmosphere.

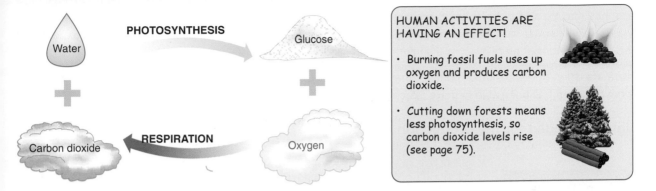

Hydrogen carbonate indicator can be used in this experiment to check the levels of carbon dioxide.

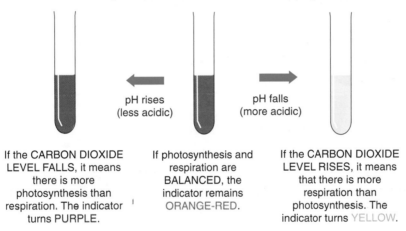

pH rises
(less acidic)

pH falls
(more acidic)

If the CARBON DIOXIDE LEVEL FALLS, it means there is more photosynthesis than respiration. The indicator turns PURPLE.

If photosynthesis and respiration are BALANCED, the indicator remains ORANGE-RED.

If the CARBON DIOXIDE LEVEL RISES, it means that there is more respiration than photosynthesis. The indicator turns YELLOW.

Factors affecting photosynthesis

Any food that the plant has left over, after it has used some for energy, can be used for growing. The plant will be able to grow, so long as it can photosynthesise more than it respires. The four factors that affect photosynthesis are:

● **Light intensity:** Light provides the energy needed to join carbon dioxide and water together. The more light there is, the greater the rate of photosynthesis.

● **The level of carbon dioxide:** The air must provide carbon dioxide. There is very little carbon dioxide in the normal atmosphere (see page 197), so this gas must be quickly replaced by respiration.

● **Temperature:** Thermal energy is needed so that all the chemical reactions in the plant can happen quickly enough. The best temperature for photosynthesis is around 25 °C. Temperatures above 40 °C damage plant cells, and photosynthesis comes to a halt.

● **Water:** Water is needed to combine with carbon dioxide, and to carry foods around the plant's body. Water is important for photosynthesis but it is not as important as the other factors.

Checking how factors affect photosynthesis

Scientists are very interested in how different factors affect photosynthesis. If they can understand how plants grow, then they may be able to make plants grow more quickly. This could provide more food for humans and other animals. When a scientist has an idea that he or she wants to check, then he or she will need to carry out an **experiment**. The experiment must be reliable, or the information it gives will not be useful (see page 3).

There are different ways in which photosynthesis by the plant can be measured. The easiest method is to show whether or not the plant has been able to make starch.

Light is needed for the production of starch

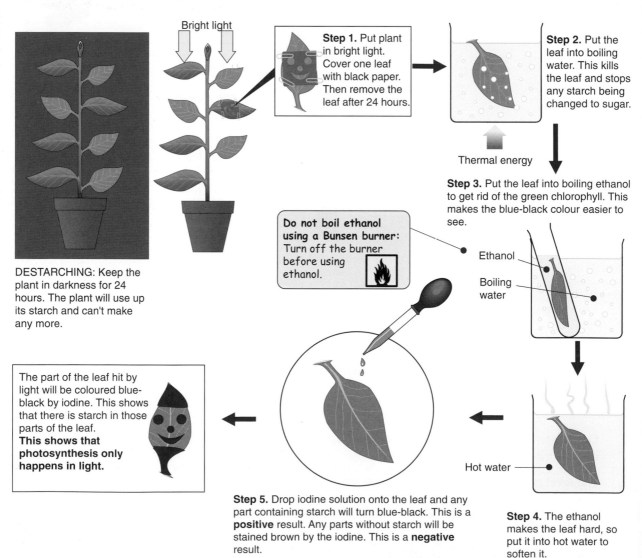

Bright light

Step 1. Put plant in bright light. Cover one leaf with black paper. Then remove the leaf after 24 hours.

Step 2. Put the leaf into boiling water. This kills the leaf and stops any starch being changed to sugar.

Thermal energy

Step 3. Put the leaf into boiling ethanol to get rid of the green chlorophyll. This makes the blue-black colour easier to see.

Do not boil ethanol using a Bunsen burner: Turn off the burner before using ethanol.

Ethanol

Boiling water

DESTARCHING: Keep the plant in darkness for 24 hours. The plant will use up its starch and can't make any more.

The part of the leaf hit by light will be coloured blue-black by iodine. This shows that there is starch in those parts of the leaf. **This shows that photosynthesis only happens in light.**

Step 5. Drop iodine solution onto the leaf and any part containing starch will turn blue-black. This is a **positive** result. Any parts without starch will be stained brown by the iodine. This is a **negative** result.

Hot water

Step 4. The ethanol makes the leaf hard, so put it into hot water to soften it.

If the scientist wanted to check how variations in temperature, light, water or carbon dioxide affected the growth of a plant, then it would be necessary to use many plants. The different tests could be carried out on different plants. It would be important, though, to carry out the tests at the same time on plants that were the same size at the start of the experiment.

Oxygen and photosynthesis

When glucose is produced from carbon dioxide and water, the gas oxygen is produced as a waste product. We can't see oxygen in the atmosphere, but we **can** see oxygen bubbles **in water.** This is useful for two reasons:

● we can prove that the gas given off **is oxygen**; and

● we can therefore use this to show **how fast** photosynthesis is happening.

The experiment shown below explains both of these points.

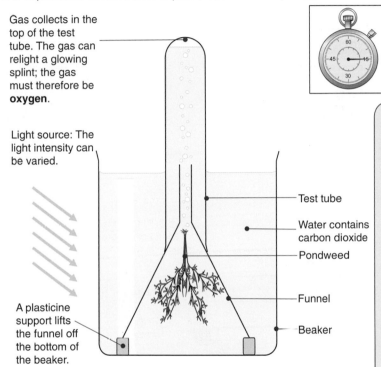

Gas collects in the top of the test tube. The gas can relight a glowing splint; the gas must therefore be **oxygen.**

Light source: The light intensity can be varied.

A plasticine support lifts the funnel off the bottom of the beaker.

Test tube

Water contains carbon dioxide

Pondweed

Funnel

Beaker

A stopwatch can be used to count the number of bubbles in a fixed time. This means you can measure the **rate** of photosynthesis.

IS IT A FAIR TEST (see page 3).
If a scientist wants to investigate the effect of light intensity on the rate of photosynthesis, he would set the following parameters:

- LIGHT INTENSITY would be the INDEPENDENT (INPUT) variable.
- THE RATE OF PHOTOSYNTHESIS would be the DEPENDENT (OUTPUT) variable.
- ALL OTHER FACTORS would be the FIXED variables.

For example:
temperature;
the amount of pondweed; and
the concentration of carbon dioxide.

The experiment would be repeated several times to make the results more reliable. An average result would then be calculated.

Getting it right: Growing plants in greenhouses

It is possible to control the process of photosynthesis by growing plants in greenhouses. The owner of a greenhouse can control the amount of light, the temperature and the amount of carbon dioxide, as well as making sure that the plants never run out of water.

Key words

Biomass – material made by the process of photosynthesis and built into the body of a plant.

Greenhouse – an environment where the ideal conditions for photosynthesis can be created.

Chloroplast – the structure in the plant cell where photosynthesis takes place.

Chlorophyll – the green pigment in plant cells that can absorb light energy for photosynthesis.

Exercise 7.1: Photosynthesis

1. During the preparation for the starch test, a leaf is warmed in ethanol. The ethanol turns green – why is this?

2. A bluebell grows from an underground stem called a bulb. The leaves make glucose and this is stored as starch in the bulb.

    (a) Describe the process by which glucose is made in leaves.

    (b) How could you test to show that starch has been stored in the bulb?

    (c) Bluebells grow in the Spring, before most trees have their leaves. Explain why this is the case.

3. Using the apparatus shown on page 71 to collect gas for measurement (not as a bubble count), Felix and Gena obtained the following results:

Light intensity in arbitrary units	Volume of oxygen released in mm^3 per minute
1	7
2	14
3	21
4	28
5	34
6	39
7	42
8	44
9	45
10	45

    (a) Plot this information as a line graph.

    (b) At what light intensity did the shoot produce 25 mm^3 of oxygen per minute?

    (c) What was the maximum light intensity that seemed to affect the rate of photosynthesis? How could this information be useful to a grower of greenhouse tomatoes?

4. Complete this table to show that you understand the idea of a fair test.

Factor to be varied	Factor to be measured	Factors to be kept constant
Light	Length of plant	
Amount of carbon dioxide	Length of plant	
Amount of water	Length of plant	
Temperature	Length of plant	

Leaves and roots help plants to grow

Remember

● Plants make food during a process called photosynthesis.

● Photosynthesis needs carbon dioxide, water and chlorophyll to absorb light energy.

We have learnt so far that plants need to trap light energy, so that they can combine carbon dioxide gas and water into molecules of glucose. They have to do this in order to make the food they require to supply energy and raw materials. It shouldn't be a surprise to find out that much of the plant's structure is very well adapted to this process. The diagram shows this:

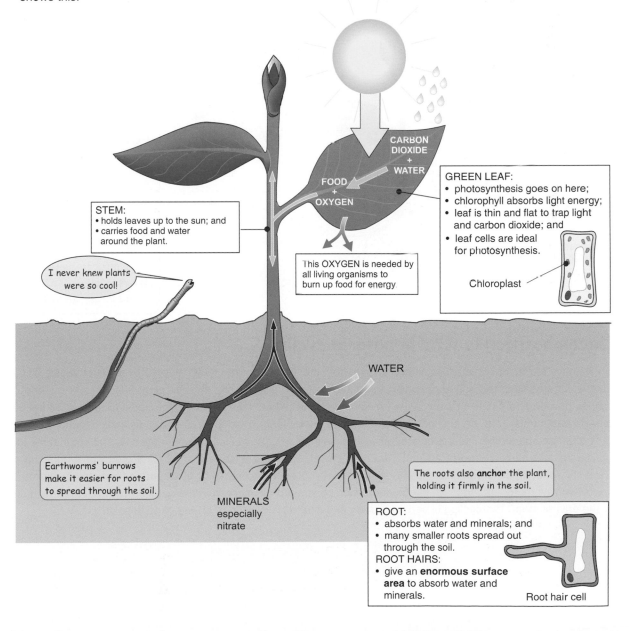

CARBON DIOXIDE + WATER

FOOD + OXYGEN

STEM:
• holds leaves up to the sun; and
• carries food and water around the plant.

I never knew plants were so cool!

This OXYGEN is needed by all living organisms to burn up food for energy.

GREEN LEAF:
• photosynthesis goes on here;
• chlorophyll absorbs light energy;
• leaf is thin and flat to trap light and carbon dioxide; and
• leaf cells are ideal for photosynthesis.

Chloroplast

WATER

Earthworms' burrows make it easier for roots to spread through the soil.

The roots also **anchor** the plant, holding it firmly in the soil.

MINERALS especially nitrate

ROOT:
• absorbs water and minerals; and
• many smaller roots spread out through the soil.
ROOT HAIRS:
• give an **enormous surface area** to absorb water and minerals.

Root hair cell

Plants and minerals

By now we know that plants can make glucose during the process of photosynthesis. But that is not necessarily enough. They also need some mineral nutrients to produce some of the other food molecules that they need. The most important of these minerals is **nitrate**. The plant requires nitrate to make its proteins. Remember that these proteins are part of the food for herbivores. The plants take up their mineral nutrients, including nitrates, which are dissolved in water, from the soil via their roots. If the soil does not have enough of these mineral nutrients, the plant cannot grow properly. Farmers can test the soil to see if there are enough minerals for their crops to grow. If the minerals are in short supply, the farmer can add fertilisers. A **fertiliser** usually contains all the main minerals that a plant needs, particularly large amounts of nitrate, which can be a problem, as you will see below.

Plants and minerals

Minerals are needed for:
· healthy green leaves;
· widespread roots; and
· large, plentiful fruits or flowers.

Plants without minerals have:
· withered, yellow leaves;
· short roots without branches; and
· tiny fruits, or no fruits at all.

Important minerals include:
· **nitrates** for growth of roots and leaves; and
· **magnesium** to help in the production of chlorophyll.

But there's bad news. Excess nitrates can be washed out of the soil into lakes and rivers. This can:
● turn rivers green from the growth of algae;
● pollute drinking water which can be especially harmful to babies; and
● eventually kill off fish and larger animals.

Decomposition is vital in natural cycles

So we have learnt that plants take carbon dioxide from the air and convert it into glucose by photosynthesis. They also absorb nitrates from the soil and convert them into proteins. This means that the plant has locked up some of the carbon dioxide and nitrate present in the environment. It would not take very long for plants to remove all the carbon dioxide and nitrate from the environment and then no more plants could grow. Since all animals depend on plants for their food (see page 99), if plants cannot grow, then animals will die. It is important for the environment that the locked-up nitrate and carbon dioxide are put back into the environment. This is the job of a group of organisms called decomposers. These organisms – bacteria and fungi – convert the remains of plants and animals back into these important raw materials. Animals, plants and decomposers are all involved in the natural cycling of the raw materials in the environment. The cycling of carbon dioxide and nitrates is described on the page opposite.

The carbon cycle

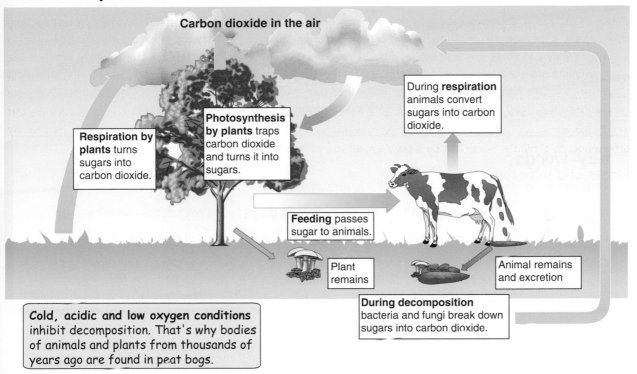

Carbon dioxide in the air

Respiration by plants turns sugars into carbon dioxide.

Photosynthesis by plants traps carbon dioxide and turns it into sugars.

During **respiration** animals convert sugars into carbon dioxide.

Feeding passes sugar to animals.

Plant remains

Animal remains and excretion

Cold, acidic and low oxygen conditions inhibit decomposition. That's why bodies of animals and plants from thousands of years ago are found in peat bogs.

During decomposition bacteria and fungi break down sugars into carbon dioxide.

The nitrogen cycle

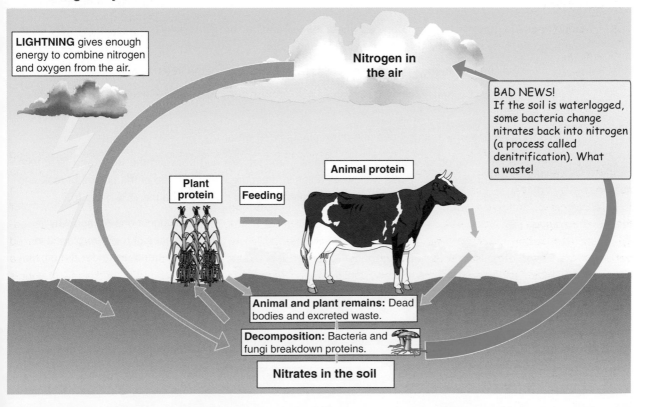

LIGHTNING gives enough energy to combine nitrogen and oxygen from the air.

Nitrogen in the air

BAD NEWS! If the soil is waterlogged, some bacteria change nitrates back into nitrogen (a process called denitrification). What a waste!

Animal protein

Plant protein

Feeding

Animal and plant remains: Dead bodies and excreted waste.

Decomposition: Bacteria and fungi breakdown proteins.

Nitrates in the soil

Plants and animals

Plants can produce food as long as they have a supply of carbon dioxide, water, light energy and minerals. They break down some of the food they make to release energy for their life processes. Any extra food they make can be used for growth, or they can **store** it in their bodies. This stored food provides animals with a useful food supply, which is why many animals eat plants. Sometimes the animal eats the whole plant, and sometimes it may just steal the food store. Plants are the only living organisms that can make their own food in this way. One way or another, all animals depend on plants for their food. This will be studied more in a later section (page 99 – Food Chains).

Key words

Fertiliser – a group of minerals added to soil to help plant growth.

Nitrate – a common mineral ion in fertilisers – it is needed by plants for the production of proteins.

Decomposer – an organism that can break down molecules from the bodies of other dead organisms.

Carbon cycle – a set of chemical reactions that follow what happens to carbon dioxide and sugars in the environment – it links photosynthesis and respiration.

Exercise 7.2: Plant nutrition

1. Write down two jobs carried out by the stem of a plant.

2. What is the main job of a leaf? Give two ways in which the leaf is well adapted for this job.

3. Mango trees are grown in hot, dry countries where the soil can be hard and tightly compacted. Farmers water the mango trees by spraying water onto the soil around them.

   (a) (i) Only a small amount of the water actually reaches the roots of the trees. Suggest one reason why.

      (ii) Suggest one other reason why mango trees do not grow well in soil which is hard and tightly packed.

   (b) Give two reasons why mango trees and other plants need water.

   (c) There is a new method of watering mango trees. Trenches are dug between the trees and filled with small pieces of rock. Plastic pipes with small holes in them are placed on top of the pieces of rock and water is pumped along the pipes. Mango trees watered by this method produce 15% more fruit.

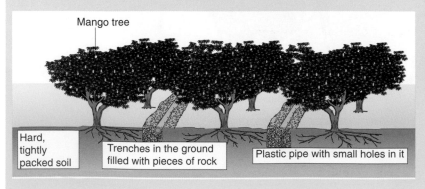

Mango tree

Hard, tightly packed soil

Trenches in the ground filled with pieces of rock

Plastic pipe with small holes in it

   (i) Suggest one reason why pieces of rock are placed in the trenches under the pipes.

   (ii) With the new method, farmers can also add nitrates to the water in the pipes. Give one reason why plants need compounds which contain nitrogen.

4. The drawing shows a plant called *Tillandsia*.

   (a) (i) The leaves of this plant absorb light. Why do plants need light?

   (ii) *Tillandsia* plants grow on the high branches of trees in rainforests. These plants cannot grow well on the lowest branches. Explain why.

   (b) *Tillandsia* plants do not have root hairs on their roots. What two substances do most plants absorb through their root hairs?

   (c) Which diagram below shows a root hair?

A	B	C	D

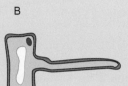

Extension question

5. Five sets of plants were grown. Each one had a slightly different treatment. The plants were weighed after two weeks of growth. How they were treated and how they grew is shown in this table.

Treatment	Ideal conditions for air, water, light and minerals	Ideal conditions for air, water and light **but** only half minerals	Ideal conditions for air, water and minerals, **but** only half light	Ideal conditions for water, light and minerals **but** only half the amount of air	Ideal conditions for air, light and minerals, **but** only half the amount of water
Weight in grams	34	32	18	28	19

   (a) Plot the results on a bar chart.

   (b) Which treatment had the greatest effect on the plants' growth?

   (c) Explain why this treatment had such an effect on the plant.

Chapter 8
Variation and classification

Here is a reminder of some of the things we should know by now:

- **All** living organisms can carry out the seven life processes (growth, nutrition, reproduction, movement, excretion, respiration and sensitivity).

- Different organisms have different features that make them able to survive in different environments.

The variety of living organisms

Differences between living organisms are called **variations**. Even humans show variations; they come in many different shapes, sizes and colours. Just imagine how many variations humans show in such features as eye colour, skin colour and shape of earlobes and so on, and now think about how many variations there must be between humans and other species.

The accumulation of these variations means that we can more easily recognise different organisms. It helps in the grouping of organisms into different categories (see page 85). The overall appearance of an organism is a result of the characteristics that it has **inherited** from its parents and the characteristics that result from the **effects of the environment**.

It is possible to produce an **equation to summarise this:**

genes   +   effects of the environment ➡ appearance

The full set of
information
passed on from
the parents.

The observable
characteristics
of an organism.

Appearance is affected by genes and environment

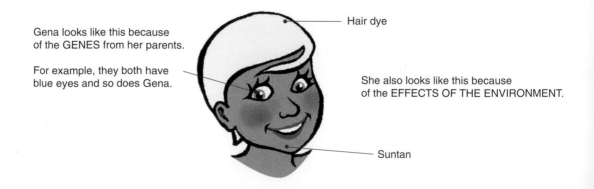

Gena looks like this because
of the GENES from her parents.

For example, they both have
blue eyes and so does Gena.

Hair dye

She also looks like this because
of the EFFECTS OF THE ENVIRONMENT.

Suntan

Different kinds of variation

Humans, like other organisms, show many variations between individuals. There are two kinds of variations:

- **Discontinuous** variations which can be very easily put into different groups. For example, you are either male or female and there aren't any in-between groups. Discontinuous variations depend only on your genes.

- **Continuous** variations fall into many groups. These groups almost run into one another. For example, there are many groups for height or for weight. You don't just have very tall or very short – there are many groups in-between. Continuous variations depend on the environment as well as on your genes.

These characteristics result from **GENES (DISCONTINUOUS VARIATION)**.

These characteristics result from **GENES** and **EFFECTS OF THE ENVIRONMENT (CONTINUOUS VARIATION)**.

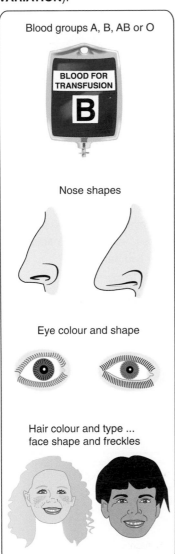

Blood groups A, B, AB or O

Nose shapes

Eye colour and shape

Hair colour and type ...
face shape and freckles

Height

Shape and build

TRAINING AND MUSCLES
We inherit genes for fast or slow muscles. Training is an environmental effect that can change the size and efficiency of what we have inherited.

AMAZING BUT TRUE!
The importance of genes in affecting height is shown by the fact that girls are rarely, if ever, taller than their fathers. Girls haven't inherited the male gene, and this is the gene that has a great effect on height.

How do variations come about?

The characteristics of an organism may change **temporarily** due to some environmental effect. For example, a pale-skinned person may develop a suntan after sunbathing. These temporary variations may be of great importance to the individual organism (for example, a suntan protects a human from dangerous radiation) but they are of less importance to the species because they cannot be inherited. The characteristics that are of most interest to biologists are those which are **permanent** and **can** be inherited – gender (whether you are male or female) is a good example. These variations come about because of your genetic make-up and that is what you have inherited from your parents.

Genes and characteristics

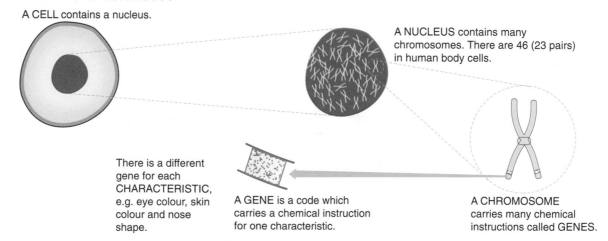

A CELL contains a nucleus.

A NUCLEUS contains many chromosomes. There are 46 (23 pairs) in human body cells.

There is a different gene for each CHARACTERISTIC, e.g. eye colour, skin colour and nose shape.

A GENE is a code which carries a chemical instruction for one characteristic.

A CHROMOSOME carries many chemical instructions called GENES.

Fertilisation joins up genes from two parents

You are the result of a fertilisation process (see page 31). In fertilisation the sex cells from your two parents combine. These sex cells contain a set of genes from each parent. Because of this process, you have two sets of genes and therefore it is not surprising that you show a mixture of the characteristics of your two parents.

Fertilisation combines genes from two parents

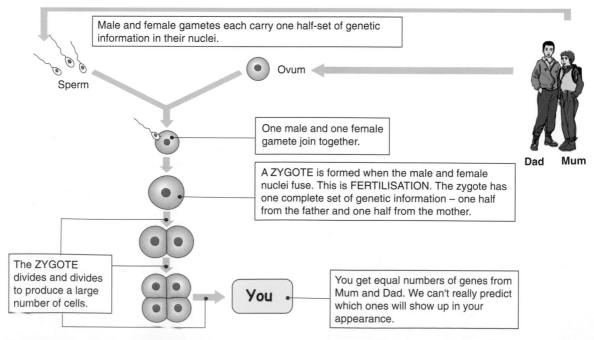

Male and female gametes each carry one half-set of genetic information in their nuclei.

Sperm

Ovum

One male and one female gamete join together.

A ZYGOTE is formed when the male and female nuclei fuse. This is FERTILISATION. The zygote has one complete set of genetic information – one half from the father and one half from the mother.

The ZYGOTE divides and divides to produce a large number of cells.

You

You get equal numbers of genes from Mum and Dad. We can't really predict which ones will show up in your appearance.

Dad   Mum

Twins show the effects of the environment

Identical twins are formed from a single fertilised egg. When the fertilised egg divides into a small ball of cells (see page 12), and the ball splits into two, each of the two sets of cells develops into a new person – identical twins. These identical twins have exactly the same genes, although they may have a slightly different appearance. Any slight differences in their appearance will be due to the effects of their environment. The most likely cause of any environmental variation is diet.

The development of twins

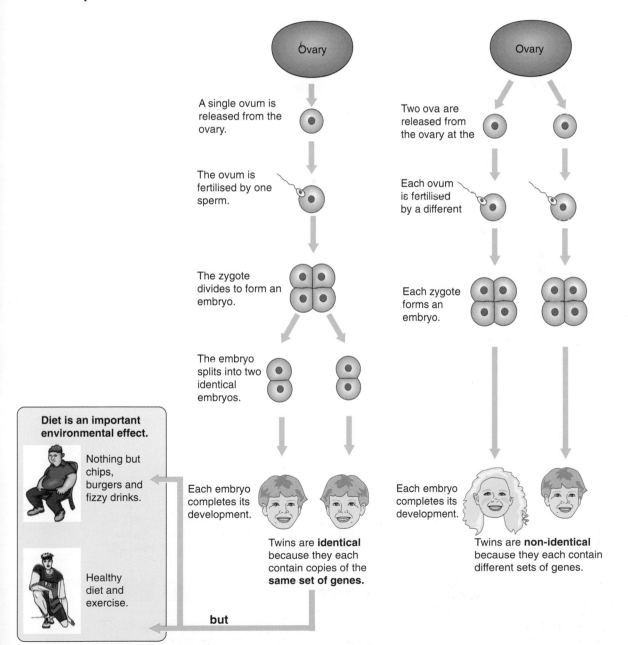

Ovary

Ovary

A single ovum is released from the ovary.

Two ova are released from the ovary at the

The ovum is fertilised by one sperm.

Each ovum is fertilised by a different

The zygote divides to form an embryo.

Each zygote forms an embryo.

The embryo splits into two identical embryos.

Diet is an important environmental effect.

Nothing but chips, burgers and fizzy drinks.

Each embryo completes its development.

Each embryo completes its development.

Healthy diet and exercise.

Twins are **identical** because they each contain copies of the **same set of genes.**

Twins are **non-identical** because they each contain different sets of genes.

but

Genes and environment also affect the characteristics of plants

Plants inherit characteristics, just as animals do. They too receive genes from the parent plants. Plants are affected much more by their environment than animals are, mainly because the plants can't move to a more suitable environment. As you know, plants are affected by the four main growth factors (see page 69).

● **Light** – is needed directly for photosynthesis and so for growth.

● **Temperature** – affects how quickly the chemical reactions needed for life can go on in the plant.

● **Water** – is needed for photosynthesis and to make plant cells swell to their full size.

● **Minerals in the soil** – nitrate, in particular, is needed for the growth of new cells.

Is it genes or the environment?

We can use sets of plants to carry out experiments to see whether some variation is inherited or due to the environment. One of these experiments is shown in here.

Testing for variation: Genes or environment?

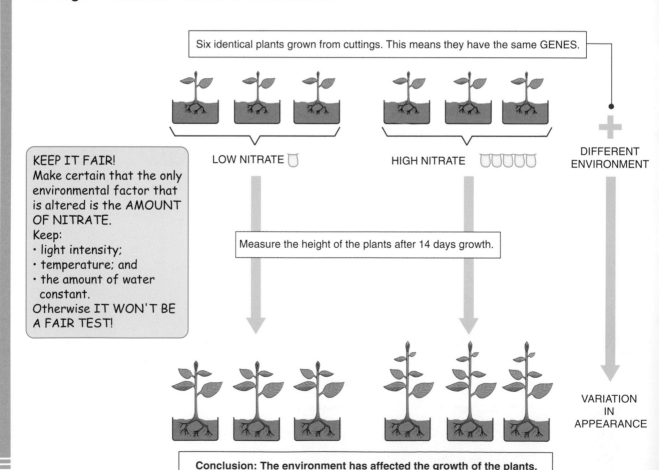

Six identical plants grown from cuttings. This means they have the same GENES.

LOW NITRATE

HIGH NITRATE

DIFFERENT ENVIRONMENT

KEEP IT FAIR!
Make certain that the only environmental factor that is altered is the AMOUNT OF NITRATE.
Keep:
· light intensity;
· temperature; and
· the amount of water constant.
Otherwise IT WON'T BE A FAIR TEST!

Measure the height of the plants after 14 days growth.

VARIATION IN APPEARANCE

Conclusion: The environment has affected the growth of the plants.

It is not so easy to carry out experiments like this on animals but sometimes they are important. For example, a food company might want to test whether a new food helps growth or not. Scientists can now produce batches of identical animals. The animals can then be fed with different amounts of the new food and their growth measured. Because these animals have identical genes (the scientific word is that they are a **clone**), any difference in growth must be due to the different amounts of food. Do you think it is acceptable to use animals in this way?

Key words

Discontinuous variation – differences that fall into very clear classes, for example, male and female.

Continuous variation – differences that can easily overlap, for example, body mass.

Genes – chemicals in the chromosomes that control the characteristics of living organisms.

Chromosome – a thread inside the nucleus of a cell – it is made of many genes.

Exercise 8.1: Variation

1. Match up the words from the first column with the definitions from the second column.

Gene	A process that joins sex cells together.
Chromosome	All factors affecting an organism.
Variation	The first cell that contains genes from two parents.
Environment	A chemical that controls a characteristic of an organism.
Zygote	The differences between organisms.
Fertilisation	A thin strand, found in the nucleus, that carries a set of genes.

2. Complete the following paragraphs.

    (a) Variation occurs in two forms. .... variation shows clear cut separation between groups, and .... variation of groups, which almost run into each other. The first of these is the result of .... alone, whilst the second is affected by both .... and .... factors.

    (b) The genes inherited by an organism come from its .... One set comes from the .... and one set from the .... The overall appearance of an organism can be explained in a simple equation: .... plus .... equals ....

3. Which of the following is an example of discontinuous variation?

    Body mass, chest circumference, blood group, hairstyle, height.

    Explain (a) why you chose one of these alternatives and (b) why you rejected the others.

Extension question

4. Two students in the first year of secondary school were carrying out a mathematical investigation. They decided to measure the heights of all the other pupils in their class. Here are their results:

Height category in cm	Number in category
121 – 125	2
126 – 130	4
131 – 135	9
136 – 140	6
141 – 145	4
146 – 150	1

(a) Plot these results as a bar chart.

(b) Explain how these differences in height could have come about.

(c) Suggest one characteristic that the students could have studied and which would have given only two different groups.

The variety of life

Don't forget

- Living organisms show variation which means there are differences between them.

- Scientists can use these differences to produce keys. Remind yourself how organisms can be classified using **branching** keys, **spider** keys and **numbered** keys. (See *Science* Book 1 chapter 8.)

Putting living things into groups

We know that a key is a very useful way to identify living things. A key works by asking a set of questions about the features an organism has. The answers we give to the questions begin to split up a large group of living things into individual organisms.

Scientists can use the answers to these questions to put all known living organisms into groups, by grouping together all the organisms with similar features. This grouping together is called **classifying**.

All living organisms can be put into very large groups called kingdoms. There are **five kingdoms** and every living organism can be placed into one or other of them.

The five kingdoms of living organisms

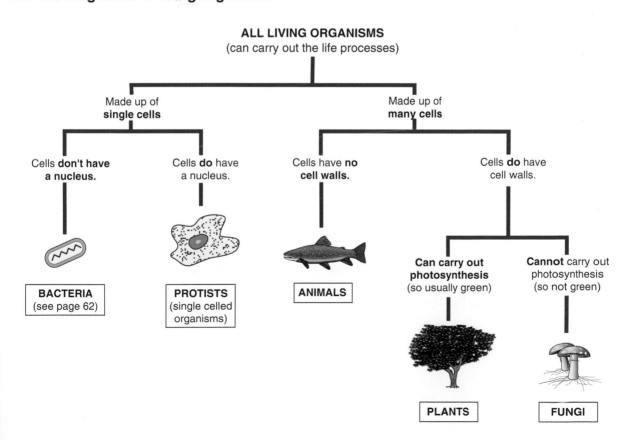

The animal kingdom

All the animals in the world can be put into one of two groups, either as a **vertebrate** or an **invertebrate**. We can put animals into the correct group by answering just one question.

Vertebrates and invertebrates

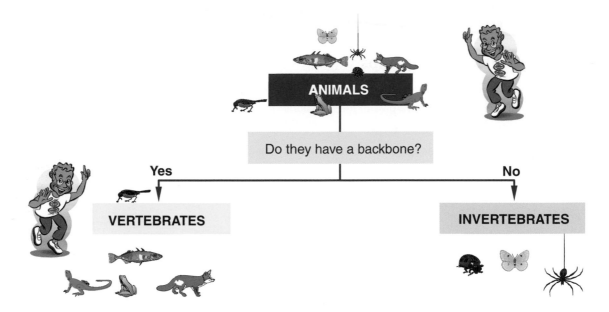

> IT'S NOT JUST A BACKBONE!
> Vertebrates don't just have a backbone; they have a complete bony skeleton (see page 27). It's amazing to think that the femur (thigh bone) of a frog weighs less than a millionth of the femur of an elephant.

There are many times more invertebrates than vertebrates, but most of us recognise vertebrates more easily. There are **five groups of vertebrates** (animals with backbones). We can easily recognise the five groups by looking at their skin, although there are other important differences between the groups.

The five groups of vertebrates

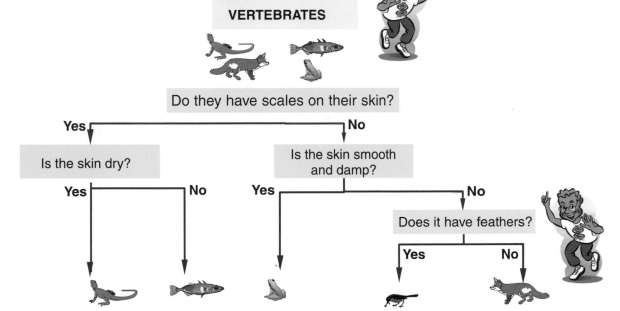

VERTEBRATES

Do they have scales on their skin?

Yes — Is the skin dry?

No — Is the skin smooth and damp?

Yes · No

Yes · No

Does it have feathers?

Yes · No

Other Important differences	REPTILE	FISH	AMPHIBIAN	BIRD	MAMMAL
Constant body temperature	No	No	No	Yes	Yes
Does it lay eggs?	Yes – with soft shells	Yes – in water	Yes – in water	Yes – with hard shells	No
Does it feed it's young on milk?	No	No	No	No	Yes

Humans are vertebrates, and belong to the class called the **mammals**.

KEEPING WARM

Fur (on mammals) and feathers (on birds) are vital. These coverings act as insulation, so that mammals and birds can keep a constant body temperature in the environment.

Arthropods are invertebrates

The invertebrates are animals without backbones. It's not always easy to tell that they haven't got backbones because some of them have very hard covers to their bodies. This hard body is good for protection against predators, but can make movement difficult. To make movement easier, one group of invertebrates – called the **arthropods** – consists of animals that have many joints in their limbs (the word arthropod actually means 'jointed foot'). Two different kinds of arthropod are the **insects** and the **spiders**. Some people think of them both as 'creepy-crawlies', but there are some important differences between these two groups.

Insects and spiders are arthropods

INSECT	SPIDER
Three main body parts:	**Two** main body parts:

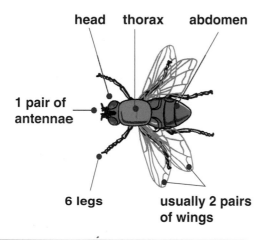

head   thorax   abdomen

1 pair of antennae

6 legs   usually 2 pairs of wings

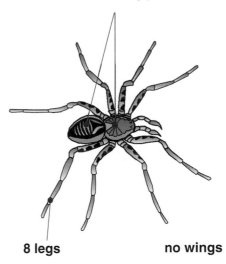

8 legs   no wings

> SCARY STUFF!
> No matter how hard we've tried, humans have never wiped out an insect pest species! (We have killed off some non-harmful species by accident though.)

Mexican red-leg tarantula

European hornet

> DID YOU KNOW?
> Every spider is a meat-eater – there are no vegetarians.

The plant kingdom

All plants have one thing in common: they have a pigment that can absorb light energy, so that they can make their own food by photosynthesis. We can divide up all the plants into two main groups, by asking just one question.

The plant kingdom

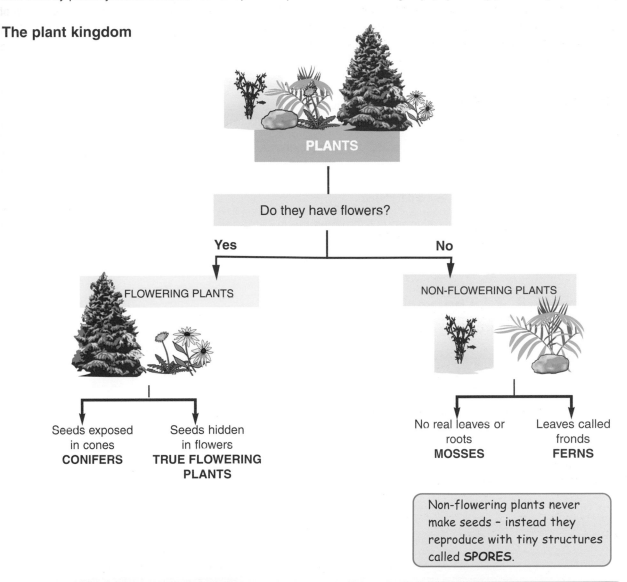

PLANTS

Do they have flowers?

Yes   **No**

FLOWERING PLANTS   NON-FLOWERING PLANTS

Seeds exposed in cones
CONIFERS

Seeds hidden in flowers
TRUE FLOWERING PLANTS

No real leaves or roots
MOSSES

Leaves called fronds
FERNS

Non-flowering plants never make seeds – instead they reproduce with tiny structures called **SPORES**.

FUNGI NEED FOOD!
Fungi have no chlorophyll, so must feed by digesting other foods. They use enzymes (just like humans do) to **decompose** animals and plants, or their remains.
FUNGI ARE NOT PLANTS. Can you explain this to your parents?

Scientists used to believe that fungi were plants. They thought this because they knew fungi definitely weren't animals. In fact, even though mushrooms and toadstools look more like plants than animals, **fungi cannot carry out photosynthesis and so cannot be called a plant**.

What is a species?

There are many other questions that can be asked to split these large groups into smaller and smaller groups. The smallest of all groups is called the **species**. Members of the same species are so much alike that males and females can mate and produce offspring just like themselves. Humans are one species, oak trees are another and barn owls are another and so on. Scientists have found that there are over five million species on Earth.

Key words

Classification – a way of placing living organisms into groups with similar characteristics.

Kingdom – a very large classification group, for example, the animal kingdom.

Vertebrate – an animal with a backbone.

Invertebrate – an animal without a backbone.

Species – a very small classification group – the organisms in it are so similar to each other that they can breed with one another.

Exercise 8.2: The variety of life

1. Copy this table. Use information from this section to fill in the gaps. Put a + if a feature is present and a – if it is absent.

Feature	Fish	Amphibian	Reptile	Bird	Mammal
Backbone					
Scales					
Feathers					
Hairy skin					

2. Match up the description from the first column with the group from the second column.

Has wings, a constant body temperature and lays eggs with hard shells.	Insect
Has no backbone, two body parts and eight jointed legs.	Fungus
Has a body made of a single cell with a clear nucleus and cytoplasm.	Fish
Has no backbone, three body parts and six jointed legs.	Mammal
Has cells with a definite cell wall but does not feed by photosynthesis.	Flowering plant
Has hair, provides milk for its young and has a constant body temperature.	Protist
Has a backbone, gills, fins and scales.	Bird
Has flowers for reproduction and green leaves.	Spider

Extension question

3.   The system for giving all living things a name in Latin was suggested by a scientist called Linnaeus.

(a)   Use the Internet or your library to complete this table.

Latin name	Common name
Fraxinus excelsior	
	English oak
Pan troglodytes	
Loxodonta africana	
	Foxglove
	Common frog

(b)   What are the advantages of a common system of names?

(c)   Try to find the name for the Lion in French, German and Swahili.

Selective breeding

Variation occurs naturally in all living organisms. This means that they have different characteristics. It is possible to mix characteristics deliberately to produce useful varieties of animals and plants. Ever since the early humans began to domesticate animals and plants, they have been trying to improve them. This improvement is brought about by choosing or selecting the individual organisms with the most useful – useful to humans, that is – characteristics, allowing only these individuals to breed. This process is called **selective breeding**. Here are some examples of selective breeding:

- **Jersey cattle** have been bred to produce milk with a very high cream content.

- All domestic **dogs** are the same species but some have been bred for *appearance* (e.g. Pekinese), some as *hunting companions* (e.g. Springer spaniels), some as *guard dogs* (e.g. Rottweilers) and some for *racing* (see below).

- **Wheat** has been bred so that all the stems are the same height. This makes harvesting easier and makes collection of the grain easier because the ears separate easily from the stalk.

Selective breeding of animals

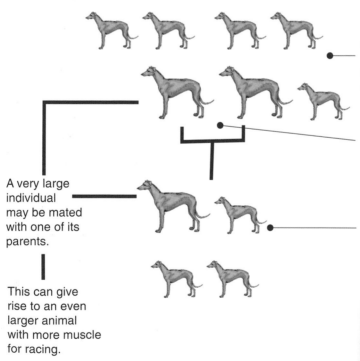

In this litter of greyhounds two are larger than the others. Large greyhounds carry more muscle which is valuable to a racing animal.

These two dogs with the desirable characteristic are allowed to breed and produce a litter.

A very large individual may be mated with one of its parents.

This can give rise to an even larger animal with more muscle for racing.

If the size characteristic is inherited, the next generation may contain individuals which are even bigger.

Selective breeding of plants

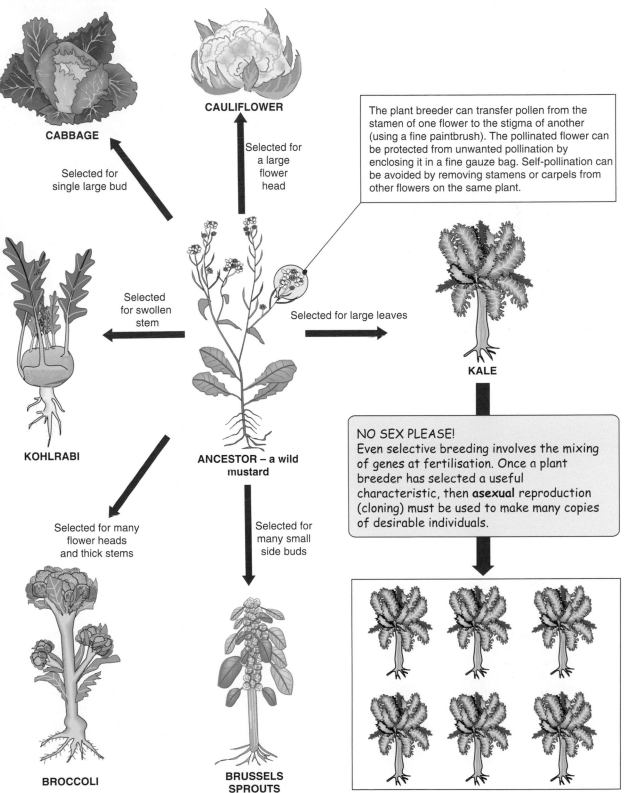

CABBAGE

Selected for single large bud

CAULIFLOWER

Selected for a large flower head

The plant breeder can transfer pollen from the stamen of one flower to the stigma of another (using a fine paintbrush). The pollinated flower can be protected from unwanted pollination by enclosing it in a fine gauze bag. Self-pollination can be avoided by removing stamens or carpels from other flowers on the same plant.

Selected for swollen stem

Selected for large leaves

KOHLRABI

ANCESTOR – a wild mustard

KALE

Selected for many flower heads and thick stems

Selected for many small side buds

NO SEX PLEASE!
Even selective breeding involves the mixing of genes at fertilisation. Once a plant breeder has selected a useful characteristic, then **asexual** reproduction (cloning) must be used to make many copies of desirable individuals.

BROCCOLI

BRUSSELS SPROUTS

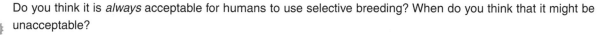

Of course, what *humans* consider a valuable characteristic might not actually be valuable in a *natural* situation. A pet animal such as a Chihuahua dog would probably not survive in the wild because its hunting instincts have been bred out to make it more useful as a house pet.

These characteristics are controlled by genes (see page 80). However, it is very important that humans preserve unpopular genes, i.e. genes which control characteristics that do not currently offer any advantage to us. It may be that a cow with a very limited milk yield in fact carries a gene that makes it resistant to a disease which is not yet a problem in domestic herds. This resistance gene might be extremely valuable if ever such a disease did threaten our herds of cows. For this reason many varieties of animals and plants are kept in small numbers, in rare breed centres up and down the country.

Plant genes may be conserved in their seeds, which make them easy to store. Some animal genes may be kept as frozen eggs, sperm or embryos. It is likely that selective breeding will be replaced by **genetic engineering** in the future. This technique is very much more predictable than selective breeding and is even quicker in producing results which might be of benefit to humans.

Do you think it is *always* acceptable for humans to use selective breeding? When do you think that it might be unacceptable?

Adaptation

Adaptation means being well suited to the environment. You need to remember:

- A habitat must provide a living organism with food, shelter and a breeding site.

- A habitat can change for many reasons.

- In our world, such a huge variety of life exists because different organisms have different features.

Living organisms have features that enable them to survive in their environments. These features are called **adaptations**. These features result from the variations between different organisms. There are many different adaptations that allow living organisms to carry on with the life processes in a range of different habitats. These adaptations fall into different groups, according to how they help the organism to survive.

Feeding: Animals have many features that help them to feed. For example, hunting animals (predators – see page 103) often have sharp teeth and claws to kill their prey, powerful muscles to chase them and very sensitive eyes to find them in the first place *(e.g. a cheetah)*.

Plants often have very large leaves to trap light and deep roots to reach water. Some plants even have sticky leaves to trap insects *(e.g. Venus fly trap)*.

Protection: Not all animals are hunters – some of them are chased by the hunters. These prey animals (see page103) need to protect themselves. Some of them have a hard covering to their bodies *(e.g. a tortoise)*.

Some of them are coloured to blend into their background – they are **camouflaged** *(e.g. a peppered moth)*.

Camouflage can also be used by predators. The polar bear, for example, has a white coat that helps it to hide from the prey animals it is trying to catch.

Its great size and large volume means that there are more cells to generate internal/thermal energy by respiration.

The polar bear also has the adaptations of a carnivore which enable it to feed on meat.

Small ears and tail means that there is less surface area for loss of internal/thermal energy by radiation.

Pads on the feet provide:
- insulation against loss of internal/thermal energy by conduction; and
- grip on slippery surfaces.

A **thick layer of fat** provides:
- good insulation against loss of internal/thermal energy; and
- can be used as a food store during hibernation. Polar bears will hibernate to avoid the most severe weather conditions.

SLEEPING THROUGH THE WINTER
Polar bears spend the long, dark winters hibernating. The female must save enough fat to be able to feed her new-born cubs, as well as keeping herself warm.

Plants that live in dry environments often have a waxy covering to cut down the loss of water from their bodies and spines to stop animals eating them. These adaptations are shown below.

Cacti are well adapted to hot, dry environments

A swollen stem stores water.

Stomata are sunk in grooves to avoid drying winds.

The leaves are reduced to **spines** this reduces the surface area for water loss. They also deter grazing animals.

Deep roots penetrate to very low water tables.

The green **stem** carries out photosynthesis.

Shallow roots absorb water from the lightest of rainfalls.

Movement: Whether an animal is a predator or is prey, it will need to be able to move. There are many adaptations to make this possible. Birds have feathers that are light and give a big surface to help them fly. Fish are streamlined to cut through the water and have fins to push against the water. Camels have big, flat feet, so that they can walk on sand without sinking.

The camel is adapted to dry, desert conditions

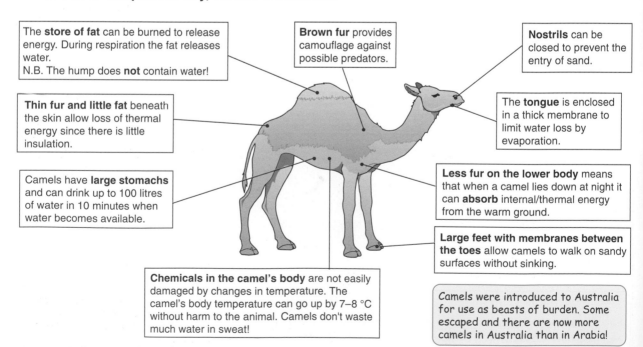

The **store of fat** can be burned to release energy. During respiration the fat releases water.
N.B. The hump does **not** contain water!

Brown fur provides camouflage against possible predators.

Nostrils can be closed to prevent the entry of sand.

Thin fur and little fat beneath the skin allow loss of thermal energy since there is little insulation.

The **tongue** is enclosed in a thick membrane to limit water loss by evaporation.

Camels have **large stomachs** and can drink up to 100 litres of water in 10 minutes when water becomes available.

Less fur on the lower body means that when a camel lies down at night it can **absorb** internal/thermal energy from the warm ground.

Large feet with membranes between the toes allow camels to walk on sandy surfaces without sinking.

Chemicals in the camel's body are not easily damaged by changes in temperature. The camel's body temperature can go up by 7–8 °C without harm to the animal. Camels don't waste much water in sweat!

Camels were introduced to Australia for use as beasts of burden. Some escaped and there are now more camels in Australia than in Arabia!

The diagrams in **Science** Book 1 of the freshwater pond and the oak woodland showed some of the many ways in which living organisms are adapted to their habitats. In this book we will look at the hedgerow and what its habitat provides its occupants.

Hedgerows and habitats

ANNUAL CHANGES DEPEND ON THE SEASONS (see page 355).
Living organisms have to be adapted to deal with changes in:
* temperature;
* availability of water;
* winds;
* light intensity;
* length of daylight; and
* availability of food.

HEDGEROWS ARE WILDLIFE CORRIDORS where animals can move from one piece of woodland to another, without being seen by their predators.

HEDGEROWS ARE IDEAL HABITATS because they provide:
* food, such as berries, seeds and insects;
* shelter, from wind and rain and from predators; and
* breeding sites, such as nests for birds and burrows for small mammals like mice.

ANIMALS ADAPT TO ANNUAL CHANGES. For example in winter:
* Hedgehogs **hibernate** to avoid food shortages.
* Butterflies and other insects lay eggs, then die. The next generation spends the winter as **pupae** (like butterfly chrysalids).
* Some mammals **store food** for times when no food can be found.
* Many birds **migrate,** which means they move to a warmer place where they can still find food.

HEDGEROWS AFFECT THE ENVIRONMENT

WIND: One side of a hedge is usually sheltered from the wind. This side is usually more humid (damper air) and warmer. The temperature can easily be measured with a thermometer.

LIGHT: The hedgerow bushes will cast a shadow, so the bottom of the hedge may be much darker than an open field. Light intensity can be measured with a light meter.

SOIL MOISTURE: The roots of the hedgerow plants absorb a lot of water, so soil near the hedge may be quite dry. Soil moisture can be measured by weighing a sample of soil, drying it out and then weighing again.

PLANTS ADAPT TO ANNUAL CHANGES. For example in winter:
* Deciduous trees **shed their leaves** because there's less light for photosynthesis and it's harder to pull cold water out of the soil.
* Flowers form seeds and then **die off** because there are very few insects left to pollinate them.
* Leaves of many flowers die back, and food is **stored in bulbs underground** until conditions improve next spring.

NITRATES: Minerals such as nitrates can be taken up by the roots of the hedgerow plants. On the other hand, fallen leaves and fruits decompose to replace many minerals (see page 75).

Key words

Adaptation – a feature of an organism that makes it very well suited to its environment.

Camouflage – a pattern or colour that allows an animal to blend in with its background.

Nocturnal – being active at night.

Migration – moving to a new habitat, usually to obtain enough food.

Hibernation – sleeping through the winter, to save energy and to avoid having to find food when there isn't much available.

Exercise 8.3: Adaptation

1. Why do small birds that eat insects migrate south for the winter? Name two such birds.

2. How does a caterpillar avoid being eaten by a small bird?

3. How are daffodils adapted to survive winter conditions?

4. Name two hedgerow animals that hibernate. Why do they hibernate?

Extension questions

5. Use a book or an Internet website to find out about how birds know which way to fly when they migrate. Write a short paragraph describing the process.

6. Use a book or the Internet to find out about two other animal migrations. Write a short paragraph on each, explaining why they migrate.

Chapter 9
Feeding relationships

● All living organisms need a **supply of food** to carry out their life processes.

● **Plants** use light energy and chemicals from their surroundings to make their own food.

● **Animals** cannot *make* their own food but they get their energy and raw materials from the food they eat.

● **Decomposers** obtain energy and raw materials from the remains of other living organisms.

Animals (and that includes humans) depend on plants for survival. There may be many different animals and plants in one habitat (see page 97, for example) but they are all linked together by food. An example of the way living organisms are linked by food is shown below.

Feeding links are called food chains

As we know, these feeding links between different organisms make up a **food chain**. (See *Science* Book 1 chapter 11.) A food chain shows how energy and raw materials are passed from one organism to another by feeding. There are certain **rules** about food chains:

● They always start with a green plant because only green plants can make their own food. Plants make their own food by photosynthesis, so they are called **producers**.

● Animals eat or consume food, so they are called **consumers**.

● The arrows in a food chain mean 'food for'. These arrows always point in the direction in which the energy and raw materials are moving as the organisms feed.

A food chain shows feeding links

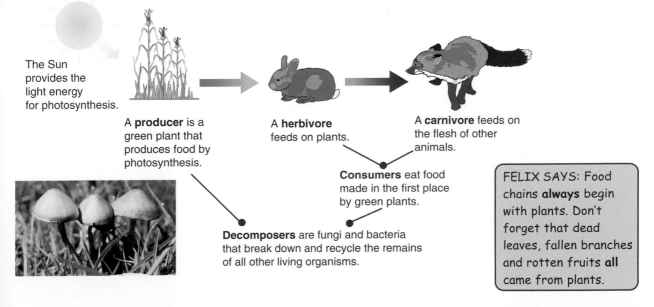

The Sun provides the light energy for photosynthesis.

A **producer** is a green plant that produces food by photosynthesis.

A **herbivore** feeds on plants.

A **carnivore** feeds on the flesh of other animals.

Consumers eat food made in the first place by green plants.

Decomposers are fungi and bacteria that break down and recycle the remains of all other living organisms.

FELIX SAYS: Food chains **always** begin with plants. Don't forget that dead leaves, fallen branches and rotten fruits **all** came from plants.

There are different types of consumers

Because animals cannot make their own food, they must obtain their food by eating other organisms. Animals are very well adapted to the type of food they eat. Some animals are called **herbivores** because they eat plants (*herba* means 'plant' or 'grass' in Latin). Other animals are called **carnivores** because they eat meat (*caro, carnis* means 'meat' in Latin). Some animals get the best of both worlds; they eat plants *and* meat. These animals are called **omnivores** (*omni* means 'all'). Before you move on, make sure you can name a herbivore, a carnivore and an omnivore.

Some microbes (bacteria and fungi) feed on the remains of dead plants and animals, or the waste that animals produce during excretion. These microbes are **decomposers** (see page 75). Every habitat needs decomposers so that supplies of minerals and other food materials can be recycled.

All change

If one organism in a food chain is affected in some way, then other organisms in the same food chain will also be affected. One example is shown in the diagram below:

Lettuces fall in number because more snails eat them.

Snails increase in number because no thrushes eat them.

Thrushes fall in number because somebody shoots them.

Hawks fall in number because there are fewer thrushes to eat.

A change in the number of thrushes can cause ...

Organisms are less likely to be affected if they can feed on more than one kind of food, in other words if they can take part in more than one food chain.

Food webs

Most animals and plants actually play a part in more than one food chain. Feeding relationships in a habitat are in fact very complex because food chains overlap. These interlinked food chains are called food webs.

A food web is a set of linked food chains

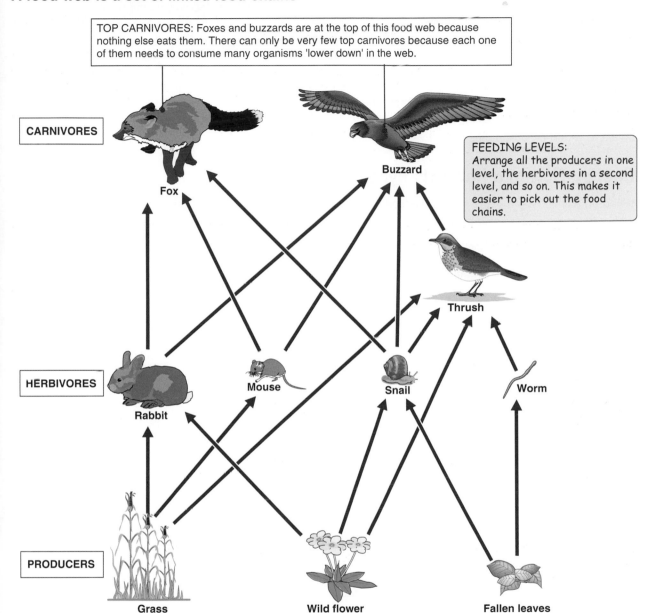

TOP CARNIVORES: Foxes and buzzards are at the top of this food web because nothing else eats them. There can only be very few top carnivores because each one of them needs to consume many organisms 'lower down' in the web.

FEEDING LEVELS:
Arrange all the producers in one level, the herbivores in a second level, and so on. This makes it easier to pick out the food chains.

CARNIVORES

Fox

Buzzard

Thrush

HERBIVORES

Rabbit

Mouse

Snail

Worm

PRODUCERS

Grass

Wild flower

Fallen leaves

Food webs:

● Give a more realistic picture of the feeding relationships in a habitat. For example, the diagram shows that a fox can feed on more than one kind of herbivore and that grass is eaten by more than one kind of consumer.

● Show how many animals can survive changes in their environment. For example, cold weather might reduce the number of earthworms and snails available to a thrush but it can feed itself on grass seeds and fruits.

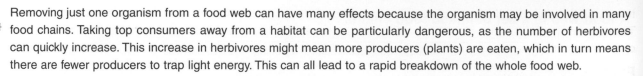

Removing just one organism from a food web can have many effects because the organism may be involved in many food chains. Taking top consumers away from a habitat can be particularly dangerous, as the number of herbivores can quickly increase. This increase in herbivores might mean more producers (plants) are eaten, which in turn means there are fewer producers to trap light energy. This can all lead to a rapid breakdown of the whole food web.

Adding a new organism to a food web can be just as dangerous as taking one away. Rats were introduced to the islands around New Zealand when they escaped from ships stopping to take on food and water. The rats killed off many ground-nesting birds. The situation was made worse by introducing stoats to try and kill off the rats. The stoats also killed and ate the ground-nesting birds. The conservation of wild organisms is a very complicated business and should be left to expert biologists (see page 115).

Energy flow in a habitat: Pyramids of numbers

When an animal eats a plant, it uses the food to supply raw materials and energy (see page 46). Some of the food molecules in the plants never become food molecules in the animal for the following reasons:

- Some of the plant material is wasted. For example, roots and stem may be left behind. (Do you eat all of a sprout plant?)

- Some of the plant material passes right through the animal's digestive system and is passed out in the faeces.

- Some of the energy is lost to the environment as thermal energy.

Energy is lost at every stage in the food chain. In fact, only about 10% of the available energy passes from one feeding level to the next.

Food chains and energy

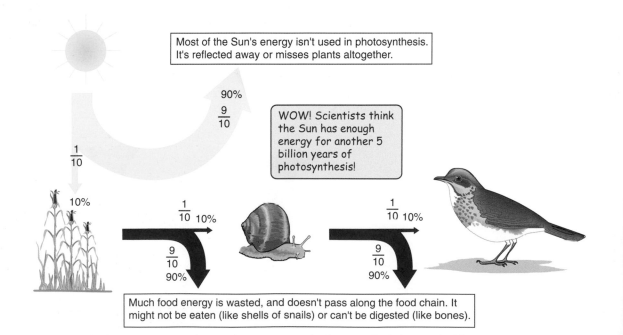

Most of the Sun's energy isn't used in photosynthesis. It's reflected away or misses plants altogether.

WOW! Scientists think the Sun has enough energy for another 5 billion years of photosynthesis!

Much food energy is wasted, and doesn't pass along the food chain. It might not be eaten (like shells of snails) or can't be digested (like bones).

If you count the number of organisms at each feeding level in a food chain, you can produce a **pyramid of numbers**. The pyramid shape is a result of the energy loss at each stage. The consumers must always eat large numbers of the organisms below them in the pyramid.

Pyramid of numbers

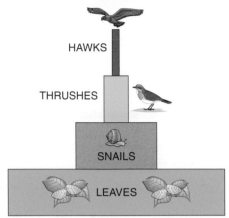

HAWKS

THRUSHES

SNAILS

LEAVES

A pyramid of numbers is constructed by counting the number of organisms at each stage of a food chain.

Odd numbers

A pyramid of numbers may not be a pyramid! Just counting the organisms can give strange results, like these:

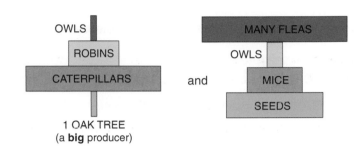

OWLS

ROBINS

CATERPILLARS

1 OAK TREE
(a **big** producer)

and

MANY FLEAS

OWLS

MICE

SEEDS

Predators and prey

Animals that eat other animals are called **predators**, and the animals that they catch are called **prey**. The numbers of predators and their prey depend on each other. For example, if there are a lot of foxes (predators) in one habitat, then the rabbit (prey) numbers will quickly fall. If the number of rabbits falls, then there may not be enough food for all the foxes. Some of the foxes will die unless they move to a place where there is more food, or learn to eat other things. In Britain, many foxes have moved into cities where they have learned to feed on food thrown away by humans. The same thing can happen with insects. Greenfly can breed very quickly if the weather is warm and moist. There can be millions of them in one garden, much to the horror of the gardeners. However, a plague of greenfly is a heavenly situation for the animals that love to eat them, such as ladybirds. The ladybird numbers increase and, because there are so many of them, the number of greenfly falls again. There is a cycle between the numbers of predators and their prey.

Predators and prey

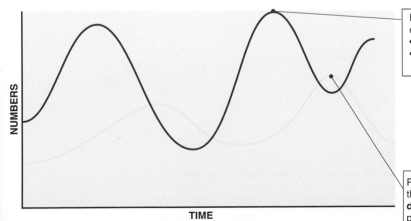

NUMBERS

TIME

PREY numbers go up and down depending on:
• how quickly they breed; and
• how many are eaten by predators.

PREDATOR numbers go **up** when the number of prey rises, then **down** again when the number of prey falls.

FELIX SAYS: Don't forget - there must always be more prey than predators!

Key words

Food chain – the flow of food energy between living organisms.

Producer – an organism that can trap light energy to supply food energy to a food chain.

Consumer – an organism that obtains its food energy by eating another organism.

Predator – an animal that chases and catches other living organisms.

Pyramid of numbers – a way of drawing out the number of organisms at different stages in a food chain.

Food web – a set of different food chains that overlap and link up with one another.

Exercise 9.1: Food chains

1. Look at the diagram of the hedgerow (page 97). Identify and write down a food chain from this habitat.

2. Give an example of a herbivore, a carnivore and an omnivore that would live in a hedgerow habitat. Name one decomposer and explain why it is so important in this habitat.

3. A sparrow hawk consumes 25 blue tits. 25 000 leaves are eaten by 2500 worms. Each blue tit eats 100 worms. Use this information to draw a pyramid of numbers (your pyramid does not need to be drawn exactly to scale).

Extension question

4. Some students made a survey of a freshwater pond. After many visits they put together their results in this list:

    Hydra feeds on water fleas.

    Diving beetles feed on water fleas and on mayfly larvae.

    Pond snails feed on algae and on pondweed.

    Pond skaters feed on water fleas and tadpoles.

    Perch feed on tadpoles, diving beetles, water fleas and pond skaters.

    Herons feed on perch.

    Mayfly larvae feed on algae.

    Water fleas feed on algae.

    Tadpoles feed on algae and on water fleas.

    (a) Use this information to construct a food web for this pond.

    (b) What is the top consumer for this food web?

    (c) What happens to the animals and plants that die before they are eaten?

    (d) Choose one food chain from your food web. Draw the pyramid of numbers that you would expect for this food chain.

Food chains and pollution

Remember

- All living organisms need food to supply raw materials and energy.

- Food is transferred from one organism to another along food chains.

Improving our food supply

Humans, like all other animals, require food. We are different from other animals because we can do a lot to alter our food supply. The population of humans on the Earth has increased because we have been able to improve our food supply in two ways:

- By making food **more nutritious** (**additives**, such as preservatives, help us to keep food for longer), and by adding **extra nutrients**, such as vitamin D and calcium, which are added to many dairy products.

- By producing **greater quantities** of food. **Fertilisers** such as nitrate and phosphate help crop plants to grow more quickly and **pesticides**, such as DDT, kill organisms that might reduce the amount of food for humans.

Unfortunately, the use of fertilisers and pesticides has caused some **problems for the environment**. The delicate balance between animals and plants in food webs (see page 101) can be seriously affected by both fertilisers and pesticides.

Overuse of nitrates

Here's one particular problem. Farmers use fertilisers to increase their crop yield (see page 74). Now most fertilisers contain large amounts of **nitrate.** This mineral can easily be washed into rivers, streams and lakes. The problem with this is that simple plants living in the water (algae) also thrive on these nitrates and reproduce very quickly. The build up of algae blocks out light and so other plants die. Once these plants have died, they are decomposed by bacteria. The bacteria use up a lot of oxygen as they respire (see page 45) and soon most of the oxygen in the water is used up. Animals, such as fish, water fleas and other animals that need oxygen for respiration, die. They decompose too and the problem just gets worse and worse until almost nothing except bacteria is left alive in the water. As you can imagine, the food webs in the water can be seriously upset.

Fertilisers cause water pollution

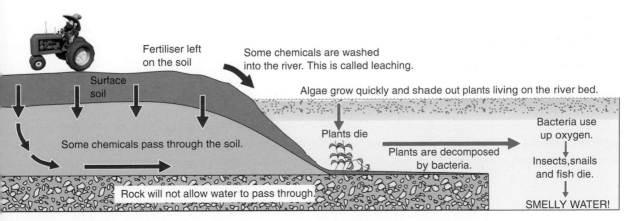

Pesticides and food chains

A **pest** is an organism that competes with us for our food supplies. Some scientists believe that as much as one third of all the food produced in the world is eaten by pests and so is not available to humans. Crops can be protected from pests if they are sprayed with chemicals called **pesticides**. Unfortunately, it means that if crops are sprayed with these pesticides, they too can enter food chains because they gradually build up in the bodies of animals. This problem is explained below.

Pesticides can be poisonous

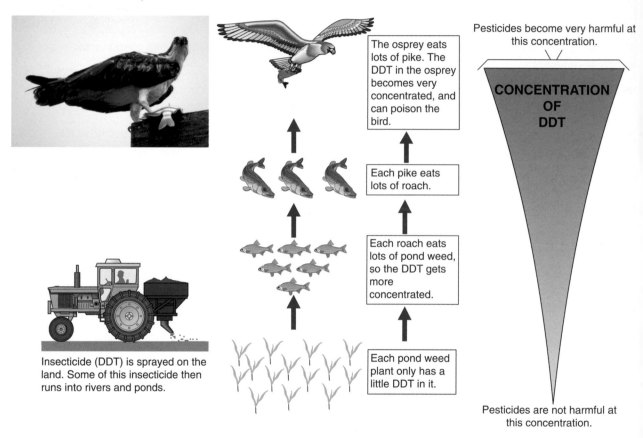

Insecticide (DDT) is sprayed on the land. Some of this insecticide then runs into rivers and ponds.

The osprey eats lots of pike. The DDT in the osprey becomes very concentrated, and can poison the bird.

Each pike eats lots of roach.

Each roach eats lots of pond weed, so the DDT gets more concentrated.

Each pond weed plant only has a little DDT in it.

Pesticides become very harmful at this concentration.

CONCENTRATION OF DDT

Pesticides are not harmful at this concentration.

One pesticide that has been used to kill many types of insect is **DDT**. In the 1960s, the numbers of peregrine falcon, a bird of prey, were falling very quickly. Scientists discovered that DDT in the food chain was causing the birds to lay eggs with very thin shells. These eggs cracked as soon as a parent bird tried to incubate them. The use of DDT was banned in Britain and the population of peregrine falcons has now grown again.

Other toxins

Any substance that can act as a poison to a living organism is called a **toxin**. There are other toxins in the environment, apart from pesticides. Heavy metals, such as **lead,** can build up in humans. The Japanese fishermen in Minimata Bay suffered terrible illnesses when **mercury** was allowed to enter the waters where they caught their fish.

Mercury caused Minimata disease

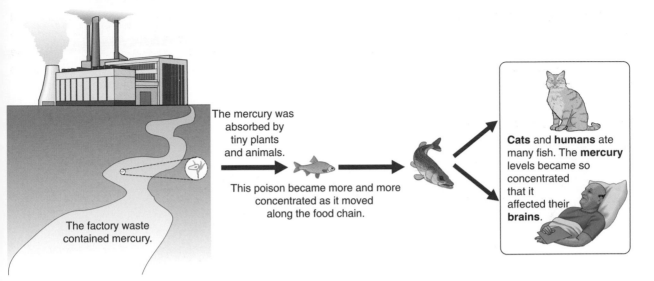

The mercury was absorbed by tiny plants and animals.

This poison became more and more concentrated as it moved along the food chain.

The factory waste contained mercury.

Cats and **humans** ate many fish. The **mercury** levels became so concentrated that it affected their **brains**.

Key words

Fertiliser – a group of minerals added to soil to help plant growth.

Pesticide – a chemical used to control pests.

Pest – an organism that competes with humans for food.

DDT – a very dangerous pesticide that can build up in food chains.

Pollution – a harmful effect of human activities on the environment.

Exercise 9.2: Food chains and pollution

1. Read through the following paragraph, and then use words from the list below to complete it.

   pollution   algae   oxygen   fertilisers   bacteria   leaching   light
   nitrates   cloudy   decomposed

   Farmers use ……… to increase the yield of their crops. The fertilisers are spread onto the fields and supply several minerals, including ……… which are needed for plant growth. Sometimes farmers spread too much fertiliser on the fields and when rain falls, ……… occurs. The fertilisers are washed into nearby streams and rivers. The fertilisers are used by tiny plants called ……… . This causes them to reproduce very quickly. This makes the water go very ………, which cuts out the ……… to other plants rooted at the bottom of streams and rivers. These rooted plants die and are ……… by ……… . The bacteria use up all the ……… . This causes many fish and aquatic insects to die. The water becomes very smelly and very few organisms can live there. This is an example of ……… .

Extension question

2. A scientist noticed that some plants were never bothered by insects. He was interested in whether the plants contained their own natural insecticide. He ground up the plants so that he could collect the natural insecticide which he thought could be dissolved in water.

    (a) Which technique would he use to separate the dissolved insecticide from the crushed-up remains of the plant? Draw a simple diagram to explain how he would do this (try page 167 for a clue).

    He thought that the juice would be able to kill insects and decided to try to find out whether spraying more pesticide juice would kill more insects.

    (b) What would his **hypothesis** be and what **prediction** might he make?

    To carry out this investigation, the scientist and his team of workers made up a number of different concentrations of the natural insecticide and then sprayed the insecticide solutions onto a series of plants. Each plant was of the same species and each plant had 100 aphids feeding on it. The team kept all the plants in the same room and later counted how many aphids were left alive after 24 hours.

    (c) What was the **input (independent) variable** in this experiment?

    (d) What was the **outcome (dependent) variable**?

    (e) Do you think that this was a fair test? Explain the answer that you give.

    This table shows the results obtained in this experiment.

Concentration of insecticide (in g per 1000 litres)	0	5	10	15	20	25	30	40	50	100
Number of aphids alive after 24 hours	99	97	96	95	55	40	25	20	21	20

    (f) Plot a graph of these results. Include a title on your graph.

    (g) Use your graph to calculate the concentration of pesticide needed to kill 50% of the aphids.

    (h) Do the results support the prediction that the scientist made? Use the graph to explain your answer.

Chapter 10
Populations and competition

A **population** is the number of organisms of the same species living in the same habitat at the same time. The size of a population does not remain the same from day to day or from year to year. Whether a population gets larger, smaller or stays the same depends on the balance between several different processes. These processes affect whether organisms join the population (making it get bigger) or leave it (making it get smaller). These processes are described below.

Population changes

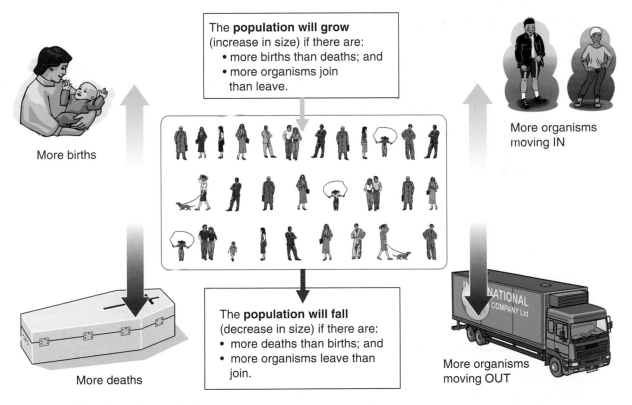

More births

The **population will grow** (increase in size) if there are:
- more births than deaths; and
- more organisms join than leave.

More organisms moving IN

More deaths

The **population will fall** (decrease in size) if there are:
- more deaths than births; and
- more organisms leave than join.

More organisms moving OUT

Here's an equation to help you remember the factors that affect population growth:

population change = (number of births + number moving in) – (number of deaths + number moving out)

Counting living organisms

Biologists who are interested in populations can count the number of organisms in an area at a particular time. It would be very difficult and would take too long to count every individual organism of that species, so biologist take a **sample** of the population. The way they do this is explained below. Quite simply taking samples has several advantages:

●   it is much quicker than trying to count every individual; and

●   it does much less damage to the environment.

One simple way to do take a sample is to use a **quadrat**. A quadrat is a square, usually made of wood or metal, that can be placed on the ground where the organisms are living. What the biologist needs to work out is:

●   how many organisms of a particular species are present inside the quadrat; and

●   how many of the quadrats would fit into the area that the biologist is studying.

The population is then calculated by using this equation:

total population = no. of organisms in one quadrat x no. of quadrats that fit in the area

Reliable results

Living organisms do not spread out equally through their environment. There may be more of one species in one part of the habitat than in another, so a single quadrat might give unreliable results. The biologist should count the number of organisms in several quadrats (probably ten is best) and then find out the average (mean) number in one quadrat. Using this mean value will give a much more reliable count of the population.

Measuring a population using a quadrat

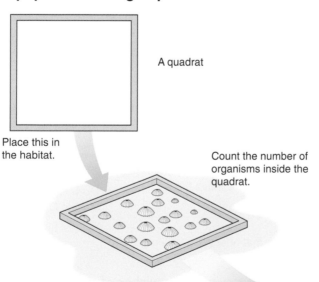

A quadrat

Place this in the habitat.

Count the number of organisms inside the quadrat.

You might have problems counting these organisms!

Now calculate how many organisms are in the whole of the habitat.

TAKE AN AVERAGE!
• First count the organisms in ten quadrats.
• Then divide the total number by 10
• You do this because a mean (average) value gives a more reliable result.

Work out how many quadrats fit into the habitat.

What about animals?

Quadrats are very easy to use with plants, like dandelions, or with animals that stay still while they are being counted (like limpets on a rocky shore). Unfortunately, animals that can move will usually run, swim or fly away while they are being counted. Luckily, there are other methods that can be used for counting animals. Here are some of the methods that can be used:

Counting animals that move

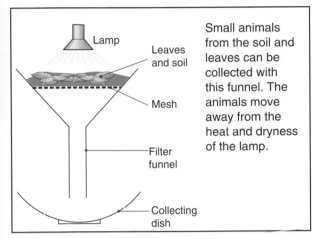

Small animals from the soil and leaves can be collected with this funnel. The animals move away from the heat and dryness of the lamp.

Lamp

Leaves and soil

Mesh

Filter funnel

Collecting dish

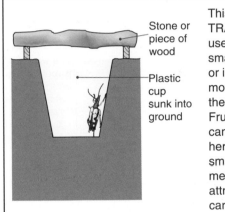

This PITFALL TRAP can be used to catch small animals or insects moving across the ground. Fruit or leaves can attract herbivores or a small piece of meat could attract carnivores.

Stone or piece of wood

Plastic cup sunk into ground

USE A NET: A net can catch flying or swimming organisms.

Understanding the results

A population curve can be drawn by plotting the results of counting populations at different times. A population curve usually has the same shape, whichever organism is being counted. A population curve is shown below.

Population curve

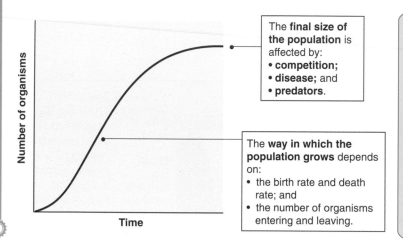

The **final size of the population** is affected by:
• **competition**;
• **disease**; and
• **predators**.

The **way in which the population grows** depends on:
• the birth rate and death rate; and
• the number of organisms entering and leaving.

USING YOUR KNOWLEDGE!
If you understand what affects the shape of this population curve, you can:

• **Prevent a population from growing**.
  e.g. The growth of a population of bacteria can be prevented by making sure that they are starved of a resource they need. Bacteria need water to multiply, so food can be preserved by dehydration.

• **Make a population grow more quickly**.
  e.g. Removing weeds will mean that the crop plants don't have to compete for nitrates. The crop population can then grow to a higher level.

The shape of this curve can be understood by thinking about what a living organism needs from its environment. A **habitat** is an area of the environment that can provide food, shelter and breeding sites for an organism. If there is plenty of food, a number of places to shelter and no shortage of breeding sites, then the organisms can breed and new members of the same species can move into the area. The population will increase but, as this happens, the organisms become more crowded. This overcrowding will eventually mean that the population will no longer increase. There are two main reasons for this:

● **Disease**: As the population becomes more crowded, it becomes easier for the microbes that cause disease to spread. The disease may kill some organisms and make others too unwell to breed. As a result, the population will fall. As the number of organisms falls, they spread out more, so it becomes harder for the disease to spread. The population can increase again. Usually a balance is reached, and the population size will probably become more or less constant.

● **Competition**: As the population increases, each organism has less space and less food (and less light in the case of plants) and so competition increases. Competition happens when two organisms are both trying to get the same resource from their environment. Competition for food is one of the reasons why animals try to set up a **territory**. The territory can supply them with the food, shelter and breeding sites they need. The territory will usually be small if there is plenty of food but may need to be much larger if there is very little.

The size of a population will also be affected by **predators**. There is usually a good balance between the numbers of predators and their prey (see page 103).

Key words

Population – all the members of the same species living in one area.

Competition – when two or more organisms are trying to obtain the same thing from their environment.

Quadrat – a wooden or metal square that can be used in the counting of populations.

Habitat – a part of the environment that can provide food, shelter and a breeding site.

Exercise 10.1: Populations

1. Twenty moose swam across a river to a large grassy island. At first, the moose population rose very rapidly, but then it levelled out. Give two reasons why the numbers stopped rising.

2. Felix wanted to discover the number of small invertebrate animals living in leaf litter (decomposing leaves in a woodland). After obtaining his samples of leaf litter, he used this apparatus to extract the animals.

   (a) Suggest two reasons why the animals move into the container.

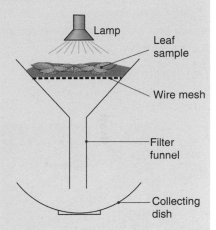

   Among the animals collected were a number of springtails which feed on soil fungi. These animals have a tail which is normally folded under the body but can be suddenly released to propel the animal several centimetres forward.

   (b) (i) What is the importance of fungi in the leaf litter?

   (ii) To which group of animals does the springtail belong?

   (iii) What is the advantage to the springtail of its ability to jump?

3. The graph below shows how the size of the population of a certain species of animal changes with time.

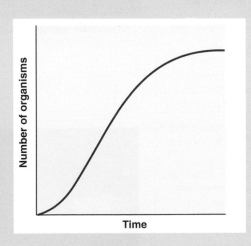

   (a) Describe what the graph tells us.

   (b) Suggest a reason for the shape of the graph.

   (c) Suggest two factors which may cause the population size of an animal species to fall suddenly in its natural habitat.

Humans may have a positive effect on the environment: Conservation

Humans may cause damage to the environment, but they can also do good things to the environment. Many people are now involved in **conservation**. Conservation involves looking for ways to protect the environment. Before we look at some of the ways in which we can preserve the environment, let's look at how it can be destroyed. The picture below shows how humans have been responsible for cutting down huge numbers of trees (deforestation) over much of the Earth's surface:

Deforestation is a disaster

Soil fertility is reduced:
• Trees contain most of the forest's minerals and when trees are cut down and taken away, the minerals can't be recycled.
• Wind and water can cause soil erosion, because the tree roots aren't there to bind the soil together.

Scientists believe that one plant and one animal species become extinct every 30 minutes due to deforestation.

Flooding and landslides:
• Once trees are cut down, they cannot absorb water. Heavy rainfall is not absorbed and can result in flooding and landslides from steep hillsides.

Even nature reserves can be cut down for road building.

Changes to the atmosphere:
Fewer trees mean:
• **More carbon dioxide** because the gas is not absorbed for photosynthesis.
• **Less oxygen** because it is not produced by photosynthesis.
• **Drier air**, because there are fewer leaves to give out water.

Extinction of species:
For example:
• The mountain gorilla depends on the rain forest for its habitat.
• Osprey depend on pine forests.
• **Many plants provide medicines,** e.g. contraceptive chemicals, anti-cancer drugs and painkillers.

In comparison to this, humans have also set up schemes for the large-scale planting of trees (**reforestation**). Large numbers of trees may be planted in areas which had previously been cleared or which are thought likely to benefit from tree cover. For example, millions of trees were planted when the M25 motorway around London was built.

There are a number of reasons for carrying out these programmes:

- The trees may be a valuable cash crop, providing timber for building purposes (as with many of the coniferous plantations in this country) or for fuel (as with the quick-growing Eucalyptus trees which are planted in Central Africa).

- The trees may help to reverse soil erosion, and are particularly valuable in areas which have become deserts.

- The forests may be valuable wildlife habitats. For example, Red Squirrels can thrive in Scots Pine plantations (see page 118).

- The forests may be valuable recreational areas, providing opportunities for leisure activities, such as camping, mountain-biking and orienteering.

In a well-managed forest all these requirements can be met. Indeed, the Forestry Commission in the UK *must* take all these into account when managing its plantations. Forests in Britain are a good example of sustainable development. **Sustainable development** means that we should *not* take too much from our environment now, because it will affect its value *for future generations*. Forests with a single species of tree may be very good for growing wood for building or for paper manufacture, but they are:

- very likely to be damaged by pests (any pest does not have far to go to find another tree of the same type);

- very limited in value to wildlife because there is not a great variety of food; and

- often very boring to look at.

It **is** possible to use biological knowledge carefully in the management of forests. A forest can provide wood for now and wood and wildlife for the future.

The picture on the next page suggests that human effects on the environment may not always be negative ones. We sometimes believe that humans only damage the environment, but the growing numbers of **conservationists** are looking for ways to **manage** the environment. Conservationists try to balance the human demands on the environment with the need to maintain wildlife habitats. This is an important part of sustainable development.

Sustainable development

Deciduous trees are planted along the edges of forests that are grown to provide wood for paper or for building.
- They improve the appearance of the woodland, so visitors are happier.
- They provide seeds used as food by wildlife.
- Many insects live in this kind of tree, so there's a greater variety of food for different species of wildlife.

All this helps to save wildlife for the future.

There are **blocks of trees of different ages,** so:
- some can be cut for wood;
- some are just the right age to produce seeds; and
- some are still short enough to provide good hiding places.

Brash (thin branches) is not burned, because:
- it is an excellent habitat for insects which can be food for birds and small mammals; and
- it is a very good provider of hiding places and nesting sites.

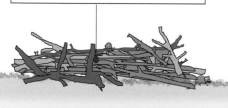

Open space provides extra light and warmth. This encourages:
- more wild flowers; and
- more butterflies.

Dead wood is left to rot naturally, even though it takes up space:
- it provides a habitat for mosses and ferns, and for insect larvae which are a good food source for birds; and
- minerals like nitrates are naturally returned to the soil.

Why is conservation necessary?

The competition between humans and other living organisms means that many species have disappeared completely or fallen in number.

Conservationists therefore really have two jobs:

- they must try to slow down or stop the fall in **biodiversity** (the number of different species); and

- they must try to make the **public aware** of the need to maintain species and their habitats.

What is conservation?

Conservation always involves some form of **management**. Conservation almost always involves a balance. For example, a farmer might be encouraged to replant hedgerows but must still be able to make a profit from growing crops. Conservation may involve a number of strategies:

● **Preservation**: In its strictest sense this involves keeping some part of the environment **without any change**. This **might** be possible in an enormous area such as Antarctica but is of less significance in a densely-populated area like Britain.

● **Reclamation**: This involves the restoration of damaged habitats. It might include the replacement of grubbed-out hedgerows or the recovery of former industrial sites.

● **Creation**: This involves the production of new habitats. It might include the digging of a garden pond or the planting of a forest.

If conservation is to be successful, careful planning is necessary. A **conservation plan** involves several stages:

● **Sampling**: The number of organisms present at the start of the conservation work needs to be counted (see page 110).

● **Devising a management plan**: This involves considerable biological knowledge. For example, trying to increase the population size of a species will involve knowing what its breeding requirements are.

● **Carrying out the plan**: This will probably involve cost to the conservation organisation involved in the work. Many people become involved in voluntary work which reduces the financial cost of conservation work.

● **Resampling**: The number of the conserved species needs to be counted again, otherwise the conservationists won't know whether their plan has worked or not. This might be five or ten years after the first sampling, if the organism is a slow-breeding species.

Two examples of conservation work are described in the next section. Firstly, the **Red Squirrel**: in Britain the Red Squirrel is a very endangered species; some scientists suggest it may become extinct. Suggestions for its conservation largely involve careful **management of habitat**. Secondly, **zoos** which are extremely popular in many countries: zoo managers now stress the importance of zoos in conservation rather than as places of entertainment.

The Red Squirrel in Britain

The Red Squirrel (*Sciurus vulgaris*) used to be very widespread in Britain but in most areas it has now been replaced by the larger Grey Squirrel (*Sciurus carolinensis*) which was introduced into Britain from North America. There are a number of possible reasons for the decline of the red squirrel.

● **Competition with the Grey**: The Red feeds on conifer seeds from pine cones and eats very little of other foods, such as acorns, fruits and berries. The Grey can survive on a very monotonous diet of a wider range of foods. For example, it can cope with a diet which is almost completely acorns. In a broad-leaved (deciduous) woodland the Greys can always find something to eat, especially as they are more willing to feed at ground level and can take advantage of food sources which the more tree-loving Reds would ignore (including cast-off sandwiches!).

● **Disease**: It is believed that the Grey Squirrel carries a virus which usually only causes disease and death in Red Squirrels. Thus in mixed populations the Reds are at a disadvantage.

- **Habitat loss**: Although the Red survives better in coniferous forest, it must have access to trees of different ages to provide food throughout the year. In many recent forest plantings, the trees are all the same age and largely Sitka Spruce, which produces small seeds which are shed early in the year, leaving little food for the Reds in the winter.

Conservation plans to support Red Squirrel numbers must take all of these points into account. One very important point to note is that the introduction of a species from another country is often the cause of problems for native wildlife!

Saving the Red Squirrel

The key to sucessful conservation in this case seems to be the management of a habitat which provides food.

Habitat management
Choose tree species that provide food for Red Squirrels, e.g. birch. Remove oak and beech because these provide food for Grey Squirrels. Good conifers include Scots pine because these provide seeds very late in the year for Red Squirrels.

Supplementary feeding
Selective hoppers have been developed which only allow access to Red Squirrels. These are placed in clusters of 2 or 3, 20 to 30 metres apart, and filled with a mixture of yellow maize, wheat, peanuts and sunflower seeds. They have the disadvantage that they must be visited regularly and frequently filled.

Elimination of competitors
- poison or shoot them; or
- use a chemical to sterilise them (this is a good solution because it doesn't actually kill any animals).

Habitat management
Red squirrel reserves should be surrounded by at least 3 km of conifer forest or open land to stop entry by Grey Squirrels.

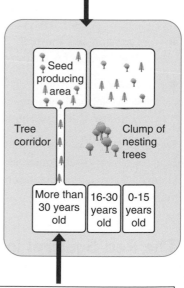

Reintroduction of Red Squirrels
Small numbers might be released to test the success of habitat management techniques. Survival and behaviour of the introduced Reds would be carefully monitored by radio and regular observation.

Forestry practice
The forest should be managed to provide both food and shelter. This typically involves a structure where 30% of trees are 0 to 15 years old, 30% are 16 to 30 years old and 40% are more than 30 years old.
When tree felling, some single seed-producing trees should be left in small groups, in order to provide nesting sites. Seed-producing areas should be connected by corridors of trees to prevent isolation and make movement between them easier for Red Squirrels.

Zoos and conservation

Zoos, or zoological gardens, are areas of confinement for keeping animals in captivity. For many people the fact that the animals *are* in captivity means that zoos can never be justified – these people say that the animals are being exploited for the amusement of humans. Other people have a different point of view, and suggest that *without* zoos many species would be extinct. For example, there are more Siberian Tigers in zoos than there are in the wild. The supporters of zoos argue that animals can be bred in zoos until their habitat is secured for their eventual release. The anti-zoo people argue back that breeding animals *in* captivity is breeding animals *for* captivity, and point out that reintroduction to the wild is very rarely successful.

Zoo visits *are* extremely popular. In the United States more people visit zoos than visit Disneyland. It is extremely important to note that zoo directors justify keeping large, attractive animals because they say that these species generate income which can then be used to conserve less glamorous species. Tigers, pandas and elephants are examples of these **flagship** species. Many zoo visitors will contribute money to conserve elephants, but this money also conserves those species which live in the same habitat as the elephant. Some of the possible benefits of zoos to conservation are explained below.

GOOD POINTS

Animals get food and shelter and are looked after by a vet.

Animals may breed which is important in preserving endangered species.

People enjoy visiting zoos. Entry fees can be spent on animals' welfare and people may give money for conservation work.

Zoos may get people interested in animals and conservation.

BAD POINTS

Animals may not have mates for breeding.

Animals may be in the wrong groups, e.g. wolves like to live in packs.

Cages may be small, so animals get bored.

Zoo keepers may not be able to provide food that the animals are used to.

Throughout these sections on pollution and conservation you should be able to see how humans have the potential to alter their environment (see page 114). It is vital that future generations of scientists use this power carefully, that they live up to the name *Homo sapiens* – the 'wise man' – if the Earth is to remain habitable for other species as well as our own.

Key words

Conservation – managing the environment for the benefit of wildlife.

Deforestation – cutting down large areas of trees.

Sustainable development – only taking enough from the environment to make sure that there will be some left for future generations.

Biodiversity – the range of different living organisms.

Exercise 10.2: Conservation

1. Find a book about conservation. Try to find an example of an animal and a plant in Britain that have been protected by conservation work.

2. Find an Internet site dealing with zoos. What can you find about the conservation work of zoos?

Extension questions

3. Read the following passage carefully and then answer questions (a) to (d).

> *Between 1947 and 1963 hedges were being removed at an average rate of over 3000 miles per year. This increased to 5000 miles per year by 1968.*
>
> *A recent report claims that, between 1980 and 1985, 5000 miles of hedgerow were removed and 2500 miles were planted in England and Wales.*
>
> *Older hedges generally provide a richer habitat with a wider variety of plants and animals.*
>
> *Both during and after World War Two, farmers were encouraged to grow more food, to do so more efficiently and at less cost.*
>
> *On one Devon farm with small fields, removing 1 mile of hedges provided another 3 acres of arable land and reduced by one third the average time taken to harvest a field of cereal crops.*
>
> *In 1987, British tax-payers spent about £1 578 000 000 to buy and store surplus UK farm produce. In the European Economic Community, stored surplus food includes 1 500 000 tonnes of beef.*
>
> *Farmers are now being encouraged by the European Community to grow less food.*
>
> The above material has been adapted from the Nature Conservancy Council publication 'Points of View No 1: Hedgerows'.

(a) What was the highest average rate of removal of hedges before 1969?

(b) If that rate of hedge removal had continued, what effect would it have had on the variety of wild animals and plants in the countryside and the amount of arable land for farming?

(c) How did the removal of hedges per year differ in the period between 1980 and 1985 from that in 1968?

(d) Why is it less important now to gain extra arable land than it was immediately after World War Two?

Read the following and answer question (e).

> *A Hedges provide an important habitat for wildlife which can help with pollination and biological control.*
>
> *B Hedges can provide a home for weeds, insect pests, rabbits and crop diseases.*
>
> *C Hedges take up space which could be planted with crops.*
>
> *D Hedges are an attractive feature in the rural landscape.*
>
> *E Expensive labour is needed to maintain hedges.*
>
> *F Hedges provide a wind break for crops, shelter and shade for farm animals and a barrier to disease spread.*
>
> *G Hedges shade part of the crop, which reduces yield.*

H   *Hedges help to prevent topsoil from blowing away.*

I   *Hedges provide cover for game, such as pheasants and partridges.*

J   *Hedges obstruct the efficient use of modern farm machinery.*

The above material has been adapted from the Nature Conservancy Council publication 'Points of View No 1: Hedgerows'.

(e)   Choose five statements from the list above to support a case against removing hedges.

4.   Read the following and then answer the questions (a) to (e).

The publication of newspapers uses up an enormous quantity of paper every day. Paper is manufactured from wood. Large numbers of trees are cut down every year to provide the raw material for the paper industry.

(a)   How does the publication of newspapers affect the world's timber resources?

Timber is a very important natural resource. In terms of conservation, it would be helpful if used-paper could be collected and repulped. The organisation, collection and sorting of waste paper is an expensive process. As a result very little paper is recycled.

Trees cut down for use must be replaced. The planting of trees to replace those felled is called reforestation. Schemes of reforestation must be established and well managed if supply is to keep up with demand. The quicker-growing tree species are the conifers (softwoods), such as pine and spruce. These are grown over large areas of land, producing forests with relatively few species but giving high productivity quickly and are, therefore, an attractive investment.

There is also a need for the deciduous hardwoods, such as oak and beech. These are much slower growing, taking longer to establish and are therefore, in the short-term, a less attractive crop. As a habitat, a mixed deciduous woodland will support a greater variety of species than a conifer plantation.

(b)   What do the terms recycling and reforestation mean?

(c)   (i)   Name one coniferous tree.

(ii)   Name one hardwood tree.

(d)   How do coniferous woodlands differ from deciduous ones as commercial crops and as habitats for wildlife? Support your answer with reasons.

In overcoming one problem reforestation schemes may produce secondary conservation problems. More and more frequently large areas of moorland, important habitats themselves, are being used as sites for conifer plantations.

(e)   What could happen to Britain's moorland habitats and communities if reforestation schemes were allowed to go on unchecked?

You have now completed the 'Life processes and living things' section of your science course. You should have a good idea of the workings of the human body, and about what can go wrong with it. This should enable you to make some important decisions about your own body. You will remember that the body requires a source of raw materials – foods – to grow and develop. Your study of plants will have shown you that plants can make their own food by photosynthesis, and that animals depend on plants for all their foods. Finally, you will have seen that all living organisms form part of larger communities and that damage to any one member of the community can have serious effects on the other living organisms that make it up. Don't forget that humans have the power to alter their environment – as a scientist you will have the understanding to make sure that we use our environment in a sustainable way.

What is chemistry?

What is chemistry and why do we want to study it? For many people the first contact with chemistry involves watching films showing strange scientists messing about with bubbling liquids, smelly gases, loud explosions and bright flashes. These things can be explained by chemistry, but the subject involves a lot more.

In the simplest terms, chemistry is the study of materials. Chemists study the physical properties of different substances and they also try to understand the reactions between different substances. Everything in our world is made of materials – all these materials are chemicals. Chemicals are found in chemistry laboratories, but you are far more likely to come across them in your food, in detergents, medicines, cosmetics, in your car, your clothes or in the decoration in your bedroom. The air you breathe is made up of chemicals and so is your body.

Chemistry has helped us to explain how one substance can be changed into another. These changes, called chemical reactions, occur all around us. They include:

● the burning of fuels;

● the cooking of foods;

● the rusting of cars and bicycles;

● the breakdown of household waste; and

● the growth of plants and animals.

The study of chemical reactions, especially finding out the most efficient way of making new substances, is the basis of the chemical industry. Understanding chemistry helps us to make the best use of our environment while limiting the damage we cause. An important example studied later in this book is the efficient extraction of metals from the Earth.

There are several important branches of the chemical industry:

- The petrochemical industry uses oil as a raw material to produce fuels, plastics and building materials.

- The pharmaceutical industry uses many different raw materials to produce drugs and medicines for the treatment of disease and the relief of pain and hormones to increase the growth of animals and plants.

- The agrochemical industry produces pesticides, fertilisers and other products required for farming.

Why do we study chemistry?

Some of us will study chemistry just because we find it interesting. Finding out about the properties of different chemicals, and working out how they react together, can occupy a lifetime of research.

Fred Sanger is one of the few people to have been awarded two Nobel prizes. In Cambridge he developed a new chromatographic method. He published the complete sequence of insulin in 1955 and was awarded the Nobel prize in 1958 for his work on sequencing proteins.

Over the next 15 years Fred and his team developed several ever-improving methods to sequence nucleic acids (DNA and RNA). It was for this work that he was awarded his second Nobel prize in 1980. This method, developed nearly 25 years ago, is still in use today.

Frederick Sanger in his laboratory

However, chemistry is not just interesting, it is also useful. Many important advances in science, medicine and technology have been made possible by the production of new chemicals. Silicon chips in computers, drugs for helping asthma sufferers and super-strong alloys in racing cars would not exist without the efforts of chemists. Nowadays many chemists are involved with caring for the environment. We are beginning to understand how to recycle many of the materials we have developed for our use. Everyone can benefit from the study of chemistry.

This kit car has been made from recycled products.

Chapter 11
Experiments in chemistry: Important apparatus and skills

Chemistry is a practical subject. The laws of chemistry have been worked out by scientists who have carried out experiments to test their ideas (see page 2). The results collected by these scientists will only be acceptable if:

●   they have designed their experiments carefully (see page 3);

●   they have been able to use the correct apparatus; and

●   they have been able to measure variables accurately.

Apparatus

Apparatus is the name we give to the equipment used in a chemistry laboratory. A diagram of apparatus is often very useful when a chemist has to describe an experiment. Each piece of apparatus can be drawn in an outline form. An outline diagram is quick to produce and should be clear to any other user.

Throughout this book you will see both 3-D pictures of apparatus and scientific drawings. It is very important that you learn how to draw apparatus correctly, otherwise you may be drawing experiments that wouldn't work at all or that may even blow up. The table below shows the 3-D pictures and the way you must draw these pieces of apparatus.

Each piece of apparatus has a particular function.

3-D Picture	Description	Scientific drawing
	● **Conical flask:** used for mixing solutions, without heating.	
	● **Watch glass:** used for collecting and evaporating liquids without heating (see page 166).	
	● **Gas jar:** to collect gases for testing (see page 135).	
	● **Filter funnel:** used to separate solids from liquids, using a filter paper (see page 167).	
	● **Measuring cylinder:** used for measuring the volume of liquids (see page 127).	

The other very important measuring device in the laboratory is a balance (weighing machine).

3-D Picture	Description	Scientific drawing
	● **Thermometer:** used to measure temperature (see page 126).	
	● **Spatula:** used for handling solid chemicals; for example, when adding a solid to a liquid (see page 161).	
	● **Pipette:** used to measure and transfer small volumes of liquids (see page 135).	
	● **Stand, boss and clamp:** used to support the apparatus in place. This reduces the risk of dangerous spills (page 140). This is not generally drawn. If the clamp is merely to support a piece of apparatus, it is usually represented by two crosses as shown.	
	● **Bunsen burner:** used to heat the contents of other apparatus (e.g. a liquid in a test tube) or for **directly** heating solids (see page 133).	THERMAL ENERGY
	● **Tripod:** used to support apparatus above a Bunsen burner (see page 140). The Bunsen burner, tripod and gauze are the most common way of heating materials in school science laboratories.	
	● **Gauze:** used to spread out the thermal energy from a Bunsen burner and to support the apparatus on a tripod (see page 140).	
	● **Test tube and boiling tube:** used for heating solids and liquids. They are also used to hold chemicals while other substances are added and mixed. They need to be put safely in a test tube rack (page 135).	
	● **Evaporating dish:** used to collect and evaporate liquids with or without heating (see page 166).	
	● **Beaker:** used for mixing solutions and for heating liquids (see page 140).	
	● **Round bottom flask:** used for heating liquids: for example, during distillation (see page 140).	
	● **Flat bottom flask:** used for mixing liquids. It should **not** be heated strongly or it may crack (see page 140).	

Measurement of variables

In many experiments chemists need to measure variable quantities, such as volume, temperature, mass and time. It is very important to be able to read scales accurately and to choose the correct units for the quantities that have been measured. Some of the common measuring equipment used in chemistry laboratories is shown below:

Measuring temperature using a thermometer

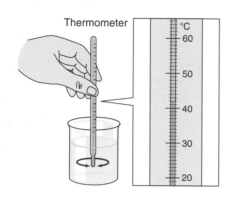

Thermometer

°C
60
50
40
30
20

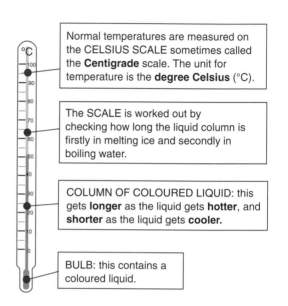

°C

Normal temperatures are measured on the CELSIUS SCALE sometimes called the **Centigrade** scale. The unit for temperature is the **degree Celsius** (°C).

The SCALE is worked out by checking how long the liquid column is firstly in melting ice and secondly in boiling water.

COLUMN OF COLOURED LIQUID: this gets **longer** as the liquid gets **hotter**, and **shorter** as the liquid gets **cooler.**

BULB: this contains a coloured liquid.

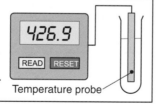

An electronic thermometer and probe. Equipment like this will be necessary if a scientist needs to measure temperatures above 100°C or below 0°C.

426.9

READ   RESET

Temperature probe

Measuring mass using an electronic pan balance

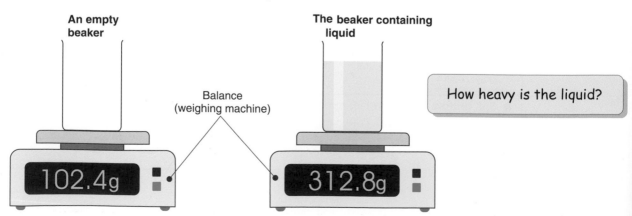

An empty beaker

The beaker containing liquid

Balance (weighing machine)

How heavy is the liquid?

102.4g

312.8g

Measuring volume using a beaker or a measuring cylinder

BEAKER
It is not accurate to use a beaker because the scale is not fine enough.

MEASURING CYLINDER

When using a measuring cylinder, stand the measuring cylinder on a level table or bench, so that the liquid is level.

Make sure that you read the level carefully. You may notice that the surface of the fluid is curved; this is called the **meniscus**.

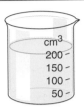

Is it cm^3 or ml? Some equipment is scaled in cm^3, and some is scaled in ml. It really doesn't matter – 1cm^3 has exactly the same volume as 1ml.

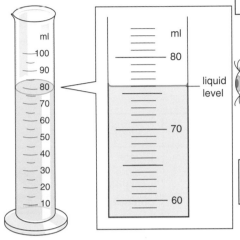

liquid level

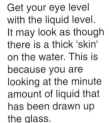

Get your eye level with the liquid level. It may look as though there is a thick 'skin' on the water. This is because you are looking at the minute amount of liquid that has been drawn up the glass.

The volume of liqiuid is represented by the **bottom of the meniscus**.

Interestingly, plastic beakers and measuring cylinders often do not give rise to a meniscus!

Reading the measurement from a measuring cylinder by getting your eye level with the liquid level.

This table gives a summary of the measuring equipment used in chemistry laboratories

QUANTITY	UNITS	EQUIPMENT
Volume (fluid)	Cubic centimetres (cm^3) Litres (dm^3) 1 litre = 1000 ml	Measuring cylinder or beaker
Temperature	Degrees Celsius (°C)	Thermometer
Time	Seconds (s) Minutes (min)	Stopclock (can be analogue or digital)
Mass	Grams (g) Kilograms (kg) 1 kg = 1000 g	Balance (usually top pan balances and electronic)

Chemicals

Doing experiments in chemistry often involves making changes to materials. We often call the materials we use in experiments chemicals. It is extremely important that these chemicals are used safely. Some chemicals are too dangerous to be used in school laboratories and all of them must be used with great care. To help us identify which chemicals are particularly dangerous, we have a series of hazard symbols which appear on containers holding chemicals. These symbols warn us of special dangers and they also help teachers and technicians decide on the best thing to do if a chemical is spilled or swallowed by mistake. These symbols, and some examples of the chemicals that are marked with them, are shown below:

Hazard symbols

Symbol	Description	Examples
	Oxidising These substances provide oxygen which allows other materials to burn more fiercely.	Bleach, sodium chlorate, potassium nitrate
	Highly flammable These substances easily catch fire.	Ethanol, petrol, acetone
	Toxic These substances can cause death. They may have their effects when swallowed or breathed in or absorbed through the skin.	Mercury, copper sulphate

Symbol	Description	Examples
	Harmful These substances are similar to toxic substances but less dangerous.	Dilute acids and alkalis
	Corrosive These substances attack and destroy living tissues, including eyes and skin.	Concentrated acids and alkalis
	Irritant These substances are not corrosive but can cause reddening or blistering of the skin.	Ammonia, dilute acids and alkalis

LAB RULES OK!

- Always wear eye protection when handling or heating chemicals.

- Wear a long-sleeved overall to protect clothes and skin if handling corrosive materials.

- Tie back long hair.

Some chemicals can have more than one label.

For example, petrol:
- is flammable;
- harmful; and
- an irritant!

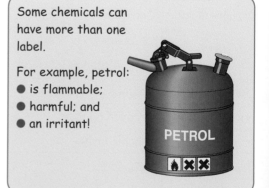

Key words

Apparatus – the equipment used for scientific experiments.

Variable – something (a factor) that changes during the course of an experiment.

Exercise 11.1: Experiments in chemistry

1. Look at these diagrams. A scientist has measured the volume and the mass of some water and some alcohol. What can you tell from your measurements?

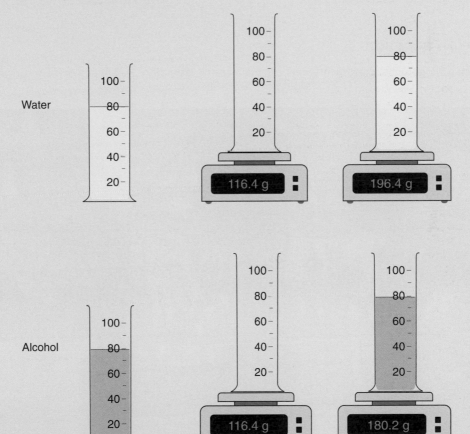

2. India is going on a trip and she wanted to take some water. She has a water container that weighs 95 grams. She doesn't want to take more than 260 grams altogether. What is the maximum mass of water she can take?

3. Briefly describe what each of the following pieces of apparatus is used for:

   (a) conical flask   (c) measuring cylinder   (e) spatula

   (b) tripod   (d) filter funnel   (f) pipette

4. Make the following conversions of units:

    (a) 1.22 kg to g

    (b) 4 min 19 s to s

    (c) 1320 s to minutes and seconds

    (d) 2340 cm^3 to litres

    (e) 3400 g to kg

    (f) 2984 cm^3 to ml

Extension question

5. Identify the potential hazards of working in this wizard's laboratory. How many of them can you identify? What advice would you give to prevent them?

Using a Bunsen burner

Remember

● Chemical reactions always involve an energy change.

● Some chemical reactions are **exothermic** (give out thermal energy) and some are **endothermic** (take in thermal energy).

Chemical reactions often require some form of heating. Even reactions which are exothermic (give out thermal energy) may need some thermal energy to get them started. A good example of this kind of reaction is using a match. The match gives out energy when it burns, but won't even start to burn until some thermal energy is provided by friction when the match is struck against a rough surface.

Experiments in the chemistry laboratory often need some type of heating. This heating must be reliable (you can get it whenever you need it) and it must be controllable (you can vary the amount of thermal energy). The **Bunsen burner** is the most common source of thermal energy used in the laboratory. It is safe and easy to use, but the user needs to stick to some rules!

● Have a **flame** ready to light the Bunsen burner before turning on the **gas supply**.

● Check that the **air hole** is closed before turning on the gas supply and lighting the Bunsen burner.

● When you are not using the Bunsen burner, either turn it off or close the air hole to give a **yellow** flame. The yellow flame is **luminous** so that it can be seen easily. This means that there is less risk of someone accidentally being burned.

● For gentle heating, half open the air hole to give a **quiet blue** flame.

● For strong heating, have the air hole wide open. This will give a **roaring blue** flame.

The burner was invented by Robert Wilhelm Bunsen's lab assistant, Peter Desolega, based closely on an earlier design by Michael Faraday. They were studying the spectrum of light and needed a non-luminous flame to burn the substances they were studying. The only way they could get this kind of flame was to mix gas and air before it burned. It bears Bunsen's name because he used it very effectively and championed its use to the scientific community.

Using a Bunsen burner

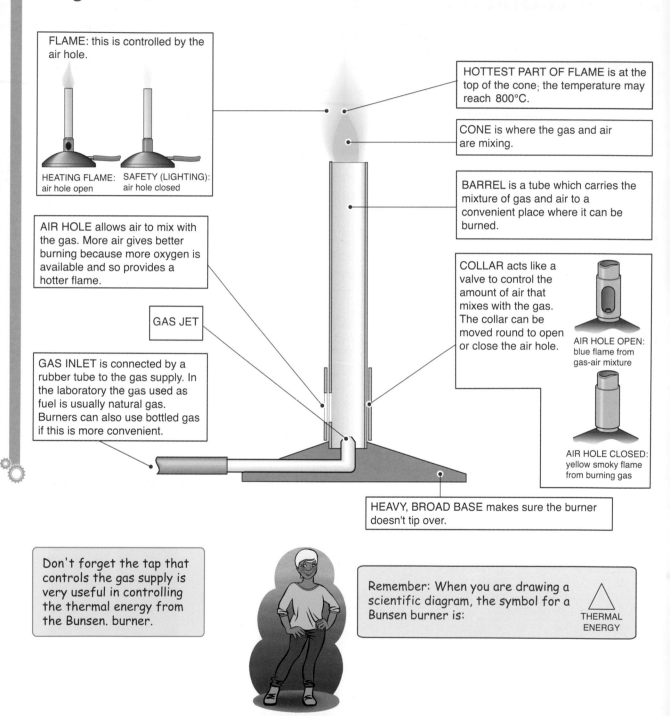

FLAME: this is controlled by the air hole.

HEATING FLAME: air hole open

SAFETY (LIGHTING): air hole closed

HOTTEST PART OF FLAME is at the top of the cone; the temperature may reach 800°C.

CONE is where the gas and air are mixing.

BARREL is a tube which carries the mixture of gas and air to a convenient place where it can be burned.

AIR HOLE allows air to mix with the gas. More air gives better burning because more oxygen is available and so provides a hotter flame.

GAS JET

GAS INLET is connected by a rubber tube to the gas supply. In the laboratory the gas used as fuel is usually natural gas. Burners can also use bottled gas if this is more convenient.

COLLAR acts like a valve to control the amount of air that mixes with the gas. The collar can be moved round to open or close the air hole.

AIR HOLE OPEN: blue flame from gas-air mixture

AIR HOLE CLOSED: yellow smoky flame from burning gas

HEAVY, BROAD BASE makes sure the burner doesn't tip over.

Don't forget the tap that controls the gas supply is very useful in controlling the thermal energy from the Bunsen. burner.

Remember: When you are drawing a scientific diagram, the symbol for a Bunsen burner is:

THERMAL ENERGY

The size of the flame can also be adjusted by altering the gas flow to the Bunsen burner. This is done at the gas tap. If there is a risk of someone burning, or the Bunsen burner has tipped over, always **STOP THE GAS SUPPLY BY CLOSING OFF THE TAP.**

There are some other important safety issues to remember whilst conducting experiments which involve heating or burning. These are shown below:

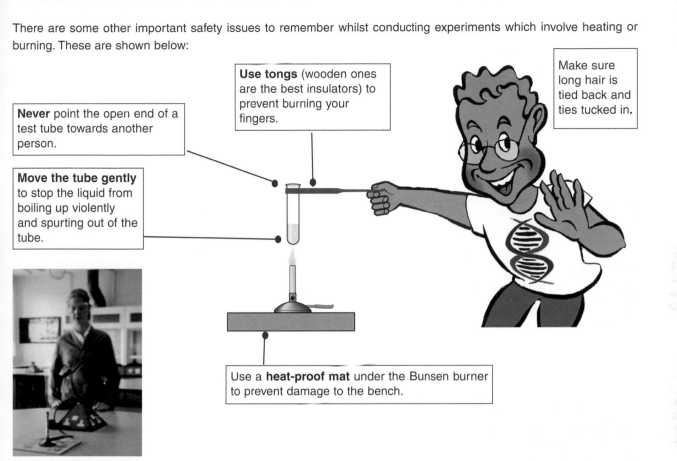

Use tongs (wooden ones are the best insulators) to prevent burning your fingers.

Make sure long hair is tied back and ties tucked in.

Never point the open end of a test tube towards another person.

Move the tube gently to stop the liquid from boiling up violently and spurting out of the tube.

Use a **heat-proof mat** under the Bunsen burner to prevent damage to the bench.

Exercise 11.2: The Bunsen burner

1. Gena and Louis were carrying out an experiment to find out whether a Bunsen burner delivers more thermal energy with the air hole open or with it closed. They were measuring the thermal energy from the Bunsen burner by finding out the time taken for some water to boil.

   (a) What is the input variable in this experiment?

   (b) What is the outcome variable in this experiment?

   (c) Gena and Louis knew that there should also be controlled variables, i.e. things that had to be kept constant for this to be a fair test. If any of these were changed, the outcome of the experiment could be affected. Which variables from the list below should be controlled?

      (i)   The size and shape of the beaker.

      (ii) The starting temperature of the water.

      (iii) Which day of the week they did the experiment.

      (iv) The position of the Bunsen burner below the beaker.

      (v)   The position of the gas tap (how much flow of gas).

      (vi) The volume of water in the beaker.

2. Gena carried out a series of experiments to investigate how much thermal energy could be produced by a Bunsen burner. She used a stopwatch to measure how long it took for some water in a beaker to boil. She altered some of the conditions from one experiment to the next. The results of her experiments are shown in the table below:

Experiment	Volume of water in cm³	Temperature at start of heating in °C	Gas tap	Air hole in Bunsen burner	Time for water to boil in seconds
I	100	20	Fully on	Open	155
II	100	50	Fully on	Open	85
III	200	20	Half on	Open	275
IV	200	20	Half on	Closed	425
V	200	20	Fully on	Open	300

(a) Why is it not a fair test to compare the results for experiments II and III?

(b) (i) What is Gena testing when she compares results for experiments III and IV?

(ii) What conclusion can she come to?

(c) (i) What is Gena testing when she compares results for experiments I and II?

(ii) What conclusion can she come to?

(d) Which results should Gena compare to find the effect of the volume of water on the time taken for the water to boil?

Useful chemical tests

Don't forget

- During a chemical reaction new products are formed.
- The new product could be a solid, a liquid or a gas.

Testing for gases

Many gases are colourless, so we can't see them. We may be aware that a gas has been produced because we see some fizzing or a release of bubbles. If we get a colourless gas formed in a chemical reaction, we will need to use a test to find out what it is. Three gases that are commonly involved in chemical reactions are oxygen, carbon dioxide and hydrogen. There are simple tests for each of these gases:

Testing for carbon dioxide

For example:

calcium carbonate ➡ calcium oxide + carbon dioxide

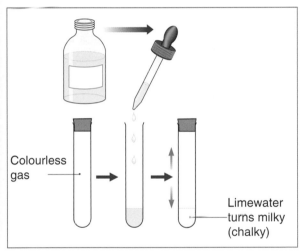

Colourless gas → → Limewater turns milky (chalky)

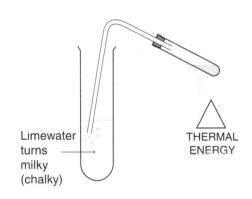

Limewater turns milky (chalky)

THERMAL ENERGY

Testing for oxygen

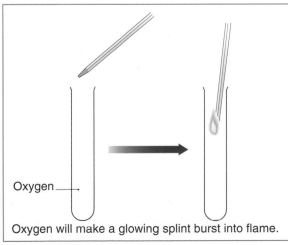

Oxygen

Oxygen will make a glowing splint burst into flame.

For example:

mercury oxide ➡ mercury + oxygen

 Glowing splint

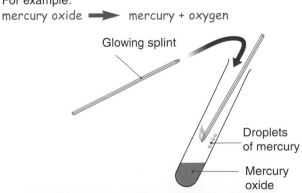

Droplets of mercury

Mercury oxide

SAFETY! This is not an experiment for the classroom as it releases poisonous mercury vapour. You can safely test for oxygen during the thermal decompostion of potassium manganate (VII).

Testing for hydrogen

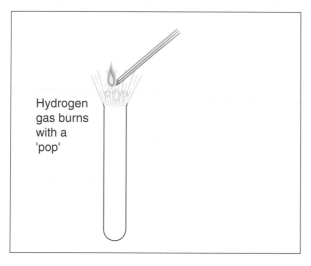

Hydrogen gas burns with a 'pop'

For example:

hydrochloric acid + zinc ➡ zinc chloride + hydrogen

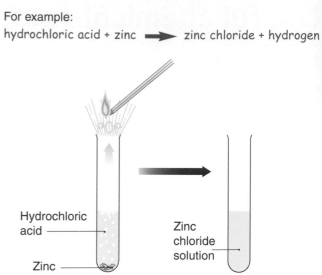

Hydrochloric acid

Zinc

Zinc chloride solution

Some gases are **coloured** (chlorine gas is green, for example) or they have a definite **smell** (hydrogen sulphide smells like rotten eggs, for example). The smelly gases can be quite dangerous, and if there is any danger at all that a gas could be poisonous or an irritant, it should never be produced except in a fume cupboard (by a teacher). Some very dangerous gases, for example, carbon monoxide – are colourless and don't smell at all.

Testing for water

A useful and safe experiment to test for the presence of water uses anhydrous copper sulphate. This white powder turns blue in the presence of water.

Anhydrous copper sulphate is WHITE.

Copper sulphate is BLUE.

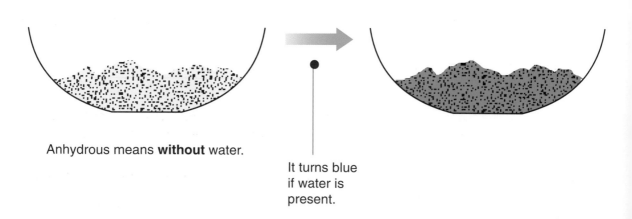

Anhydrous means **without** water.

It turns blue if water is present.

Some crystals can remove water from the air. This can be useful. For example, silica gel can keep water out of the air around delicate electronic equipment.

Many colourless liquids are neutral, which means they are neither acid nor alkali. Water is neutral along with many other clear liquids. To find out whether a clear liquid, produced during a chemical reaction, is in fact water, we can test it with blue **cobalt chloride** paper:

Blue cobalt chloride paper ...

... turns pink if water is present.

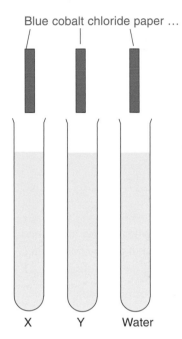

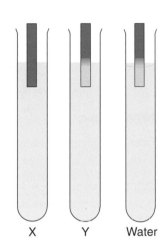

X is definitely not water.

Y contains water. You would need to carry out further tests such as:

● Does it boil at 100 °C?

● Is it neutral?

to see if the water is pure.

SAFETY! Cobalt chloride paper should always be handled with forceps or when wearing gloves.

Exercise 11.3: Testing

1. Name two different acidic gases. What effect does an acid gas have on litmus solution? (Hint: See page 218).

2. A chemical reaction gives out a vapour that can be cooled to give a colourless liquid. Name two tests that could help you to decide if this liquid is water. What would the results be if the liquid were water?

3. Complete this paragraph, using words from the list below:
   carbon dioxide   re-light   pop   milky   hydrogen   oxygen

   Limewater can be used to test for .... The limewater will turn .... if carbon dioxide is present. The gas called .... will make a glowing splint .... A lighted splint will make the gas called .... produce a sound like a ....

4. Which indicator is used by biologists to test for the presence of carbon dioxide? (Hint: look in Chapter 7 in the 'Life and living processes' section of this book.)

Chapter 12
States of matter: Solids, liquids and gases

Remember

All the materials on the Earth can be placed into three groups: **solids**, **liquids** and **gases**.

These three different groups of materials have different properties which can affect the jobs they are used for. The most important properties are:

- Whether or not the material can **flow**. Gases and liquids flow, but solids do not.

- Whether or not the material can **change shape**.

  Solids keep the same shape, liquids change shape to match the shape of the container they are in, and gases spread out to fill any space they can reach. We can change the shape of a solid, but only by getting rid of some of it or by bending it.

- Whether or not the material can be squeezed to **change its volume** (can it be compressed).

  It is easy to change the volume of a gas by squashing it. But liquids and solids normally don't change very much in volume (some can expand very, very slightly when heated).

Matter is the scientific word used to describe all of the different substances and materials found on the Earth (and in all other parts of the Universe, too!). We call **solid**, **liquid** and **gas** the three **states of matter**.

Changing states

Here is some important information:

- Most substances can exist in all three states.

- The state of a substance depends on the temperature.

- Changes of state are brought about by changes in temperature.

  Raising the temperature causes solids to change to liquids (**melting**) and, eventually, liquids to change to gases (**boiling** and **evaporation**). In the same way, cooling a gas will eventually change it into a liquid (**condensation**) and if the cooling is continued, the liquid will eventually change into a solid (**freezing**).

  These changes of state are described in the next diagram:

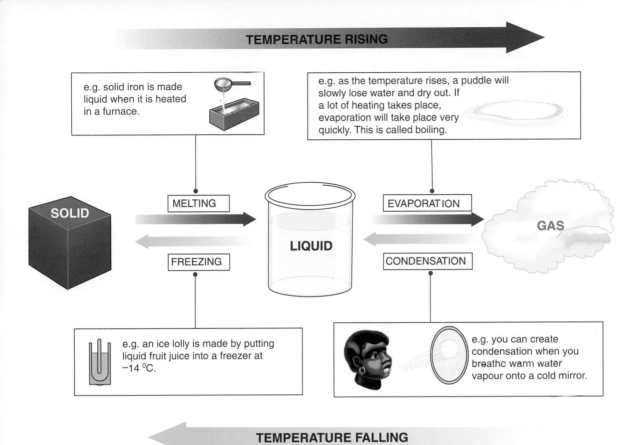

In a pure substance these changes of state always occur at the same particular temperatures: the **boiling point (bp)**, the **melting point (mp)** and the **freezing point (fp)**.

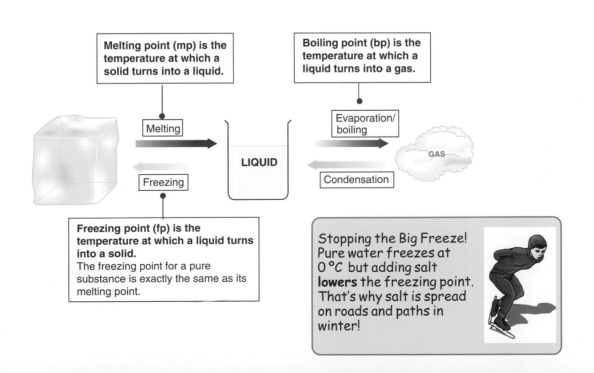

Melting point: Every pure substance has its own particular melting point. Checking the melting point is one way to test how **pure** a substance is. A **mixture** of substances melts over a range of temperatures.

Boiling point: Every **pure** substance has its own particular boiling point. A **mixture** of substances would boil over a range of temperatures.

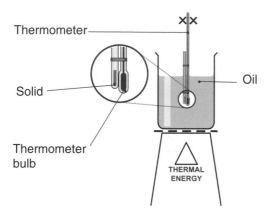

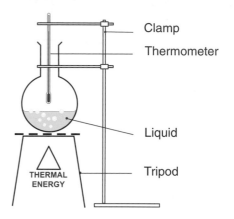

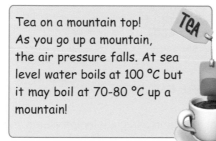

Tea on a mountain top! As you go up a mountain, the air pressure falls. At sea level water boils at 100 °C but it may boil at 70-80 °C up a mountain!

Because these temperatures are always the same for one particular substance, they can be counted as **properties** of the substance. Like other properties, they can help us to explain what a substance or material can be used for.

Substance	Melting point in °C	Boiling point in °C
Oxygen	⁻218	⁻183
Mercury	⁻39	357
Water	0	100
Alcohol	⁻114	78
Aluminium	660	2467

Why does the water in an aluminium pan boil before the pan melts? Aluminium has a useful property for pan making.

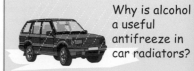

Why is alcohol a useful antifreeze in car radiators?

The water cycle

Scientists think that the amount of water on the Earth has stayed the same for millions of years. However, the water is constantly recycling as it changes from one state to another. Water **evaporates** from the sea into the air and then **condenses** back from the air into the sea. In between evaporation and condensation, water may be moved over thousands of kilometres by winds. These natural changes in the state of water are called the **water cycle**, and are shown in this diagram:

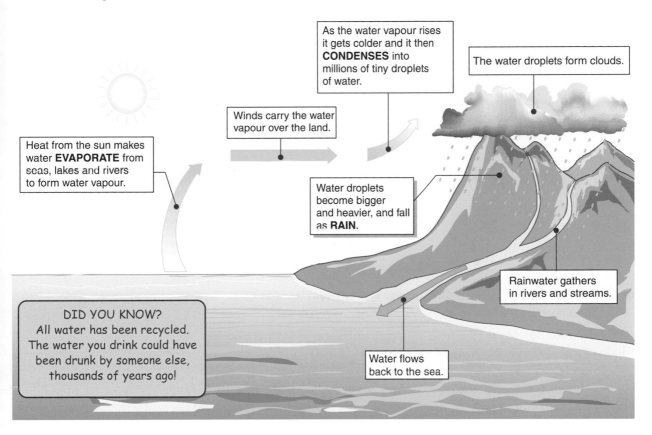

As the water vapour rises it gets colder and it then **CONDENSES** into millions of tiny droplets of water.

The water droplets form clouds.

Winds carry the water vapour over the land.

Heat from the sun makes water **EVAPORATE** from seas, lakes and rivers to form water vapour.

Water droplets become bigger and heavier, and fall as **RAIN**.

Rainwater gathers in rivers and streams.

DID YOU KNOW?
All water has been recycled. The water you drink could have been drunk by someone else, thousands of years ago!

Water flows back to the sea.

The heating of water to evaporate it from the sea is caused by the Sun. Remembering how the Sun also supplied the energy for plants to make their food, and that water is one of the raw materials for this process (check photosynthesis on page 71), you can see why the Sun and water are absolutely essential for all life on Earth.

Air flow and temperature affect evaporation of water

Winds and solar energy affect the water cycle. Increased temperature makes water evaporate more quickly from the sea and from rivers and lakes, and winds move the water vapour in the air from place to place. Scientists are very concerned about the effects of global warming caused by the production of greenhouse gases (see page 217) and try to predict how rising temperatures will affect our climate and our lives. So that they can predict what will happen in nature, scientists carry out experiments in the laboratory and use the results to explain what might happen in the outside environment. Carrying out an experiment and using the results to make predictions like this is called **making a model**.

Experiments on evaporation

The amount of a substance is its **mass**. As you know, we can measure mass using an electronic top pan balance (a weighing machine). We can measure changes in the mass of a certain volume of water and then calculate how much water has been lost by evaporation.

● The experiment can be repeated at **different temperatures** to make a model of the effect of temperature on loss of water by evaporation.

Measuring the evaporation of water

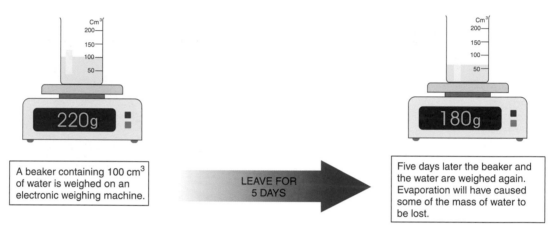

A beaker containing 100 cm³ of water is weighed on an electronic weighing machine.

LEAVE FOR 5 DAYS

Five days later the beaker and the water are weighed again. Evaporation will have caused some of the mass of water to be lost.

● The experiment can also be repeated with **different speeds of air flow** to make a model of the effect of windspeed on the loss of water by evaporation.

Measuring the effect of airflow on evaporation

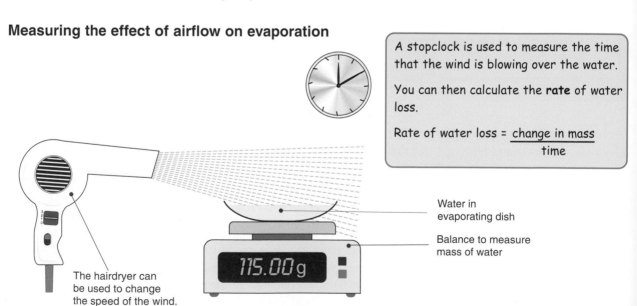

A stopclock is used to measure the time that the wind is blowing over the water.

You can then calculate the **rate** of water loss.

Rate of water loss = $\dfrac{\text{change in mass}}{\text{time}}$

Water in evaporating dish

Balance to measure mass of water

The hairdryer can be used to change the speed of the wind.

After carrying out many experiments of this type, experts in the study of weather have predicted that global warming will make the seas evaporate more quickly. There will be many more violent rainstorms and strong winds (more hurricanes) as all this extra water is carried over the land.

Exercise 12.1: Water and the water cycle

1. Copy and complete this paragraph:

    Pure water boils at .... and freezes at .... A simple chemical test uses cobalt chloride paper to test for the presence of water. The cobalt chloride paper changes from .... to .... if water is present. Seawater is a .... of many different substances. The presence of these impurities .... the freezing point and .... the boiling point of water.

2. Look at this experiment, set up to study the effect of temperature on evaporation:

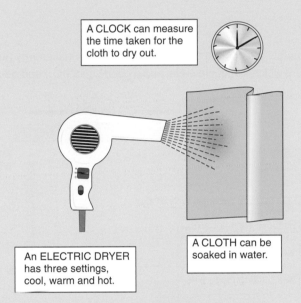

A CLOCK can measure the time taken for the cloth to dry out.

An ELECTRIC DRYER has three settings, cool, warm and hot.

A CLOTH can be soaked in water.

EXPERIMENT: DOES WARM AIR SPEED UP EVAPORATION?

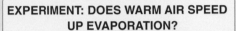

CHANGE ONE FACTOR: the thermal energy from the dryer.

MEASURE ONE OTHER FACTOR: the time taken for cloth to dry out.

MAKE IT A FAIR TEST! Keep the other factors the same:
- the speed the fan is blowing;
- the distance between the dryer and the cloth;
- the size of the cloth; and
- the amount of water added to the dry cloth.

How could you change the experiment to test:

(a) whether the speed of blowing the air affected the rate of evaporation;

(b) whether different types of cloth dry off at different rates.

Write your answers in a table like this:

Experiment	Factor to change (input variable)	Factor to measure (outcome variable)	Factors to keep constant (controlled variables)
(i)			
(ii)			

Extension project

Use the Internet or textbooks in a library to find out about hurricanes. What can scientists measure about hurricanes? Give some examples of the results they have obtained.

Other properties of solids, liquids and gases

Don't forget

- Any **pure** substance can be identified by its melting point and boiling point.

- Solids and liquids cannot be compressed (squashed), but gases can easily be compressed.

There are several other important properties of substances that can help us to decide whether they are solids, liquids or gases:

Conduction of internal/thermal energy: Solids that are metals are good at transferring internal/thermal energy (they are good **conductors**). Liquids (with the exception of mercury which is a liquid metal and a good conductor) and gases are not good conductors.

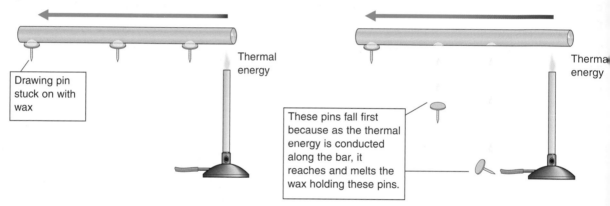

Drawing pin stuck on with wax

Thermal energy

Thermal energy

These pins fall first because as the thermal energy is conducted along the bar, it reaches and melts the wax holding these pins.

Expansion: All states of matter expand when they are heated, but this is usually easier to see with solids.

These experiments show that:

- all matter – solid, liquid or gas, expands when heated;

- gases expand more than liquids and liquids expand more than solids.

When you put a thermometer under your tongue, the internal/thermal energy makes the alcohol expand. This then gives a reading on the thermometer.

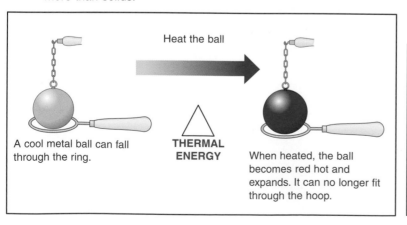

Heat the ball

A cool metal ball can fall through the ring.

THERMAL ENERGY

When heated, the ball becomes red hot and expands. It can no longer fit through the hoop.

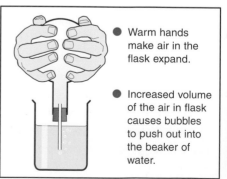

- Warm hands make air in the flask expand.

- Increased volume of the air in flask causes bubbles to push out into the beaker of water.

Expansion could cause problems

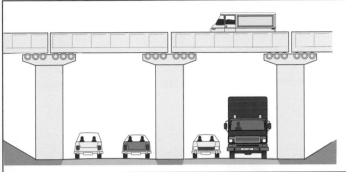

- In hot weather the bridge sections expand.
- Gaps between the sections expand without damage.
- The rollers let the sections move as they expand.
- You will often see that the gaps in concrete roads are filled with tar. When the concrete expands, it just squashes the tar.

Diffusion: Particles can spread out through liquids and gases, but not through solids. This spreading out is called **diffusion**. The particles spread out from where there are a lot of them to where there aren't very many. Diffusion goes on much more quickly if the temperature is raised. Think how smelly a changing room is in summer compared with in the winter!

The smell of fish and chips can spread out through the air. This process is called diffusion.

Diffusion takes place:

- when gases or liquids mix;
- until the concentration of the two gases or liquids becomes the same everywhere.

Density: The density of a substance tells us how much of the substance is packed into a certain volume. Solids are usually denser than liquids and liquids are denser than gases. Look at the diagram below. Of course a kilogram of feathers has exactly the same mass as a kilogram of iron! However, the kilogram of feathers will take up more space than the kilogram of iron. We say that the feathers have a lower **density** than the iron.

We can work out the density of any substance using the following equation:

$$\text{Density} = \frac{\text{mass}}{\text{volume}}$$

Where: density is in grams per cubic centimetre (g/cm³) or kilograms per cubic centimetre (kg/cm³)
mass is in grams (g) or kilograms (kg)
volume is in cubic centimetres (cm³)

Example 1: Finding the volume of a regular shape

A gold bar measures 12 cm × 5 cm × 4 cm and has a mass of 4632 g.

What is the density of gold? First find the volume of the gold bar:

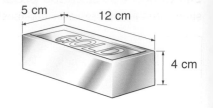

$$Volume = length \times width \times height$$

$$= 12 \times 5 \times 4$$

$$= 240 \ cm^3$$

Now use the equation to calculate the density of the gold.

$$Density = \frac{mass}{volume}$$

$$Density = \frac{4632 \ g}{240 \ cm^3}$$

$$= 19.3 \ g/cm^3$$

> Repeat the calculation taking the mass of gold as 4.632 kg.
>
> Check your units for the density of the gold.

Example 2: Measuring volume by displacement

As we saw above, the volume of a regular object, like a cube, can be found by doing a little calculation. However, find the volume of an irregular shaped object, you can use the displacement of water in a measuring cylinder.

The diagram shows how to measure the volume of a small stone.

The measurements are:

$Volume \ of \ water \ with \ small \ stone \ added \quad = 75 \ cm^3$

$Volume \ of \ water \ at \ the \ start \quad\quad = 60 \ cm^3$

$Therefore, \ volume \ of \ small \ stone \quad\quad = 15 \ cm^3$

This stone weighed 30 grams. What was its density?

$$Density = \frac{mass}{volume}$$

$$Density = \frac{30 \ g}{15 \ cm^3}$$

$$= 2 \ g/cm^3$$

How could you check this earring is really gold?

Which is heavier:
A kilogram of feathers ...
... or a kilogram of horseshoes?

Stretch and flow: Some substances can stretch or flow to fill a space. Solids do **not** stretch very easily, liquids can stretch and flow **quite** easily and most gases can flow **very** easily into new spaces.

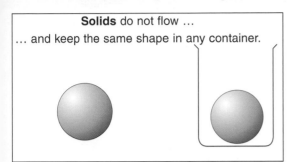

Solids do not flow …
… and keep the same shape in any container.

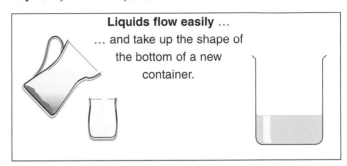

Liquids flow easily …
… and take up the shape of the bottom of a new container.

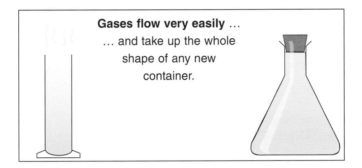

Gases flow very easily …
… and take up the whole shape of any new container.

Exercise 12.2: Other solids, liquids and gases

1. Classify each of these materials into solid, liquid or gas:

    Wood, carbon dioxide, snow, plastic, salt, vinegar, stone, lime juice, water vapour, tomato ketchup.

2. (a) Complete this table about the properties of solids, liquids and gases:

Does it …?	Solid	Liquid	Gas
Melt			
Freeze			
Boil			
Compress			
Conduct thermal energy			
Expand			
Diffuse			
Stretch			
Flow			

(b) Give the density of (choose high, medium or low):

(i)   a solid

(ii) a liquid

(iii) a gas

Extension questions

3. This table lists the properties of some common metals.

Metal	Melting point in °C	Density in g/cm³	Cost per tonne in £
Aluminium	659	2.7	1900
Magnesium	1117	1.7	7200
Iron	1540	7.9	280
Lead	328	11.3	625
Copper	1083	9.0	2200
Nickel	2837	8.9	8150
Silver	961	10.5	320 000
Tin	232	7.3	19 100
Zinc	420	7.1	1200

(a) Rearrange these metals from lowest to highest density, then make a bar chart of the densities.

(b) Use the table above to write an explanation of the following:
   (i)   Why deep sea divers use boots made of lead.
   (ii)   Why tent poles are made from aluminium, not iron.
   (iii) Why dustbins are made from iron coated with zinc, not coated with tin.
   (iv) Why overhead electrical cables are made from aluminium, not copper.
   (v)   Why ovens are not made from tin.
   (iv) Why the wheels of racing cars are made from a mixture of magnesium and aluminium and not from a mixture of iron and lead.

4. The density of a substance can be measured in g/cm³.

   (a) If 10 litres of a liquid has a mass of 975 g, what is its density?

   (b) A metal has a density of 9.0 g/cm³. What is the mass of a cube of this metal which has sides that are 3 cm long?

   (c) If a salt solution has a density of 1.2 g/cm³, what volume of the solution would have a mass of 840 g?

Particle theory

Explaining these properties

All materials are made up of tiny **particles**. The particles in matter can be arranged in different ways. The simplest particles are called **atoms**. An **atom** is the smallest particle that can make up a substance. Some substances are made up of **molecules**. A **molecule** is made up of two or more atoms that are joined together.

Scientists have a theory that the way in which these particles are arranged helps to explain the different properties of solids, liquids and gases. Where did this **particle theory** come from? You will need to think back to how you would design an experiment or investigation.

The theory about particles

Any theory about the nature of matter must be able to explain our observations (in other words, what we actually see happening to solids, liquids and gases). A **theory** is an idea that explains observations and these observations are the results obtained by carrying out experiments. This diagram shows how a theory can be developed:

Creating a scientific theory

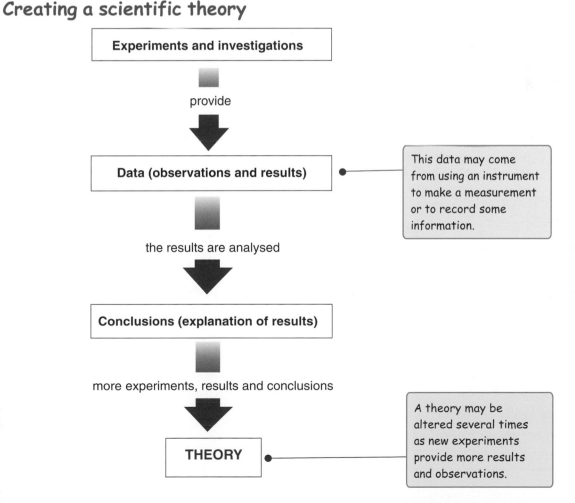

Experiments and investigations

provide

Data (observations and results)

This data may come from using an instrument to make a measurement or to record some information.

the results are analysed

Conclusions (explanation of results)

more experiments, results and conclusions

THEORY

A theory may be altered several times as new experiments provide more results and observations.

The way in which a particle theory can help to explain our observations on the properties of solids, liquids and gases is explained below:

Observations on the **properties** of solids, liquids and gases ...

Vibrations move along and conduct thermal energy.

Thermal energy

Conduction (internal/thermal energy transfer). The particles in the solid must be close together to allow the energy to passed from one particle to another along the bar.

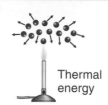

Thermal energy

Expansion (getting bigger on heating). The particles must move further apart from each other when they are heated as they have more energy. This could explain why the material **expands**.

... create ...

Density (how heavy something is for its size). Very **dense** materials (like metals) must have a lot of particles of the material packed into a small space.

Compressibility (squashiness). Solids and liquids don't **compress** very much, so there can't be much space between the particles. Gases must have some space between particles, as they can be pushed together.

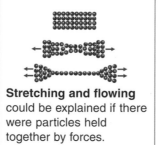

Stretching and flowing could be explained if there were particles held together by forces.

Diffusion could be explained if particles could move and spread out among themselves.

... THE PARTICLE THEORY

- All **solids**, **liquids** and **gases** are made up of **very small particles**.
- **Particles** are **always moving** and have **spaces between them**.
- **Particles** are held **together by forces**.

The particle theory and states of matter

We can explain the three states of matter - solid, liquid and gas - by the way the particles in the substances are arranged. Remember that the particles in the substance can be either atoms or molecules.

Atoms in a gas

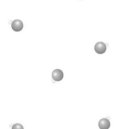

Molecules in a gas

In **gases** the particles are relatively a long way away from each other but they all bounce around, hitting each other, and this keeps them apart. This is why gases flow so easily and spread out to fill any available space. A gas is mostly empty space, so you can easily squeeze the particles together into a smaller space, which is why it is so easy to change the volume of a gas.

Atoms in a liquid

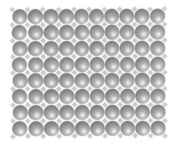

Molecules in a liquid

In **liquids** the particles are very close together but they don't hold onto each other very strongly. Although the particles in a liquid stay close together, they are always moving around one another; in fact they change places all the time. This is why liquids flow so easily and why they can take up the shape of the container they are in. There is no space between the particles, so you can't squeeze a liquid into a smaller space.

Atoms in a solid

Molecules in a solid

In **solids** the particles are packed very closely together and hold onto each other so tightly that they can hardly move at all. This is why solids don't flow and why they keep their shape. Because the particles are so close together, solids can't be squashed into a smaller volume.

Popping popcorn

This is all about liquids and vapours – actually **water** and **steam** (see page 139).

Each kernel (seed) of popcorn contains a tiny drop of water. The water is stored inside a circle of soft starch, and the soft starch is surrounded by a hard coat.

Heat in a pan or microwave oven.

Liquid water changes to vapour. This expands and puts pressure on the inside of the seed coat. This pressure gets too much, the popcorn 'pops' and the steam escapes.

The bits left in the bottom of the popcorn are called 'old maids'. They are too dry to have a 'pop' in them!

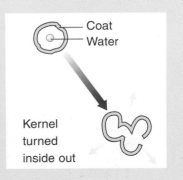

Coat
Water

Kernel turned inside out

Particle theory and changes of state

When a substance changes state – from liquid to gas, for example – it does so because it absorbs energy. These changes of state can be explained by the particle theory shown below:

The particle theory explains changes of state

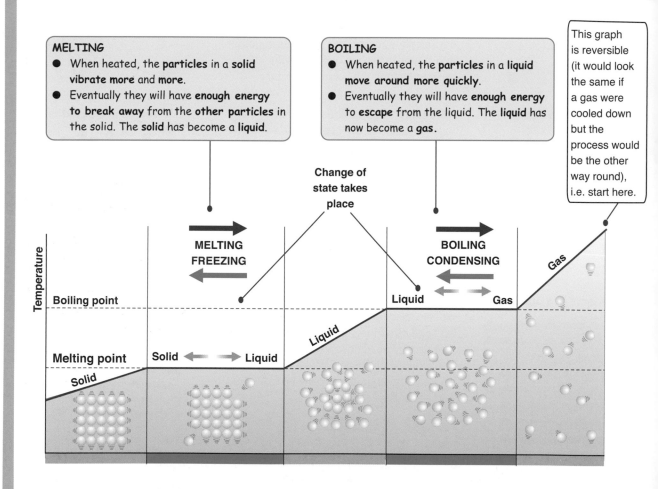

MELTING
- When heated, the **particles** in a **solid** **vibrate more** and **more**.
- Eventually they will have **enough energy to break away** from the **other particles** in the solid. The **solid** has become a **liquid**.

BOILING
- When heated, the **particles** in a **liquid** move around **more quickly**.
- Eventually they will have **enough energy** to **escape** from the liquid. The **liquid** has now become a **gas**.

This graph is reversible (it would look the same if a gas were cooled down but the process would be the other way round), i.e. start here.

Change of state takes place

MELTING
FREEZING

BOILING
CONDENSING

Gas

Temperature

Boiling point

Liquid   Gas

Melting point

Solid ⟷ Liquid

Liquid

Solid

KEY In these periods of time, **energy** is **used to push the particles apart** (so the 'line' graph stays flat).   In these periods of time, **energy is used to raise the temperature of the substance** (so the 'line' graph goes upwards).

Sublimation is when a substance changes directly from a solid state to a gaseous state.

Heating and cooling of water

Water is a liquid at the sort of temperatures we find in a laboratory (that is, around 20 °C). When water is cooled, its temperature falls and the water eventually freezes. The liquid water changes state into solid water, or **ice** (see page 139 for more on changes of state). We can draw a graph of the temperature changes as water is cooled. This **cooling curve** for water is shown below:

A cooling curve

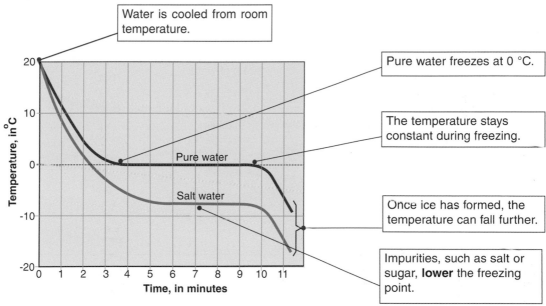

Water is cooled from room temperature.

Pure water freezes at 0 °C.

The temperature stays constant during freezing.

Once ice has formed, the temperature can fall further.

Impurities, such as salt or sugar, **lower** the freezing point.

When water is heated, its temperature rises as the water molecules absorb thermal energy. Eventually the water boils and turns into **water vapour** (the gas state for water). The **heating curve** for water is shown below.

A heating curve

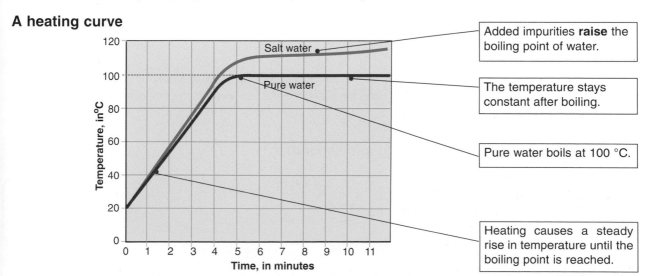

Added impurities **raise** the boiling point of water.

The temperature stays constant after boiling.

Pure water boils at 100 °C.

Heating causes a steady rise in temperature until the boiling point is reached.

In summary, therefore, water is a compound with a freezing point defined at 0 °C and a boiling point at 100 °C. There are two simple **chemical tests** for water. These have already been described on page 136.

Physical changes and conservation of mass

Physical changes cause the particles of a substance to be rearranged. No chemical bonds are formed, and no particles are lost or gained. If no particles are lost or gained, there should be no change in the mass of a substance when it goes through a physical change. If you measure an exact mass of water, freeze it (and weigh it again), then thaw it out, you will find that the freezing and thawing have had no effect on the mass of the water. This is called **conservation of mass**.

Conservation of mass during a change of state

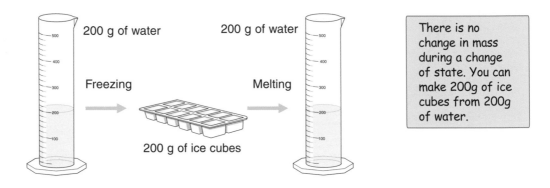

200 g of water   200 g of water

Freezing   Melting

200 g of ice cubes

There is no change in mass during a change of state. You can make 200g of ice cubes from 200g of water.

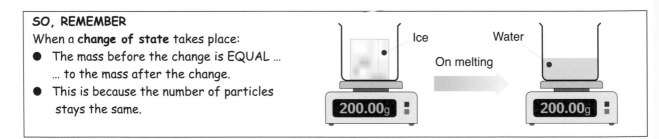

SO, REMEMBER

When a **change of state** takes place:
- The mass before the change is EQUAL ...
  ... to the mass after the change.
- This is because the number of particles stays the same.

Ice   Water

On melting

200.00g

200.00g

If you add 10 g of sugar to a dish of water and stir the two substances together, the sugar will dissolve and become invisible. You can collect the sugar again by allowing the water to evaporate away. At the end of this experiment you will find that there are still 10 g of sugar.

Conservation of mass during mixing and separation

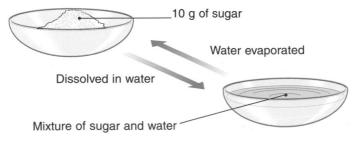

10 g of sugar

Water evaporated

Dissolved in water

Mixture of sugar and water

The law of **conservation of mass** applies to **all** physical changes.

Key words

States of matter – the forms in which a substance can exist, as solid, liquid or gas.

Change of state – the conversion of a substance from one form to another.

Property – any characteristic of a substance, such as colour, compressibility or shape.

Exercise 12.3: Solids, liquids and gases

1. Copy and complete this table about the properties of solids, liquids and gases.

	Solids	Liquids	Gases
Do they flow easily?			
Can they be compressed?			
Can they change their shape?			
Are the particles close together or far apart?			
Do the particles hold onto each other tightly or not?			

2. Select a type of material for the following uses. Choose from solid, liquid or gas:

   (a) To act as a roof support ....

   (b) To be squeezed into a container ....

   (c) To be pushed through a pipe ....

   (d) To fill up a balloon ....

   (e) To make into a tool ....

   (f) To pour from one container into another ....

3. The tyre on a racing car is hard because of the pressure of air inside the tyre.

   (a) What causes the air pressure inside the tyre?

   (b) Why does the air pressure increase when the mechanics pump up the tyre?

   (c) What happens to the air pressure inside the tyre as the tyre gets hotter during the race? Explain your answer to this part of the question.

   (d) How can tyres that contain air absorb some of the bumps on the racing circuit?

Internet project

Find out what a **barometer** is. How does it work? How is it useful to a weather forecaster?

Chapter 13
Mixtures: Pure substance or mixture?

Starting points

- Chemistry is the study of the properties and reactions of substances.

- All substances, solid, liquid or gas, are made of particles.

A chemist is interested in how different substances are made up, and how they can be changed. It is very important in chemistry to know whether a substance is pure, or whether it is made of several different substances mixed together. A pure substance may behave in a different way from a mixture. A doctor, for example, would want to be absolutely sure that a drug was pure before he or she offered it to a patient. Remember:

- In a pure substance **all the particles are the same** and so they all behave in the same way.

- In a mixture there is **more than one type of particle**. The particles are not joined together, and the mixture can react in different ways, depending on how many of each type of particle is present.

Pure ethanol contains only ethanol particles and all of them are very poisonous.

Lager beer contains a **mixture** of different particles: alcohol, minerals, sugars, carbon dioxide and about 95% water.

Testing for purity

There are different methods that can be used to test whether a substance is pure or a mixture:

Appearance: sometimes the particles are big enough to be seen, perhaps with a microscope. For example, looking at a sample of soil shows that it is made up of several different types of particle, so it is a mixture.

Melting and boiling point measurements: a pure substance always melts at one fixed temperature and boils at another fixed temperature (see page 139). A mixture can have very different melting and boiling points, depending on how much of each substance is present.

Looking for particular physical properties: some metals are magnetic, for example, and can be separated from mixtures using a magnet.

Soil sample

This is a soil sample. The particles are large enough to see that it is a mixture. Different types of soil have different properties, depending on how many of each type of particle are present.

Pure water

This is pure water. We can tell because it boils at 100 °C. A mixture, for example salt solution, has different boiling and melting points, depending on the amount of each substance in it.

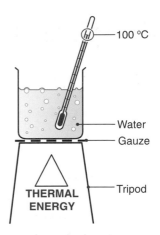

100 °C

Water
Gauze

THERMAL ENERGY

Tripod

Mixture of iron filings and copper

This is a mixture of iron filings and copper. We can tell that this is a mixture because the iron is attracted to the magnet but the copper is left behind. Some mixtures can easily be separated like this. For more information on the separation of mixtures, see page 166.

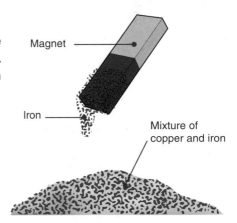

Magnet

Iron

Mixture of copper and iron

Exercise 13.1: Pure substance or mixture?

1. How could you check that a mixture of sand, salt and sugar actually contained several different types of particle?

2. A delicatessen sells bottles of 'pure mountain spring water'. How could you check whether this claim is true?

3. A popular brand of orange juice claims to be 'pure orange juice, containing only natural fruit sugar, vitamin C, citric acid and water'. Why doesn't this sentence make sense?

4. How could you tell whether a metallic powder contained only iron filings or whether it also had some magnesium mixed in with it?

More about mixtures: Solutions and solubility

Don't forget

- A pure substance is made up of only one type of particle.

- A mixture is made up of different types of particle.

- Making a mixture is an example of a physical change.

As you know, the appearance of some substances changes when the substances are mixed with water. You can see this if you drop a soluble aspirin into a glass of water; the aspirin seems to disappear. In fact what has happened is that the aspirin has **dissolved** in the water to form a mixture. This mixture is a **solution** and the aspirin has not disappeared at all. The particles of the aspirin have spread so that you can't see them, but they are still there.

Solids can dissolve to make solutions

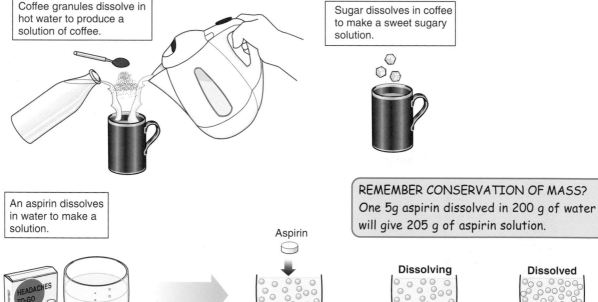

Coffee granules dissolve in hot water to produce a solution of coffee.

Sugar dissolves in coffee to make a sweet sugary solution.

An aspirin dissolves in water to make a solution.

REMEMBER CONSERVATION OF MASS?
One 5g aspirin dissolved in 200 g of water will give 205 g of aspirin solution.

Aspirin

Water (solvent) full to brim

The solvent particles have space between them and can move about.

Aspirin (solute)

Dissolving

The solute particles dissolve ...

Dissolved

... and spread out between the solvent particles.

> GASES AND LIQUIDS ALSO DISSOLVE!
> Gases, for example oxygen, can dissolve in water. This is good for fish!
> Some liquids can also dissolve in water (for example, alcohol).

Exactly the same thing happens when you add a spoonful of sugar to your tea, or make a cup of coffee by adding boiling water to coffee granules.

What makes up a solution?

If a substance will dissolve to form a solution, we say that the substance is **soluble**. The substance that dissolves is called the **solute** and the substance it dissolves in is called the **solvent**.

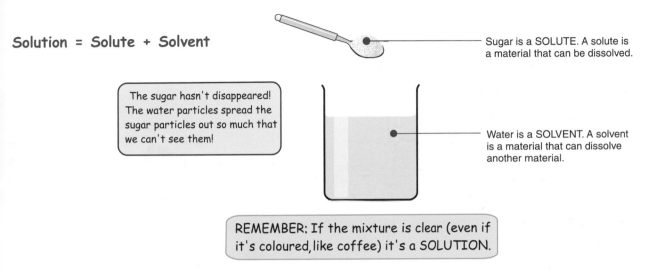

Solution = Solute + Solvent

Sugar is a SOLUTE. A solute is a material that can be dissolved.

The sugar hasn't disappeared! The water particles spread the sugar particles out so much that we can't see them!

Water is a SOLVENT. A solvent is a material that can dissolve another material.

REMEMBER: If the mixture is clear (even if it's coloured, like coffee) it's a SOLUTION.

If a substance won't dissolve in a solvent, we say that the substance is **insoluble**. A good example is chalk in water; chalk is insoluble in water. This means that when they are mixed, the mixture stays cloudy because the chalk particles stay stuck together in pieces that are big enough for us to see. This kind of mixture is called a **suspension**. You see a good example when carbon dioxide is bubbled through limewater; the cloudy liquid is actually a suspension of chalk (calcium carbonate, to give chalk its chemical name). Another good example is sand; sandy water is very cloudy indeed!

Insoluble solids form suspensions

Cloudy suspension of calcium carbonate (CO_2 in limewater).

Quicksand is a suspension of sand and water. There are so many sand particles that you can't really tell there's any water there!

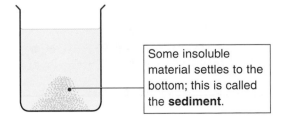

Some insoluble material settles to the bottom; this is called the **sediment**.

Sedimentation occurs when soil and rock particles settle out of water.

Water as a solvent

Water is a very common solvent, but it isn't the only one. A substance that is insoluble in one solvent can be soluble in a different one. The **solubility** of a substance is a measure of the amount of a substance that will dissolve in a particular solvent. Many industries depend on substances having a different solubility in different solvents.

Not all solutes are soluble in water

Some stains aren't removed by water, especially greasy or oily stains.

But other solvents (like those used by dry cleaners) can dissolve and remove these difficult stains.

Nail varnish is dissolved in **propanone**, so it can be spread onto your nails. It is insoluble in water, so it won't easily wash off.

SUBSTANCE (Solute)	SOLVENT	IMPORTANT POINT
Pigment in gloss paint	White spirit	Paint colour does not dissolve when it rains.
Pleasant smelling oils in perfume and aftershave	Alcohol	Alcohol evaporates after spraying, leaving a pleasant smell behind.
Correcting fluid (Tipp-ex) is white pigment in a fatty solvent.		Solvent evaporates and leaves white pigment particles behind.

SOME SOLVENTS ARE HARMFUL!
Some solvents can dissolve away fats in the cell membranes. Cells can burst and injury or death can result.
DON'T SNIFF SOLVENTS!

Temperature and solubility

You can tell if a substance has dissolved in water because the substance seems to disappear and the solution is clear. However, you can't just keep on dissolving a substance; eventually no more will dissolve and some of the substance will begin to settle out at the bottom of the container. When this happens, we say that the solution is **saturated**. No more particles of the solute can be fitted between the particles of the solvent and so the undissolved particles of the solute stick together. Scientists can use this to check on how different conditions affect the solubility of substances. Some important factors that affect the **rate** at which a substance will dissolve are:

● The amount of **mixing** or **stirring** that goes on.

● The **temperature** of the solvent.

● The **size of the solute particles** (whether the solute is in lumps or has been ground down to a powder).

The way temperature affects solubility can be investigated by measuring the amount of solute that will dissolve in 100 g of water at different temperatures. The results of an example of this type of investigation are shown on the graph below.

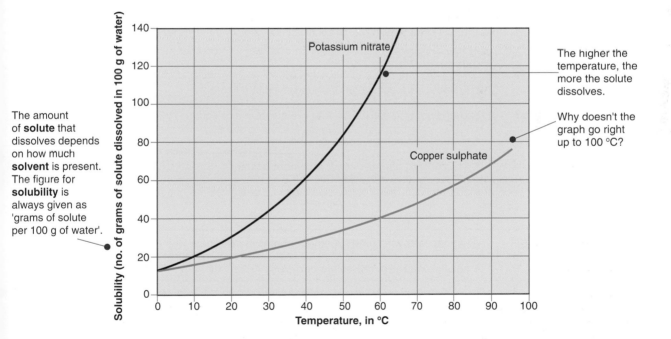

The amount of **solute** that dissolves depends on how much **solvent** is present. The figure for **solubility** is always given as 'grams of solute per 100 g of water'.

The higher the temperature, the more the solute dissolves.

Why doesn't the graph go right up to 100 °C?

Dilute or concentrated?

A solution with many solute particles in a certain volume of solvent is **concentrated** (this is a more scientific term than saying it is strong), and a solution with very few solute particles in the same volume of solvent is **dilute** (or weak). We can concentrate a solution by adding more solute to it, and we can dilute a solution by adding more solvent to it.

You will find out how to separate the different substances in a solution on page 170.

Key words

Solution – a mixture of a solute in a solvent.

Solute – the substance that dissolves in a solvent when a solution is made.

Solvent – the liquid that dissolves a solute.

Insoluble – unable to dissolve in a solvent.

Solubility – means how much of a substance will dissolve in a certain volume of a solvent.

Saturated – a solution made when the maximum amount of a solute that can dissolve has been added to a solvent.

Suspension – a mixture made of a liquid and an insoluble substance.

Exercise 13.2: Solutions and solubility

1. Match up words from the first column with the correct definitions from the second column:

Word	Definition
Dissolve	The name for a substance that dissolves in a liquid
Concentrated	The amount of a substance that will dissolve in a liquid
Dilute	A mixture of a solvent and a solute
Solute	A solution that cannot accept any more solute
Soluble	A solution with many solute particles in a small volume of solvent
Solvent	This means 'can dissolve'
Solution	What happens when one substance seems to disappear when it is mixed with a liquid
Insoluble	A solution with very few solute particles
Saturated	The name for the liquid part of a solution
Solubility	This means 'cannot dissolve'

2. Coca Cola is a solution:

    (a) Find out three main solutes and the solvent in Coca Cola.

    (b) Coca Cola manufacturers want the manufacturing process to take as little time as possible. How can they make sure that the solutes dissolve quickly in the solvent?

3. Look at the diagram below which shows an experiment on dissolving a solute:

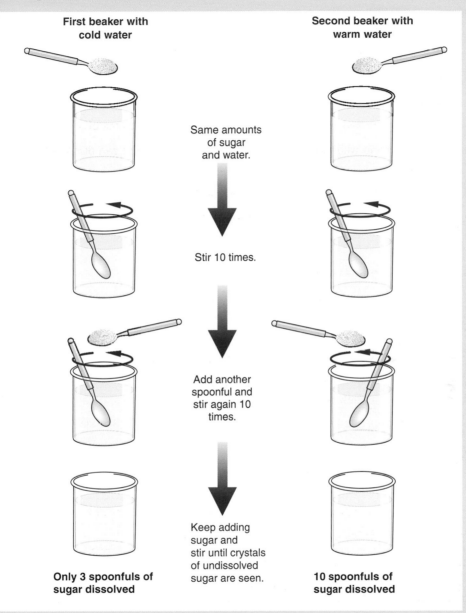

First beaker with cold water

Second beaker with warm water

Same amounts of sugar and water.

Stir 10 times.

Add another spoonful and stir again 10 times.

Keep adding sugar and stir until crystals of undissolved sugar are seen.

Only 3 spoonfuls of sugar dissolved

10 spoonfuls of sugar dissolved

(a) What is the input (independent) variable in this experiment?

(b) What is the outcome (dependent) variable in this experiment?

(c) What has the scientist done to make sure that this is a fair test?

(d) How could you alter the experiment to investigate the effect of lump size on the solubility of sugar?

Extension question

4. Gena and her friend Izzy decided to investigate the solubility of sugar in water. They added weighed amounts of sugar to a beaker containing 100 g of water until no more sugar could dissolve. They repeated the experiment but varied the water temperature. Here are their results:

Temperature in °C	Mass of sugar that dissolves in 100 g of water in grams
0	180
10	192
20	205
30	220
50	265
70	365
80	425
90	475

(a) Plot their results in a line graph.

(b) How much sugar dissolves in 100 g of water at 40 °C?

(c) How much sugar would dissolve in 250 g of water at 50 °C?

(d) Give two factors that they would need to keep constant if this were to be a fair test.

(e) Suggest two ways in which they could have improved the reliability of their results.

Separating mixtures of materials

Starting points

* A **pure substance** is one in which all of the particles (atoms or molecules) are the same.

* A **mixture** contains different types of particle.

* Different materials have **different useful properties**.

Air, tap water and sea water are good examples of mixtures. They are made up of different particles that are not combined with one another. Because they are **not joined by chemical bonds**, these particles can be separated using **physical methods**.

Mixtures contain more than one type of particle

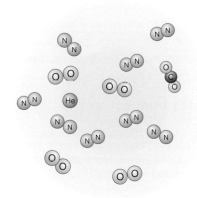

You can find the actual proportions of the different substances in these mixtures on page 197.

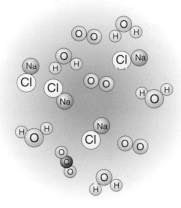

Air is a mixture of elements and compounds.

Seawater is a mixture of elements and compounds.

What is separation?

We often want to separate the different materials in a mixture. We usually want to do this because one material is very useful for a particular reason (getting pure drinking water out of sea water, for example). There are many ways in which you can separate the different materials in mixtures; all of these methods depend on some difference between the materials in the mixture. The sort of questions a chemist might ask before trying to carry out a separation would include:

* Do all the materials have the same solubility?

* Do all of the materials have the same boiling point?

* Are some of the materials solid while the others are liquid?

* Do any of the materials have some special physical property that none of the others has?

We have already seen that iron can be separated from other elements because iron is magnetic (see page 157). This is an unusual method of separation. Usually other methods – decanting, filtration and evaporation, for example – are used when you need to separate materials from a mixture (see **Science** Book 1, pages 157-159).

Separating a solid from a liquid: Decanting

Decanting is a process that you should all by now be very familiar with. In many parts of Africa and Asia, for example, drinking water is collected from the nearest river in large jars. Sometimes the water is quite muddy or sandy because there are soil particles floating in the water. The people who collect the water leave the jars to stand, so that the mud, sand and silt will settle out at the bottom of the jar. The clear water can then be poured off and the solid materials from the mixture can be left behind at the bottom of the jar.

Separating a solid from a liquid: Filtration

A filter is a layer with many tiny holes in it. The tiny holes allow small particles in a liquid through, but keep the larger particles of the solid back. Many filters are made from paper, and these can hold back extremely small particles of solid. Using filter paper is very important in scientific experiments.

Separating solids and water: Evaporation

We can use filter paper to separate an insoluble substance from a liquid because the particles of the insoluble substance (the solid) are too big to get through the gaps in the filter paper. However, when a substance dissolves in a liquid, the tiny particles of the dissolved substance are so spread out that they can pass through these gaps. This means that you can't use filtration to separate a solute and a solvent. The way in which you can separate a solute and a solvent is by getting rid of the solvent. You can do this by evaporation (the changing of a liquid into a gas).

The process of evaporation and crystallisation separates solutes from solvent

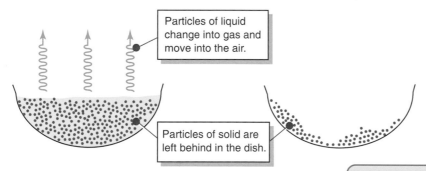

Particles of liquid change into gas and move into the air.

Particles of solid are left behind in the dish.

This process can be used to show that **sea water, tap water and distilled water** are different from each other. Distilled water gives **no** crystals, tap water gives a **few** but sea water gives **many** crystals of **several different types**.

If the liquid is water, it is safe to speed up evaporation using a flame.

NEVER do this with a flammable solvent, such as ethanol or propane.

As the liquid evaporates slowly and the solid dries out, the solid forms **crystals**. This process is called **crystallisation** and can produce a pure solid. An example is the formation of copper sulphate crystals from copper sulphate solution.

Evaporation takes place if a liquid is left to stand in a warm place. The process is very much quicker if the solution is gently heated, using a low Bunsen flame, but slow evaporation is best if you want to collect **crystals** of the pure solute. Be careful, never heat the solution until its completely dry, otherwise hot crystals of salt could spit out.

In the process of crystallisation most of the solvent is removed by heating but then the solution is allowed to cool slowly. This process works because crystals form as the saturated solution cools. Remember that the solubility of a solute falls as the temperature is reduced.

Filtration and evaporation can be used in the same separation

Sometimes a mixture can be quite complicated. There may be a solvent, a solute and an insoluble substance all together! A mixture like this can be separated into the different substances if two methods, **filtration** and **evaporation**, are combined. Evaporation would mean that the solvent would be lost, so a third process, **condensation**, can be included.

One mixture of this type is **rock salt** which is made up of sand and salt. The steps in the separation are:

●   Crush the rock salt to make the particles smaller.

●   Mix the rock salt with water to dissolve the soluble salt.

●   **Filtration**, when the mixture is filtered through filter paper. This leaves the sand as a residue and the salt solution passes through as the filtrate.

●   **Evaporation**, when the salt solution is warmed. The water evaporates and leaves the salt behind as crystals in the evaporating dish.

●   You could also collect the water by **condensation**. This is when the water vapour is cooled, so that it is turned back to water.

The process of separating a mixture

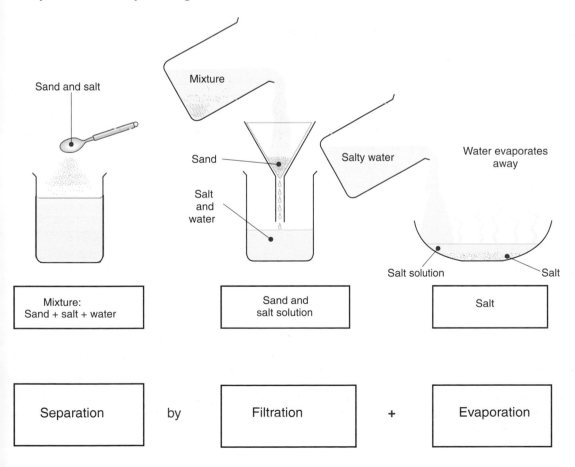

Separation of a solvent from a solution: Simple distillation

So we now know that evaporation separates a solute from a solution, but the solvent is usually lost unless special precautions are taken. Sometimes the solvent is valuable and needs to be saved. This can be achieved by evaporating the solvent and then condensing it in a piece of apparatus where the solvent can be collected. The solution is heated, so that the solvent boils quickly and evaporates. **Simple distillation** can be performed using this apparatus:

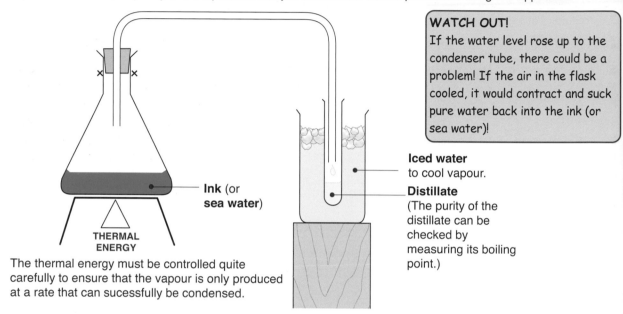

WATCH OUT!
If the water level rose up to the condenser tube, there could be a problem! If the air in the flask cooled, it would contract and suck pure water back into the ink (or sea water)!

Ink (or **sea water**)

THERMAL ENERGY

The thermal energy must be controlled quite carefully to ensure that the vapour is only produced at a rate that can sucessfully be condensed.

Iced water to cool vapour.

Distillate (The purity of the distillate can be checked by measuring its boiling point.)

Simple distillation can also be performed using the apparatus shown below. Here the vapour is directed into a **water-cooled condenser**. This piece of apparatus has a central tube for condensing the solvent and an outer tube that carries cold water. It is more efficient at cooling the vapour than the apparatus shown above. The condenser is often known as the **Liebig condenser**, after the scientist who first worked out how to perform this kind of separation. The separation of pure water from sea water is described below:

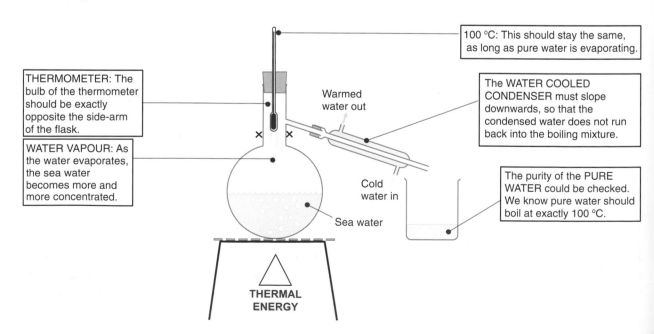

THERMOMETER: The bulb of the thermometer should be exactly opposite the side-arm of the flask.

WATER VAPOUR: As the water evaporates, the sea water becomes more and more concentrated.

Warmed water out

100 °C: This should stay the same, as long as pure water is evaporating.

The WATER COOLED CONDENSER must slope downwards, so that the condensed water does not run back into the boiling mixture.

Cold water in

Sea water

The purity of the PURE WATER could be checked. We know pure water should boil at exactly 100 °C.

THERMAL ENERGY

Notice how the diagrams on the previous page are drawn in **cross section**. This helps us to see how the apparatus works. From the the bottom picture on page 168 we can see that the steam passes through the middle part of the condenser and is cooled by the cold water on the outside.

SAUDI SPRING WATER!

In Saudi Arabia and other desert countries drinking water is obtained by distillation of sea water.

Separation of two liquids from a mixture: Fractional distillation

Some liquids, like ethanol and water, mix together. Liquids that mix together in this way are said to be **miscible**. Miscible liquids can be separated as long as they have **different boiling points**. Remember that every pure substance has a fixed boiling point. Ethanol boils at 78 °C and water boils at 100 °C, so when a mixture of the two is heated the ethanol will evaporate first. Ethanol vapour starts to reach the condenser, cools down and drips into the collecting beaker. Some water does evaporate from the mixture but the cool glass beads in the fractionating column turn the water vapour back to liquid which trickles back into the flask. If the temperature is kept at 78 °C, almost pure ethanol can be collected.

Fractional distillation can separate ethanol from beer or wine

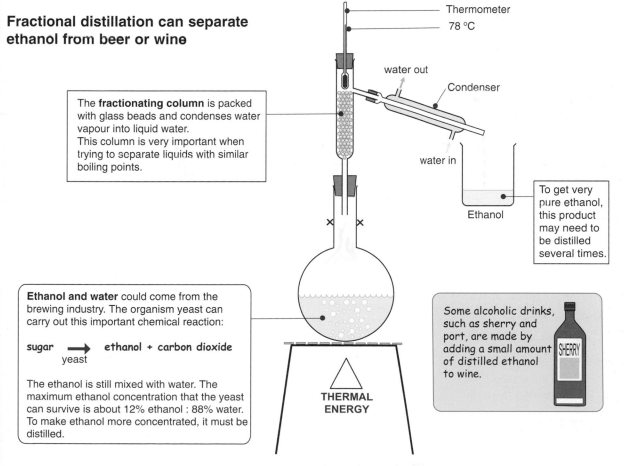

Thermometer
78 °C

water out

Condenser

The **fractionating column** is packed with glass beads and condenses water vapour into liquid water.
This column is very important when trying to separate liquids with similar boiling points.

water in

Ethanol

To get very pure ethanol, this product may need to be distilled several times.

Ethanol and water could come from the brewing industry. The organism yeast can carry out this important chemical reaction:

sugar   ⟶   ethanol + carbon dioxide
    yeast

The ethanol is still mixed with water. The maximum ethanol concentration that the yeast can survive is about 12% ethanol : 88% water. To make ethanol more concentrated, it must be distilled.

THERMAL ENERGY

Some alcoholic drinks, such as sherry and port, are made by adding a small amount of distilled ethanol to wine.

SHERRY

Strong alcoholic drinks (spirits like brandy and whisky) are made in this way. Great care is taken to make sure that the ethanol is separated from other substances with very similar boiling points, because some of these substances can be poisonous. Cheap spirits may not have been distilled very carefully and can cause great harm to anyone who drinks them.

Separation of several different soluble substances: Chromatography

Chromatography can be used to separate mixtures of different soluble substances. This process depends on substances having **different solubilities** in a certain solvent. The process is also affected by how much the substances stick to the paper used in the separation. The method for separating a mixture of coloured inks is shown below:

Using water as a solvent in simple paper chromatography

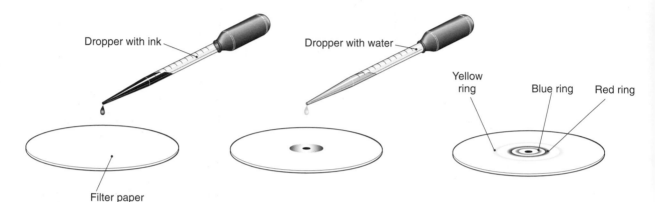

Dropper with ink

Dropper with water

Yellow ring   Blue ring   Red ring

Filter paper

Step1:
Place a drop of black ink at the centre of a piece of filter paper and let it dry.

Step 2:
Carefully squeeze small drops of water onto the ink. Leave a little time between drops to let the ink spread out. As the water moves across the filter paper, it will carry the colours with it. However, what you will see is that different colours travel at different speeds.

Step 3:
In this ink there are three coloured substances: blue, red and yellow. Notice that the blue dye didn't move as fast as the others. It got left behind and so formed its own ring. Next the red stopped moving. The yellow substance was the most soluble and so moved the furthest.

Chromatography can be used to identify unknown substances in a mixture. Look at the experiment on the opposite page (page 171):

- A spot of the mixture is placed on a baseline drawn on a piece of chromatography paper. The baseline must be drawn in pencil, or any colours in the baseline will interfere with the result!

- A separating solvent is placed in a jar and the sample paper is allowed to stand in the solvent, until the solvent nears the top of the paper.

- The separating solvent runs up through the paper and pulls the different substances from the spot. The most soluble substance travels furthest up the paper, and the least soluble substance travels the shortest distance. Each different dye in the coloured mixture will form a spot in a different place.

- The unknown spots can be compared with spots of known substances, so that the unknown materials can be identified.

Chromatography can identify unknown substances in a mixture

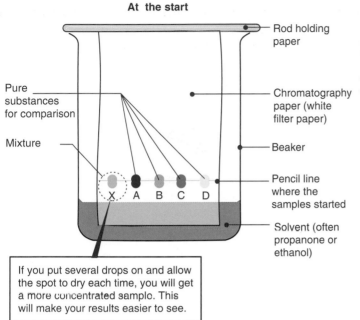

At the start

Rod holding paper

Pure substances for comparison

Chromatography paper (white filter paper)

Mixture

Beaker

X A B C D

Pencil line where the samples started

Solvent (often propanone or ethanol)

If you put several drops on and allow the spot to dry each time, you will get a more concentrated sample. This will make your results easier to see.

After the solvent has soaked up the paper

Solvent has reached this far up the paper.

X A B C D

Sample X was a mixture of pure substances, C and D. We can tell this because it formed two spots of colour. The yellow travelled the same distance as D and the blue travelled the same distance as C.

Some mixtures are not soluble in water, so other solvents must be used to separate them by chromatography. Two important solvents used in this way are **propanone** and **ethanol**. Chromatography is not only used for checking the dyes in different inks, it is also important in:

● checking the sugars in different kinds of foods;

● identifying different parts of the blood, including tests on blood at crime scenes; and

● comparing the pigments (colours) in different types of flowers and leaves.

Key words

Pure – describes a substance that is made of only one type of particle.

Mixture – contains more than one type of particle, not linked to one another.

Filtrate – the liquid that can pass through a filter paper.

Filtration – the process of separation that uses a paper to separate a solid from a liquid.

Decanting – separation of a solid from a liquid by careful pouring.

Evaporation – the change of state from liquid to gas (vapour), speeded up by heating.

Condensation – the change of state from vapour to liquid, speeded up by cooling.

Distillation – the process of separation that depends on substances in a mixture having different boiling points.

Chromatography – separation of dissolved materials depending on how well they are carried through a special kind of paper by a moving solvent.

Exercise 13.3: Separating mixtures

1. Copy and complete these paragraphs, using words from the list below:

   physical   evaporation   alcohol   boiling points
   identical   mixtures   chromatography   gold/salt

   (a) Most natural substances are ...., they are not pure. The particles of each substance in a mixture are not .... to each other and so these substances can often be separated because they have different .... properties.

   (b) There are several different ways of separating substances, including .... which can separate different soluble substances in a mixture and .... which can provide pure crystals of a solute from a solution.

   (c) The process of distillation depends on the fact that different substances have different .... The process can be used to collect .... from sea water and .... from beer or wine.

2. Freddie has a motorcycle and he likes to clean it in his garage.

   (a) After cleaning it, he sweeps up the floor of the garage, so that it's tidy for next time. The sweepings contain iron filings, aluminium shavings, salt and sand. Explain how the different substances in the sweepings could be separated from each other.

   (b) Freddie noticed some liquid on the floor. He thought that it was probably just water, but wanted to check that it wasn't leaking fluid from his brakes. Describe one test he could do to check whether the liquid was just water.

3. Gena loves Smarties. She wanted to look at the colourings used to give the colour to different Smarties, so she tested different coloured Smarties and compared her results with a similar test she did on some artificial colourings, identified with E-numbers. The results of both tests are shown below:

   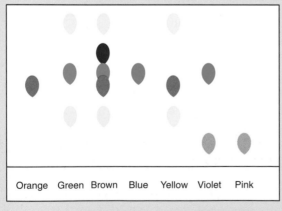
   Orange Green Brown Blue Yellow Violet Pink

   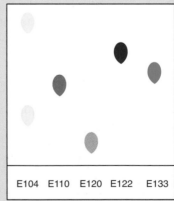
   E104 E110 E120 E122 E133

   (a) What is this method of separation called?

   (b) Which colours contain more than one colouring?

   (c) How many of the 'E' numbered colourings are there in brown Smarties?

   (d) Gena is sensitive to E110 (it makes her hyperactive). Which colours of Smarties must she avoid?

Chapter 14
Acids, bases and indicators

Think back to what you already know about acids:

● There is hydrochloric acid in your stomach, where it helps to digest proteins.

● Many people enjoy the smell of vinegar on fish and chips.

Acids in everyday life: Natural acids

We come across many acids in our everyday lives. If you eat yoghurt, the slightly sour taste is because you are eating lactic acid (made from the sugar in milk). If you are bitten by an ant, the sting you feel is because the ant has injected methanoic acid under your skin. If you add vinegar to fish and chips (mmm... – that delicious smell!), the vinegar is partly made of ethanoic acid. We don't just come across these acids by accident; they usually have a particular purpose.

● Acids often slow down the growth of microbes and so can be used to preserve foods. For example, vinegar has been used for centuries to pickle foods, such as onions and cabbage.

● Ascorbic acid (Vitamin C), found in foods such as oranges and lemons, helps to maintain healthy (connective) tissues and prevent scurvy. Ascorbic acid is also added to many foods because it prevents the oxidation of food molecules, a process which makes stinking and unpleasant smells.

Some of these natural acids are shown in the table below:

Name of acid	Where it is found
Ascorbic acid	In some fruits (like oranges) and vegetables (like potatoes)
Citric acid	Lemon juice
Ethanoic acid	Vinegar
Hydrochloric acid	Stomach juices
Lactic acid	Sour milk and yoghurt
Methanoic acid	Stings from ants and stinging nettles
Tannic acid	Tea

Acids in the home and car

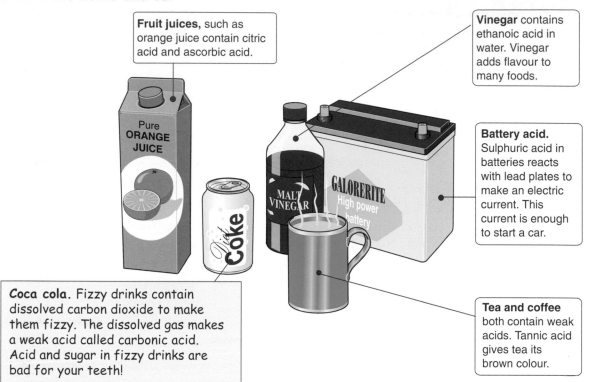

Fruit juices, such as orange juice contain citric acid and ascorbic acid.

Vinegar contains ethanoic acid in water. Vinegar adds flavour to many foods.

Battery acid. Sulphuric acid in batteries reacts with lead plates to make an electric current. This current is enough to start a car.

Coca cola. Fizzy drinks contain dissolved carbon dioxide to make them fizzy. The dissolved gas makes a weak acid called carbonic acid. Acid and sugar in fizzy drinks are bad for your teeth!

Tea and coffee both contain weak acids. Tannic acid gives tea its brown colour.

Laboratory acids

Acids used in the laboratory are more corrosive than natural acids – this means that they can damage clothing, eyes or skin. All containers of laboratory acids must have the warning symbol for corrosive on them. Here is a reminder of what that symbol is, and a few hints about using acids:

Working with acids

Acids are corrosive, and eyes and skin must be protected.

Remember this poem!
Here lie the bones of Samuel Jones,
He'll never breathe no more.
What he thought was H_2O was H_2SO_4

CORROSIVE

8

REMEMBER! This symbol is part of the **Hazchem** system. These symbols tell us which chemicals are safe and which dangerous. Check back to page 128 to remind yourself of the other symbols.

HAZARD!

In the laboratory **never** add water to an acid in a test tube or beaker. **Always** add acid to water. This is because some acids give out thermal energy when diluted. The water can boil and 'spit' into your face!

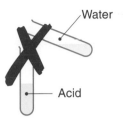

Dealing with spills

In the laboratory	● Wash the affected area with a lot of water.
	● **Tell the teacher**.
	● Mop up the area, then wash it again with water.

On roads or in factories:

Symbols on the lorry tell police and firefighters which chemicals the lorry is carrying. If it is acid, it is diluted with lots and lots of water.

John Haig was the 'Acid Bath Murderer' in 1949. He murdered a woman and tried to destroy her body in a bath of sulphuric acid. Unfortunately for him, sulphuric acid does not destroy plastics. She was identified by her false teeth, and Haig was sentenced to death by hanging.

One material that is not corroded by acid is glass. This is why glass bottles are used for keeping and storing acids in the laboratory. The three common laboratory acids are hydrochloric acid, nitric acid and sulphuric acid. They are used in many chemical experiments and they also have important uses in industry.

This table shows what the three common laboratory acids can do:

Acid	Salts made in laboratory reactions	Important uses in industry
Hydrochloric acid (HCl)	Chlorides	In metal processing and purification of ores
Nitric acid	Nitrates	Making fertilisers and explosives
Sulphuric acid	Sulphates	Making fertilisers, making paints and plastics; used in car batteries

Strong and weak acids

It is very important not to get mixed up between how **strong** an acid is and how **concentrated** it is.

- **Strength** is a chemical property of an acid. It tells us how easily the hydrogen in an acid combines with another substance. For example, a strong acid will react very quickly with a metal.

- **Concentration** is a physical property of the acid. It depends on how much water is present in the solution of the acid.

It is quite possible to have a dilute solution of a strong acid. For example, dilute nitric acid is a dilute solution of a strong acid – it is not very concentrated but still reacts quickly with metals. It is also possible to have a strong solution of a weak acid. Many metal cleaners are solutions of weak acids, like methanoic acid; these cleaners will remove the lime scale from inside a kettle but will not attack the metal of the kettle itself.

If a large amount of an acid or an alkali is spilt, the fire brigade will often hose down the area with large volumes of water. The corrosive substance will become less concentrated. Dilute acids and alkalis are less hazardous than concentrated ones.

Bases and alkalis

There are so many different chemicals in the world that it is impossible to remember them all. What scientists like to do is to put chemicals into groups. All the chemicals in the same group have similar properties and this helps scientists to predict what they can be used for. **Acids** make up one of these groups, and **bases** and **alkalis** make up another.

- A base is a substance that can neutralise an acid. Metal oxides, carbonates and hydroxides are all examples of bases.

- An alkali is a base that can dissolve in water. The oxides of reactive metals, e.g. sodium and calcium, are alkalis. Hydroxides, e.g. ammonium hydroxide, sodium hydroxide and calcium hydroxide (lime water), are also alkalis.

- Alkalis can be strong or weak. Oxides and hydroxides of sodium and calcium are stronger than those of less reactive metals.

Bases and alkalis are the chemical opposite of acids.

Uses of alkalis

Alkalis can be just as corrosive as acids and can be very dangerous to humans. We say that these substances are **caustic**. We use many alkalis as cleaning materials:

The importance of alkalis

SODA CRYSTALS can dissolve in water to clean pans and sinks.

OVEN CLEANER sometimes contains very concentrated and very strong alkalis. This reacts with fats and burned-on grease and makes them easier to dissolve in water.

MILK OF MAGNESIA neutralises stomach acid (see page 20) to overcome upset stomachs.

HAZARD! Alkalis can be even more corrosive than acids. For this reason, gloves, overalls and eye protection should be worn when using oven and drain cleaners.

SOAP is alkaline. It is made by mixing together fat and caustic soda (sodium hydroxide).

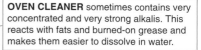

TOOTHPASTE is an alkali which helps to whiten the teeth and neutralise acids from food.

Key words

Acid – a substance that can give up hydrogen in a chemical reaction.

Base – a substance that can neutralise an acid.

Alkali – a base that is dissolved in water.

Corrosive – able to attack other materials, including skin.

Strength – how easily an acid or alkali reacts with other substances.

Concentration – how many particles of a substance there are mixed with a certain number of particles of water.

Exercise 14.1: Acids and bases

1. Why does pickling food help to preserve it?

2. Give two uses of acids in industry.

3. What is an alkali? Give one important use of alkalis.

4. Copy and complete this paragraph, using words from the list below:

   water   corrosive   goggles/eye protection   overalls/lab coat   acid

   Acids and alkalis are ...., which means that they can cause damage to the skin. If one of these substances is spilt or splashed onto the skin, plenty of cold water must be run over the splashed area. In the laboratory, you should always add .... to .... and never the other way round. When working with acids or alkalis, you should always wear .... and ....

Extension questions

5. What is the benefit of having hydrochloric acid in your stomach? Why could this be harmful?

6. Ascorbic acid (Vitamin C) is an antioxidant. Use the Internet or your library to find out what an antioxidant does, and which kinds of food contain antioxidant.

Acid or alkali? Using indicators

Starting point

●   Acids and alkalis are important chemicals but can be dangerous if they are not used properly.

●   Acids have the opposite chemical properties to alkalis.

Strong acids and alkalis are corrosive and so could be very harmful to humans. Even so, there are many chemical and industrial reactions where we need to use these chemicals. How can we test for these chemicals without harming ourselves? You can find out if a substance is an acid or an alkali by using an indicator. An indicator contains a dye that changes colour, depending on whether it is mixed with an acid or an alkali.

Plant dyes can be used as indicators

You can make an indicator from the dye in some coloured plants. Red cabbage, blackcurrant and raw beetroot are all suitable plants and the indicator can be obtained as shown below:

> Why do you think pickled cabbage is red?

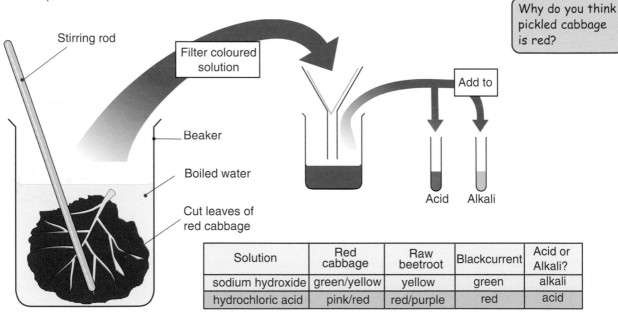

Solution	Red cabbage	Raw beetroot	Blackcurrent	Acid or Alkali?
sodium hydroxide	green/yellow	yellow	green	alkali
hydrochloric acid	pink/red	red/purple	red	acid

Using litmus

An indicator which is often used in laboratories is called **litmus**. This can be used as a liquid, or as papers which have been soaked in the liquid and then dried out. The colour changes for litmus with acid and alkali are shown in the diagram below:

> Two common acidic gases are carbon dioxide and sulphur dioxide.

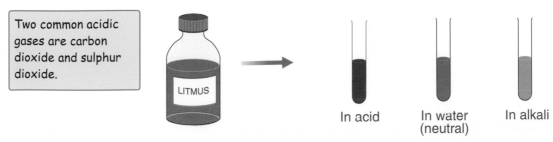

Universal indicator and the pH scale

Litmus and plant dye indicators only tell us whether a substance is acid or alkaline. These indicators do not tell us how strongly acidic or alkaline the substance is. Some indicators can measure how strong an acid or alkali is and give us a **numerical value on the pH scale**. On this scale the values run from 0 to 14. Neutral substances have a pH value of 7, acid substances have a pH below 7 and alkaline substances have a pH value above 7.

One very useful **indicator**, which shows a range of colours, is **Universal Indicator** (or Full Range Indicator). This indicator can show whether a substance is acid or alkali and how strong it is.

Universal indicator and the pH scale: How to find out if a substance is acid or alkali

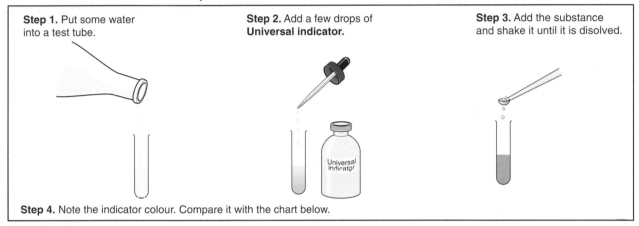

Step 1. Put some water into a test tube.

Step 2. Add a few drops of **Universal indicator.**

Step 3. Add the substance and shake it until it is disolved.

Step 4. Note the indicator colour. Compare it with the chart below.

Universal indictor (has a whole range of colours).

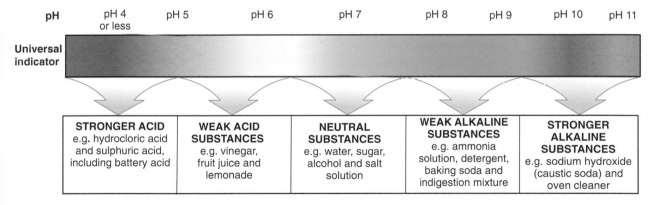

| pH | pH 4 or less | pH 5 | pH 6 | pH 7 | pH 8 | pH 9 | pH 10 | pH 11 |

| STRONGER ACID e.g. hydrocloric acid and sulphuric acid, including battery acid | WEAK ACID SUBSTANCES e.g. vinegar, fruit juice and lemonade | NEUTRAL SUBSTANCES e.g. water, sugar, alcohol and salt solution | WEAK ALKALINE SUBSTANCES e.g. ammonia solution, detergent, baking soda and indigestion mixture | STRONGER ALKALINE SUBSTANCES e.g. sodium hydroxide (caustic soda) and oven cleaner |

pH scale (a scale of numbers ranging from 1 to 14).

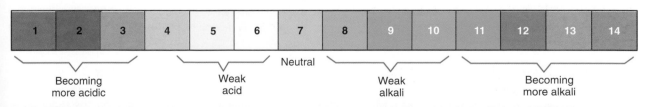

| 1 | 2 | 3 | 4 | 5 | 6 | 7 | 8 | 9 | 10 | 11 | 12 | 13 | 14 |

Becoming more acidic — Weak acid — Neutral — Weak alkali — Becoming more alkali

---

STRANGE BUT TRUE!
Each unit on the pH scale means a change in strength of 10 times! An acid with pH3 is 10 times stronger than an acid with pH4, and 100 times stronger than one with pH5!

Substances with very low or very high pH values are the most dangerous.

It was a Danish chemist called Sørensen who invented the pH scale. He worked for the Carlsberg brewery. The pH level is very important in the process of fermentation by yeast.

Neutralisation: Reactions between acids and alkalis

When acids and alkalis are mixed, they cancel each other out. If the correct amounts are added to each other, a neutral solution can be formed. This kind of chemical reaction is called **neutralisation** and is a very common reaction in chemistry. Universal indicator can be used to show a neutralisation taking place.

Checking neutralisation with Universal indicator

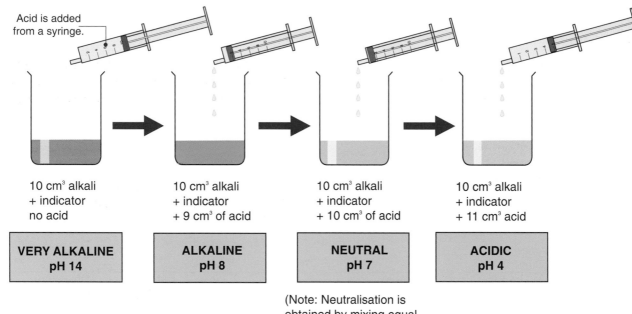

Acid is added from a syringe.

| 10 cm³ alkali + indicator no acid | 10 cm³ alkali + indicator + 9 cm³ of acid | 10 cm³ alkali + indicator + 10 cm³ of acid | 10 cm³ alkali + indicator + 11 cm³ acid |

| **VERY ALKALINE** pH 14 | **ALKALINE** pH 8 | **NEUTRAL** pH 7 | **ACIDIC** pH 4 |

(Note: Neutralisation is obtained by mixing equal quantities of acid and alkali of the same concentration.)

The chemistry of neutralisation produces a salt and water. This is a word equation for this type of reaction:

$$acid + base \longrightarrow salt + water$$

One example is:

$$hydrochloric\ acid + sodium\ hydroxide \longrightarrow sodium\ chloride + water$$

Universal indicator gives us the pH value as a whole number, but sometimes we could disagree about the exact value because we each see colours slightly differently. The pH scale actually has values between these whole numbers – there can be a pH of 4.2 or 9.3, for example. A pH probe can be used to measure the pH of a solution when an exact value of pH is required.

Using a pH probe to study neutralisation

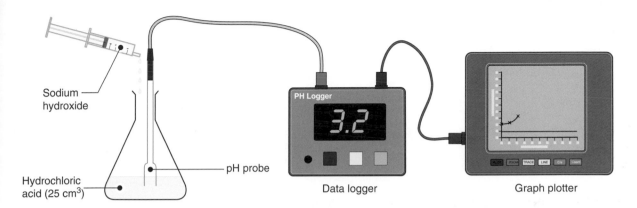

Sodium hydroxide

pH probe

Hydrochloric acid (25 cm³)

Data logger

Graph plotter

Making salts

Neutralisation reactions are important because they can be used to make salts. Some of these salts are very useful chemicals, for example as fertilisers, weedkillers or drugs. It is important to measure the pH during neutralisation, because the acid needs to be exactly neutralised by the base. The diagram below shows how a salt can be made using neutralisation.

Remember: **acid + base ⟶ salt + water**

Salts can be made by neutralisation

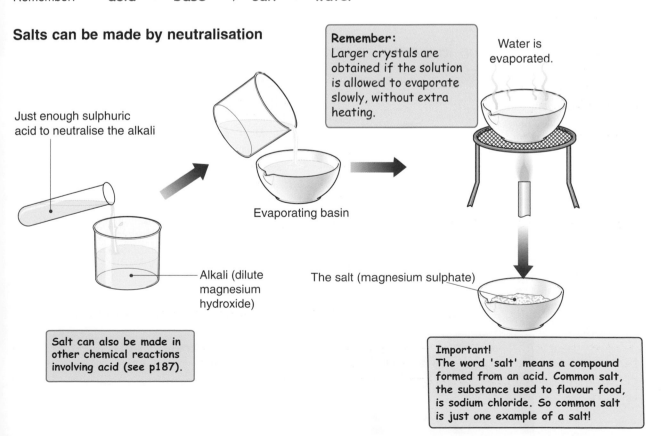

Remember:
Larger crystals are obtained if the solution is allowed to evaporate slowly, without extra heating.

Water is evaporated.

Just enough sulphuric acid to neutralise the alkali

Evaporating basin

Alkali (dilute magnesium hydroxide)

The salt (magnesium sulphate)

Salt can also be made in other chemical reactions involving acid (see p187).

Important!
The word 'salt' means a compound formed from an acid. Common salt, the substance used to flavour food, is sodium chloride. So common salt is just one example of a salt!

Acids can be **neutralised by insoluble bases** as well as alkalis. For example, sulphuric acid is neutralised by copper oxide to form copper sulphate and water.

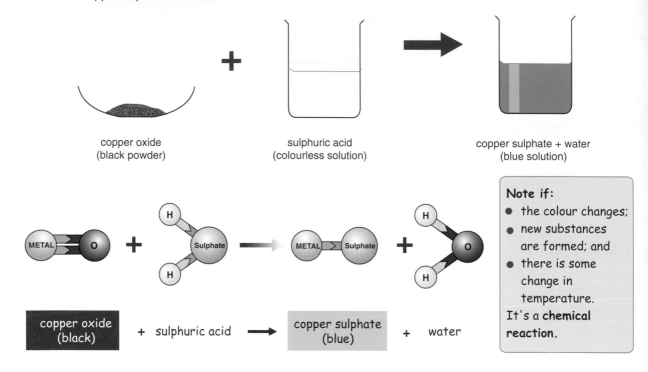

copper oxide
(black powder)

sulphuric acid
(colourless solution)

copper sulphate + water
(blue solution)

| copper oxide (black) | + | sulphuric acid | → | copper sulphate (blue) | + | water |

Note if:
- the colour changes;
- new substances are formed; and
- there is some change in temperature.

It's a **chemical reaction.**

Using neutralisation in medicine and industry

Neutralisation can be useful. Here are some examples of important commercial neutralisations:

ANTACID: Too much acid in the stomach causes indigestion. Medicines to cure this can contain alkalis (usually magnesium hydroxide) to neutralise the acid.

BETTER SOIL: Most crop plants do not grow well in acidic soils. Farmers add lime to neutralise the acid and make the soil more suitable for plant growth.

DEALING WITH STINGS: Wasps and bees give painful stings, but ...
- a weak **acid**, like vinegar, can neutralise a **wasp** sting, because a wasp sting is alkaline;
- a weak **alkali**, like ammonia or baking soda, can neutralise a **bee** sting or a nettle sting because bee and nettle stings are acidic.

MANUFACTURE OF FERTILISER: Plants need nitrogen to grow well. Farmers add nitrogen fertilisers to increase the soil fertility. Fertilisers can be made by neutralisation.

nitric acid + ammonium hydroxide
(acid)   (alkali)

ammonium nitrate + water
(salt)   (water)
(fertiliser)

Fast growing
Organic

MAXI-GRO
Fertiliser

Plants cannot absorb minerals in acidic soils. Carnivorous plants, such as sundew, obtain their nitrate from the bodies of insects they catch.

STRANGE BUT TRUE!
Prisoners-of-war used sweat (acid) and saliva (alkali) to write invisible messages!

GET ME OUT OF HERE!

It's a secret! Invisible ink
When you want to send a secret note you can use neutralisation. Here's how to do it:

- Write using a cotton bud dipped in a solution of baking soda (an alkali).
- Show up the writing by painting over the paper with vinegar or grape juice (both are acids).
- The acid and the alkali react together to produce a coloured salt, so that it can be read.

Key words

Acid – a substance that can give up hydrogen in a chemical reaction and always has a pH less than 7.

Alkali – a base that is dissolved in water and always has a pH more than 7.

Neutral – a solution that is neither acid nor alkaline and has a pH of 7.

Indicator – a substance that changes colour according to the pH of another substance.

pH – a scale of numbers, from 0 – 14, that gives a measurement of acidity or alkalinity.

Neutralisation – a chemical reaction between an acid and an alkali or base.

Salt – one of the products of a neutralisation reaction.

Exercise 14.2: Neutralisation

1. Nettle stings contain methanoic acid. What would you rub on a nettle sting to make it less painful?

2. Aspirin solution turns Universal Indicator pink. What does this show?

3. This table lists the pH of several solutions:

Solution	A	B	C	D	E
pH	7	5	1	10	3

Name the solution or solutions that:

(a) would turn litmus blue.

(b) would turn universal indicator orange or red.

(c) is neither acidic nor alkaline.

(d) could be used on a wasp sting.

Extension questions

4. You have four different antacid treatments (indigestion remedies). Describe how you would tell which one was most powerful. Include a list of the apparatus you would use and the steps you would take.

5. Gena and Felix carried out a neutralisation reaction. They slowly added sodium hydroxide to 25 cm³ of hydrochloric acid and used a pH probe to measure the pH of the solution. Here are their results:

Volume of sodium hydroxide added (cm³)	0	5	10	20	25	30	40	50	60
pH	1	1	1.3	2.5	7	10	12.5	13	13

(a) Plot their results in a line graph.

(b) Try to explain the shape of the graph.

(c) How could they improve their results?

More reactions of acids

Don't forget

- Some metals react with acids to produce a salt and hydrogen gas.
- Alkalis react with acids in a process called neutralisation to produce a salt and water.

Acids and metal carbonates

Metal carbonates are compounds that contain a metal and a **carbonate**. The carbonate is made up of carbon and oxygen. An acid always reacts with a carbonate by breaking it down to give off carbon dioxide gas. The carbon dioxide makes the mixture fizz (this fizzing is sometimes called **effervescence**). It also turns limewater milky. The diagram below shows how you can test that this is happening.

Reaction of acids and carbonates

This reaction goes on for longer if the salt is soluble. For example, **hydrochloric acid** and **calcium carbonate** make calcium chloride. This dissolves away and lets the reaction carry on. **Sulphuric acid** and **calcium carbonate**, however, make **calcium sulphate.** This salt is insoluble and makes a layer around the **calcium carbonate.** This keeps the acid away from the carbonate and the reaction is stopped.

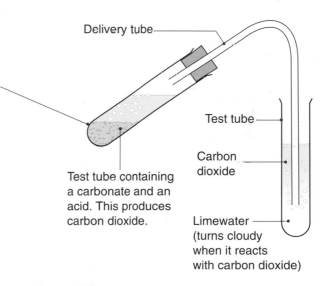

Delivery tube

Test tube

Carbon dioxide

Test tube containing a carbonate and an acid. This produces carbon dioxide.

Limewater (turns cloudy when it reacts with carbon dioxide)

A good example is:

copper carbonate (Green) + sulphuric acid ⟶ copper sulphate (Blue) + water + carbon dioxide

Sherbet sweets contain **sugar, citric acid and carbonate**. The saliva in your mouth dissolves the acid and the acid reacts with the carbonate. This produces **carbon dioxide** which fizzes on your tongue!

CARBONATES AND CAKES!
Some cake recipes use flour and baking powder. Baking powder contains weak acid and **sodium hydrogen carbonate**. When the baking powder is heated, carbon dioxide bubbles are made. These tiny bubbles make the cake rise, giving it a light and fluffy texture.

The general word equation for this type of reaction is:

acid + metal carbonate ➝ salt + water + carbon dioxide

You can see that a salt is formed, as well as the carbon dioxide. Remember that salts are very important chemicals, so this is another good method for the production of salts. Some real word equations for acids reacting with metal carbonates are:

nitric acid + lead carbonate ➝ lead nitrate + water + carbon dioxide

hydrochloric acid + calcium carbonate ➝ calcium chloride + water + carbon dioxide

Limestone contains the compound calcium carbonate. Rainwater contains weak acids and these react slowly with limestone and break it down. Buildings, pavements and statues made of limestone are attacked by rain and can be severely damaged over a long period of time. The problem is made worse if the rain becomes more acidic. Acid rain (see page 211) contains extra acids and so speeds up the breakdown of limestone rocks. The importance of these reactions with limestone is described below:

Reaction of limestone with acid

Limestone

Marble

Limestone contains calcium carbonate (and so does marble).
Calcium carbonate reacts with the acids:

● calcium carbonate + hydrochloric acid ➝ calcium chloride + water + carbon dioxide

This is very soluble and easily washed away – the limestone seems to disappear!

This fizzes and so is an excellent test to check whether a rock contains a carbonate.

● Acid rain damages buildings made of limestone and makes underground caves in areas of limestone rock.

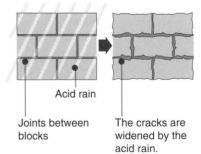

Acid rain

Joints between blocks

The cracks are widened by the acid rain.

EXTENSION IDEAS!
For a chemical reaction to occur, particles of different substances must come into contact with one another. The reaction goes more quickly if more particles bump into each other more often. This can be done by:
● Increasing the surface area – many small particles react faster than a few large ones.
● Increasing the concentration – more particles in the same space.
● Raising the temperature – so more particles move faster.
● Adding a catalyst – to hold the particles in contact with one another.

Acids and metals

Acids react with metals to produce salts and hydrogen gas (see page 136).

For example: **zinc + sulphuric acid → zinc sulphate + hydrogen**

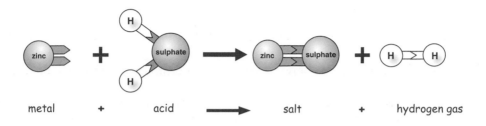

metal   +   acid   ⟶   salt   +   hydrogen gas

Summary of acid reactions

Acids are very important chemicals. We have spent a lot of time looking at their properties and their reactions. There is a lot to learn, so here is a useful summary of these properties and reactions:

Properties of acids

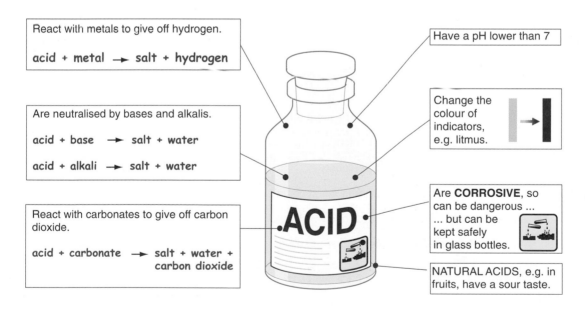

React with metals to give off hydrogen.

acid + metal ⟶ salt + hydrogen

Have a pH lower than 7

Are neutralised by bases and alkalis.

acid + base ⟶ salt + water

acid + alkali ⟶ salt + water

Change the colour of indicators, e.g. litmus.

React with carbonates to give off carbon dioxide.

acid + carbonate ⟶ salt + water + carbon dioxide

Are **CORROSIVE**, so can be dangerous ... ... but can be kept safely in glass bottles.

NATURAL ACIDS, e.g. in fruits, have a sour taste.

Remind yourself!

Test for hydrogen: The
SQUEAKY POP.

Test for carbon dioxide:
The **MILKY LIME WATER**.

Bacteria in your
mouth feed on sugar
and create acids.
These acids can
cause tooth decay.

Key words

Carbonate – a compound that contains a metal, carbon and oxygen, and always gives off carbon dioxide when it reacts with an acid.

Lime – a compound made when limestone is crushed and heated strongly.

Exercise 14.3: More reactions of acids

1. Copy and complete the following word equations:

    (a)   zinc + ... ➜ zinc chloride + hydrogen

    (b)   nitric acid + magnesium ➜ .... + ...

    (c)   .... + potassium hydroxide ➜ potassium sulphate + ...

    (d)   copper carbonate + hydrochloric acid ➜ .... + ... + ...

    (e)   lead + ... ➜ lead sulphate + ...

2   Which acid and base would you use to produce the following salts?

    (a)   copper chloride   (c)   iron chloride

    (b)   lead nitrate   (d)   zinc sulphate

3. Why is acid kept in glass bottles and not in metal containers?

4. Read this passage and answer the questions which follow:

    When an excess of calcium carbonate is added to dilute hydrochloric acid, a chemical reaction occurs. Some of the powder dissolves and a gas is given off. Once the reaction is finished, the excess calcium carbonate can be filtered off. The salt formed can be obtained by evaporation of the filtrate.

    (a)   How can you tell that this is a chemical change?

    (b)   What is the name of the gas given off? How can you test for this gas?

    (c)   How can you tell when the reaction is finished?

    (d)   What is the name of the salt formed during the reaction?

    (e)   How could you make sure that you obtained large crystals of this salt?

5. Copy and complete this paragraph, using words from the list below:

   carbonate   hydrogen   salt   (squeaky) pop   calcium carbonate

   Acids react with most metals to produce a .... and a gas called .... This gas makes a .... when tested with a lighted splint. Acids react with .... to make a salt, water and carbon dioxide gas. Limestone contains the compound .... which can be dissolved by acid in rainwater.

Extension questions

6. A well-known recipe for making blackcurrant and apple jam recommends that the fruit is boiled in a copper pan and not in an iron pan. Can you explain this?

7. Gena and her friend Charles were interested in the reaction between marble chips and dilute hydrochloric acid. They added 20 g of large marble chips to 50 cm³ of dilute hydrochloric acid in a large conical flask, as shown in this diagram.

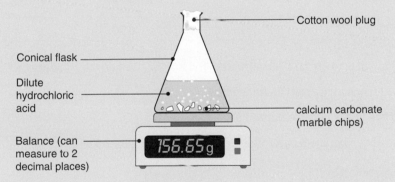

The decrease in mass during the experiment is noted at one minute intervals.

calcium carbonate + hydrochloric acid ➔ calcium chloride + carbon dioxide + water

They measured the loss in mass every minute for ten minutes. This was their first experiment. Gena and Charles then repeated the experiment, but this time they crushed the 20 g of marble into very small pieces before they added it to the hydrochloric acid. This was their second experiment. The results of their experiments are shown in the table on the following page.

Time in min	First experiment: Loss of mass in grams	Second experiment: Loss of mass in grams
1	1.10	2.15
2	1.90	3.05
3	2.50	3.45
4	2.95	3.65
5	3.20	3.70
6	3.40	3.70
7	3.50	3.70
8	3.60	3.70
9	3.70	3.70
10	3.70	3.70

(a)   Plot a graph of these results. Put time on the x (bottom) axis and loss in mass on the y (side) axis.

(b)   Which experiment goes the fastest at the start of the reaction?

(c)   Why do both of the graphs eventually become horizontal?

(d)   What do the results tell you about the effect of surface area on the rate of a chemical reaction?

Project

Acid rain is partly caused by chemicals in the exhaust gases from car engines. These gases can be collected and quickly converted to less harmful gases if a catalytic converter is fitted to the exhaust system of the car. Find out how a catalytic converter works. Use a diagram to explain your answer to a friend.

Chapter 15:
Elements and compounds

Remember

- Atoms are the simplest particles found in matter.

- Molecules may contain more than one atom.

Elements

A substance that is made of only one type of atom is called an **element**. For example, in the element aluminium there are only aluminium atoms. Aluminium, like every other element, cannot be broken down into simpler substances in the laboratory. There are more than 100 different kinds of atom, which means that there are more than 100 different elements. About 90 of these elements occur naturally on Earth. The other elements are made by nuclear reactions in special laboratories.

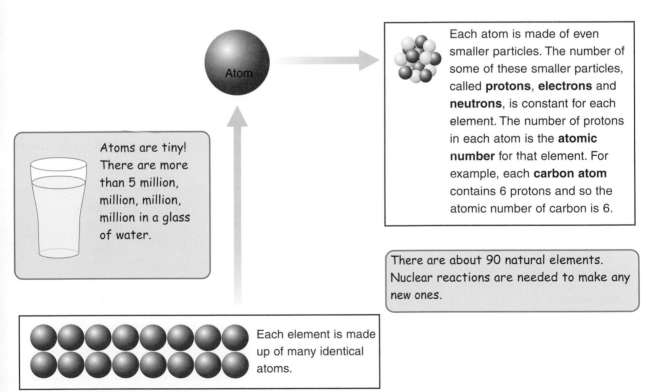

Atoms are tiny! There are more than 5 million, million, million, million in a glass of water.

Each atom is made of even smaller particles. The number of some of these smaller particles, called **protons**, **electrons** and **neutrons**, is constant for each element. The number of protons in each atom is the **atomic number** for that element. For example, each **carbon atom** contains 6 protons and so the atomic number of carbon is 6.

There are about 90 natural elements. Nuclear reactions are needed to make any new ones.

Each element is made up of many identical atoms.

All the atoms within an element behave in the same way, but they are different from the atoms in other elements. For example, atoms of gold are heavier than atoms of aluminium, so gold is a heavier metal than aluminium.

Symbols and formulae for elements

Scientists have made up a series of **symbols** for describing elements; this saves a lot of time when they need to write down the names of the elements many times! The symbol given to an element usually comes from the first one or two letters of its name. The symbol for oxygen is O, for example, and the symbol for calcium is Ca. Some elements have symbols that aren't so obvious. The symbol for iron is Fe, for example. This is because this element was named when scientists still wrote down much of their work in Latin. The Latin name for iron is *ferrum*. The diagram below points out some of the rules for chemical symbols:

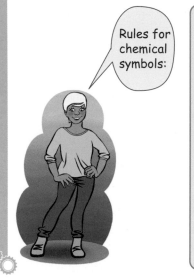

Rules for chemical symbols:

- The first letter of a symbol is **always** a capital letter. If there is a second letter it is always lower case.

- The symbol is usually the first one or two letters of the name.

- Every element has a different symbol.

- Some elements get their symbol from an old name, often from Latin.

Here are some common elements with their symbols:

aluminium	Al	hydrogen	H	oxygen	O
calcium	Ca	iron	Fe	sodium	Na
chlorine	Cl	lead	Pb	sulphur	S
gold	Au	nitrogen	N	zinc	Zn

In most elements the particles are individual atoms, but in a few elements the particles are molecules (that is, made up of two or more identical particles bonded together). The **formula** for an element tells us whether it is made of single atoms or of molecules. Some examples are shown in this table:

Name	Symbol of atoms	Diagram of particles	Formula of particles	Description of particles
helium	He	He	He	atoms
magnesium	Mg	Mg	Mg	atoms
hydrogen	H	H H	H_2	molecules (each with two atoms)
sulphur	S	S S S S S S S S	S_8	molecules (each with eight atoms)

The Periodic Table

All the elements are listed in the **Periodic Table**. In this table:

- The elements are listed in the order of their atomic number.

- The elements are shown as their symbols, and not their formulae.

- The elements are arranged in natural **groups** (particular types of metals, for example). Each **group** is a vertical column of elements.

- There is always a gradual change (called a 'trend') in the properties of the elements as you look across the table. Each horizontal row showing this trend in properties is called a **period**. Part of the Periodic Table is shown below:

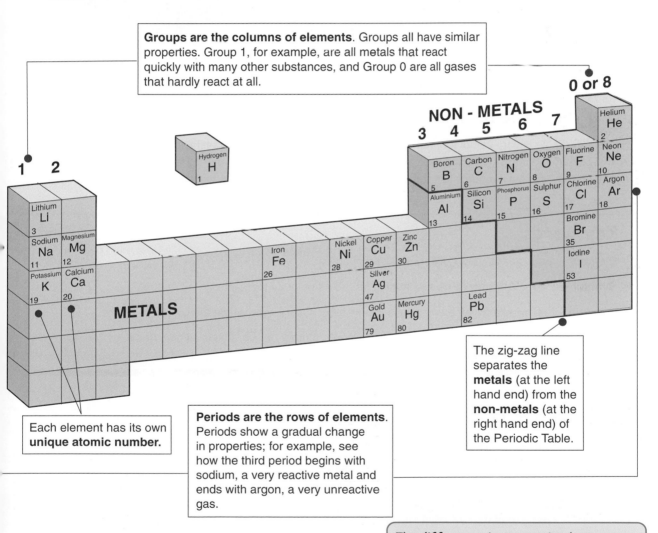

Groups are the columns of elements. Groups all have similar properties. Group 1, for example, are all metals that react quickly with many other substances, and Group 0 are all gases that hardly react at all.

Each element has its own **unique atomic number.**

Periods are the rows of elements. Periods show a gradual change in properties; for example, see how the third period begins with sodium, a very reactive metal and ends with argon, a very unreactive gas.

The zig-zag line separates the **metals** (at the left hand end) from the **non-metals** (at the right hand end) of the Periodic Table.

The **difference in properties between metals and non-metals** is one of the most important pieces of information given by the Periodic Table.

This arrangement of the elements was worked out by a Russian scientist called Mendeléev.

Dimitri Ivanovich Mendeléev was born in 1834 in Siberia, the youngest of 15 children. His father went blind when Dimitri was young and his mother struggled to bring up the family while running a glass factory. She saved to send Dimitri to be educated, though she died exhausted shortly after he started his studies at St. Petersburg.

As well as his famous work in chemistry, Dimitri was a brilliant chemistry teacher. Everyone wanted to come to his lectures. At that time women were not allowed in university classes, so Dimitri gave extra classes for women in his spare time.

He was very down to earth, he always travelled third class in trains along with the peasants and he swore like a trooper. He cut his hair once a year, in spring when the warm weather set in.

Using the Periodic Table

The Periodic Table is very useful for predicting the properties of elements we don't know very much about. As long as we know its atomic number, we will have some idea of an element's properties. The table is also very useful in letting us predict how different elements listed in different parts of the table will react together.

Key words

Element – a substance made of only one type of atom.

Symbol – a letter or group of letters standing for the name of an element.

Formula – the formula for an element tells you whether it is made of single atoms or a molecule.

Periodic Table – a chart that arranges all the elements in order of their atomic number and in groups according to their properties.

Exercise 15.1: The Periodic Table

1. Complete these sentences using words from this list:

    nuclear   molecular   elements   atoms   hundred

    .... are substances that cannot be broken down into simpler substances. Some, such as carbon, are made of particles called ...., and others, such as oxygen, are made of particles called .... There are about a .... of these substances; the heaviest ones can only be made during .... reactions.

2. Which of these substances are elements?

    Carbon, water, sugar, magnesium, sulphur, air, lead.

Metals and non-metals

Don't forget

● An element is a substance made of one type of particle.

● Elements can be arranged into the Periodic Table.

There are two types of element: **metals** and **non-metals**. Of the elements that occur naturally, about three-quarters are metals and one quarter is non-metal. The metals are arranged on the left-hand side of the Periodic Table with the non-metals on the right. Look back at the Periodic Table on page 193 to remind yourself that the metals and non-metals are separated by a zig-zag line. The metals close to the line have some of the properties of non-metals and the non-metals close to the line have some of the properties of metals. The important physical properties of metals are shown below and the properties of metals and non-metals are compared in the table on the next page.

Metal properties can be explained by particle theory

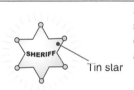

Some metals are **tough**; they don't break easily because there are very strong bonds between the particles.

Steel Blade

Most metals have high melting points (mp) and boiling points (bp) this means they can absorb a great deal of energy before they melt. This is because the metal particles (atoms) are joined to each other by strong bonds.(Sodium and mercury are exceptions with low mps.)

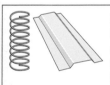

Some metals are **shiny;** they reflect light, especially when they are polished or cut.

Tin star

Most metals have high densities which means they feel heavier for their size because they have many particles packed closely together into a small volume. (Sodium and potassium are exceptions, they float on water.)

Metals can be **stretched or hammered into different shapes.** The bonds between the particles are strong enough to stop the metal from breaking, even when the particles are re-arranged.

Some metals are magnetic which means they can be attracted by magnets (see page 315). Only iron, nickel or cobalt (or alloys made from these metals) are magnetic.

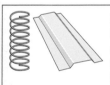

Copper wire

Buzz!

4.5V

Metals **conduct electricity**. This happens because metal particles can pass on the electrical charge from one to another.

Metals can make alloys:
• an alloy is a combination of different metals; and
• an alloy has a combination of the properties of different metals.
For example, an alloy wheel combines **lightness** from one metal with **strength** from another.

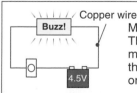

Aluminium pan

Metals **conduct internal/ thermal energy.** The hot particles vibrate strongly. They move and pass energy from particle to particle.

MERCURY is the only metal that is a liquid at room temperature. Mercury is used in some thermometers.

BUT metals can corrode (go rusty, for example) if they react with air and water.

There is one non-metal, GRAPHITE (a form of carbon), which is a good conductor of electricity.

Table 1: The properties of metals and non-metals compared

METALS	NON-METALS
Found on the left-hand side of the Periodic Table.	Found on the right-hand side of the Periodic Table.
Usually solids at room temperature.	Usually solids or gases at room temperature.
Good conductors of electricity.	Poor conductors of electricity.
Good conductors of internal/thermal energy.	Poor conductors of internal/thermal energy.
Shiny (**lustrous**) when they are polished or cut.	Do not reflect light very well and so are usually dull.
Malleable (can be hammered into a different shape).	Most are brittle (they break if they are hammered).
Sonorous (sound like a bell when they are hit).	Not sonorous.
Ductile (can be stretched).	Not ductile.
Usually very dense.	Have a low density.
Have high melting and boiling points.	Usually have low melting and boiling points.
Strong and tough, so they are very hardwearing.	Not strong or tough, so not hardwearing.

There are also some important differences in the chemical properties of metals and non-metals. These will be looked at when we study some of the chemical reactions of metals and non-metals on page 199.

Non-metals

The simplest way to tell a metal from a non-metal is that **most non-metals do not conduct thermal energy or electricity**. The diagram on the right shows a simple circuit that can be used for testing the electrical conductivity of a material.

Many non-metals are very good **thermal insulators** (they do not **conduct** thermal energy very well). Gases are especially poor conductors of thermal energy because the molecules of a gas are too far apart to pass thermal energy from one to another. It is very important to look at more than one property if you are trying to decide whether a material is a metal or non-metal. For example, most metals are solids but mercury is a liquid at room temperature and most solid non-metals are very brittle, although the hardest natural substance is

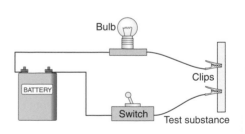

diamond (a form of carbon, which is a non-metal). The table shows that almost all non-metals have certain properties.

The group of photographs on the next page show how non-metals can be very different from one another – some are solids, some are gases and one is a liquid!

Sulphur powder

Carbon (diamond)

Carbon (graphite)

Phosphorus under water in a jar

Chlorine gas in a jar

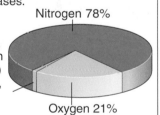
Bromine liquid and vapour in a jar

Although there aren't as many non-metals as metals, most of the objects around us are made from non-metals.

Non-metals form much of our world

Many **man-made (synthetic) substances** contain large amounts of non-metals. For example, plastics are mostly made up of carbon and hydrogen.

Dry **air** is a mixture of non-metals. These are all gases.

Nitrogen 78%

Other elements, including carbon (carbon dioxide) and inert gases, 1%

Oxygen 21%

That's weird! The elements of the human body would only cost £15-20 to buy (unless you have gold fillings in your teeth!).

The **body** is mainly made up of non-metals. Most of the metal is calcium in teeth and bones, sodium in the blood plasma and iron in red blood cells.

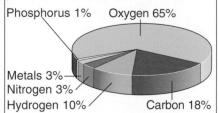

Phosphorus 1%   Oxygen 65%

Metals 3%
Nitrogen 3%
Hydrogen 10%   Carbon 18%

Strange but true! One cubic kilometre of sea water contains 6 tonnes of gold – worth about £60 000 000 in 2003.

The **sea** is a mixture of substances. Because the sea is mainly water, most of it is made up of the elements hydrogen and oxygen. There are still quantities of metals dissolved in sea water.

Oxygen 91%

Other elements including silicon, aluminium, gold, calcium, potassium, iodine, bromine 0.4%

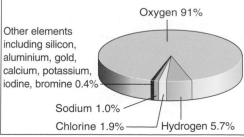

Sodium 1.0%
Chlorine 1.9%   Hydrogen 5.7%

Key words

Metal – an element on the left of the Periodic Table that usually conducts internal/thermal energy and electricity.

Non-metal – an element on the right of the Periodic Table that usually does not conduct internal/thermal energy or electricity.

Exercise 15.2: Metals and non-metals

1. Complete the following sentences:

    (a) .... form much of our world.

    (b) Air is mostly a mixture of nitrogen and .... Other elements, such as .... and ...., are found in much smaller proportions.

    (c) The most common element in the sea is ...., followed by ....

    (d) Most metals are solids. The exception is .... which is liquid at room temperature. Metals are usually much tougher than non-metals, although the non-metal .... is the hardest natural material on the Earth.

    (e) The most common difference between metals and non-metals is that metals are good .... of thermal energy and electricity, whereas non-metals tend to be .... These properties are explained by the .... Theory of Matter.

2. This table shows the percentage, by weight, of different elements in the Earth's crust:

Aluminium	8.0
Calcium	3.5
Magnesium	2.0
Iron	5.0
Oxygen	46.5
Potassium	2.5
Sodium	3.0
Silicon	27.5
Other elements	2.0

    (a) Plot a pie chart of these percentages.

    (b) Which is the most abundant metal on Earth?

    (c) Find out where would you find most of the silicon on the Earth?

    (d) If you had a sample of these pure elements, how could you separate the iron from the other elements?

    (e) Which non-metal is not shown here but is a large part of the human body?

Comparing oxides of metals and non-metals

Remember

Metals and non-metals can be told apart because they have many different physical properties (see table on page 196). They also have some different chemical properties. The oxides formed when metals and non-metals react with oxygen can be either **acidic** or **basic**. The diagram below shows how oxides can be tested to see if they are acidic or basic.

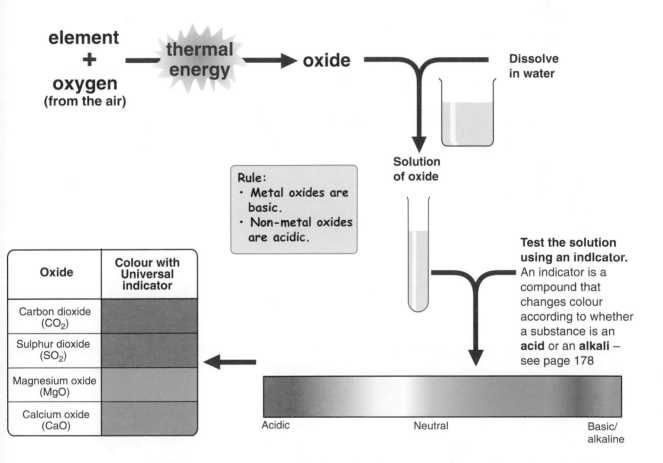

Oxide	Colour with Universal indicator
Carbon dioxide (CO$_2$)	
Sulphur dioxide (SO$_2$)	
Magnesium oxide (MgO)	
Calcium oxide (CaO)	

These chemical reactions show us another difference in the properties of metal and non-metals – that metal oxides are basic and that non-metal oxides are acidic.

Compounds

Compounds are made when elements combine.

● An element is made of only one type of atom.

● Each element has its own particular properties.

● Metallic and non-metallic elements have very different properties.

● During chemical reactions new substances are formed.

Elements can combine during chemical reactions. When two or more elements combine they form a **compound**. The particles in a compound are called **molecules**. These molecules are all the same in one particular compound but they contain atoms of more than one element. When atoms of different elements combine during a chemical reaction, the link between them is called a **chemical bond**.

Different elements can combine to produce a new compound

Here are **atoms** of carbon and oxygen. They are two different elements. These are the **reactants** in this chemical reaction.	These atoms can combine to form a **molecule** of carbon dioxide. The atoms of carbon and oxygen are linked by **chemical bonds**. Carbon dioxide is the **product** of this chemical reaction.

Extra information

Forming these chemical bonds depends on the electrons in the atoms:

● Sometimes electrons are **shared** between atoms, making **covalent bonds**.

● Sometimes electrons **pass from** one atom to another, making **ionic bonds**.

Elements and compounds have different properties

Hydrogen and oxygen are elements. Hydrogen is a colourless gas that is flammable (will burn) and oxygen is a colourless gas that helps other substances to burn. If these two substances are mixed and then the mixture is heated, a **chemical reaction** takes place. This reaction produces a new substance, water, and this new substance has very different properties from the two elements that made it. Water is a colourless liquid that puts fires out! This new substance is a **compound**.

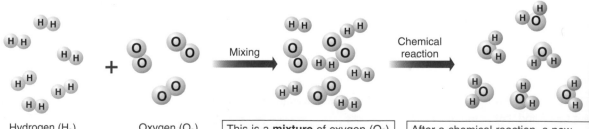

Hydrogen (H_2)   Oxygen (O_2)

This is a **mixture** of oxygen (O_2) and hydrogen (H_2). This mixture would have the **same** properties as the two elements.	After a chemical reaction, a new compound, water (H_2O), has been formed. This compound has totally different properties from the two elements which reacted together.

We can write a shorter version of what has happened in this reaction in the form of a **chemical word equation**. The word equation for the reaction between oxygen and hydrogen is:

$$\text{hydrogen} + \text{oxygen} \longrightarrow \text{water}$$

Another important example that shows the main features of a chemical reaction is the reaction between the two elements iron and sulphur:

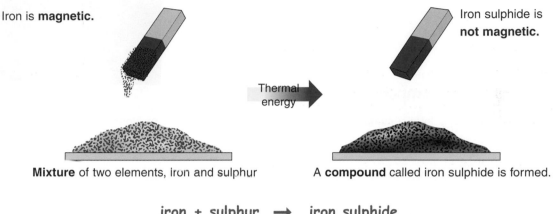

Iron is **magnetic.**

Iron sulphide is **not magnetic.**

Mixture of two elements, iron and sulphur   A **compound** called iron sulphide is formed.

$$\text{iron} + \text{sulphur} \longrightarrow \text{iron sulphide}$$
(thermal energy)

Reacting with oxygen

Many elements combine with oxygen, in a process called **oxidation,** to form compounds called oxides.

Burning, also called **combustion**, needs thermal energy to get it started. Once it is started, it will give out both thermal and light energy. The light can look like a flame or even like a bright flash.

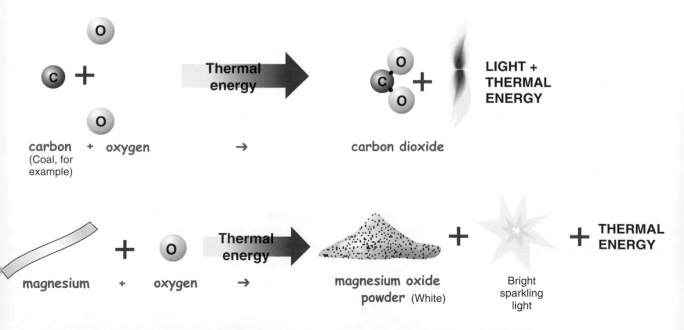

carbon   +   oxygen   →   carbon dioxide
(Coal, for
example)

LIGHT + THERMAL ENERGY

magnesium   +   oxygen   →   magnesium oxide   +   Bright sparkling light   +   THERMAL ENERGY
                                         powder (White)

Oxidation by burning provides light. The following are used to make fireworks:

- Magnesium gives a bright, white light.

- Calcium gives a red, sparkling light.

Firework display over Tower Bridge, London

The formulae of compounds

When elements combine to form a compound there is always a fixed number of atoms. This allows us to write a **formula** for the compound.

A formula is a way of showing a compound as a set of symbols

COMPOUNDS AND MIXTURES
The fixed number of atoms in a compound is very different from a mixture. In a mixture there could be any number of atoms. For example, CO_2 is a **compound** but a **mixture** of carbon and oxygen could have 1000 times as much carbon as oxygen, or only $1/10^{th}$ as much!

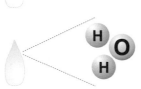

We can write the formula as...

$$H_2O$$

Rule 1: The number of atoms is always written below the line.

Rule 2: We never write the number 1, because a single atom needs no number.

It is **very** important to remember that a formula like CO means that the compound contains carbon (symbol C) and oxygen (symbol O). If you mixed up capital and small letters, you might write Co which is the symbol for the element cobalt. **So be very careful not to mix up capital and small letters!**

Names for different compounds

If you just learn these simple rules, you will easily be able to work out the name of a compound:

● If **two elements** are combined, then the name of the compound ends in -**ide**. If one of the elements is a metal, then the name of the metal comes first.
  For example:
  Sodium chlor**ide** (NaCl) is made from sodium and chlorine.
  Magnesium ox**ide** (MgO) is made from magnesium and oxygen.

● If the compound contains **more than one atom of one of its elements** then you might use **mono-, di-** or **tri-** in its name. This can be very useful in telling some similar compounds apart.
  For example:
  Carbon **mon**oxide (CO) has only one oxygen atom, whereas carbon **di**oxide (CO₂) has two oxygen atoms.

● When **three or more different elements** combine, and the third one is oxygen, the name will end in –**ate**.
  For example:
  Potassium sulph**ate** (K₂SO₄) contains potassium, sulphur and oxygen.
  Sodium nit**rate** (NaNO₃) contains sodium, nitrogen and oxygen.
  Calcium carbon**ate** (CaCO₃) contains calcium, carbon and oxygen.

Note: Compounds called 'hydroxides' are an exception. They contain a metal, oxygen and hydrogen but the oxygen and hydrogen are both included in the name of the compound. For example, KOH is potassium hydroxide **not** potassium hydrate.

Exercise 15.3: Compounds

1. Complete this table to compare the properties of elements and compounds:

Name of substance	Solid, liquid or gas	Colour	Is it flammable?	Any special property
Iron				
Sulphur				
Iron sulphide				
Oxygen				
Hydrogen				
Water				

2. What is a compound? Which of the following substances are compounds?

   Al₂O₃   NaCl   He   HCl   CO   Cl₂   K   H₂O   Na   Co

3. Which elements are found in the following compounds?

   (a) sodium nitrate

   (b) magnesium carbonate

   (c) calcium carbide

   (d) nitrogen hydroxide

   (e) aluminium oxide

   (f) hydrogen sulphate

4. Look at these diagrams:

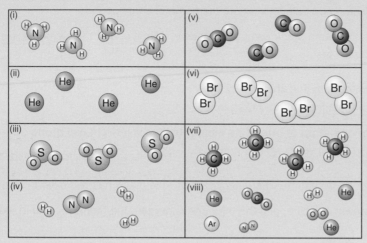

Which of these are:

(a) elements?

(b) compounds?

(c) mixtures?

(d) made up only of atoms?

(e) made up only of molecules?

Extension question

5. Look at this simplified Periodic Table, and then answer the questions that follow:

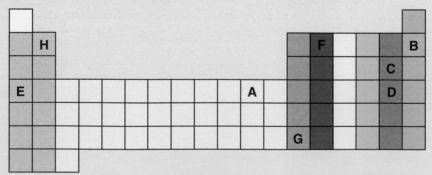

(a) Which two elements would you expect to have very similar properties?

(b) Which element is likely to form a basic oxide?

(c) Which element is a very unreactive gas?

(d) Which element is likely to have some properties of a metal and some properties of a non-metal?

Chapter 16: Chemical reactions

Remember

- Everything that we use is made of materials. These materials are chemicals.
- Each material has properties that might make it useful to humans.
- The properties of materials may be altered by chemical changes.

Almost all materials are made through **chemical reactions**, which means that chemical changes are extremely important in everyday life. Some materials are obviously man-made, such as concrete, plastics, medicines, fertilisers and detergents. Some other materials are made by 'natural' chemical reactions. For example, oxygen in the air and starches in plants are made by photosynthesis.

In a chemical change:

- the starting materials are called the **reactants**;
- the new materials made during the reaction are called the **products**;
- there is always an **energy change**; and
- the reaction is **difficult to reverse**.

How to recognise a chemical reaction

There are definite signs that we can look for to check whether a chemical reaction has occurred. These changes are described below:

How to spot a chemical change: The reactants will be changed and difficult to reverse.

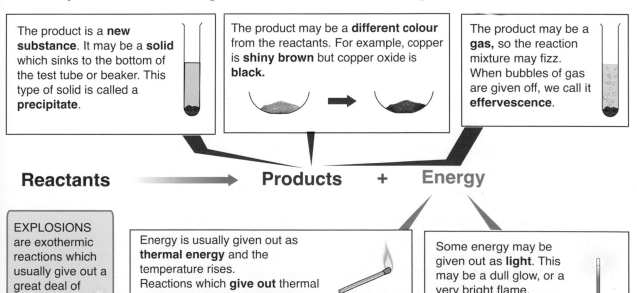

The product is a **new substance**. It may be a **solid** which sinks to the bottom of the test tube or beaker. This type of solid is called a **precipitate**.

The product may be a **different colour** from the reactants. For example, copper is **shiny brown** but copper oxide is **black.**

The product may be a **gas,** so the reaction mixture may fizz. When bubbles of gas are given off, we call it **effervescence**.

Reactants ⟶ **Products** + **Energy**

EXPLOSIONS are exothermic reactions which usually give out a great deal of light and sound!

Energy is usually given out as **thermal energy** and the temperature rises. Reactions which **give out** thermal energy are called **exothermic reactions**. Some reactions **take in** thermal energy – these are called **endothermic reactions**.

A burning match is an exothermic reaction.

Some energy may be given out as **light**. This may be a dull glow, or a very bright flame. Burning magnesium gives the sparkle to sparklers.

This type of apparatus can be used to observe some chemical reactions:

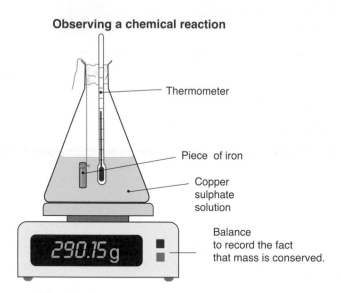

Observing a chemical reaction

Thermometer

Piece of iron

Copper
sulphate
solution

Balance
to record the fact
that mass is conserved.

290.15 g

Describing chemical reactions

Chemical reactions can be described by **word equations**. Word equations are like short sentences that describe chemical reactions. In a word equation:

●   We list the reactants first, and then the products.

●   We change some of the words from the sentence into symbols, to save space. The '+' sign means 'and', and an arrow (➔) means 'changed into'.

$$\textbf{reactants} \quad \rightarrow \quad \textbf{products}$$

Here are some examples of word equations:

●   The burning of carbon in oxygen:

exothermic

carbon + oxygen ➔ carbon dioxide

●   The reaction between iron with sulphur:

exothermic

iron + sulphur ➔ iron sulphide

Many chemical changes are useful to humans. There are also some that are not useful. Whether a reaction is useful or not, it is important that scientists work out how a chemical reaction might be controlled. Science allows us to understand how chemical reactions take place; once we understand what is happening in a chemical change, we might be able to control it, so that it suits our human purpose. **It is, however, important that we always consider how these reactions might affect the world around us.**

Key words

Chemical change – a reaction which results in new products and an energy change and which is very difficult to reverse.

Physical change – a change of state which involves no new products and which can be reversed.

Reactant – the starting material in a chemical change.

Product – the material present after a chemical change has taken place.

Equation – a scientific way of writing out what happens during a chemical change.

Exercise 16.1: Chemical changes

1. Write down two things that you might **see** when a chemical change takes place.

2. Write down two things that you might **hear** when a chemical change takes place.

3. Read this description of a chemical reaction demonstrated by a teacher:

    "A small quantity of the metal sodium was placed into a gas jar containing green chlorine gas until a dirty-white solid was formed. Although the reaction was slow to start, eventually a lot of thermal energy was given out."

    (a) Write out a word equation for the reaction which has taken place.

    (b) Give three reasons why you believe a chemical reaction has taken place.

4. Gena investigated differences between physical and chemical changes. She put three chemicals in separate crucibles and weighed each one. She then heated each crucible. She weighed each crucible again when it had cooled down.

    She recorded her observations in a table as shown below:

Experiment	Name of chemical	Observations	Change in mass
A	Magnesium (a silvery solid)	The silvery magnesium burned brightly in air. A white powder was formed.	Increase
B	Potassium manganate VII (purple crystals)	The purple crystals crackled and turned black. A colourless gas was given off.	Decrease
C	Zinc oxide (a white powder)	The white powder turned pale yellow on heating. It turned white again on cooling.	No change

    (a) (i) In experiment A, magnesium reacts with a gas in the air. Complete the word equation for the reaction:

    magnesium + ...➞ ....

    (ii) Explain the increase in mass in experiment A. Use your word equation to help you.

    (b) The gas given off in experiment B relit a glowing splint. Give the name of this gas.

    (c) Name the white powder left at the end of experiment C.

    (d) In each experiment, A, B and C, state whether a chemical change or a physical change has taken place.

Useful chemical reactions: Science and technology

Scientists and technologists have discovered that there are many reactions that are useful to humans. The diagram below illustrates some of these.

Chemical reactions can make useful products

Separate reactants can combine with a chemical change to make **superglue**.

Raw reactants can be made into **tasty products** by **cooking!**

Neutralisation removes **acid** or **alkali**, which could be harmful reactants.

One example of neutralisation removes **excess stomach acid**.

hydrochloric acid + magnesium oxide
(acidic)

↓

magnesium chloride + water
(neutral)

Reactants

↓

Products

Useful metals are products of **smelting**:

- An **ore** is a rock with a high percentage of metal in it.
- This chemical change releases a **metal element** from a **compound**.

For example:
iron oxide + carbon monoxide ⟶ iron
+ carbon dioxide

- Another metal extracted from ores in this way is **copper**.

Blast Furnace

Fermentation makes **ethanol** and **carbon dioxide**:

sugar $\xrightarrow[\text{no oxygen}]{\text{yeast}}$ ethanol + carbon dioxide

Sugar and oxygen are products of **photosynthesis**.

- Plants convert:
carbon dioxide + water $\xrightarrow{\text{light}}$ sugar + oxygen

Reactions may release **useful energy**. For example:

- **Combustion** (burning) gives out thermal energy and light.
  Combustion requires fuel + oxygen $\xrightarrow{\text{thermal energy}}$ carbon dioxide + water + energy

- **Respiration** gives out **energy** from **food**.
  In living cells sugar + oxygen ⟶ carbon dioxide + water + energy

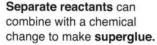

Some of these useful reactions are explained in more detail in other parts of this book. However, it is worth just summarising them here before we move on.

- **Combustion** gives out **energy**. This energy can be used for heating homes, factories and hospitals, for example. It can also be used for making other chemicals react together, or for generating electricity. Combustion only goes on if oxygen is present (see page 214).

- **Neutralisation** involves the removal of acid or alkali because these substances may be harmful (see page 180).

- **Smelting** is the extraction of metals from ores. This provides us with purified metals that have many important properties and uses (see page 247).

- **Fermentation** is the production of alcohol (and carbon dioxide). This chemical reaction only goes on properly if no oxygen is present and was one of the earliest chemical reactions that humans used.

- **Photosynthesis** is the production of sugar and oxygen using light energy. This process is the start of all the food chains in nature: no food chains, no humans (see page 99).

- **Respiration** is the process that releases energy from food molecules inside our cells. This energy is used to keep all of the life processes going. Without this chemical reaction there would be no living things (see page 45).

- **Cooking of food** makes food safer, tastier and easier to eat. Molecules in the food are changed during cooking. For example, frying an egg alters proteins and fats in the egg so that the cooked egg has products that are more solid and taste differently from a raw egg.

- **Glues and adhesives** work by forming a bond between different materials. Some glues stick because different substances in the glue react together. Superglue works because the molecules of glue change the way in which they are arranged (they become much more sticky) when they contact **moisture** or **alkali**. This is why this type of glue is sometimes called **contact adhesive**.

ENZYMES ARE CATALYSTS

Yeast is a living organism. Yeast cells contain molecules called **enzymes**. These molecules can speed up a chemical reaction without being changed themselves. Enzymes are damaged by thermal energy and acids and alkalis. Enzymes in yeast work best at 28 °C and in neutral conditions, and the yeast is killed above 45 °C.

FERMENTATION is a chemical reaction, so:
- We can tell which are reactants and which are products.
- The arrow shows the direction of change.
- New substances are produced and there is an energy change.
- The process cannot be reversed.

This **energy** is needed by the yeast to carry out its life processes. The yeast cells reproduce using this energy, so some yeast cells may remain in the bottle.

glucose ⟶ ethanol + carbon dioxide + energy

Glucose (sugar) is the reactant. This substance comes from a fruit (e.g. grapes) or a seed (e.g. malt).

Ethanol is important in brewing

Hops (for flavour)

Yeast
28 °C

Germinating barley (for malt sugar)

Alcohol solution (flat, since all the carbon dioxide has escaped)

more sugar

stoppered bottles

The beer is made fizzy by carbon dioxide from a second fermentation.

It's a matter of taste! Fruits and seeds contain other chemicals as well as glucose. These chemicals give different tastes to different alcoholic drinks. For example, potatoes can be used to make Vodka!

ROXCOFF VODKA
40% PROOF

Carbon dioxide is especially important in bread making

Baking:
- kills yeast; and
- evaporates the alcohol.

Yeast + sugar warmed together = **raising agent**

flour, salt

warm water

Dough

fermentation

Rising dough

Bread

(Carbon dioxide bubbles cause the dough to swell.)

N.B. Ethanol is a poison. It will eventually kill the yeast cells which produce it and does the same to human cells if taken in too large a quantity.

Fermentation can only produce a mixture of ethanol and water. Distillation (see page 168) is needed to purify the ethanol. Spirits, such as gin, whisky and brandy, are made from distillation.

Chemical reactions that are not useful

Many materials can take part in chemical reactions, although some materials are much less reactive than others. Sometimes these materials are useful as they are and it is a nuisance if they change into something else. Some 'non-useful' chemical reactions are shown below:

Some chemical changes cause damage or danger

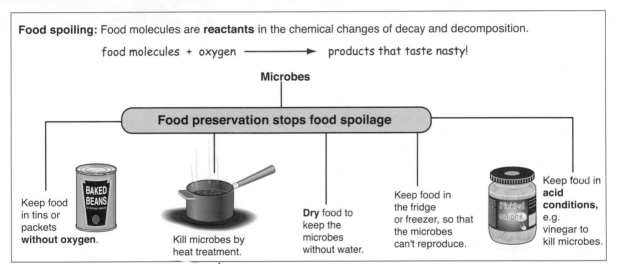

Food spoiling: Food molecules are **reactants** in the chemical changes of decay and decomposition.

food molecules + oxygen ⟶ products that taste nasty!

Microbes

Food preservation stops food spoilage

Keep food in tins or packets **without oxygen**.

Kill microbes by heat treatment.

Dry food to keep the microbes without water.

Keep food in the fridge or freezer, so that the microbes can't reproduce.

Keep food in **acid conditions,** e.g. vinegar to kill microbes.

Reactants ➤ Products

Corrosion converts useful metal into a damaged product.

- The process is called **oxidation**. It uses oxygen from air or water.

  metal + oxygen ⟶ metal oxide

- **Metal oxide** is weaker and softer than the metal, so corroded objects break easily.

- The most important example of corrosion is **rusting.**

Pollution is caused by **products** of chemical reactions which take place in industry.

Acid rain:
- Combustion of fuels produces **oxides of sulphur and nitrogen.**
- Oxides react with the water in clouds to make **acid rain.**
- Acid rain irritates our lungs and eyes, damages leaves on trees and dissolves some building materials.

Greenhouse effect:
- Carbon dioxide is a **product** of burning fossil fuels.
- Methane is a **product** of cows' digestion of grass.
- These gases trap warm air close to the Earth's surface.

Melting of ice caps – bad news for penguins!

This list gives a summary of these reactions and tells you where you can find out more about them:

1. **Decay and decomposition** are processes that break down other materials. This includes the rotting or spoiling of food and some diseases. When food rots, it reacts with oxygen in the air to form new compounds that taste unpleasant; we say that the food is **rancid**. This happens most often with foods that contain fat, so foods such as cheese and crisps are often sealed up in bags filled with nitrogen. Because there is no oxygen in the bags, the fats are not oxidised and the food is **preserved**. Some foods **rot** because microbes called **decomposers** use the food molecules to carry out the chemical reactions needed for the microbes to stay alive.

Rotting and mouldy figs

2. **Corrosion** is the oxidation of metals. This includes rusting which damages many structures and buildings (see page 238).

3. **Acid rain** is formed from the products of burning fossil fuels. It can cause damage to buildings, trees and your lungs (see page 186).

4. **The greenhouse effect** is caused by certain gases which trap internal/thermal energy close to the Earth's surface. One way in which these gases are produced is by the combustion of fossil fuels (see page 217).

Key words

Chemical change – a reaction which results in new products and an energy change and which is very difficult to reverse.

Reactant – the starting material in a chemical change.

Product – the material present after a chemical change has taken place.

Exercise 16.2: Important chemical changes

1. A baker wanted to try out a new dough mix. He needed to know how long it would take to swell to a certain size; the dough needs to swell before the bread is baked in the oven.

   He made up a sample of the dough and dropped it into a measuring cylinder, as shown in the diagram. He left the dough standing on a radiator and went back to check it every five minutes, for half an hour.

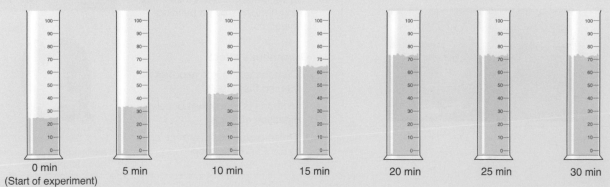

Copy this table and complete it, using the baker's results:

Time in minutes	Volume of dough in cm³
0	
5	
10	
15	
20	
25	
30	

(a) Draw a line graph to show how the amount of dough changed over the half-hour period.

(b) Use your graph to work out how long he would need to leave the dough for it to swell to twice its original size.

(c) The baker decided to try to find out how much the amount of sugar in the dough affected the volume of the dough.

    (i) What would be the **input** (independent) variable in this experiment?

    (ii) What would be the **outcome** (dependent) variable in this experiment?

    (iii) Give two important variables the baker would need to control if this experiment were to be a fair test. Explain how these variables could be checked.

2. Give two examples of useful chemical reactions that occur naturally and two examples of natural chemical reactions that are not useful.

3. Make a list of ten substances that you could find at home. Pick out which of the substances have been made by a chemical reaction. Choose one substance from your list and find out which reactants were needed to make it.

Combustion

Burning is a chemical change called **combustion**.

●   Combustion is a chemical reaction in which **thermal energy** and **light energy** are produced.

●   During combustion, **oxygen** from the air combines with another element to form an **oxide**.

Some substances burn when they are heated in air. When these substances burn, they are changed completely. The burning process cannot be reversed. Burning happens when substances react with **oxygen** in the air and give out **thermal** and **light energy**. Burning makes new substances. The substance that burns is called the **fuel**, and is often changed into another solid material (ash). It is easy to see the ash but there are in fact other substances that are created during the burning process. One of these is a gas, called carbon dioxide, and the other is water.

Products of burning

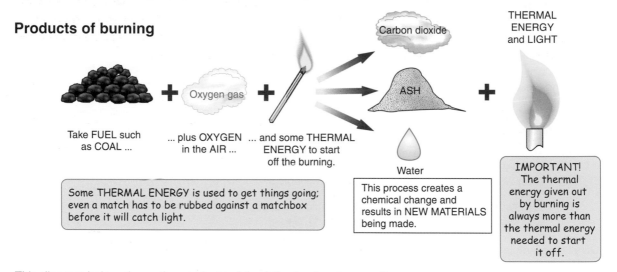

Take FUEL such as COAL ...

... plus OXYGEN in the AIR ...

... and some THERMAL ENERGY to start off the burning.

Carbon dioxide

ASH

Water

THERMAL ENERGY and LIGHT

Some THERMAL ENERGY is used to get things going; even a match has to be rubbed against a matchbox before it will catch light.

This process creates a chemical change and results in NEW MATERIALS being made.

IMPORTANT! The thermal energy given out by burning is always more than the thermal energy needed to start it off.

This diagram below shows the products of the following burning reaction:

hydrocarbon + oxygen → water + carbon dioxide
   (from fuel)   (from air)

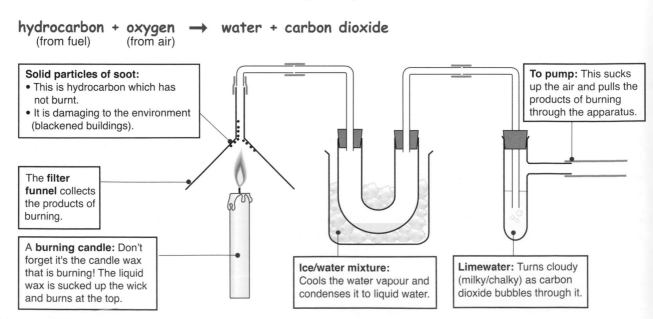

Solid particles of soot:
• This is hydrocarbon which has not burnt.
• It is damaging to the environment (blackened buildings).

The **filter funnel** collects the products of burning.

A burning candle: Don't forget it's the candle wax that is burning! The liquid wax is sucked up the wick and burns at the top.

Ice/water mixture:
Cools the water vapour and condenses it to liquid water.

To pump: This sucks up the air and pulls the products of burning through the apparatus.

Limewater: Turns cloudy (milky/chalky) as carbon dioxide bubbles through it.

Combustion is a chemical reaction (see page 205) and when combustion occurs new products are formed. It is important that you know what these products are and how you can test for them. These tests are described in Chapter 11 (page 135).

Air contains only about 20% oxygen (the rest is mostly nitrogen and materials will not burn in nitrogen). Oxidations occur much more quickly if pure oxygen is used. The reactions may be so quick that an explosion occurs, so using pure oxygen for combustion is very dangerous!

Using fuels

Burning fuels is an important chemical change.

The energy that is given out in this process is useful to humans. The thermal energy can warm our homes and cook our food and the light can help us to see when it is dark. Very large amounts of fuel can be burned in power stations. The thermal energy given out can be converted into electricity. Electricity is a more useful kind of energy because we can send it along wires. This means that humans can use even more energy and they can use it in a different place from where it was released. This means that our lives can be cleaner and more convenient.

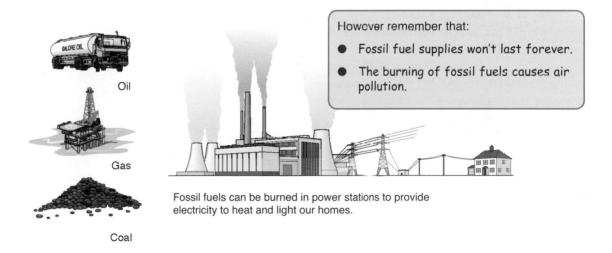

Oil

Gas

Coal

However remember that:

● Fossil fuel supplies won't last forever.

● The burning of fossil fuels causes air pollution.

Fossil fuels can be burned in power stations to provide electricity to heat and light our homes.

Combustion and the environment: Problems with fossil fuels

Natural gas, coal and oil are called **fossil fuels**. Fossil fuels are substances that were formed millions of years ago from the remains of dead animals and plants. These fuels contain many of the chemicals that were present in the live animals and plants. These chemicals are made up of different elements, including carbon, hydrogen, sulphur and nitrogen.

As we learnt earlier on, when fuel is burned (combustion), these elements combine with oxygen from the air to make oxides. Because these reactions are all chemical changes, we can write out word equations to describe them.

Burning fossil fuels

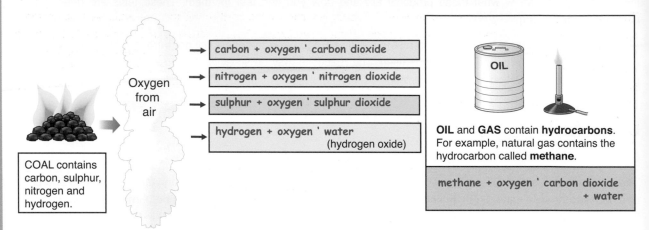

carbon + oxygen ' carbon dioxide

nitrogen + oxygen ' nitrogen dioxide

sulphur + oxygen ' sulphur dioxide

hydrogen + oxygen ' water
(hydrogen oxide)

COAL contains carbon, sulphur, nitrogen and hydrogen.

OIL

OIL and **GAS** contain **hydrocarbons**. For example, natural gas contains the hydrocarbon called **methane**.

methane + oxygen ' carbon dioxide + water

CARBON MONOXIDE KILLS!
If there is too little oxygen present, carbon may react with oxygen to form carbon monoxide (CO). This gas binds onto the haemoglobin in the red blood cells which means that less oxygen can be carried by the haemoglobin. This can be fatal.

ELEPHANTS HAVE WIND!
Did you know that a single elephant 'farts' enough methane every day to run a small gas stove for 8 hours!

Burning fossil fuels gives out very large amounts of energy, but there are two important problems:

● Fossil fuels are **non-renewable**: in other words they are not being made any more, so that once they are used up, there won't be any more available for us to use.

● Fossil fuels cause **pollution**: smoke, ash and waste gases cause damage to our environment, especially to the air. Some of this damage affects humans as well as other living organisms (see page 218).

The greenhouse effect

The Earth is warmed by **radiation** from the Sun. The radiation reaches the Earth and is then reflected back out towards space. Some of the reflected radiation is **trapped** by the atmosphere. Layers of gases stop this reflected internal/thermal energy from escaping back into the atmosphere and reflect it back towards the Earth's surface. This is a natural effect and keeps the surface of the Earth at an ideal temperature for life (the average over the Earth's surface is about 16 °C). This effect is very similar to the way in whicht the glass in a greenhouse lets light energy in but stops internal/thermal energy from escaping. This is why the layers of gas are called **greenhouse gases**.

The greenhouse effect

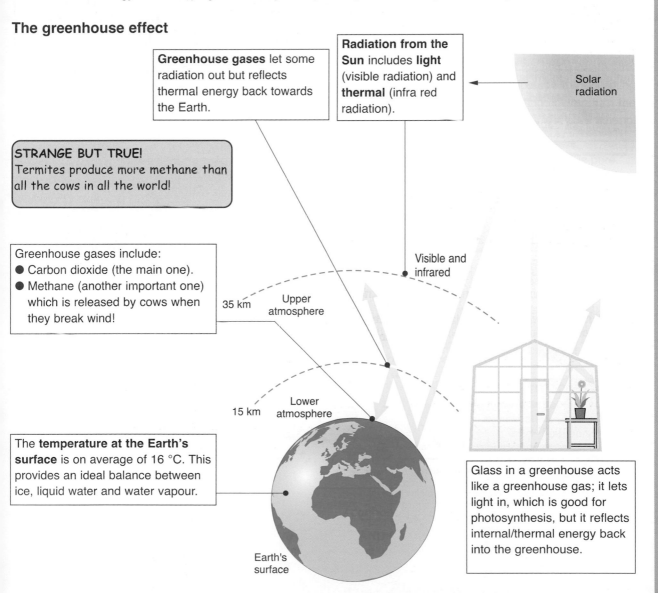

Greenhouse gases let some radiation out but reflects thermal energy back towards the Earth.

Radiation from the Sun includes **light** (visible radiation) and **thermal** (infra red radiation).

Solar radiation

STRANGE BUT TRUE!
Termites produce more methane than all the cows in all the world!

Greenhouse gases include:
● Carbon dioxide (the main one).
● Methane (another important one) which is released by cows when they break wind!

Visible and infrared

35 km — Upper atmosphere

15 km — Lower atmosphere

The **temperature at the Earth's surface** is on average of 16 °C. This provides an ideal balance between ice, liquid water and water vapour.

Earth's surface

Glass in a greenhouse acts like a greenhouse gas; it lets light in, which is good for photosynthesis, but it reflects internal/thermal energy back into the greenhouse.

Burning fossil fuels produces more of these greenhouse gases and so more thermal energy is continually reflected back towards the Earth's surface. This makes the Earth warmer. Scientists have measured the Earth's temperature for hundreds of years and they think that the Earth has become about 2 °C warmer in the last 100 years. This is called **global warming**.

We think that global warming might have some very serious effects. These effects are shown below:

The effects of global warming

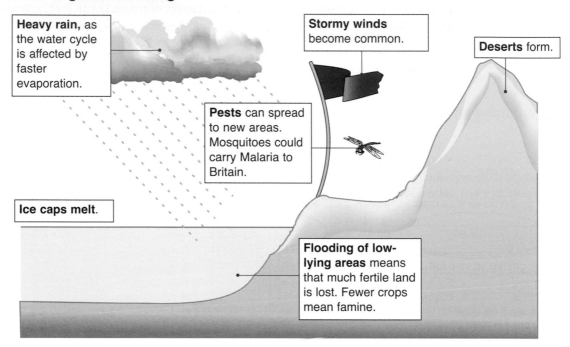

Heavy rain, as the water cycle is affected by faster evaporation.

Stormy winds become common.

Deserts form.

Pests can spread to new areas. Mosquitoes could carry Malaria to Britain.

Ice caps melt.

Flooding of low-lying areas means that much fertile land is lost. Fewer crops mean famine.

Acid rain

Combustion produces new products called oxides. Some of these oxides are acid gases (see page 199). Two of these acid gases are sulphur dioxide and nitrogen dioxide. The acid gases dissolve in water in clouds and form acids. When it rains, these acids fall and land on the Earth. This **acid rain** causes many problems, as you can see below:

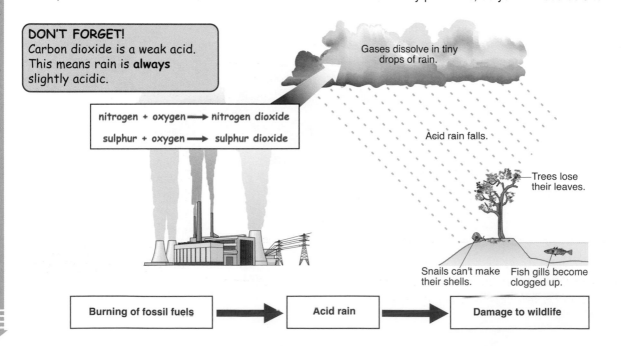

DON'T FORGET!
Carbon dioxide is a weak acid. This means rain is **always** slightly acidic.

Gases dissolve in tiny drops of rain.

nitrogen + oxygen ⟶ nitrogen dioxide

sulphur + oxygen ⟶ sulphur dioxide

Acid rain falls.

Trees lose their leaves.

Snails can't make their shells.

Fish gills become clogged up.

| Burning of fossil fuels | ⟶ | Acid rain | ⟶ | Damage to wildlife |

Dealing with air pollution

Although humans can cause damage to the environment, they are also the only ones who are able to work out the best way of reducing this damage. Because scientists understand what a greenhouse gas does and why rain becomes acid, they can suggest ways to deal with these problems. For example, the greenhouse effect can be reduced by:

● reducing the cutting of forests for cattle ranches and rice fields (burning the forests produces more carbon dioxide and reduces the number of plants that can absorb carbon dioxide);

● planting more forests (plants absorb carbon dioxide for photosynthesis); and

● reducing the burning of fossil fuels by trying to find alternative energy sources.

Estimated carbon dioxide emissions

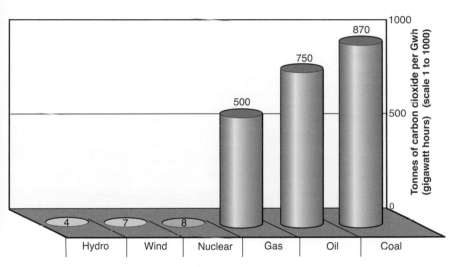

Carbon dioxide emission from various energy sources (Nuclear Issues, January 1995)

All countries are being put under pressure to reduce their carbon emissions. In many countries rising energy demands are being met by coal or oil power stations, which, as you can see from the chart above is not the way to reduce these greenhouse gases. Interestingly, nuclear power stations emit hardly any carbon dioxide, so countries with a substantial nuclear power programme have managed to reduce these emissions significantly. For example, France (80% nuclear) has, since 1970, halved its emissions of carbon; Japan (32% nuclear) has achieved a reduction of 20%.

Acid rain can be reduced by:

● not burning coal which has a high sulphur level;

● building more efficient power stations that can clean the gases they let out into the atmosphere; and

● designing cars with catalytic converters (these get rid of acid gases from the exhaust fumes).

Farmers sometimes add crushed chalk to their fields or lakes to neutralise the acid rain, but this is very expensive and takes a lot of time.

Key words

Combustion – is a chemical change that releases energy by combining a fuel with oxygen.

Acid rain – happens when oxides made in combustion combine with water vapour in the air.

Fuel – is a substance that can be burned to release energy.

Greenhouse effect – is the trapping of internal/thermal energy close to the Earth by a layer of gases.

Global warming – is the raising of the Earth's temperature and is a result of pollution and the greenhouse effect.

Exercise 16.3: Burning

1. Which one of these is not a fossil fuel?

   natural gas, wood, oil, coal.

2. Give a reason why covering burning wood with a blanket will put out a fire.

3. A scientist wanted to find out how much thermal energy is given out when fuels burn. He took different fuels, burned them and measured the thermal energy released. Here are the results:

Type of fuel	Units of thermal energy released	Amount of fuel burned in grams	Units of thermal energy from 100 grams of fuel
Coal	40	60	
Gas	54	80	
Paraffin	36	50	
Petrol	60	50	
Diesel oil	54	75	

(a) Copy out the table and complete the final column. Why is it important to complete this final column?

(b) The scientist always used the same amount of air for his experiment. Why is this important?

(c) Draw a bar chart of the results from the final column. Which is the most useful heating fuel?

Exercise 16.4: Air pollution

1. Acid rain is harmful to the environment. How could you test whether a sample of rain was acid rain?

2. Why do we say that carbon dioxide is a greenhouse gas?

Extension questions

3. Two students were interested in the effects of sulphur dioxide on living organisms. They decided to investigate the effect of sulphur dioxide on the germination of oat seeds. Twenty-five sets of apparatus were set up, five sets of apparatus for each of five different concentrations of sodium disulphite solution. Sodium disulphite breaks down to release sulphur dioxide into the atmosphere. The table below shows the results obtained one week after setting up the experiment:

Concentration of sodium disulphite (%)	Number of seeds germinated out of twenty (five experiments)					Percentage germination
0.00	19	19	17	20	18	
0.05	18	19	18	19	19	
0.10	12	13	14	11	12	
0.50	0	1	0	0	1	
2.50	0	0	0	0	0	

(a) Complete the table to show the percentage germination of the oat seeds at each sodium disulphite concentration.

(b) Plot the results in the form of a bar chart.

(c) Why was the experiment repeated five times at each concentration?

(d) Water (i.e. 0% sodium disulphite solution) is used as a control. What is the purpose of this control?

(e) What is the lowest concentration of sodium disulphite which had a harmful effect on seed germination?

(f) How could the students modify the experiment to find a more accurate value for the concentration of sodium disulphite which had a harmful effect on seed germination?

(g) For this experiment, what are the input (independent) and the outcome (dependent) variables? Suggest two factors which might affect seed germination and which are controlled variables in this experiment.

(h) The sodium disulphite in the experiment released sulphur dioxide into the atmosphere in the apparatus.

 (i) Which human activity releases large amounts of sulphur dioxide into the natural environment?

 (ii) Suggest two other effects, apart from reducing seed germination, of sulphur dioxide on living organisms.

4. The following table contains information about the sources and effects of greenhouse gases:

Gas	Sources of gas	Percentage overall contribution to the greenhouse effect
Carbon dioxide	Burning forests, burning fossil fuels, production of cement	54
Chlorofluorocarbons (CFC's)	Aerosol propellants, refrigerants, coolants in air conditioners	21
Methane	Waste gases from domestic animals, rotting vegetation, rice growing	14
Nitrogen oxides	Exhaust gases from internal combustion engines, breakdown of fertilisers	7
Low level ozone	Combination of nitrogen oxides with oxygen	2

(a) Present these results in the form of a bar chart.

(b) The only other greenhouse gas is water. Use the above data to calculate the greenhouse effect of water.

(c) Which of the gases shown in the table is produced by natural processes?

(d) What, exactly, is a greenhouse gas?

(e) Suggest three possibly harmful effects of greenhouse gases.

(f) Use the data in the table to suggest why the following are valuable conservation measures:

    (i) reducing forest clearances for cattle ranches;

    (ii) improved insulation for houses;

    (iii) the use of alternative energy sources, such as nuclear, windmills and wave machines.

(g) In 1900 the concentration of carbon dioxide in the atmosphere was 0.03%. In 1990 this had risen to 0.035%, and is expected to rise further to 0.055% by 2030.

    (i) By how much did the carbon dioxide concentration increase between 1900 and 1990?

    (ii) What is the expected increase in carbon dioxide concentration between 1990 and 2030?

    (iii) Suggest why the figure you calculated in (ii) is so much higher than your answer to (i).

Conservation of mass during chemical changes

All chemicals are made up of particles (see page 150). During a chemical reaction these particles are rearranged into a new pattern **but they are never broken down**.

Particles in a chemical change

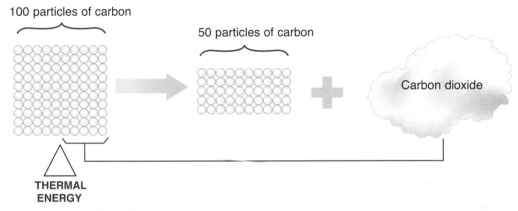

100 particles of carbon

50 particles of carbon

Carbon dioxide

THERMAL ENERGY

Before this experiment began, the carbon particles were packed tightly into a solid. When the carbon burns, it reacts with oxygen particles in the air. A new substance called carbon dioxide is made. Each particle of carbon reacts with two particles of oxygen to produce carbon dioxide. The carbon dioxide gas spreads out into the air, but if it were collected and weighed it would contain the missing 50 grams of carbon.

The particle theory explains why, during any chemical reaction, there is **conservation of mass**. This means the total mass of the reactants used is the same as the total mass of the products formed. The diagram below shows a demonstration of the conservation of mass during a chemical change:

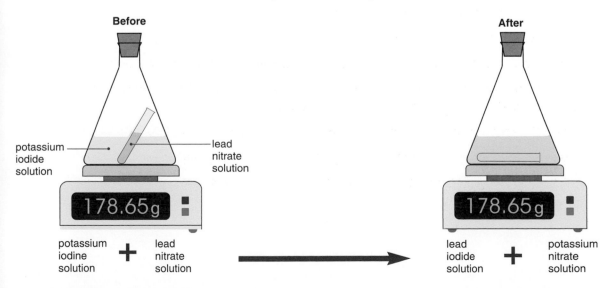

Before

potassium iodide solution

lead nitrate solution

178.65g

potassium iodine solution + lead nitrate solution

After

178.65g

lead iodide solution + potassium nitrate solution

Exercise 16.5: Conservation of mass

1. Look at the diagram below. It shows an experiment where magnesium ribbon is burned in air.

    Step 1: Before heating, weigh the magnesium ribbon, crucible and lid.

    Step 2: Heat the ribbon strongly.

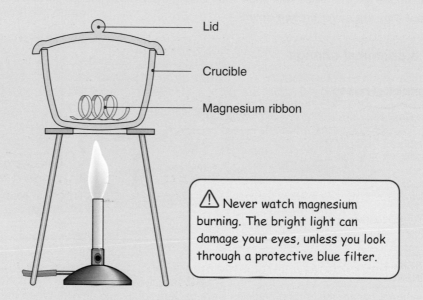

Lid

Crucible

Magnesium ribbon

⚠ Never watch magnesium burning. The bright light can damage your eyes, unless you look through a protective blue filter.

    Step 3: After heating, weigh the magnesium oxide and crucible lid.

    The following results were obtained:

    Mass of crucible   50 g

    Mass of crucible + magnesium ribbon   62 g

    Mass of crucible + contents after heating   70 g

    Explain these results.

Chemical reactions can be reversed

The different substances in a mixture can usually be separated quite easily (see page 156). The methods used for these separations involve physical changes because the substances in the mixture have not been changed into different substances. It is more difficult to break up a compound into its elements but it is sometimes possible.

In Book 1 you will have learnt that chemical reactions are normally non-reversible. The honest truth is that some chemical reactions are in fact reversible but under special circumstances. Another chemical reaction is needed. The type of chemical reaction that can break up a compound is called a **decomposition**, and usually requires a great deal of energy.

The energy to break up some compounds can be supplied by thermal energy, in a type of reaction called a **thermal decomposition**. Other compounds can be broken up using electricity, in a type of chemical reaction called **electrical decomposition** or **electrolysis**. To break up a compound by electrolysis, the compound needs to be molten or dissolved.

Some compounds are not very strongly bonded together and can be broken down into simpler materials by heating. The thermal decomposition of hydrated copper sulphate is reversible and forms a test for water (see below).

Examples of decomposition reactions are shown below:

Thermal decomposition uses thermal energy to break up a compound into elements

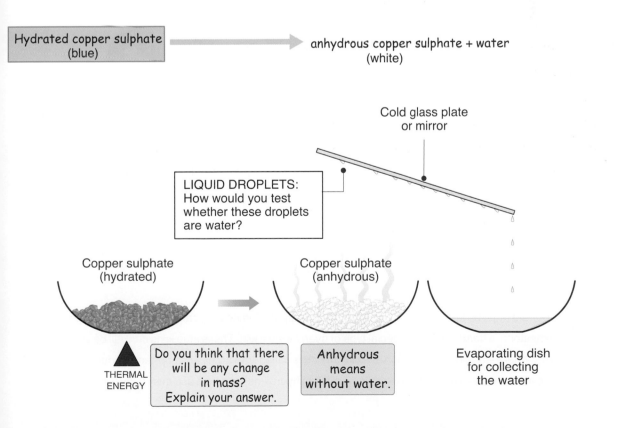

Hydrated copper sulphate (blue) → anhydrous copper sulphate + water (white)

Cold glass plate or mirror

LIQUID DROPLETS: How would you test whether these droplets are water?

Copper sulphate (hydrated)

Copper sulphate (anhydrous)

THERMAL ENERGY

Do you think that there will be any change in mass? Explain your answer.

Anhydrous means without water.

Evaporating dish for collecting the water

Here are some other **important thermal decompositions**.

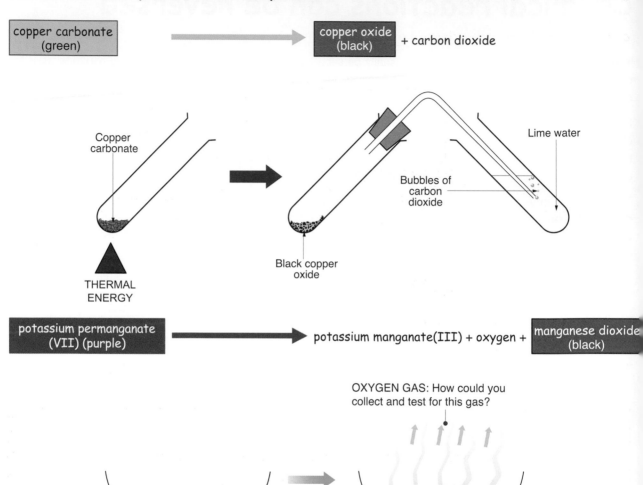

copper carbonate
(green) ⟶ copper oxide
(black) + carbon dioxide

Copper carbonate

Bubbles of carbon dioxide

Lime water

THERMAL ENERGY

Black copper oxide

potassium permanganate (VII) (purple) ⟶ potassium manganate(III) + oxygen + manganese dioxide (black)

OXYGEN GAS: How could you collect and test for this gas?

potassium permanganate (VII)

potassium manganate (III) + manganese dioxide

Finally, the thermal decomposition of calcium carbonate in limestone.

calcium carbonate
(white) ⟶ calcium oxide + carbon dioxide

The calcium carbonate must be heated very strongly for this to happen. The heating can take place on a large scale, where crushed limestone is heated inside a special type of oven called a kiln. These lime kilns can still be seen in many parts of the country where limestone is common. Calcium oxide is called lime and is an important product for agriculture. Chemists dissolve lime in water to produce slaked lime (calcium hydroxide) and then use this slaked lime to neutralise acidic soils.

Electrolysis uses electrical energy to break up a compound into elements

copper chloride → chlorine + copper

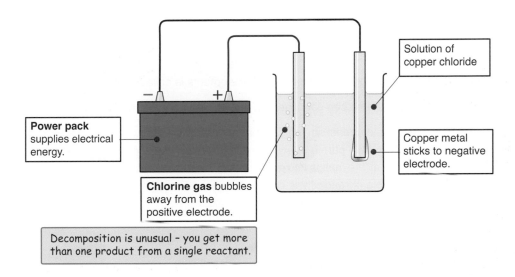

Power pack supplies electrical energy.

Solution of copper chloride

Copper metal sticks to negative electrode.

Chlorine gas bubbles away from the positive electrode.

Decomposition is unusual – you get more than one product from a single reactant.

Key words

Compound – a chemical substance made of different elements linked to one another.

Mixture – a group of different substances that are not linked to one another.

Combustion – a chemical reaction that involves a substance burning in oxygen and giving out thermal energy.

Corrosion – a chemical reaction between a metal and the air without any burning.

Decomposition – a chemical reaction in which one substance is broken down into several products.

Formula – a shorthand version of the name for a compound, written using chemical symbols.

Chapter 17
The reactions of metals

We already know that

● During chemical reactions new substances are formed.

● A new substance formed by combining two or more different elements is called a compound.

● During combustion, oxygen from the air can combine with another element to form an oxide.

If an element easily takes part in a chemical reaction, we say that it is **reactive**. Some metals are very **unreactive**; gold and silver, for example, do not easily take part in many chemical reactions. Most metals are reactive, and some are very reactive indeed. We can arrange all the metals into a sort of league table of reactivity, depending on how easily they react with other substances. This table of reactivity is usually called the **Reactivity Series**. It can be worked out by comparing the reaction of different metals with oxygen, water and acids.

Metals and oxygen

You should already have an idea of how metals react with oxygen (see page 199), and we also know that some metals react much more quickly than others do. Reactions with oxygen are called **oxidations**. Products of oxidation reactions are called **oxides**. The equation for one of these oxidation reactions is shown below:

$$\text{metal} + \text{oxygen} \longrightarrow \text{metal oxide}$$

The different metals can be compared in their reaction with oxygen using the apparatus shown below:

Metals and oxygen

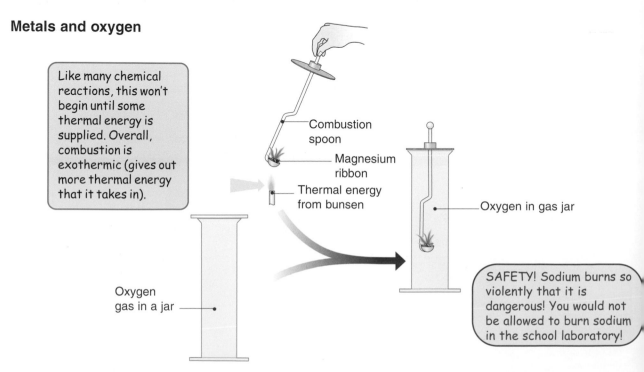

Like many chemical reactions, this won't begin until some thermal energy is supplied. Overall, combustion is exothermic (gives out more thermal energy that it takes in).

Combustion spoon

Magnesium ribbon

Thermal energy from bunsen

Oxygen in gas jar

Oxygen gas in a jar

SAFETY! Sodium burns so violently that it is dangerous! You would not be allowed to burn sodium in the school laboratory!

This table lists the results obtained in a series of experiments:

Metal	Reaction with oxygen	Product
Sodium	Burns very quickly even after gentle heating.	Sodium peroxide (a pale yellow powder)
Calcium	Burns easily with gentle heating.	Calcium oxide (white powder)
Magnesium	Burns easily with a brilliant white flame.	Magnesium oxide (grey-white powder)
Iron	Burns slowly and only if there is strong heating and the iron is powdered or in strands.	Iron oxide (black powder)
Copper	Does not burn, but a black layer is formed on the surface of the metal.	Copper oxide (black powder)
Gold	No reaction, even with strong heating.	

If the metal is reactive, an oxide is formed; this oxide is a **base** (remember that this is a comparison with non-metal oxides – see page 199). If a base dissolves in water, it makes an **alkaline** solution.

Metals and water

If a **reactive metal**, for example sodium or calcium, is placed in water, it reacts vigorously to form the **hydroxide**. For example:

water + sodium ⟶ sodium hydroxide + hydrogen

This reaction is strongly exothermic and the thermal energy ignites the hydrogen. The reaction of potassium with water is even more exciting (see page 235).

Less reactive metals react with **steam** to form the oxide and hydrogen:

water + metal ⟶ metal oxide + hydrogen

This occurs with magnesium, iron, aluminium and zinc.

water   +   magnesium ⟶   magnesium oxide +   hydrogen

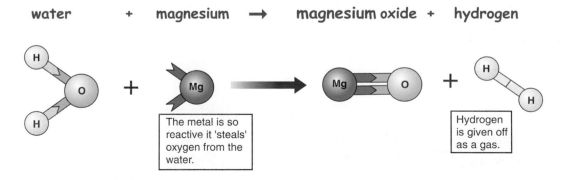

The metal is so reactive it 'steals' oxygen from the water.

Hydrogen is given off as a gas.

ALUMINIUM SEEMS TO BE ODD!

It is very hard to make aluminium react with water, **because it's already reacted with oxygen!**

Aluminium metal very quickly gets covered with a thin layer of aluminium oxide. This layer stops water molecules reaching the metal, so they can't react with it! This means we can use aluminium for very lightweight pans and kettles without worrying about any reaction with water.

Some metals do not react with water. Imagine what would happen if a copper pan reacted with water, or if gold reacted with water and you forgot to remove a gold ring when you washed your hands! Some metals react quite slowly with water (magnesium is an example), but some react so violently that they must be kept under a layer of oil or they would react with the water vapour in the air!

This table lists the results of experiments in which metals and water are allowed to react together:

Metal	Reaction with water	Products
Sodium	Reacts very violently and catches fire.	hydrogen gas + sodium hydroxide solution
Calcium	Reacts quite quickly.	hydrogen gas + calcium hydroxide in solution
Magnesium	Reacts slowly with water but quite vigorously with steam.	hydrogen gas + solid magnesium oxide
Iron	No reaction in cold water, but iron will react with steam.	hydrogen gas + solid iron oxide
Copper	No reaction.	
Gold	No reaction.	

Metals and acids

Acids are compounds and include hydrogen in their structure. When a metal reacts with an acid, the metal replaces the hydrogen and the hydrogen is given off as a gas. As well as hydrogen, another product, called a **salt**, is produced.

Most metals react with acids. For example, if magnesium is put into hydrochloric acid, this reaction takes place:

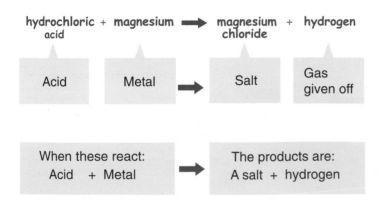

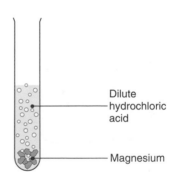

This diagram shows what is happening in the reaction of magnesium with hydrochloric acid.

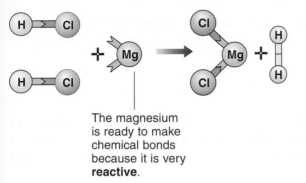

The magnesium is ready to make chemical bonds because it is very **reactive**.

The magnesium (Mg) has **displaced** the hydrogen (H) ('displaced' means 'has taken the place of').

The presence of hydrogen can be tested using a lighted splint.

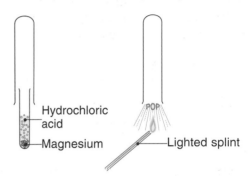

Hydrochloric acid

Magnesium

Lighted splint

An acid reacts with a metal, and gas is collected in an upturned test tube.

This test shows that the gas is hydrogen.

If we are going to compare the reactivity of metals with acids, we should always use the same acid in the tests. This table gives results for the reaction of some different metals with dilute hydrochloric acid.

Metal	Reaction with dilute hydrochloric acid	Products
Magnesium	Reacts very quickly.	Hydrogen gas + magnesium chloride in solution
Zinc	Reacts slowly.	Hydrogen gas + zinc chloride in solution
Iron	Reacts slowly, unless the mixture is warmed.	Hydrogen gas + iron chloride in solution
Copper	No reaction.	
Gold	No reaction.	

This next table gives results for the reaction of some different metals with sulphuric acid.

Metal	Reaction with dilute sulphuric acid	Products
Magnesium	Reacts very quickly.	Hydrogen gas + magnesium sulphate in solution
Zinc	Reacts slowly.	Hydrogen gas + zinc sulphate in solution
Iron	Reacts slowly, unless the mixture is warmed.	Hydrogen gas + iron sulphate in solution
Copper	No reaction.	
Gold	No reaction.	

The Reactivity Series

If you look back at these three tables of results, you should be able to see that we can arrange the metals in a list according to how reactive they are. This list is called the **Reactivity Series** and a short version is shown below:

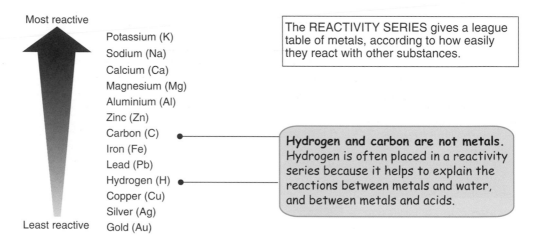

Most reactive

Potassium (K)
Sodium (Na)
Calcium (Ca)
Magnesium (Mg)
Aluminium (Al)
Zinc (Zn)
Carbon (C)
Iron (Fe)
Lead (Pb)
Hydrogen (H)
Copper (Cu)
Silver (Ag)
Gold (Au)

Least reactive

The REACTIVITY SERIES gives a league table of metals, according to how easily they react with other substances.

Hydrogen and carbon are not metals. Hydrogen is often placed in a reactivity series because it helps to explain the reactions between metals and water, and between metals and acids.

Hydrogen and carbon are not metals, but they are often placed in the Reactivity Series. These elements play a useful part in some reactions with metals, so it is useful to know where they fit (see page 236).

Metals from the Earth

Metals are found underground, in rocks. The rocks that contain metals are called **ores**. They are dug out of the ground by miners, so that the rocks can be crushed and the metals extracted. The unreactive metals, such as gold and silver, do not easily form compounds, so that they can be found as tiny pieces of pure metal. The more reactive metals form compounds, and are not found as pure metals. They need to be separated from other elements before they can be used. This separation process is described on page 247.

Competition between metals: Displacement reactions

Metals that are high in the Reactivity Series are more likely to react than metals that are low in the series. If two metals are present in the same solution, the more reactive metal will bind onto any other chemical in the solution. For example, a chemical reaction occurs when a piece of zinc is placed in a solution of blue copper sulphate. The zinc turns darker and the blue copper sulphate turns paler. If this sounds complicated, have a look at the diagram below; it should help you to understand the process.

zinc + copper sulphate

↓

zinc sulphate + copper

The zinc and copper compete for the sulphate. Zinc is more reactive, which means it can form stronger bonds, so it displaces the copper from the copper sulphate.

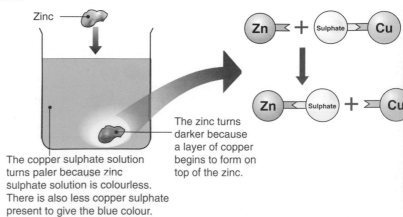

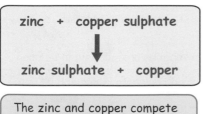

Zinc

The zinc turns darker because a layer of copper begins to form on top of the zinc.

The copper sulphate solution turns paler because zinc sulphate solution is colourless. There is also less copper sulphate present to give the blue colour.

The kind of reaction, in which one metal replaces another, is called a **displacement reaction**. The metals displace one another in a regular order, and we can predict this order from the Reactivity Series. The predictions can be checked by carrying out a series of experiments; in these experiments different metals are added to different solutions of metal salts.

The results of one set of experiments are shown in the table below:

Metal	Reaction with magnesium chloride solution	Reaction with iron nitrate solution	Reaction with lead chloride solution	Reaction with copper sulphate solution	Reaction with silver nitrate solution
Magnesium	✗	✔	✔	✔	✔
Zinc	✗	✔	✔	✔	✔
Iron	✗	✗	✔	✔	✔
Lead	✗	✗	✗	✔	✔
Copper	✗	✗	✗	✗	✔
Silver	✗	✗	✗	✗	✗

In this table, a ✔ sign means that a displacement reaction took place and a ✗ sign means that no displacement reaction took place.

These results show a pattern that confirms the order of metals in the Reactivity Series. A displacement reaction only takes place when the metal being added is higher in the Reactivity Series than the metal that is already present (in the salt solution).

For example, iron **can** displace lead from a lead chloride solution because iron is higher in the series (i.e. more reactive) than lead.

iron + lead chloride ⟶ iron chloride + lead

However, iron **cannot** displace magnesium from magnesium chloride solution because iron is lower in the series than magnesium.

We can use displacement reactions to make new salts from salts we already have. If we need some magnesium sulphate and we have some copper sulphate and some magnesium, we can make magnesium sulphate by mixing the two chemicals in water. The magnesium will displace the copper and magnesium sulphate will be formed.

magnesium + copper sulphate ⟶ magnesium sulphate + copper

Displacement from solids: Metals and metal oxides

Not all displacement reactions involve solid metals and metal salt solutions. Displacement reactions can also take place between solid metals and solid metal oxides. However, these reactions can be quite dangerous and are not so easy to carry out in a school laboratory.

One example which can be demonstrated in a school laboratory involves the reaction of powdered iron and copper oxide:

Metals can be displaced from metal oxides

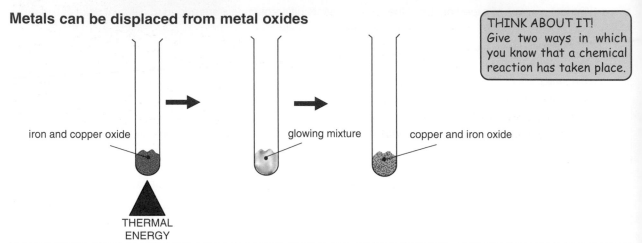

iron and copper oxide   glowing mixture   copper and iron oxide

THERMAL
ENERGY

THINK ABOUT IT!
Give two ways in which you know that a chemical reaction has taken place.

The **iron** has **gained oxygen**. We can say that:
- the iron has been oxidised; and
- that it is an **oxidation reaction.**

The **copper** has **lost** the **oxygen** to the **iron**. We can say that:
- the copper has been **reduced**; and
- that it is called a **reduction reaction**.

We can also say that:
- **iron** is a **reducing agent**; and
- **copper oxide** is an **oxidising agent for iron.**

In this reaction the iron and copper are competing for the oxygen but because iron is more reactive (higher up the Reactivity Series) than copper, it steals the oxygen away from the copper oxide.

Another well-known example of this kind of reaction occurs when powdered aluminium and iron oxide are heated together.

$$\text{aluminium + iron oxide} \longrightarrow \text{iron + aluminium oxide}$$

Once this reaction is started, it carries on very quickly and gives out enough internal/thermal energy to keep the iron molten. The reaction is called the **Thermit Reaction**. This Thermit Reaction is very useful in industry when a small amount of molten iron at a high temperature is needed. This reaction, for example, is used to join two lengths of railway line together. So much internal/thermal energy is given out that it melts the ends of the rails and they form a very strong joint as they cool together.

Using the Reactivity Series to predict chemical reactions

From the reactions you have learnt about in the last few sections, we can make a useful summary which will allow you to use the Reactivity Series to predict the outcome of chemical reactions.

- The Reactivity Series allows us to predict **what** will happen.

  For example, it tells us that sodium is a very reactive metal. If sodium is added to water, we know that there will be a violent reaction and hydrogen gas will be given off.

- The Reactivity Series can also let us predict **how fast** a reaction will occur.

For example, calcium fizzes gently when it is placed in water because bubbles of hydrogen gas are given off. Some internal/thermal energy is given off and the water becomes warm. Potassium is higher in the Reactivity Series, so we would predict that it would react more violently with water than calcium does. In fact potassium reacts so violently that it whizzes around in the water, the hydrogen bursts into flames and the water can get very hot! Potassium and hydrogen are **a long way apart** in the Reactivity Series, which is why the reaction to 'steal' the oxygen from the hydrogen in the water is so **violent**.

Potassium reacting with water

If two metals are **close together** in the Series, then the reaction between them will be **slow and gentle**. For example, when powdered lead and copper oxide are heated together, copper is displaced from the copper oxide and lead oxide is produced, but because the two metals have almost the same reactivity, the reaction goes on very slowly.

- The Reactivity Series can also predict how stable a compound is likely to be.

Metals that are **high** in the Reactivity Series form compounds so **quickly** because they can bond very tightly to other elements. Once one of these compounds has been formed, it is very difficult to break them down again – scientists say they are hard to **decompose**. For example, copper carbonate is easily decomposed by heating but potassium carbonate will not decompose, even if it is heated strongly for a long time.

copper carbonate $\xrightarrow[\text{energy}]{\text{thermal}}$ copper oxide + carbon dioxide

potassium carbonate $\xrightarrow[\text{energy}]{\text{thermal}}$ no reaction

Rules for predicting chemical changes

- Reactions of metals are faster and stronger the nearer the metal is to the top of the Reactivity Series.

- Metals higher up the Series can displace metals lower down the Series from their compounds.

- Compounds of metals higher up the Series are more stable than the compounds of metals lower down the Series.

Here is a summary that you can use to predict what will happen in chemical reactions:

Predicting chemical reactions with the reactivity series

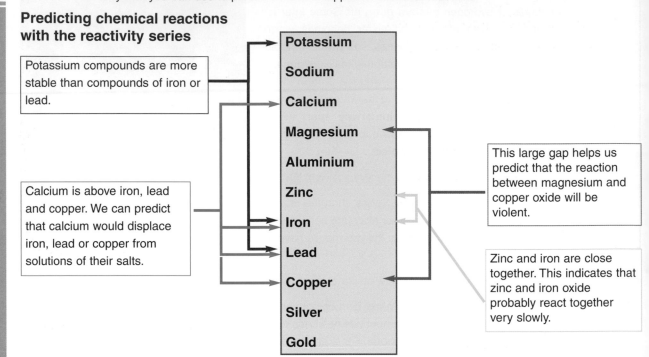

Potassium compounds are more stable than compounds of iron or lead.

Potassium
Sodium
Calcium
Magnesium
Aluminium
Zinc
Iron
Lead
Copper
Silver
Gold

Calcium is above iron, lead and copper. We can predict that calcium would displace iron, lead or copper from solutions of their salts.

This large gap helps us predict that the reaction between magnesium and copper oxide will be violent.

Zinc and iron are close together. This indicates that zinc and iron oxide probably react together very slowly.

Using the Reactivity Series: Understanding the uses of metals

Metals are used in many industries and activities. Scientists who understand the Reactivity Series can suggest which metal is most likely to be useful for a particular job. There are usually several things to think about when making a choice of a metal to use:

●   Is it cheap enough?

●   Is it unreactive, so that it will not combine with other substances and change its properties?

●   Can it easily be made into useful shapes?

Here are some ways the Reactivity Series can predict how metals may most usefully be used:

Metal	Use	How reactivity suits its purpose
Silver	Electrical contacts	Very unreactive, so it does not corrode inside electrical equipment.
Gold	Jewellery Spectacle frames	Very unreactive, so it does not corrode when in contact with skin.
Lead	Roofing	Does not react with water, so is ideal as a waterproof roof. It is also soft enough to be easily shaped.
Copper	Piping Electrical wiring	Does not react with fluids moving through pipes. Does not corrode.
Iron	Many uses in engineering	Quite reactive, but it can be protected from corrosion.

Key words

Reactive – will easily take part in a chemical reaction.

Displacement – a reaction in which one element replaces another one in a compound.

Reactivity Series – a table listing metals in order of how easily they take part in chemical reactions.

Oxidation – a chemical reaction in which oxygen is added to an element.

Base – a substance which will neutralise an acid.

Oxide – a compound formed when an element combines with oxygen.

Acid – a chemical that can give off hydrogen when it reacts with a metal.

Salt – one product of the reaction between an acid and a base.

Decomposition – a chemical reaction in which a substance breaks down to form more than one product.

Exercise 17.1: The Reactivity Series

1. A piece of zinc is placed in silver nitrate solution. As the zinc dissolves, the solution turns grey and a silver coating appears on the zinc.

    (a) Which is more reactive, zinc or silver?

    (b) Copy and complete the following word equation:

    zinc + silver nitrate ⟶ . . . .

2. Look at the following situations. For each one, say whether a reaction will take place. Give a reason for each of your answers.

    (a) Copper heated with iron oxide.

    (b) Magnesium placed in dilute hydrochloric acid.

    (c) Copper placed in dilute sulphuric acid.

    (d) Magnesium placed in copper sulphate solution.

    (e) Silver warmed with water.

Extension question

3. You have some pieces of an unknown metal, called M.

    (a) You also have solutions of copper sulphate, zinc sulphate, iron sulphate and magnesium sulphate. Metal M is thought to be either copper, magnesium, iron or zinc. How could you test to see what metal M is?

    (b) Metal M reacts with hydrochloric acid, and gives out a gas. Describe a useful test you could carry out on the gas, and suggest what the result would be.

    (c) Metal M can be converted to a carbonate. The carbonate decomposes if it is heated, and a gas is given off. What is this gas? How could you test for its identity?

Corrosion of metals

Remember

● Metals can react with oxygen to form oxides.

● Metals high in the Reactivity Series react more quickly with oxygen than metals lower in the Reactivity Series.

Most metals turn dull when they are exposed to the air. The dullness is usually a coating of metal oxide, formed when the **metal** reacts with oxygen in the air. With aluminium, for example:

$$\text{aluminium} + \text{oxygen} \longrightarrow \text{aluminium oxide}$$

This layer can be useful, because it stops the oxygen getting at the metal under the coating. The layer is so useful that sometimes it is deliberately made thicker if it is especially important that the metal does not corrode (see page 241). Copper reacts with carbon dioxide and oxygen in the atmosphere and forms a thin coat of a green compound called **verdigris**. This can often be seen where copper has been used in making a roof on a building.

Corrosion is generally a slow process, although very reactive metals, such as sodium and potassium, are kept in a bottle of oil, so that they can't react with oxygen in the air. The metals at the bottom of the Reactivity Series hardly corrode at all, which is one reason why silver and gold are so important in the production of jewellery.

Rusting is the corrosion of iron

Of all the metals that can be obtained from the Earth, iron is used more than any other. This is because:

● Iron is easy to obtain because there is a lot of iron ore in the Earth's crust.

● It is quite easy to separate iron from iron ore. Iron ores are refined in a blast furnace. The product of the blast furnace is called pig iron and contains about 4% carbon. Cast iron is made when pig iron is re-melted in furnaces (see page 248). This cast iron contains between 2% and 6% carbon.

● Iron can be mixed with other substances to make its properties suitable for a wide range of jobs.

Most iron is used in this way to make **steel** (steel contains less carbon than pig iron and doesn't shatter or crack so easily – see page 249).

Rusting is the name given to the corrosion of iron and steel. This process is a problem because so many man-made structures get their strength from iron or steel. It is therefore important that we understand the processes involved, so that we can do something to stop this process happening!

An investigation into the rusting of iron

Iron nails are a very convenient source of iron for this experiment. It is easy to get a set of nails that are all the same size and shape, so that the experiment will give reliable results. The diagram below shows an experiment to investigate the conditions that cause rusting:

An investigation into the rusting of iron

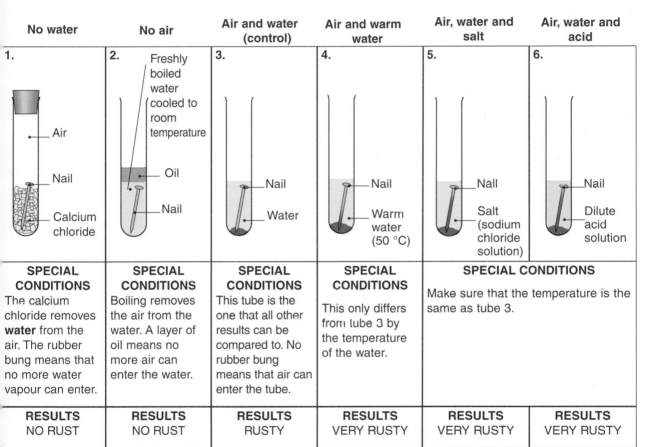

No water	No air	Air and water (control)	Air and warm water	Air, water and salt	Air, water and acid
1. Air — Nail — Calcium chloride	2. Freshly boiled water cooled to room temperature — Oil — Nail	3. Nail — Water	4. Nail — Warm water (50 °C)	5. Nail — Salt (sodium chloride solution)	6. Nail — Dilute acid solution
SPECIAL CONDITIONS The calcium chloride removes **water** from the air. The rubber bung means that no more water vapour can enter.	**SPECIAL CONDITIONS** Boiling removes the air from the water. A layer of oil means no more air can enter the water.	**SPECIAL CONDITIONS** This tube is the one that all other results can be compared to. No rubber bung means that air can enter the tube.	**SPECIAL CONDITIONS** This only differs from tube 3 by the temperature of the water.	**SPECIAL CONDITIONS** Make sure that the temperature is the same as tube 3.	
RESULTS NO RUST	**RESULTS** NO RUST	**RESULTS** RUSTY	**RESULTS** VERY RUSTY	**RESULTS** VERY RUSTY	**RESULTS** VERY RUSTY

There are three main conclusions that can be drawn from this experiment:

● Both air and water are needed for iron to rust.

● Rusting occurs more quickly in the presence of acid or salt.

● Rusting occurs more quickly at higher temperatures.

Rusting is the combination of oxygen with iron

The experiment described below shows that iron combines with **oxygen** in the air when rusting takes place.

Rusting and oxygen

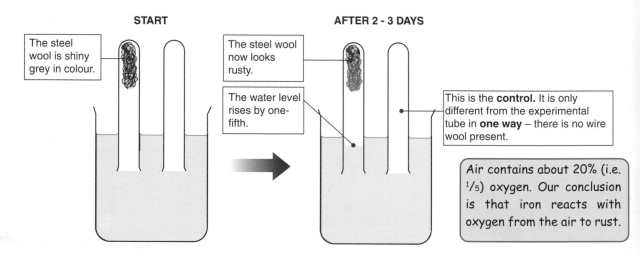

START	AFTER 2 - 3 DAYS

The steel wool is shiny grey in colour.

The steel wool now looks rusty.

The water level rises by one-fifth.

This is the **control.** It is only different from the experimental tube in **one way** – there is no wire wool present.

Air contains about 20% (i.e. $1/5$) oxygen. Our conclusion is that iron reacts with oxygen from the air to rust.

Look back at the investigation on page 239. Think about two ways in which you could speed up this experiment so that you didn't have to to wait for 2-3 days.

So, rusting is the combination of iron with oxygen. The material that we call **rust**, that is the brown flaky material that forms on iron and steel, is actually a special kind of oxide called **hydrated iron oxide**. The word equation for the formation of rust is:

$$\text{iron + oxygen + water} \longrightarrow \text{hydrated iron oxide (rust)}$$

Once we have understood the conditions needed for rusting to occur, we can explain some observations that we can make about rusting in different conditions.

Rusting is a problem because the hydrated iron oxide is very brittle (breaks easily) and weak. Since so many man-made objects get their strength from iron or steel, this weakening could be extremely dangerous. For example, many cars must be scrapped because the bodywork has rusted, even though the mechanical parts, such as the engine and gearbox, are still working quite well.

Understanding rusting

There is almost no water in the desert air.

Crashed aircraft in the desert **do not rust!**

Acid in rain water speeds up rusting.

The salt in sea water speeds up rusting.

Warning buoys soon **go rusty!**

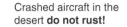

A 1960s sports car in California. Cars rust faster where there is acid rain - it doesn't rain much in California.

Deep in the ocean it is cold and there is almost no dissolved oxygen.

Sunken ships in deep oceans hardly rust at all.

Prevention of rusting

Because iron and steel are so important in, for example, building and engineering, they must be protected from corrosion. There are two ways in which iron and steel can be protected:

- by forming a **physical barrier** to keep out air and water; or

- by attaching the iron to a more reactive metal that can oxidise more easily than the iron does. This is known as **sacrificial protection**.

The diagram on the next page describes these two methods.

Prevention of corrosion

Barrier methods keep air and water out

OIL or **GREASE** keep water away from moving parts of machinery, e.g. a bike chain.

'TIN' CANS are about 99% steel (cheap) with a very thin covering of tin (very expensive). This protects the steel, especially from acid foods such as tinned fruits.

PAINTING a cover onto steel in a bridge. Paint is cheap and a large area can be covered quickly.

A PLASTIC COATING can be put on a chain-link fence.

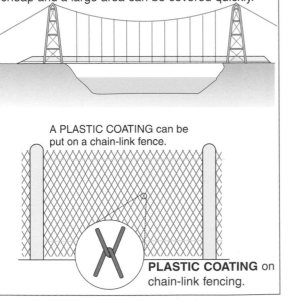

PLASTIC COATING on chain-link fencing.

Sacrificial protection

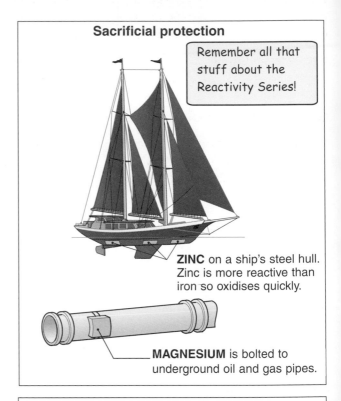

Remember all that stuff about the Reactivity Series!

ZINC on a ship's steel hull. Zinc is more reactive than iron so oxidises quickly.

MAGNESIUM is bolted to underground oil and gas pipes.

ZINC COATING (GALVANISING) on steel in buckets and screws combines a physical barrier with a sacrificial metal, but:

● it is expensive; and

● the zinc adds extra weight.

ELECTROPLATING uses electricity to put a thin layer of an attractive (but expensive) metal onto iron or steel. Chrome parts on a car or motorbike are steel with a very thin layer of chromium on top.

Once rust starts to appear on metal, it must be rubbed away (usually with sandpaper) and then the base metal can be carefully repainted.

Each method has certain advantages and disadvantages.

Physical barriers are often cheap and can be used to cover large areas of iron or steel. The main disadvantage is that once the coating is scratched or damaged, then air and water can get to the iron and rusting will begin. Physical barriers cannot be used if the iron is being rubbed or worn, such as when it is made up into railway lines.

Sacrificial protection can be used to **cover** areas of iron or steel that are often bumped or rubbed during normal use. The method is usually more expensive than coating, and the more reactive metal will eventually be used up.

Galvanising involves both types of protection

Iron and steel can be protected by coating them in a thin layer of zinc. This is usually done by dipping the metal object in a big bath of molten zinc. Thirty per cent of all the zinc extracted from the Earth is used for **galvanising**, which is the name given to this process. Galvanising is used:

- For car panels, especially in more expensive cars.
- For motorway crash barriers.
- For dustbins.
- For iron roofing sheets.
- For girders used to support parts of buildings.

The zinc acts as a barrier against corrosion by keeping out air and water. The advantage of this type of coating is that if it is scratched, the iron is still protected, as zinc is a more reactive metal.

Key words

Corrosion – damage to a metal due to combination with oxygen from the air.

Rusting – the corrosion of iron.

Oxide – a compound of an element with oxygen.

Galvanising – protection of a metal by coating it with zinc.

Oxidation – a chemical reaction in which an element is combined with oxygen.

Exercise 17.2: Corrosion

1. Copy and complete these paragraphs:

   (a) Corrosion involves a reaction between a .... and some substance in the .... In most cases an .... is formed on the surface of the metal.

   (b) Rusting is the corrosion of .... and .... This is a dangerous process because the .... is weak and brittle. Rusting can be prevented by coating the metal with, for example, ... Another method of prevention involves 'sacrificing' a second metal, such as ....

2. The rusting of car bodies is the main reason why cars need to be scrapped.
   (a) Write a word equation for the rusting of iron.
   (b) Why do cars rust more quickly in England than in California?
   (c) Give two ways in which car manufacturers can protect cars against rust.

3. Galvanising is a method used to stop corrosion.
   (a) Why is galvanising such an effective method of protection?
   (b) Give three examples of the use of galvanising.
   (c) Why can't coating be used for preventing corrosion of railway lines?

4. A scientist was trying to work out the conditions needed for rusting. She set up 5 test tubes as shown in this diagram:

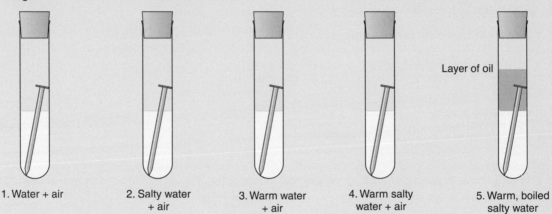

Layer of oil

| 1. Water + air | 2. Salty water + air | 3. Warm water + air | 4. Warm salty water + air | 5. Warm, boiled salty water |

After ten days she took the nails out of the tubes and measured how much of each nail was covered in rust. She wrote down the results in this Table, giving a figure of 0 if there was no rust and 1 if the nail was completely covered in rust.

Tube number	Amount of rust
1	0.4
2	0.6
3	0.7
4	1.0
5	

(a) Draw a bar chart of these results.

(b) Which had the bigger effect on rusting: salt or warmth? Give a reason for your answer.

(c) She did not write in the result for the fifth tube. What do you think the result would be? Give a reason for your answer.

Extension questions

5. Look back to question 3. Design a FAIR TEST to investigate whether galvanising offers double protection for steel.

6. Use the Internet or your library to find out about stainless steel – how is it different from iron and how is it made?

7. Gena carried out an experiment to investigate how much change in internal/thermal energy went on when magnesium reacted with a copper sulphate solution. During the reaction the magnesium replaced the copper, and the copper was left at the bottom of the tube.

She mixed different amounts of magnesium powder with copper sulphate solution in a set of boiling tubes. She carefully measured the temperature of the copper sulphate solution before she added the magnesium powder. The temperature was measured again when the reaction was completed. Her results are shown in the table below:

Mass of magnesium in g	Starting temperature in °C	Final temperature in °C	Rise in temperature in °C
0.00	22	22	
0.25	23	30	
0.50	23	38	
0.75	22	46	
1.00	22	55	
1.25	22	61	
1.50	23	68	
1.75	24	69	
2.00	23	68	
2.25	22	67	
2.50	23	68	

(a) Complete the fourth column of the table to show the **rise** in temperature.

(b) Write down a word equation for this reaction.

(c) What is the input (independent) variable for this reaction?

(d) What is the outcome (dependent) variable in this experiment?

(e) Is the reaction exothermic or endothermic?

(f) Using graph paper, plot a suitable graph of the results.

(g) Explain the shape of the curve you have plotted.

(h) What steps would need to be taken to make sure that this was a fair test?

(i) 25 g of copper sulphate solution was used in each of the experiments. What was the total mass of the chemicals in the boiling tube at the end of the experiment when 1.50 g of magnesium was added? Explain your answer.

Extraction of metals from ores

Starting point

- Metals have important properties that are useful to humans.
- Most metals are not found in a pure state in the environment but instead are found combined with other substances as ores.
- The Reactivity Series helps us to predict how difficult it will be to separate a metal from other substances.

A few metals are so unreactive that they can be found uncombined (as the element) in the ground. Because they are found as pure metals in nature, they are called **native metals**. These metals include gold, platinum and silver.

Most metals, though, are found combined with other substances in compounds – usually the compound contains the metal and either oxygen or sulphur. An **ore** is a rock or mineral that contains a metal. The rock will need to be broken down if we are to obtain the metal. There are three main steps involved in the extraction of the metal:

- Locating and mining the ore.
- Decomposing the ore to release the metal.
- Purifying the metal, so that its properties exactly suit its purpose.

Extraction

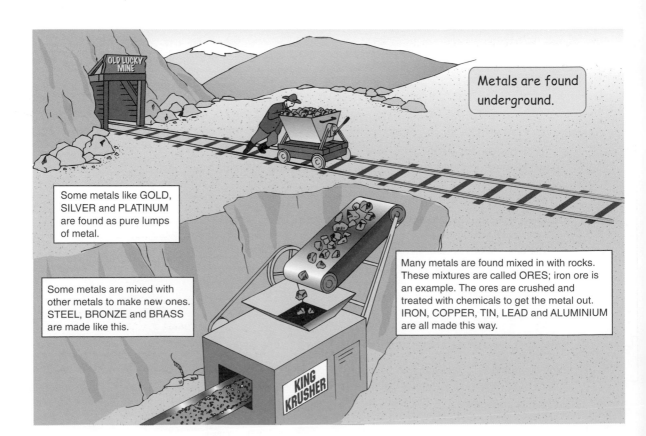

Metals are found underground.

Some metals like GOLD, SILVER and PLATINUM are found as pure lumps of metal.

Some metals are mixed with other metals to make new ones. STEEL, BRONZE and BRASS are made like this.

Many metals are found mixed in with rocks. These mixtures are called ORES; iron ore is an example. The ores are crushed and treated with chemicals to get the metal out. IRON, COPPER, TIN, LEAD and ALUMINIUM are all made this way.

IS IT WORTH IT?
To decide whether it is worth mining an ore, one needs to consider:
- How much ore there is?
- Will the mining be dangerous?
- How expensive is the extraction and purification?
- Does the metal have important uses, so that someone will want to buy it?

AND DON'T FORGET:
- Will mining and extraction damage the environment?

Methods of extraction

The extraction of metals from their ores involves chemical reactions to break down the compounds and release the metal. These chemical reactions are examples of decomposition, because the compound is decomposed (broken down). The reactions are also reduction reactions because the reactions reduce the number of elements combined with the metal. Many ores are oxides, so reduction in this case means the amount of oxygen combined with the metal is reduced.

There are three main methods that can be used to reduce ores and extract metals:

- Roasting the ore (using only thermal energy).

- Displacing the metal by heating with carbon.

- Using electrical energy to split the compound in a process called **electrolysis**.

Understanding the Reactivity Series means that scientists can predict which method will be needed. The higher up the Reactivity Series a metal is, the more stable its compounds will be. The very stable compounds will need a great deal of energy to reduce them to the pure metal. This table lists some ores, the metals they contain and the method needed to extract the metal:

Metal	Position in the Reactivity Series	Ore	Method of extraction
Aluminium	High – above carbon	Bauxite (mainly aluminium oxide)	Electrolysis
Iron	Middle – below carbon	Haematite (iron oxide)	Heating with carbon
Lead	Middle – below carbon	Galena (mainly lead sulphide)	Heating with carbon
Copper	Middle – below carbon	Malachite (mainly copper carbonate)	Heating with carbon
Mercury	Very low	Cinnabar (mainly mercury sulphide)	Heating in the air
Silver	Very low	Silver oxide (some silver is also found as 'native' silver)	Heating in the air

Thermal decomposition: Extraction by thermal energy alone

Thermal energy can decompose some compounds of the very unreactive metals. For example, silver can be produced from silver oxide by strong heating in air, as shown below:

Extraction of silver by thermal decomposition

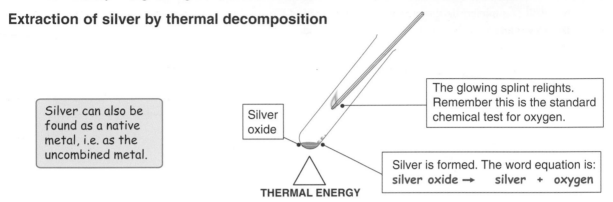

Silver can also be found as a native metal, i.e. as the uncombined metal.

Silver oxide

THERMAL ENERGY

The glowing splint relights. Remember this is the standard chemical test for oxygen.

Silver is formed. The word equation is:
silver oxide → silver + oxygen

Mercury, and sometimes copper (depending on the ore it is found in), can also be obtained in this way. This is a very inexpensive method, but it cannot be used for the compounds of the more reactive metals.

Heating with carbon: Extracting iron

Iron is the second most common metal in the Earth's crust, and is the metal most useful to humans. Fortunately the metal is not very reactive – most important is the fact that **iron is below carbon in the Reactivity Series**. The most common ore of iron is **haematite** which is made up of iron oxide and sand. The iron oxide is reduced in a set of chemical reactions that depend on the presence of carbon. This process may be carried out on an enormous scale in a Blast Furnace. Here **iron is produced by the reduction of carbon**.

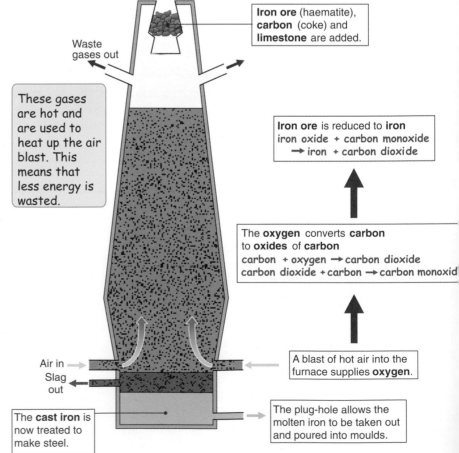

Waste gases out

These gases are hot and are used to heat up the air blast. This means that less energy is wasted.

Iron ore (haematite), carbon (coke) and limestone are added.

Iron ore is reduced to iron
iron oxide + carbon monoxide → iron + carbon dioxide

The **oxygen** converts **carbon** to **oxides** of **carbon**
carbon + oxygen → carbon dioxide
carbon dioxide + carbon → carbon monoxide

A blast of hot air into the furnace supplies **oxygen**.

The plug-hole allows the molten iron to be taken out and poured into moulds.

Air in
Slag out

Slag is a waste material, but it can be used in roof building.

Molten slag:
sand + limestone → slag

The **cast iron** is now treated to make steel.

The sand in the original ore makes the iron impure, which is why limestone is added to the furnace. The limestone reacts with silica (sand) to make a compound called calcium silicate. The molten calcium silicate, called **slag** in the steel industry, is skimmed off the top of the molten iron. This molten iron still contains about 4% carbon – it is called **cast iron** and is very brittle. Most industries need the iron to be less brittle and so the cast iron is converted to **steel**. Steel is made by removing most of the carbon and by adding small amounts of other elements. Stainless steel, for example, contains chromium and nickel as well as iron.

Decomposition by electrolysis: Extraction of aluminium

You will all have used an aluminium product, since billions of aluminium cans are made every year for the soft drinks industry! Aluminium is the most abundant metal in the Earth's crust, but it is one of the most expensive to extract. Aluminium is so high in the Reactivity Series that its compounds are very stable. A great deal of expensive energy is needed to decompose these compounds. The most common ore of aluminium is **bauxite** (mainly aluminium oxide, with some sand and some iron oxide). The extraction of aluminium has several steps:

●   Removal of impurities to make pure aluminium oxide (alumina).

●   Dissolving of the alumina in a solvent, to reduce its melting point and to make it a better conductor of electricity.

●   Electrolysis of the alumina to release pure aluminium. The most important step is the **electrolysis** stage:

Extraction of aluminium by electrolysis

Extension: How does electrolysis work?

● Electrical energy splits **aluminium oxide** into positive particles of **aluminium** and negative particles of **oxygen.**

● Positive particles move towards the negative electrode, and negative particles move towards the positive electrode.

● The negative electrode neutralises positive **aluminium** particles ➞ **aluminium metal.**

● The positive electrode neutralises negative **oxygen** particles ➞ **oxygen molecules.**

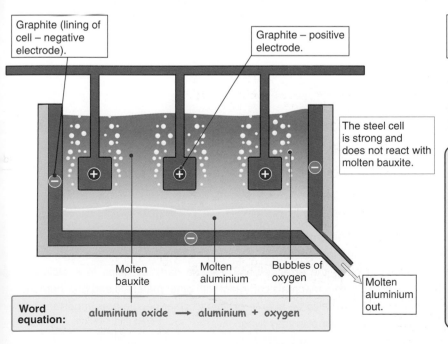

Graphite (lining of cell – negative electrode).

Graphite – positive electrode.

Electrical energy is split between the two electrodes.

This process is very expensive:
●   a lot of electricity is used; and
●   a lot of thermal energy is used to melt the Bauxite.

The steel cell is strong and does not react with molten bauxite.

Aluminium has many uses, such as making aircraft panels and window frames, for two main reasons:
●   it has a **low density**, i.e. large pieces are very light in weight; and
●   it quickly gets covered with a layer of oxide which protects it from any more corrosion.

Molten bauxite

Molten aluminium

Bubbles of oxygen

Molten aluminium out.

Word equation: aluminium oxide ➞ aluminium + oxygen

The process of electrolysis requires large amounts of electricity and so is very expensive. It is only used for metals that are high in the Reactivity Series, like calcium, magnesium and aluminium, and for those which are very valuable for human activities. Fortunately, aluminium can easily be recycled by melting down used cans etc. This is cheaper and more environmentally friendly than extracting fresh aluminium from the ore.

Key words

Ore – a rock that contains a metal.

Decomposition – a type of chemical reaction that breaks down a single substance into several products.

Reduction – a chemical reaction in which substances lose oxygen or gain hydrogen.

Electrolysis – a decomposition that uses electrical energy to split a substance into several products.

Exercise 17.3: Extraction of metals

1. Copy and complete this paragraph:

    Some metals, such as .... and silver, are found as the uncombined metal in nature. Most metals are found combined as .... in ...., such as haematite and bauxite. There are three stages in the extraction of a metal: ...., ... (which always involves some chemical reactions) and .... (which makes the metal suitable for use).

2. Copy and complete this table:

Metal	Main ore	One important use of the metal	Method of extraction
Gold			
	Haematite		
		Wire for the conduction of electricity	
Bauxite			
Mercury			

3. Write out word equations for each of the following chemical reactions:

    (a) The thermal decomposition of mercury oxide.

    (b) The use of carbon to reduce tin oxide.

    (c) The electrolysis of calcium oxide.

Everything that we know of is made up of materials. The properties of these materials have a huge impact on how useful they are to humans. Now that you have finished this section of your science course, you should understand how materials are made up of tiny particles, and how the arrangement of these particles helps to explain the properties of the materials. You will also know how different materials can react with other materials and how humans can affect how easily these reactions can go on. You will also be able to explain to other people how important it is we know something of the parts played by materials in our everyday lives.

Chapter 18
What is energy?

Nothing can happen without energy. You use energy when you lift a mobile phone to your ear and the mobile phone uses energy to send a message. Energy is used whenever a force makes something move. The more energy that is used, the greater the force generated and the further something is moved. Energy is used to heat things up; the tiny particles that make up all matter move faster when they are given more energy. Many scientists would say that life depends on using energy. Once the body cannot use energy to keep all its molecules in the right places, then the body is dead! All these different things that energy is used for are examples of **work**. So, we could define energy like this:

Energy is the measure of:

(a) **work** that **has been done**; and

(b) **work** that **is able to be done.**

There are different forms of energy

Energy can take different forms:

Chemical energy

Energy stored in a FOOD, a FUEL or in an ELECTRIC CELL. The energy is released during a chemical reaction (burning, for example – see page 214).

Electrical energy

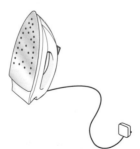

Energy due to electrical charges moving. For example, electric current in a wire.

Internal/thermal energy

Energy due to fast-moving particles in hot objects. For example, internal/thermal energy is transferred from the open fire to the room and the people sitting in it.

Electrical energy is the most convenient form of energy, because it is so easily converted into other forms, and because it can be transmitted over long distances by wires.

In addition to **chemical, electrical and internal/thermal (heat) energy,** there is:

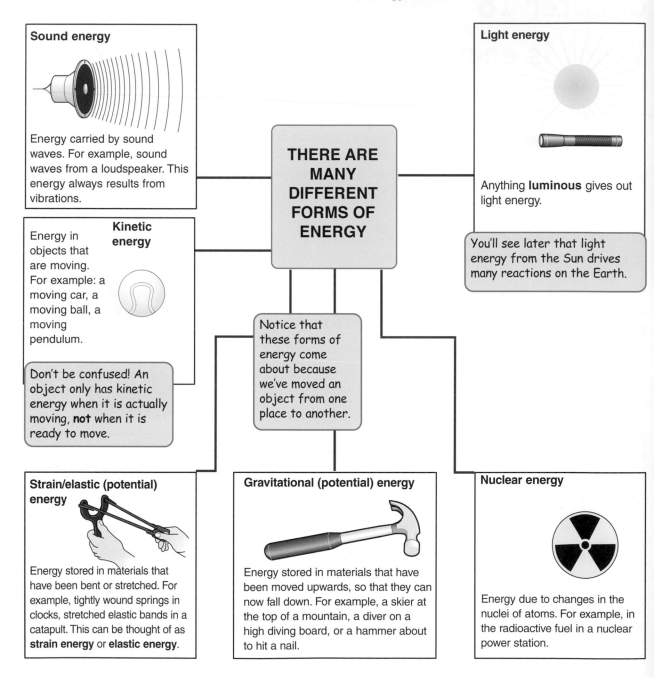

Sound energy

Energy carried by sound waves. For example, sound waves from a loudspeaker. This energy always results from vibrations.

Light energy

Anything **luminous** gives out light energy.

You'll see later that light energy from the Sun drives many reactions on the Earth.

THERE ARE MANY DIFFERENT FORMS OF ENERGY

Kinetic energy

Energy in objects that are moving. For example: a moving car, a moving ball, a moving pendulum.

Don't be confused! An object only has kinetic energy when it is actually moving, **not** when it is ready to move.

Notice that these forms of energy come about because we've moved an object from one place to another.

Strain/elastic (potential) energy

Energy stored in materials that have been bent or stretched. For example, tightly wound springs in clocks, stretched elastic bands in a catapult. This can be thought of as **strain energy** or **elastic energy**.

Gravitational (potential) energy

Energy stored in materials that have been moved upwards, so that they can now fall down. For example, a skier at the top of a mountain, a diver on a high diving board, or a hammer about to hit a nail.

Nuclear energy

Energy due to changes in the nuclei of atoms. For example, in the radioactive fuel in a nuclear power station.

These different forms of energy do not just vanish when they are used. Energy can be changed from one form into another; this is called **transforming energy**.

An every day example of transferring energy is shown below:

An athlete gives out internal/thermal energy.

Respiration releases chemical energy from food.

An athlete gains movement (kinetic) energy.

The standard unit of energy is the **joule (J)**. One joule isn't really very much energy and the number of joules used to carry out a particular piece of work might be very large, so larger amounts of energy are usually measured in **kilojoules (kJ)**. 1 kJ = 1000 joules. Here are some examples of different amounts of energy:

Joule, the scientist after whose work the unit of energy is named.

Typical energy values	Joules	Examples
Strain/elastic (potential) energy: Stretched rubber band	1 J	
Gravitational (potential) energy You, on top of a step-ladder	500 J	
Kinetic energy: Kicked football	50 J	
Small car at 70 mph	500 000 J	
Internal/thermal energy: Hot cup of tea	150 000 J	
Chemical energy: Torch battery	10 000 J	
Chocolate biscuit	300 000 J	
Litre of petrol	35 000 000 J	

How many kJ of energy are there in 10 litres of petrol?

Energy chains

Energy can be transformed from one form to another. These changes of energy are called **energy chains**. (Do you remember food chains – the flow of energy from one living organism to another? See page 99.) In every energy chain the *total* amount of energy *stays the same* even though the *energy is changed from one form to another*. Scientists have measured many different examples of these energy transformations and have written down their observations as the **Law of Conservation of Energy**:

Energy cannot be made or destroyed but it can change from one form to another.

i.e. the total amount of energy at the start = the total amount of energy at the end

Here is an example of an energy chain

| Chemical energy | Kinetic energy (movement) | Potential energy | Kinetic energy (movement) | Thermal energy Sound |

ENERGY CHAIN

● Energy is never created nor destroyed, just changed from one form to another.

● Some energy is always lost as thermal energy (for example, you get hotter when you convert chemical energy to kinetic energy when you exercise).

● Living things, machines and electrical appliances convert (transfer) energy from one type to another (see page 280).

Describing energy changes

Energy is transformed when it changes from one form to another. For example, an electric kettle can transform electrical energy into internal/thermal energy. A simple way to write down these changes is shown here:

Electrical energy ⟶ KETTLE ⟶ Internal/thermal energy

This means that electrical energy is transferred to the kettle.

This means that energy is transferred to the water as internal/thermal energy.

Anything that can change one form of energy to another is called a **transducer**. Many machines are transducers. Machines use energy to carry out work.

Key words

Work – any process that uses up energy.

Joule – a unit of energy (energy exerted when a force of one newton is applied over a displacement of one metre).

Transform – the change of energy from one form to another, e.g. electrical energy into internal/thermal energy.

Energy – the capacity for doing work (a measure of work done or able to be done).

Law of conservation of energy – energy cannot be created nor destroyed (although it can be changed from one form into another).

Machine – a device that can use energy to carry out work.

Exercise 18.1: Energy

1. Complete these paragraphs, using words from this list:

   energy   joules   elastic   electrical   light   work   kinetic

   thermal   transformed   machine

   (a) To carry out any action, ... is needed. All of these different types of action can be called ....
   Energy comes in different forms. For example, ... energy is stored in materials that have been
   stretched or bent. .... energy is the energy of movement. .... energy is the result of fast-moving
   particles in hot objects.

   (b) Energy cannot be created or destroyed, but it can be .... from one form to another. For example, a
   torch changes .... energy into .... energy. Energy is measured in units called ....

2. A fire gives out 20 kJ of energy. How many joules is this?

3. A machine is a device for doing work. Use this list of machines to complete the table below:

   torch   radio   catapult   toaster   fan   motor car

Machine (transducer)	Energy is changed from	to (mainly)
	Electrical	Sound
	Electrical	Thermal
	Electrical	Kinetic
	Chemical	Kinetic
	Potential	Kinetic
	Electrical	Light

4. Describe the energy changes that take place when:
   (a) You throw a ball up into the air.
   (b) You pull on the brakes of your mountain bike.

5. Scientists say that energy can never be created nor destroyed. Explain what they mean, and say whether you
   think this statement is true or not.

Energy resources

Starting points

- Energy is needed to do work.

- There are different forms of energy and energy can be changed from one form to another.

- Chemical energy is stored in fuels. The energy from fuel can be released by a chemical reaction, such as burning.

You would not be able to read this book without energy; your brain requires energy to form images of the words and pictures on a page and to understand what these images mean. Where does this energy come from? Your body uses **food** as a source of energy (see page 46). The food is the fuel that supplies the energy for the processes of life.

Cities and towns also need large amounts of energy. Heating, lighting, transport and industry all use up energy. Much of the energy for running cities comes from **fossil fuels**. Coal, gas and oil are called *fossil* fuels because they come from the bodies of prehistoric animals and plants. Fossil fuels took millions of years to form and we are using them up much more quickly than that. We need to conserve fuels by reducing the amount of energy that we use.

In some parts of the world, **water** can be used to generate energy, for example by harnessing tides and waves.

Electricity can also be generated by rivers in mountainous countries. Rivers are dammed to form large lakes and water is then allowed to flow steadily through large turbines. This is called **hydroelectric** power and is a well-established source that contributes to world energy production at a level approaching 3%.

Other energy sources are **solar power** in sunny regions and **wind power** in windy areas. If you go to Cornwall, for example, you will see many wind turbines perched on top of hills, turning in the wind.

Water power, wind power and solar power are all **renewable energy resources** because they can be replaced naturally and so will not run out.

Of all the renewable energy resources, hydroelectric power contributes the most energy but still produce much less than coal, oil and nuclear, all of which contribute large amounts to world energy production. The renewables contribute much lower amounts of energy, are costly or unreliable, or are only available in particular places on a small scale.

Another source of energy we must consider is the energy produced by splitting atoms (for atoms, see page 191). This breaking up of atoms can be made to happen very rapidly, with a great release of energy. This energy source is called **nuclear power**. The thermal energy produced in nuclear reactors can be used to boil water and to drive a turbine which generates electricity, just as in coal and power stations.

We can get the energy we need in many different ways. However, the information we have on existing and projected energy supplies from the traditional energy sources (coal, oil and natural gas) indicates that they will increasingly be unable to satisfy our energy needs. Unless new energy sources are developed, there is the likelihood of a serious energy shortage in the not-so-distant future. One of the challenges we face is how to choose which energy source will give the energy the world needs as reliably, safely and cheaply as possible, with the least harm to the environment. This is the basis of the **world energy crisis**.

The table below summarises some of the issues associated with these possible energy sources:

Source	Advantages	Disadvantages	Lifetime
Wood	Easy to find.	Limited amount. Destruction of rainforests.	
Biomass	Easy to do.	Uneconomic.	
Fossil fuels			
Coal	Many deposits.	Pollution.	Approx. 250 years*
Oil	Easy to extract.	Pollution.	Approx. 60 years*
Gas	Easy to extract.	Pollution.	Approx. 60 years*
Renewable			
Hydro	Uses naturally occurring valleys in mountainous regions to channel water.	Limited number of rivers. Destructive to environment when valleys are flooded.	Unlimited
Wind	Large amounts of energy.	Expensive to concentrate. Wind does not always blow. Unsightly additions to landscape. Wind farms take up large areas of land.	Unlimited
Solar	Large amounts of energy but it is not always sunny. Solar power is more economical in sunnier countries.	Expensive to concentrate. Sun does not shine all the time.	Unlimited
Wave	Large amounts of energy.	Expensive to concentrate. Damage to environment.	Unlimited
Nuclear	Non-polluting	Radioactive waste.	Unlimited

These figures are based on the lifetime of current reserves and do not account for the discovery of new reserves or new extraction technologies being developed (see page 273).

You may be wondering what we mean by 'expensive to concentrate'? Well, quite simply, concentration is a measure of how spread out the energy is. The more spread out it is, the more it costs to gather it all together to create a usable piece of electricity. For example, there is enough energy in the air of a room to boil a kettle, but how would you trap it and turn it into electricity?

In the case of wind and solar sources, the energy is spread out over a large area and so it **costs a lot** to put it in a concentrated form that can be used. In the case of coal, oil and gas, the energy is very concentrated and in the case of nuclear even more so. If energy is not concentrated, you cannot use it. So, the extent to which a fuel is concentrated plays a very important part in helping us to decide which source will provide the most reliable, safe and cheap energy, with the least harm to the environment in the future.

Key words

Biomass – material in the bodies of plants or animals. A **biomass fuel** is plant material that can be burned to release energy.

Energy – a measure of work done or able to be done.

Fuel – a store of energy that can go through a reaction to release the energy.

Fossil fuel – remains of long-dead animals and plants.

Renewable – an energy source that can be replaced naturally, and so will not run out.

Nuclear – energy released from the nucleus of an atom.

Exercise 18.2: Energy resources

1. Complete the following paragraphs. Use words from this list:

    Bunsen   energy   thermal   fossil   renewable   oxygen   natural gas   potential

    (a) A fuel is a store of .... which can be released by burning in air. The air supplies the .... required for the burning process. Burning a candle shows that .... energy and light energy are given out during the burning process. In the laboratory a .... burner can give a controllable supply of thermal energy by the burning of ....

    (b) Coal and gas are examples of .... fuels – once they are burned, they cannot be replaced. Water and wind power are .... energy resources because they can be naturally replaced and so will not run out.

Extension questions

2. This table shows how energy is being used in the United Kingdom:

Use of energy	Percentage of total energy used
Industry	29
Domestic (in homes)	31
Transport	26
Other uses	

    (a) Work out the percentage of energy used for other purposes.

    (b) Plot a bar chart of these figures.

    (c) Give two uses of energy that might be in the other uses category.

    (d) Make a list of five different ways we use energy in the home.

3. This table shows the sources of energy generated in the United Kingdom in 1999:

Source	Percentage generation
Oil	1.5
Natural gas	38.5
Coal	30.0
Nuclear	26.3
Hydro	1.5
Other	

International Atomic Energy Agency (Nuclear Issues, Nov 2000, p. 5, Vol. 22, No. 11, 1999, Electricity in the U.K.)

(a) Work out the percentage of 'other sources of energy.

(b) What is the most likely source of energy in the other category?

(c) Make a pie chart of this information.

(d) Give two reasons why we should use less coal and oil.

(e) Give one reason why we *should* use more nuclear power, and one reason why we are *anxious* about using nuclear power.

Fossil fuels

Don't forget

● A fuel can be burned to release energy.

● Fossil fuels are made from the bodies of prehistoric animals and plants.

Coal, oil and natural gas are called **fossil fuels** because they were formed millions of years ago. These fuels are the remains of organic material, such as the bodies of dead animals and plants which have not been allowed to decompose for one reason or another. Fossil fuels store **chemical energy** which can be released as other forms of energy, such as thermal and light, when the fuels are burnt. Because fossil fuels take so long to form and cannot be remade from the products of burning, they are known as **non-renewable** (sometimes called **capital**) **resources**. We cannot replace them, so they will eventually run out.

Fossil fuels are common energy resources

COAL is used for heating homes (not so much nowadays) and in power stations for generating electricity.

PETROL and DIESEL are made from oil. They are used as fuel for cars, lorries, ships and boats. More and more engines use diesel because it is more economical.

FUEL + OXYGEN

⬇

CARBON DIOXIDE + WATER
+

ENERGY

NATURAL GAS is mainly methane. It is used for heating and cooking in homes and factories, and in power stations for generating electricity.

KEROSENE (PARAFFIN) is a cheap fuel made from oil. It is used domestically for heating, and industrially as fuel for aircraft.

There may be other wastes, such as ash and sulphur dioxide.

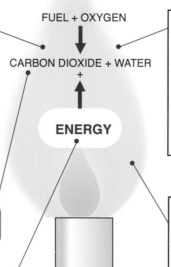

BUTANE and PROPANE are used in camping and caravan stoves for cooking and in home gas heaters. It is pressurised for storage as liquid, and can be used as LPG (Liquified Petroleum Gas) in cars and vans.

There will be light, thermal and perhaps some kinetic energy.

The formation of fossil fuels

Plants use sunlight energy to store chemical energy in the molecules that make up their bodies. Millions of years ago some of these plants would have been eaten by small animals, and some of them would have died before they were eaten. Dead animals and plants are usually quickly decomposed by the action of fungi and bacteria, but conditions in the environment might make this happen more slowly. It is the chemical energy in the bodies of these long-dead and partly-decomposed animals and plants that is released when we burn fossil fuels. Look at the diagram below to see how fossil fuels are formed:

Stages in the formation of coal: Fossil fuel from trees

Tree ferns lived 300 million years ago. As they died, they fell down and began to rot. The decay was very slow and the rotting plants formed a thick layer on the wet and swampy floor of the forest.

> Bacteria change the decaying plants to PEAT. This can be used as a fuel.

The land sank and layers of mud and rock were laid over the peat. As more and more rocks were laid down, the peat was exposed to **greater pressure and higher temperature.**

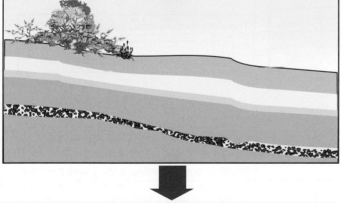

Over millions of years the layers turned into hard coal. The coal is collected by digging pits and mines.

> Because decay is slow, coal often contains fossils of plants from 300 million years ago. The period when coal was formed is called the **Carboniferous Period.**

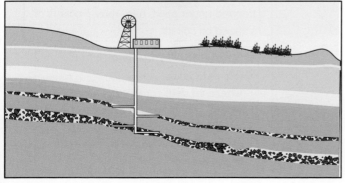

Oil and natural gas: Fossil fuels from the sea

Microscopic plants and animals have trapped chemical energy in their bodies. When these organisms die, their bodies sink to the bottom of the sea.

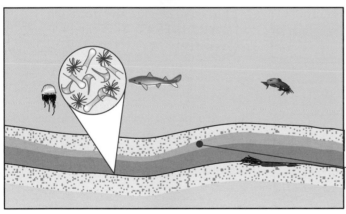

The bodies are covered by layers of mud and sand. As the bodies decay, they are changed to thick black **crude oil** by **high temperatures and pressures.**

The sedimentary rocks laid down in the sea are porous. The tiny holes allow liquids to move slowly through the rock.

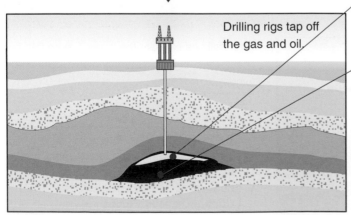

Drilling rigs tap off the gas and oil.

Some decay continues and provides gas (mainly methane). This is less dense than the oil and so collects on the top of the oil.

As the rock layers fold, crude oil becomes trapped under solid, hard rock. Pockets of trapped oil collect.

KNOWLEDGE IS POWER!
Geologists know:
- where to drill for oil;
- where sedimentary rocks are found;
- where folding has occurred; and
- where sound wave reflection tells them the rock is missing.

Using fossil fuels

Wood (not a fossil fuel) was the first fuel to be used by humans from the time they first discovered fire. But from the nineteenth century onwards, humans began to use fossil fuels extensively. Coal was the easiest to extract from the Earth, and so this was the first fossil fuel to be widely used. Oil and gas were not produced or used much until the twentieth century. By the end of the twentieth century oil and gas were more commonly used than coal. Oil can be used to make petrol and diesel fuel for motor vehicles, and to make many of the molecules needed for man-made materials, such as plastics and fabrics. All fossil fuels make carbon dioxide when they are burned, but coal is dirtier than gas and oil because it makes a lot of ash and smoke.

Check back on the sections in your book that deal with combustion (see page 214) and the use of the Bunsen burner (see page 131) and remind yourself of the disadvantages of using fossil fuels (see below).

Different fuels for different uses

A fuel is a source of energy, so we might think that the most important thing about a fuel is the amount of energy it gives out when it is burned. This is important but it is not the only thing to consider. Other important factors are:

● Can the fuel be stored?

● Can the fuel be transported?

● Is the fuel easy to extract from the Earth?

● Is the fuel clean to use?

● Is the fuel solid, liquid or gas?

● Is it easy to ignite the fuel (to start it burning)?

● How much does it cost to extract the energy from the fuel?

Some fuels are better than others for a particular job. For example, petrol is a better fuel for cars than coal; you can deliver it through a hose from a petrol pump, and it is easier to ignite. Gas is a good fuel for camping stoves because it can be compressed into lightweight gas bottles that are easy and safe to carry.

Fossil fuels and electricity

Electricity is not a fuel, but most of it is produced by burning fossil fuels. These fuels are reliable, concentrated forms of energy, but do need to be transported from where they are extracted to where they are burned in the power stations. You've seen some of this in the previous section, but let's just summarize some of the advantages and disadvantages of generating electricity from these different fossil fuels:

Fossil fuel	Advantages	Disadvantages
Coal	Still large deposits of this fuel available, enough for the next 200-300 years approximately.	Extraction and burning makes pollution.
Natural gas	Burns with less pollution than coal or oil.	Difficult to find.
Oil	Can easily be transported in pipelines.	Oil spills are very harmful to wildlife.

Conservation of fuel reserves

It is important that we save fossil fuels because:

- they are **non-renewable** and are running out; and

- burning them is the main cause of **air pollution**.

Fuels can be conserved by:

- increasing the use of alternative, renewable energy sources (see page 267) and nuclear power;

- using more efficient machines; and

- being more careful with the use of energy (see page 275).

Exercise 18.3: Fossil fuels

1. Here are some statements about coal. Sort them out to tell the story of the formation of coal:

    - The rivers washed sediment on top.

    - The material was heated under pressure for millions of years.

    - Coal is a store of chemical energy.

    - When trees died, they fell into swamps but did not decompose.

    - The Sun shone onto the Earth, and the trees absorbed light energy from the Sun.

    - More trees fell on top.

    - 300 million years ago there were huge forests of simple, fern-like trees.

2. Here are some statements about oil and natural gas. Sort them into the correct order to tell the story of the formation of these fuels:

    - People build oil platforms to drill for oil.

    - Thermal energy and pressure changed the material in the bodies of plants and animals into oil.

    - The small organisms died.

    - The plants were eaten by small animals in the sea.

    - The Sun shone on the Earth and tiny plants in the sea obtained their energy from the Sun.

    - Movements of the Earth compressed the remains of the small organisms.

    - Gas pipelines bring gas to homes and factories.

    - Sediment piled up on the bodies.

    - Conditions change, so that some bodies are allowed to decay.

    - Gas is collected from above the oil wells.

    - Over millions of years, gas given off from the decay processes is trapped.

    - When the seas dried up, the small organisms became trapped.

3. What are the two reasons why it is important to conserve fuels?

4. Wood only gives out 10 kJ of energy per gram of fuel burned, but oil gives out 46 kJ of energy per gram. Why do you think that wood is so popular as a fuel in Norway?

Extension question

5. This table contains information about the use of coal, gas and oil in the European Community (1973-1989):

Millions of tons used			
Year	Coal	Oil	Natural gas
1973	232	646	116
1979	235	622	174
1986	230	505	187
1989	229	509	199

Nuclear Power, Energy and the Environment, P.E. Hodgson

(a) Plot this information as a line graph.

(b) What percentage of the total fossil fuel used in 1973 was natural gas?

(c) Use the graph and the table to decide whether our total use of fossil fuels has changed since 1970.

Renewable energy resources

Reminders

- Energy is a measure of work done, or work able to be done.

- Energy is stored in fuels.

- When fuels are burnt to release energy, they are used up and cannot be replaced.

What does renewable mean?

Renewable energy sources do not get smaller as they are used. For example, collecting energy from the wind does not change the amount of wind energy that will be available in the future. Renewable energy resources are sometimes called **alternative** energy resources, because they are seen as an alternative to the use of fossil fuels.

There are some important points to remember about renewable energy resources:

- they are not used up; and

- they do not pollute the atmosphere.

However, with the partial exception of hydropower:

- they are several times more expensive than fossil fuels (except hydro);

- they can be unreliable and available only in particular places on a small scale;

- they contribute very little energy (except hydro); and

- they can have bad environmental effects.

What types of renewable energy are available?

Whatever form of renewable energy is available, it must be converted into a form of energy that we can use. Most of our machines and appliances work on electrical energy, so a renewable energy source must be capable of conversion into electricity (with the exception of solar panels which enable the Sun to heat the water directly, and water from hot springs and geysers).

Electricity is generated using a **turbine** and a **generator**, as shown below.

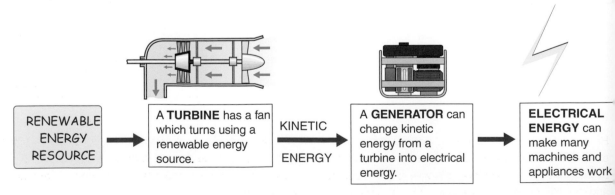

| RENEWABLE ENERGY RESOURCE | → | A **TURBINE** has a fan which turns using a renewable energy source. | KINETIC ENERGY | A **GENERATOR** can change kinetic energy from a turbine into electrical energy. | → | **ELECTRICAL ENERGY** can make many machines and appliances work |

There are several different forms of renewable energy. Engineers tend to use the one that is most available – this can be very different from one country to another. For example, **hydroelectric power** is only available in mountainous areas with swift-flowing rivers (Scotland, for example) and **geothermal power** (electric power generated using very hot water or steam which breaks through the Earth's surface from the hot interior) is only available in areas with hot springs and geysers (New Zealand, for example). Here are some alternative sources of renewable energy made available to us through the skill of engineers:

Renewable energy resources

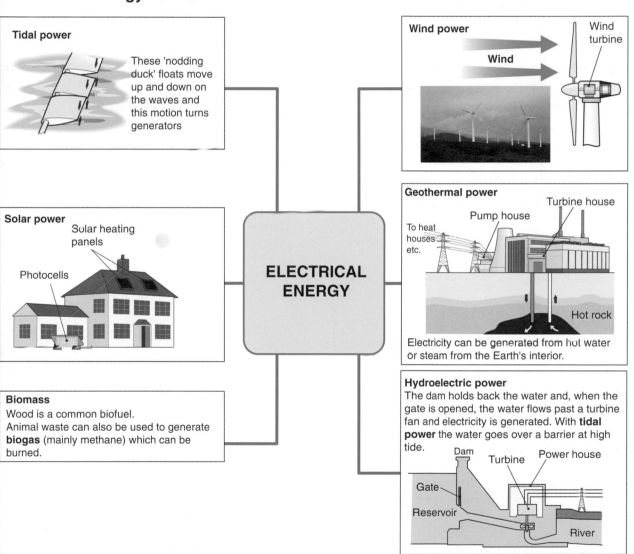

Tidal power

These 'nodding duck' floats move up and down on the waves and this motion turns generators

Solar power

Solar heating panels

Photocells

Biomass

Wood is a common biofuel.
Animal waste can also be used to generate **biogas** (mainly methane) which can be burned.

ELECTRICAL ENERGY

Wind power

Wind turbine

Wind

Geothermal power

Turbine house

Pump house

To heat houses etc.

Hot rock

Electricity can be generated from hot water or steam from the Earth's interior.

Hydroelectric power
The dam holds back the water and, when the gate is opened, the water flows past a turbine fan and electricity is generated. With **tidal power** the water goes over a barrier at high tide.

Dam

Turbine

Power house

Gate

Reservoir

River

Here is a final note on renewables before we move on. **Wind power** is the most promising of the renewables (with the exception of hydroelectric power), and it hoped that wind might provide as much as 10% of Europe's electricity needs by 2030. At the present level of power generation, the renewables are not in the same league as coal, oil and nuclear and they cannot provide a solution for the world energy crisis (see page 256).

The Sun provides many of our energy resources

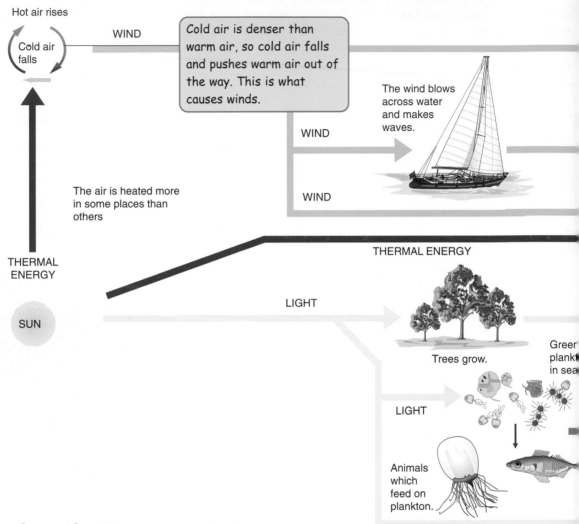

Hot air rises

Cold air falls

WIND

Cold air is denser than warm air, so cold air falls and pushes warm air out of the way. This is what causes winds.

The wind blows across water and makes waves.

WIND

WIND

The air is heated more in some places than others

THERMAL ENERGY

THERMAL ENERGY

SUN

LIGHT

Trees grow.

Green plankton in sea

LIGHT

Animals which feed on plankton.

Energy from the Sun

The Sun supplies almost all the energy on Earth. Plants trap the Sun's energy and change it into stored chemical energy in the form of food. Plants can then:

● use the food themselves;

● be eaten by animals and so pass on the chemical energy to the animals;

● die and pass on the chemical energy to bacteria and fungi; and

● die and, together with some dead animals, become trapped under conditions that favour the formation of coal, oil and natural gas.

The part that the Sun plays in the supply of our energy resources is shown above.

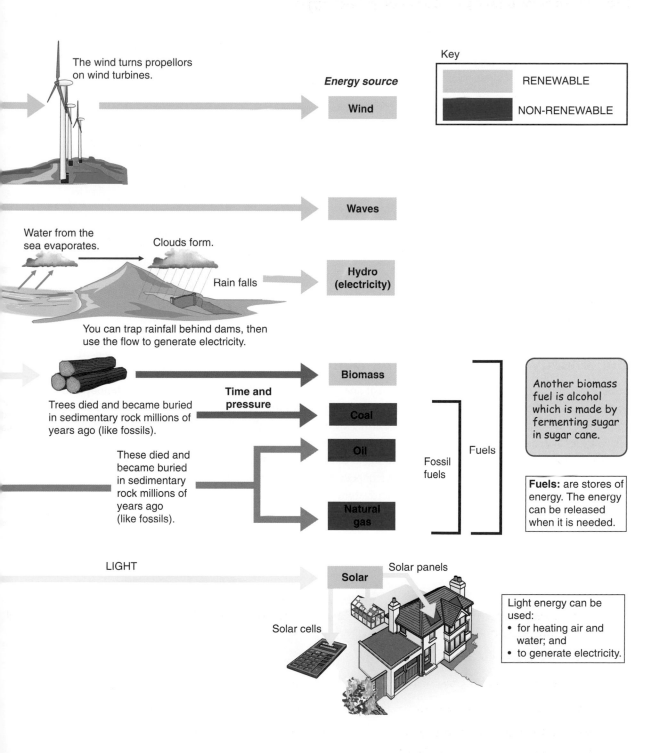

The wind turns propellors on wind turbines.

Energy source

Wind

Key

RENEWABLE

NON-RENEWABLE

Waves

Water from the sea evaporates.

Clouds form.

Rain falls

Hydro (electricity)

You can trap rainfall behind dams, then use the flow to generate electricity.

Biomass

Time and pressure

Trees died and became buried in sedimentary rock millions of years ago (like fossils).

Coal

Oil

These died and became buried in sedimentary rock millions of years ago (like fossils).

Natural gas

Fossil fuels

Fuels

Another biomass fuel is alcohol which is made by fermenting sugar in sugar cane.

Fuels: are stores of energy. The energy can be released when it is needed.

LIGHT

Solar

Solar panels

Solar cells

Light energy can be used:
- for heating air and water; and
- to generate electricity.

There are some energy sources which don't depend on the Sun.

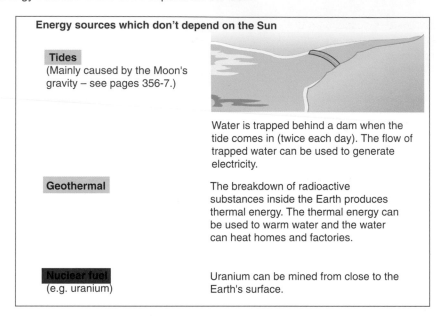

Energy sources which don't depend on the Sun	
Tides (Mainly caused by the Moon's gravity – see pages 356-7.)	
	Water is trapped behind a dam when the tide comes in (twice each day). The flow of trapped water can be used to generate electricity.
Geothermal	The breakdown of radioactive substances inside the Earth produces thermal energy. The thermal energy can be used to warm water and the water can heat homes and factories.
Nuclear fuel (e.g. uranium)	Uranium can be mined from close to the Earth's surface.

Solar energy: Energy from the Sun

All fossil fuels originally made their stored chemical energy from the sunlight energy trapped by photosynthesis (see page 68). Energy direct from the Sun is a very attractive energy source because there is no foreseeable reduction in the amount of the Sun's energy landing on the Earth. Having said that, though, it is important to remember that solar power is expensive because the Sun's energy is spread very thinly over the Earth's surface, so we have to go to a lot of trouble to concentrate it. The simplest way to make direct use of the Sun's internal/thermal energy is to put solar panels on roofs of buildings and let the Sun's rays directly heat the water running through the panels. Some solar cells (see below) change light and internal/thermal energy from the Sun into an electrical current; these are extremely useful for equipment that is a long way away from a generator, such as a space station.

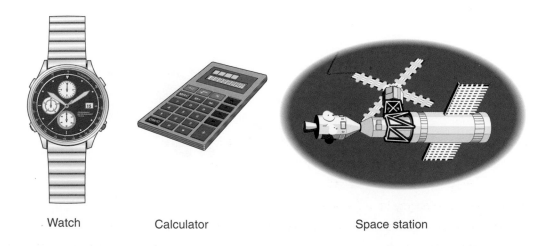

Watch   Calculator   Space station

Investigation: What factors affect the performance of solar panels?

Solar panels are designed to collect as much of the Sun's energy as possible. Several factors affect how well a solar panel absorbs solar energy. These factors are investigated here:

Step 1

- Each of the balloons contains the same volume of water.
- Both balloons are the same colour.

Step 2

- The balloons are then covered with cloth.
- The hot lamp is kept at the same distance from the balloons.
- The temperature of the water is measured at the same time for the two balloons.

Remember what makes a FAIR TEST!

- Change one variable (input or independent variable).
- Measure a second variable (outcome or dependent variable).
- Keep all other variables constant.

Step 1

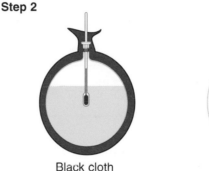

Thermometer

30 cm³ water

Step 2

Black cloth

White cloth

I.T. IN SCIENCE
The temperature can be measured with an electronic sensor.

Sensor   Datalogger

DATA logger
23°C

Lamp

Stopclock

Key words

Alternative energy – an energy source that is not a fossil fuel.

Biofuel – an energy source that is made directly by photosynthesis.

Generator – a device that changes kinetic energy into electricity.

Geothermal – thermal energy from the ground.

Renewable – an energy source that is naturally replaced (not the same as reusable!).

Turbine – a rotary engine in which kinetic energy is converted into mechanical energy by causing a blade to rotate.

Exercise 18.4: Renewable energy resources

1. Match the sentences in the second column with the resource named in the first column:

Renewable energy resource	How this resource is valuable
Solar energy	Water current turns a turbine
Geothermal energy	Can heat water or generate electricity
Wind	Sea water turns a turbine
Tides and waves	Thermal energy from underground rocks
Hydroelectric power	Material from the growth of plants
Biomass	Can move small boats or turn wind turbines

2. Why do we describe electricity as the most useful form of energy?

3. This table lists the percentage contribution of each resource to all renewable energy resources:

Energy resource	Percentage contribution
Hydroelectric	77.4
Biomass	18.6
Geothermal	1.9
Solar heating	1.9
Wind	0.2

    (a) Make a pie chart of this information.
    (b) Which renewable resource is most useful in a very forested part of the world?
    (c) Why does geothermal energy make such a small contribution?

    Energy consumption outlook in Western World 1990 (World Energy Needs and Resources)

4. This table shows the results obtained from the investigation described on page 271:

Time in minutes	Temperature in °C	
	Black cloth	White cloth
0	16	16
4	20	19
8	25	23
12	29	26
16	33	30
20	37	32

    (a) Which balloon has the warmer water after 15 minutes?
    (b) Which colour would be used for a solar panel?
    (c) Why is it important to use the same volume of water in each balloon?
    (d) Describe how you could use the same apparatus to find out whether a shiny or a dull surface is better for a solar panel.

5. Explain the difference between 'renewable' and 'reusable', when describing forms of energy.

Saving energy

Remember

- Burning fuels releases energy.
- Most of the energy we use comes from fossil fuels.
- Fossil fuels are non-renewable.

Over 70% of the energy we use in factories and for our heating, lighting and transport comes from fossil fuels.

How long will fossil fuel reserves last?

Estimate of when the World's currentlly known energy supplies will run out (1994)

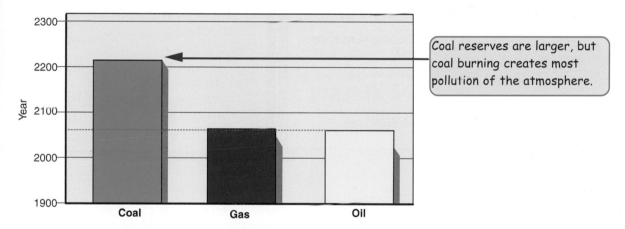

Coal reserves are larger, but coal burning creates most pollution of the atmosphere.

Nuclear Power, Energy and the Environment, P.E. Hodgson

These figures appear to be rather frightening but in fact they show what would happen if we did nothing about finding more reserves or did not develop any new technologies for extracting these fuels. As the current reserves run low, more efficient ways of extraction will be developed and we are likely to find more reserves of fossil fuels which will substantially improve the life span of oil, gas and coal.

We are getting better at using renewable energy sources (see page 266) and we are developing nuclear power but we still need to learn to make the most of the fossil fuel reserves we have. This is what is meant by **energy conservation** – using the minimum amount of energy for each particular job. Energy conservation has three main benefits:

- It will mean that the Earth's resources will last longer.
- It will cut down on costs for transport, heating, lighting and industry.
- It will reduce pollution of the atmosphere, of the land and of the sea.

However, it is interesting to note that sometimes energy conservation can make energy cheaper which can encourage people to use more of it, so it can sometimes have the opposite effect to the one we are trying to achieve.

How to save energy

There are two things to take into account when we think of ways of saving energy:

- How can we use less energy? For example, can we turn off the heating when we we do not need it?

- How can we prevent energy from being wasted? For example, can we make machines and buildings more energy efficient?

Using less energy: What can you do?

Here are some of the ways in which you can help to save energy.

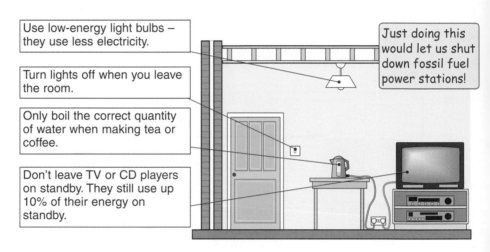

Cycle or walk to school or work – most car journeys are less than 3 miles long.

Use low-energy light bulbs – they use less electricity.

Turn lights off when you leave the room.

Only boil the correct quantity of water when making tea or coffee.

Don't leave TV or CD players on standby. They still use up 10% of their energy on standby.

Just doing this would let us shut down fossil fuel power stations!

The Government also has a part to play in helping to save energy. From the year 2000 they encouraged people to drive smaller, more efficient cars by reducing the cost of the Road Fund Licence (the tax on cars for using the roads) for cars with engines less than 1.4 litres in size.

This car does 50 miles per gallon of fuel (and the car was made completely from recycled materials).

This car does fewer than 20 miles per gallon of fuel and often carries only one passenger.

Thermal energy and the home

A lot of fossil fuel is burned so that we can heat our homes and other buildings. When the internal/thermal energy escapes into the atmosphere, it is lost to us and can never be used again. This is a waste of energy and of money. Scientists understand how thermal energy can be lost and they can give advice to builders on how to reduce losses of thermal energy.

Here are some ways to prevent internal/thermal energy loss from a house or building.

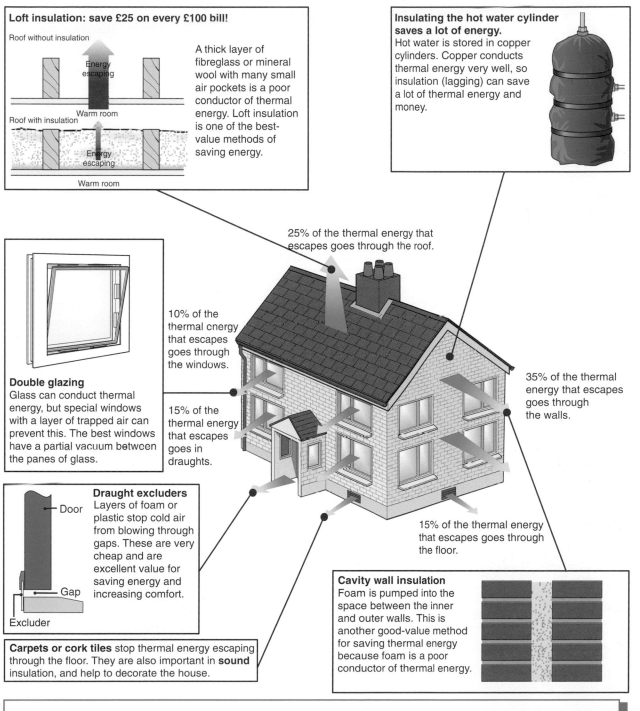

Loft insulation: save £25 on every £100 bill!

Roof without insulation

Energy escaping

Warm room

Roof with insulation

Energy escaping

Warm room

A thick layer of fibreglass or mineral wool with many small air pockets is a poor conductor of thermal energy. Loft insulation is one of the best-value methods of saving energy.

Insulating the hot water cylinder saves a lot of energy.
Hot water is stored in copper cylinders. Copper conducts thermal energy very well, so insulation (lagging) can save a lot of thermal energy and money.

25% of the thermal energy that escapes goes through the roof.

10% of the thermal energy that escapes goes through the windows.

Double glazing
Glass can conduct thermal energy, but special windows with a layer of trapped air can prevent this. The best windows have a partial vacuum between the panes of glass.

15% of the thermal energy that escapes goes in draughts.

35% of the thermal energy that escapes goes through the walls.

Draught excluders
Door
Layers of foam or plastic stop cold air from blowing through gaps. These are very cheap and are excellent value for saving energy and increasing comfort.
Gap
Excluder

15% of the thermal energy that escapes goes through the floor.

Carpets or cork tiles stop thermal energy escaping through the floor. They are also important in **sound** insulation, and help to decorate the house.

Cavity wall insulation
Foam is pumped into the space between the inner and outer walls. This is another good-value method for saving thermal energy because foam is a poor conductor of thermal energy.

Key words

Energy conservation – using the minimum amount of energy for each job.

Insulation – using a material to prevent loss of internal/thermal energy by conduction.

Exercise 18.5: Energy conservation

1. Complete this paragraph from the words in this list:

| floor | fossil | renewable | cycling | flying | walking | insulation |
| windows | doors | pollution | preservation | | | |

Reserves of .... fuels will eventually run out, so energy .... is necessary. We can use more .... energy sources which will also reduce .... Humans can use less energy by .... or .... instead of driving everywhere. We can also save energy by cutting down losses of internal/thermal energy from our buildings. .... can reduce loss of internal/thermal energy from walls and roofs, while double-glazing can reduce loss of internal/thermal energy through .... and ....

2. Complete this table about energy conservation in your home:

Do you have	Yes or no
Cavity wall insulation	
Roof insulation	
Double glazing	
Lagging on your hot water tank	
Draught excluders on external doors	
Low-energy light bulbs	

Extension question

3. Ted and Laura were investigating the effectiveness of insulation. They added 20 cm³ of boiling water to a boiling tube, and measured the temperature every two minutes. They repeated the experiment with added layers of insulating material. Their results are shown in the table below:

Time in min	Temperature in °C				
	No layers	1 layer	2 layers	3 layers	4 layers
0	94	94	94	94	94
2	88	89	90	91	91
4	80	82	84	86	86
6	72	75	77	80	80
8	67	70	73	77	77
10	61	66	69	74	74
12	55	61	66	71	71

(a) Plot these results as a line graph.

(b) What is the input (independent) variable in this experiment?

(c) What is the outcome (dependent) variable in this experiment?

(d) How can Ted and Laura make sure that this is a fair test?

(e) Each layer of insulation in a loft costs an extra £100. Does it make good sense to add five layers of insulating material? Explain your answer.

Chapter 19
Generating electricity from a fuel

Remember

● Fuels can be used to release energy.

● Electrical energy is a very useful form of energy.

Power stations

Power stations are able to change the chemical energy of fuels into electrical energy. Most power stations burn fossil fuels. The fossil fuel is tipped into a large **furnace** and oxygen is then forced into the furnace. The burning fuel gives out a large amount of **thermal energy**. The thermal energy is then used to boil **water** which turns into **steam**. The steam is forced along pipes to make powerful **jets** which hit the blades of a **turbine**. The turbine turns a shaft in the **generator** and **electricity** is made. This sequence is shown below.

How a power station works

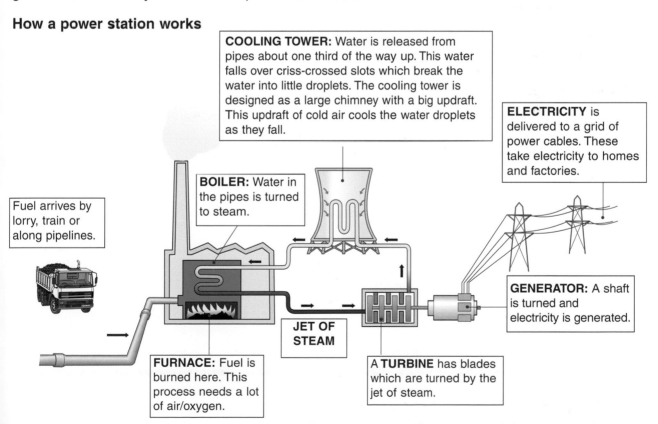

COOLING TOWER: Water is released from pipes about one third of the way up. This water falls over criss-crossed slots which break the water into little droplets. The cooling tower is designed as a large chimney with a big updraft. This updraft of cold air cools the water droplets as they fall.

ELECTRICITY is delivered to a grid of power cables. These take electricity to homes and factories.

BOILER: Water in the pipes is turned to steam.

Fuel arrives by lorry, train or along pipelines.

GENERATOR: A shaft is turned and electricity is generated.

JET OF STEAM

FURNACE: Fuel is burned here. This process needs a lot of air/oxygen.

A **TURBINE** has blades which are turned by the jet of steam.

The steam is still very hot after it hits the turbine and needs to be cooled down, so that it can be turned back into water before it is returned to the boiler. The steam is cooled in a cooling tower, where cold water is poured over the pipes that are carrying the steam. This cold water evaporates quickly. This is the steam we see coming from the cooling towers in power stations.

Efficiency of power stations

The efficiency of a power station describes how much energy is released from a certain mass of fuel. No power station is 100% efficient and they always lose some of the energy from the fuel they are using. Some power stations are more efficient than others. Gas power stations are about 50% efficient and are the best of the main power station types we use.

Making the most of electricity

Electricity is generated in power stations and then must be transferred to the homes and factories where it is needed. Most countries have a network of power cables leading from power stations to smaller sub-stations and then onto homes and factories. These power cables are often carried overhead from power stations to the sub-station, hanging from tall pylons. The cables are usually then carried underground from the sub-stations to homes.

Electricity is a very useful form of energy, because:

- It is easy to transfer along power lines and cables.

- It leaves no waste when it is used, so it is a clean form of energy.

- It is easily transformed into other forms of energy, such as the vibrations causing sound from a radio.

- It is easy to control electrical energy accurately. For example, think how fine the images can be from a digital camera.

There are one or two disadvantages when using electricity, however:

- It is not easy to store large amounts of electrical energy, so engineers have to balance carefully the production of electricity with its use.

- The transfer of electricity requires high voltages and these can be very dangerous.

Key words

Fuel – a store of energy.

Turbine – a device like a propeller that can be made to move by jets of steam (see also definition on page 271).

Generator – a device that changes kinetic energy into electrical energy.

Exercise 19.1: Generation of electricity

1. What is the difference between a turbine and a generator?

2. Why does a power station need cooling towers?

3. This table shows the percentage efficiency of different power stations:

Type of fuel used	Percentage efficiency
Coal	39
Gas	51
Oil	36
Nuclear	40

(a) Make a bar chart of these figures.

(b) Give two reasons why we would like to use less coal in power stations.

(c) Why do some people object to the use of nuclear power stations?

Electricity and energy

Starting points

- Energy is a measure of work done and able to be done.

- Fuels and renewable energy sources can release energy in various forms.

- The most useful form of energy for human activities is electricity.

Electricity is a very useful form of energy (see page 278). It doesn't produce pollution when it is used, it is easy to control and easy to send from one place to another. When we use electricity, we often change it into another kind of energy, using an electrical appliance. An **electrical appliance**, such as those shown below, can change electrical energy into another form of energy that is useful to us.

Some uses of electricity

The electric fire changes electrical energy into THERMAL and LIGHT energy.

The lamp changes electric energy into LIGHT and THERMAL energy.

The food mixer changes electrical energy into MOVEMENT, SOUND and THERMAL energy.

The television changes electrical energy into LIGHT, SOUND and THERMAL energy; so does a computer monitor.

Think back to the idea of energy chains (see page 254). You should be able to follow a chain of energy from the Sun to an appliance, such as a computer monitor, as shown here:

Energy chain: From sunlight to computer images

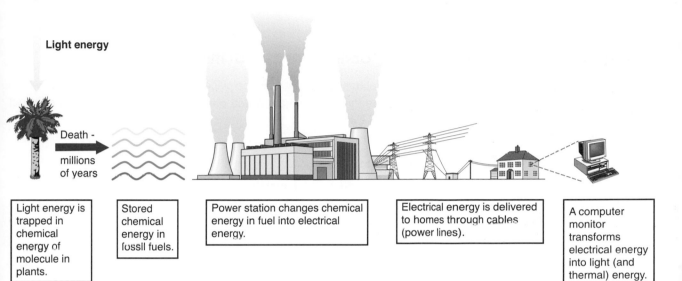

Light energy

Death -

millions
of years

| Light energy is trapped in chemical energy of molecule in plants. | Stored chemical energy in fossil fuels. | Power station changes chemical energy in fuel into electrical energy. | Electrical energy is delivered to homes through cables (power lines). | A computer monitor transforms electrical energy into light (and thermal) energy. |

Wasteful transformations

Electrical appliances transform all the energy supplied to them, but sometimes the energy is transformed into a form that isn't really useful to us. This energy will be wasted (unless we think of some very clever way of using it for something else).

> Most appliances release some energy as waste thermal energy. A computer has a fan inside it to get rid of the thermal energy – that's why it is so noisy.

A light bulb makes its surroundings warmer as well as lighter. It transfers thermal energy WWW as well as light energy ———— to its surroundings.

We will see more about the transfer of internal/thermal energy in Chapter 23, page 329.

Getting an electricity supply

Large appliances often use electricity from the **mains**, usually through a socket in the wall. Because the mains electricity is delivered from a wall socket, it means that these appliances can't be moved very far.

Smaller electrical appliances often use **batteries** to supply the energy. This means that the appliances can be moved from place to place. Batteries can store electricity, but they eventually **run down** which means they don't have enough electrical energy to run the appliance. Batteries need to be *replaced* by fresh batteries, or *recharged* so that their energy is replaced.

The passage of electricity: Conductors and insulators

As we know, electricity needs something to travel through, to get from the place where it is made to the place where it is used. Materials that allow electricity to pass through them are called **conductors** because they can **conduct** electricity.

Conductors and insulators

The materials that are used most frequently as **conductors** are **metals,** such as copper in wiring. Some non-metals, such as **graphite**, which is a form of carbon, are also used. There are other conductors but they are not so easy to use. Tap, or sea water, for example, is not so easy to control and use, but can be a very good conductor, which is why it is so dangerous to be near a source of electricity in wet conditions. (Pure water does not conduct electricity.)

Materials that do not conduct electricity are called **insulators**. Non-metallic substances are usually good insulators. Plastic, rubber, glass and wood are good examples, but you should not let them get wet.

Dangerous electricity

Electricity is a very valuable form of energy, and most of us couldn't imagine our lives without it. However, it can also be very dangerous if it is not controlled. Electrical energy can cause great damage to our bodies and could even kill us, so it is very, very important to take great care when using electrical items.

The flow of electricity can be dangerous

SHOCKING NEWS - ELECTRICITY CAN BE DANGEROUS!

MAINS ELECTRICITY can give you an ELECTRIC SHOCK that could KILL YOU!

NEVER
- stick scissors, pens or anything else into a mains socket;
- use electrical appliances near water;
- touch switches or sockets with wet hands.

ALWAYS
- hold the plastic part of a plug when plugging in or unplugging appliances because it's insulated!

ELECTRICITY FROM BATTERIES is less powerful than mains electricity, but note that rechargeable batteries can discharge quickly and can cause burns.

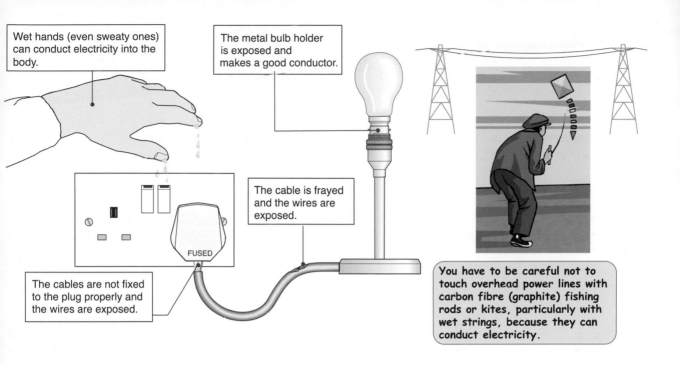

Wet hands (even sweaty ones) can conduct electricity into the body.

The metal bulb holder is exposed and makes a good conductor.

The cable is frayed and the wires are exposed.

FUSED

The cables are not fixed to the plug properly and the wires are exposed.

You have to be careful not to touch overhead power lines with carbon fibre (graphite) fishing rods or kites, particularly with wet strings, because they can conduct electricity.

Key words

Appliance – a device that can change electrical energy into a form of energy that is useful to us.

Mains – a source of electrical energy that is delivered to a house or factory from power lines.

Battery – a mobile source of electrical energy, made up of one or more cells.

Conductor – a material that allows electrical energy to pass through it.

Insulator – a material that prevents the flow of electrical energy.

Exercise 19.2: Energy and electricity

1. Give three rules for working safely with electricity.

2. Describe what a cell (battery) is and what it does.

3. Complete these sentences by choosing the missing words from this list:

    plastic   brass   conduct   insulator   lead   electricity   graphite

    The case of a plug is made from .... because it is a good .... The pins of the plug need to .... electricity, so they are made of .... The covering on a wire is made of ...., so that it will not conduct .... Some electrical machines use .... (a kind of carbon) to conduct electricity between different parts of the motor.

Extension questions

4. This question deals with electrical appliances that you could find in your home or school. Make a list of ten different appliances and use the list to complete a table like this one.

Appliance	Is it powered by mains or battery?	It converts electrical energy to ...	Some electrical energy is wasted as ...

5. Here is a drawing of an electrical circuit. If the circuit is completed and electricity can flow, then the lamp will light up. Explain how the apparatus could be used to test whether a material was an insulator or a conductor.

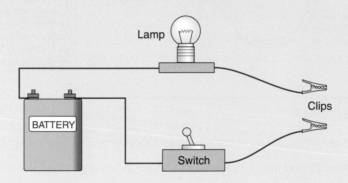

Chapter 20
Electricity on the move: Electrical circuits

Starting points

- Electricity is a convenient form of energy.

- Electricity can move from one place to another through cables or wires.

- Electrical energy can be changed into other types of energy.

What is electricity?

Electricity can provide the energy to power electrical appliances, but what is it exactly? To get an answer to this, you will need to think back to the structure of the atom (see page 191). Here's a reminder.

The structure of the atom

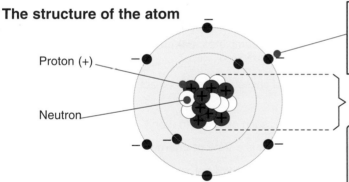

Proton (+)

Neutron

Electron (–): these can be moved and when they do move they carry a negative charge.

Nucleus

Atoms are **NEUTRAL** overall; the number of positive charges on protons is balanced by the number of negative charges on electrons.

Inside the atom there are two types of electric charge: electrons have a **negative** (–) charge and protons have a **positive** (+) charge. Electrons do not always stay attached to atoms. If electrons flow, they set up a current – scientists say that *a current is a flow of charge*.

Static electricity and electrical storms

Rubbing materials together can sometimes pull electrons from one to the other – for example, rubbing a polythene rod with a cloth will pull electrons from the cloth onto the rod.

The rod will now have a (negative) charge because of these extra electrons.

These charges stay on the material and are called STATIC ELECTRICITY.

The charges **can** move from place to place if there is a conductor (such as a metal) to let them pass through. This is like an electric current, but only lasts for a very short time (not long enough to be useful in working an electrical appliance).

Polythene rod

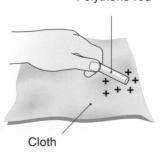

Cloth

An Electrical Storm

Thunder clouds contain tiny ice crystals and, as the clouds move around, the ice crystals rub past one another. This rubbing creates a large charge of static electricity. Each flash (bolt) of lightning during a storm is due to a huge electric spark jumping from one cloud to another, or passing down to the ground.

Multiple cloud to ground lightning, Tucson, USA

Using the knowledge

Lightning jumps the smallest gaps, and often strikes tall or pointed objects. We know that electric charge flows through conductors, so builders put a strip of metal running from the top of a tall building down to the ground. This lets the electricity take the easiest route to the ground and so stops damage to the building.

Round and round: Electrical circuits

You will remember from earlier in your work that blood flows in blood vessels around your body. The blood is pumped from the heart, round the body and then back to the heart. We say it completes a **circuit** of the body. Electricity flows in a similar sort of way around a circuit.

- Electricity flows through **wires** (also called **leads**) instead of vessels. These wires act as **electrical conductors** (see page 282).
- Electricity begins and ends a circuit in a **source of energy**, such as a cell (battery).
- Electricity flowing around a circuit is called **electric current**; it is a **flow of charge**.

Whether an electrical appliance uses the mains or a battery, the appliance will not work unless it is part of a **complete circuit**.

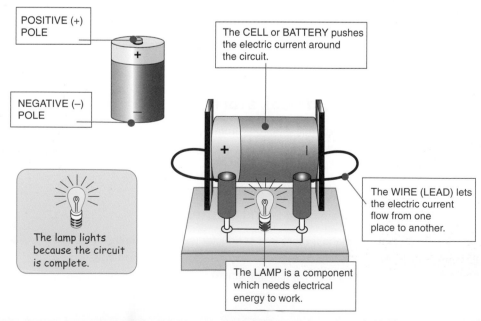

POSITIVE (+) POLE

NEGATIVE (−) POLE

The CELL or BATTERY pushes the electric current around the circuit.

The WIRE (LEAD) lets the electric current flow from one place to another.

The lamp lights because the circuit is complete.

The LAMP is a component which needs electrical energy to work.

How to connect up a complete circuit: A reminder

A cell (battery) pushes electric current around a circuit. Each cell has a **positive** end (+) and a **negative** end (-). These are called the **poles** or **terminals** of the cell. The word **polarity** is used when we describe which end of a cell is which and when we look at the direction in which the current is flowing. In order to connect up a complete circuit, you need to:

● attach a lead to the positive pole of the cell;

● connect the other end of this lead to a component, such as a bulb. If the component has a positive or negative side, connect the lead to the positive side; and

● attach another lead from the negative pole of the component to the negative pole of the battery.

There should now be a complete circuit.

Cells and batteries

A cell is a chemical source of electrical energy. Inside the cell are chemicals and, when these chemicals react together, they make the current flow in a circuit. Once the chemicals have stopped reacting, they cannot react again and the cell stops pushing charge around the circuit. The 'push' that a cell supplies to move charge around a circuit is measured in **volts** (V). The higher the voltage of a cell, the more it pushes the charge.

A **battery** is two or more cells connected together in series. An electrical appliance, such as a radio, often needs several cells to make it work – this collection of cells is the battery. People often use the word battery when they mean a single cell because it sometimes isn't possible to see all the cells. Here's a diagram to show you more about cells and batteries:

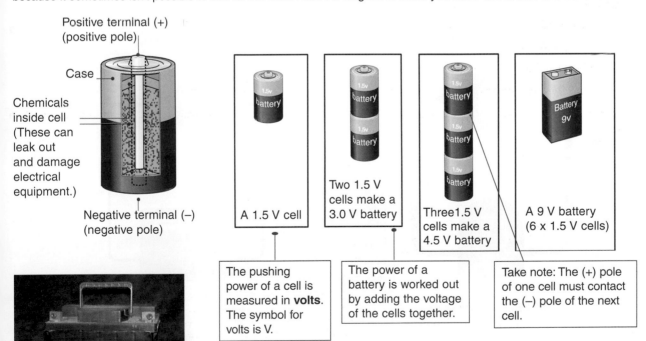

Positive terminal (+)
(positive pole)

Case

Chemicals inside cell (These can leak out and damage electrical equipment.)

Negative terminal (−)
(negative pole)

A 1.5 V cell

Two 1.5 V cells make a 3.0 V battery

Three 1.5 V cells make a 4.5 V battery

A 9 V battery (6 x 1.5 V cells)

The pushing power of a cell is measured in **volts**. The symbol for volts is V.

The power of a battery is worked out by adding the voltage of the cells together.

Take note: The (+) pole of one cell must contact the (−) pole of the next cell.

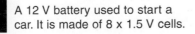

A 12 V battery used to start a car. It is made of 8 x 1.5 V cells.

BECOME A HUMAN BATTERY!
- Touch both metal plates at the same time, making sure that they are clean first.
- The ammeter shows that a current is flowing.

Copper plate   Aluminium plate

Ammeter (see page 291)

WHY DOES THIS HAPPEN?
Sweat on your hands acts like acid in a battery, starting chemical reactions with the two metals. Your hand takes negative charges away from the copper and gives negative charges to the aluminium. This flow of negative charge produces the current.
IT WON'T HURT – HONESTLY!

Inside a circuit

It can be very difficult to imagine what is going on inside an electrical circuit because we can't actually see anything moving. The flow of electric current around the circuit can be compared again with the flow of blood in the human circulation.

Human circulation

Electrical circuit

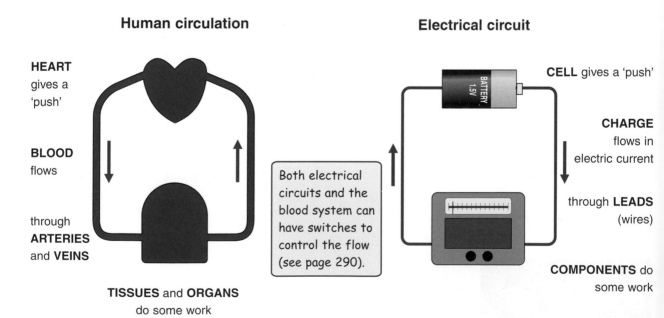

HEART gives a 'push'

BLOOD flows

through **ARTERIES** and **VEINS**

TISSUES and **ORGANS** do some work

Both electrical circuits and the blood system can have switches to control the flow (see page 290).

CELL gives a 'push'

CHARGE flows in electric current

through **LEADS** (wires)

COMPONENTS do some work

BATTERY 1.5V

A model of electricity

It is sometimes helpful in understanding things we *can't* see to make a model that we *can* see. Imagine a long tube full of small steel balls (ball bearings). Each ball bearing is the same as all the others in the tube and the ball bearings can be pushed through the tube using a handle.

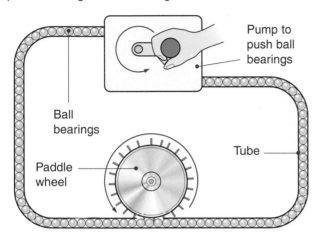

Pump to push ball bearings

Ball bearings

Paddle wheel

Tube

Turning the handle puts energy into this circuit. The energy is transmitted to the paddle wheel by the movement of the ball bearings. The paddle wheel transforms the kinetic energy (energy of movement) of the ball bearings into movement of the paddle wheel.

Key words

Current – a flow of electrons/charge.

Electron – a tiny particle that has a negative charge. Electrons can flow through conductors.

Circuit – the complete route from the positive terminal to the negative terminal of a power source.

Lead – a wire that can connect different components in a circuit.

Terminals – the positive and negative ends of a power source.

Cell – a chemical source of electrical energy. Cells may be connected in series to make up a battery.

Volt – the unit of electrical 'push'.

Component – one part of an electrical circuit.

Poles – the different ends of an electrical component – one will be positive and the other will be negative.

Exercise 20.1: Circuits

1. What three things are needed for a complete circuit?

2. What type of energy is stored in a cell?

3. What do the following represent in the model of electric current shown above?

    (a) Ball bearings

    (b) Pump

    (c) Paddle-wheel

Series and parallel circuits

Remember

- Electricity is a flow of charge.

- A current can only flow in a complete circuit.

Switches

Switches are used to control the flow of current in an electrical circuit. An *open* switch can put a deliberate break in a circuit. The circuit can be completed again when the switch is *closed*.

A SPST switch can also be used to choose between circuits (see page 296).

Switches in circuits

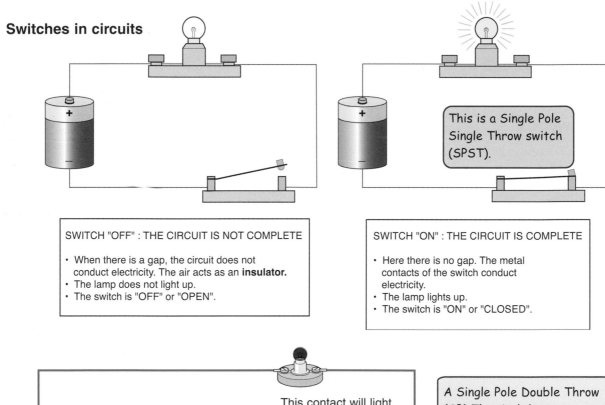

This is a Single Pole Single Throw switch (SPST).

SWITCH "OFF" : THE CIRCUIT IS NOT COMPLETE

- When there is a gap, the circuit does not conduct electricity. The air acts as an **insulator**.
- The lamp does not light up.
- The switch is "OFF" or "OPEN".

SWITCH "ON" : THE CIRCUIT IS COMPLETE

- Here there is no gap. The metal contacts of the switch conduct electricity.
- The lamp lights up.
- The switch is "ON" or "CLOSED".

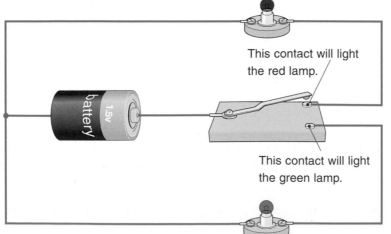

This contact will light the red lamp.

This contact will light the green lamp.

A Single Pole Double Throw (SPDT) switch lets you choose which circuit you will complete.

Circuit diagrams

As you know, you need a complete circuit for electrical current to be able to flow freely. If a circuit has any breaks or gaps in it, the electrical current will not flow freely. A **circuit diagram** is a simple version of a real circuit which makes circuit drawing easier to master. The diagram should show no breaks or gaps, unless they are put there deliberately with switches. We use **symbols** to make it easier to draw electrical circuits. Some of these symbols are shown in the table below:

Circuit Symbols

COMPONENT	SYMBOL	WHAT THE COMPONENT IS USED FOR
Cell	—||—	Provides electrical energy for the circuit.
Battery	—||||—	Provides electrical energy for the circuit.
Battery (2/more cells)	—||···||—	Provides electrical energy for the circuit.
Power supply (Lab Pack)	—o o—	Alternative to using cells.
Wire (lead) conductor	———	Lets electric current travel through it.
Wire conductor crossover		Wire conductor join
Light bulb/lamp	—⊗—	Converts electrical energy into thermal and light energy,
Motor	—(M)—	Converts electrical energy into movement energy.
Buzzer	—(	Converts electrical energy into sound energy.
Switch (open) SPST	—/ o—	Breaks the circuit and stops the flow of electric current.
SPDT Switch	—/o—	Completes one circuit from a choice of two.

This diagram shows some examples of using circuit diagrams. You can see that it is easier to work out what is happening by looking at a circuit diagram.

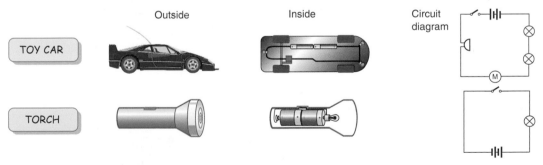

Outside   Inside   Circuit diagram

TOY CAR

TORCH

How is current measured?

If there is a light bulb in the circuit, we can judge the size of a current by looking at the **brightness** of the lamp. A large current makes the lamp glow brightly and a small current only makes the lamp glow dimly or not at all. However, this method is not accurate enough for scientific work, because one person might not agree with another person about what is bright and what isn't. For this reason, an instrument called an **ammeter** is used to measure the current.

The size of the current is measured in units called **amperes**. Amperes is usually shortened to **amps** (the symbol for amps is A).

When an ammeter is used it must be:

● connected **in** the main circuit; and

● connected with the **red** (+) terminal to the positive terminal on the cell, battery or power supply.

Using an ammeter

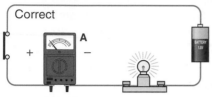

This terminal (the positive terminal) MUST be connected to the positive terminal on the power source.

Here the meter is connected in the circuit. It measures the current passing through the lamp.

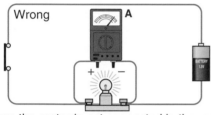

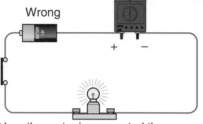

Here the meter is not connected in the main circuit. It does not measure the current passing through the lamp. The meter may be damaged.

Here the meter is connected the wrong way around. The pointer moves the wrong way. The meter may be damaged.

Series circuits

In the simplest circuits all the components are joined together in one loop. There are no branches or junctions. These are called **series circuits**.

Switch open – the switch cell and the two lamps are connected in series.

Switch closed – the circuit is complete, so both the lamps light up.

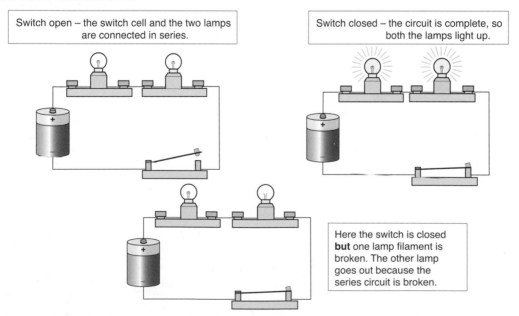

Here the switch is closed **but** one lamp filament is broken. The other lamp goes out because the series circuit is broken.

The most important thing to remember about a series circuit is that every component has to be working properly or none of them will work. Think of the Christmas tree lights not lighting up. How often do you find that the culprit is just one broken lamp?

Current in a series circuit

The current is the same at all places in a series circuit. This is because the current has only one pathway to flow through – there is no choice. It has to pass through all of the components and back to the power source.

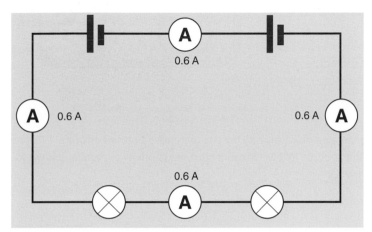

Wherever the ammeter is placed in the circuit, it gives the same reading (0.6 A). This means the current is the same everywhere in the circuit.

This result also shows that the current passes THROUGH the component and is NOT used up by the component.

The more cells we add into the series circuit the greater the amount of current that will be 'pushed' around it. Any bulbs in the circuit will be brighter or an ammeter will give a higher reading. If more bulbs or other components are added to the circuit then it will be more difficult for current to flow. Bulbs will be dimmer and an ammeter will give a lower reading. This is explained below, where we also give a model of current flow to help you understand what is going on.

Extra cells and components

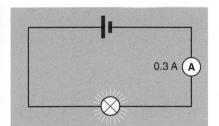

In this circuit, one cell can make a current of 0.3 A flow through one lamp.

Here an extra cell has been added. Now there is more current and the lamp will light with extra brightness.

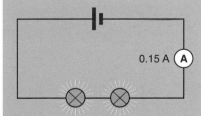

Here one cell is pushing current through two lamps. The current is only 0.15 A and the lamp merely glows dimly.

This model of current flow shows how a second pump in the circuit increases the flow of the ball bearings, which makes the paddle wheel turn faster.

In an electrical circuit this means that:
- the voltage is greater;
- the current is greater; and
- the lamp will light with extra brightness.

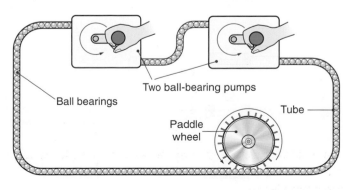

Two ball-bearing pumps

Ball bearings

Tube

Paddle wheel

Likewise the model shows that when a second paddle wheel is put in the circuit, this makes it harder for the pump to move the ball bearings. The ball bearings flow more slowly, so the paddle wheels turn more slowly.

In an electrical circuit this would mean that:

- the voltage is the same;
- the current is less; and
- the lamps become dimmer.

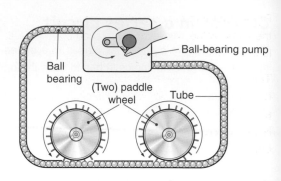

Parallel circuits

Circuits which have junctions or branches where the electrical pathway divides are called **parallel circuits**. In a parallel circuit, the current has more than one pathway that it could follow. Different currents can flow in parallel pathways and then join up again. This type of circuit is shown below:

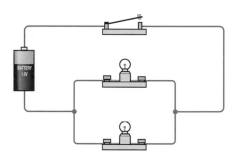

A circuit with two lamps connected in parallel.

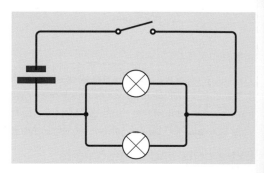

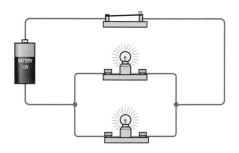

When the switch is closed, both lamps light. The switch, in this position, controls both lamps.

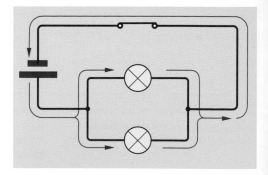

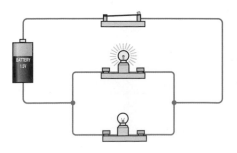

If one of the lamps blows, the other lamp stays on. There is still a complete circuit through the undamaged lamp.

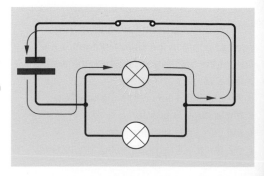

Remember that the current in a *series* circuit has to pass through all of the components and an ammeter will read just the same value wherever it is placed in the circuit. The current is the same everywhere in the circuit. As we have just learnt, if one component isn't working, the other components will stop working, even if they are not damaged.

The current in a **parallel** circuit, however, depends on the number of choices it has. An ammeter shows a different reading depending on where it is placed in the circuit and how many of the parallel lines in the circuit are being used at the time. If one component fails, the others will continue to work as long as they are in a different one of the parallel lines. Parallel circuits with switches (see below) will allow you to turn different lights on and off without affecting the others. Parallel circuits are used for house lights and power points.

Two models of parallel circuits

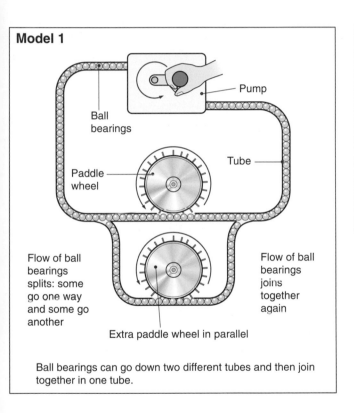

Model 1

Pump

Ball bearings

Paddle wheel

Tube

Flow of ball bearings splits: some go one way and some go another

Flow of ball bearings joins together again

Extra paddle wheel in parallel

Ball bearings can go down two different tubes and then join together in one tube.

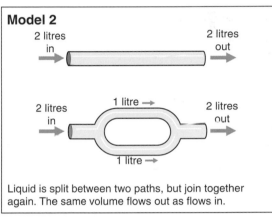

Model 2

2 litres in

2 litres out

2 litres in

1 litre →

2 litres out

1 litre →

Liquid is split between two paths, but join together again. The same volume flows out as flows in.

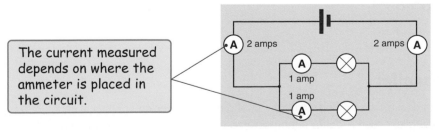

The current measured depends on where the ammeter is placed in the circuit.

(A) 2 amps

2 amps (A)

A
1 amp

1 amp

A

Working in parallel

If you look at the diagram below, you will see that in a parallel circuit each lamp is connected directly to the power supply. The voltage (push) from the power source to the lamps is the same in each case. This means that all the lamps will shine brightly. You can connect as many lamps as you like in parallel and they will always stay the same brightness. However, when you connect more lamps in parallel, the current drawn from the battery increases. A battery will quickly run down if it has a lot of lamps connected across it in parallel.

One lamp

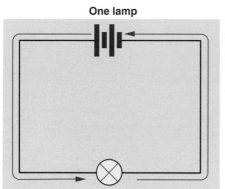

The current flows through the lamp and the lamp is BRIGHT.

Two lamps in parallel

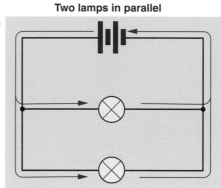

The current flows through both lamps. The lamps remain BRIGHT but twice as much current must flow from the power supply.

Switches in parallel circuits

Switches can be very useful in parallel circuits because they allow you to choose how much of a circuit the current will pass through. This illustration shows how switches can be used in this way:

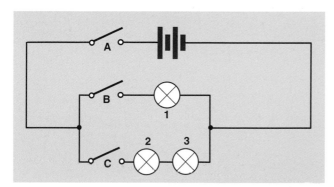

Switch **A**: Controls all bulbs
Switch **B**: Controls bulb **1**
Switch **C**: Controls bulb **2** and **3**

To light lamp **1**: **A** and **B** must be closed.

To light lamps **2** and **3**: **A** and **C** must be closed.

To light lamps **1**, **2** and **3**: **A**, **B** and **C** must be closed.

Series or parallel

When an electrician designs an electric circuit, he or she needs to decide whether a series or a parallel circuit will be best. Generally, a parallel circuit is better if the user needs to be able to control a number of components separately, but this type of circuit does take a lot of current from the power supply. A series circuit is safer because the current is smaller and is useful if you need to light several bulbs at the same time without any of them having to be particularly bright.

Series or parallel?

CHRISTMAS TREE lights use a **series** circuit.

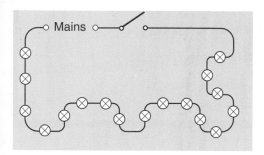

Decorative lights on tree

HOUSEHOLD lights use a **parallel** circuit.

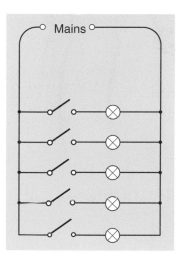

House with different rooms lit/unlit

Using the knowledge: Series or parallel?

Series circuit	Parallel circuit
One lamp damaged, none will light.	One lamp damaged, others will still light.
One switch operates all the lamps.	Each lamp can be controlled by its own switch.
Voltage from power supply is shared between all the lamps.	Voltage across each lamp is the same as the voltage across the power supply.
Current from the power supply is low: SAFER and CHEAPER TO USE.	Current from the power supply is high: MORE DANGEROUS and MORE EXPENSIVE.

> Which type of circuit would you use if you needed the lights to be on for a long time and if there was a chance that a toddler might be able to reach them?

Key words

Switch – a device that controls the flow of current in a circuit.

Symbol – a sign used for a particular electrical component.

Series circuit – an electrical circuit with all of the components joined in a single loop.

Parallel circuit – a circuit that contains junctions where the electrical pathway divides or branches.

Ammeter – an instrument for measuring electrical current.

Ampere – the unit of electrical current (often shortened to AMP).

Exercise 20.2: Series and parallel circuits

1. Match these symbols with their use. Match the letter for the symbol with the number that describes the use:

Symbol	Use
(A) ⊗	(1) Uses electric power to make a sound
(B) —Ⓜ—	(2) Can break a circuit
(C) ⊏	(3) Provides power for a circuit
(D) —o⁄o—	(4) Uses electric power to produce light
(E) —⊣⊢—	(5) Uses electric power to produce movement

2. Complete this paragraph about electric circuits. Use words from this list:

   cell   buzzer   lead   current   switch   components   lamp   conductor   filament

   Electricity can pass through any material that is a ……… . A complete circuit lets ……… flow all the way round it. The energy can be supplied by a ……… and can pass from one component to another through a ……… . When a circuit is made up, it may include a ………, which can be opened to stop the flow of current. If the ……… is closed, then a component such as a ……… will light or a ……… will sound.

3. Complete this table to compare series and parallel circuits:

Feature	Series circuit	Parallel circuit
Current in different places		
Number of pathways that current can take		
Effect of one damaged component		
Effect of opening a switch		

4. Look at the circuit in the diagram. A current of 2.6 A flows through ammeter C when switch 1 and switch 2 are closed:

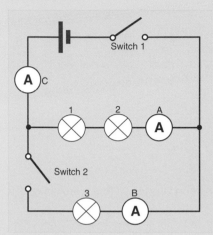

(a) What will happen to each of the lamps when switch 1 is closed with switch 2 open?

(b) If ammeter B has a reading of 1.6 A when switch 1 and switch 2 are closed, what will be the reading of ammeter A?

(c) What will be the reading on ammeter A if switch 1 is closed and switch 2 is open?

5. Six lamps were connected in a series circuit to a power supply. Six identical lamps were connected in a parallel circuit to an identical power supply.

(a) In which circuit would the lamps be brighest?

(b) Which circuit would have the highest voltage across each lamp?

(c) Which circuit would be the cheapest to use (i.e. would use the least electricity)?

Extension questions

6. Find a simple electric toy or model. Try to draw a circuit diagram for your model. Don't forget to use the correct symbols.

7. The car shown in this photograph has two headlamp lamps and two rear lights connected in parallel with the car's battery.

(a) Draw a circuit diagram to show how the four lamps are connected to the battery. Include in your diagram one switch which would allow the driver to switch all the lights on or off.

(b) Use the diagram to explain why damage to one lamp will allow the other three to continue to shine.

8. An electrical contractor sells lighting systems to fairgrounds. He wants to design a system with 20 lamps: 4 red, 4 yellow, 4 green, 4 clear and 4 blue. He wants to be able to turn all 4 lamps of the same colour on or off at the same time. If a lamp of one colour blows (stops working), all the lamps of that colour could be off but the other colours should still be capable of being switched on. Design a suitable circuit for this contractor.

Problems with circuits

Don't forget

- A circuit has a power supply and different components joined by leads.
- The power supply pushes the electric charge around a circuit.

What's wrong?

If a circuit doesn't work, there may be a very simple explanation:

- The circuit could be incomplete, which means the current can't flow around the circuit (e.g. a broken wire, a wire not connected to the power supply, a broken lamp filament).
- Polarity of cells is incorrect. If you are using more than one cell, they must all be the same way round.

Voltage, current and resistance

In a complete circuit, the current can flow because the power supply provides a voltage to 'push' the electric charge. There are some rules to remember:

- Larger voltages cause larger currents.
- A battery or cell cannot always give the same current. The current that flows depends on what is in the circuit connected to the battery.
- Some components allow electricity to pass easily; we say that these have a **low resistance**. Other components make it hard for current to flow; we say that these have a **high resistance**.

Resistance reduces the flow of current

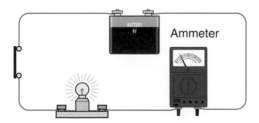

When connected to a 6 V battery, this lamp allows a current of 2 A.

When two of these lamps are connected, the resistance is higher and so the current is about 1 A.

The wires used for connecting up circuits in the laboratory or in the home have a very low resistance. They are made of copper which is a very good conductor of electricity. Very long wires, or very thin wires, make it difficult for current to flow around a circuit.

Controlling the current

Reducing the flow of current is not always a problem. When we want to control the current, we can use a resistor. The diagram below shows a **resistor** and how it can be useful in a circuit.

Controlling current with a resistor

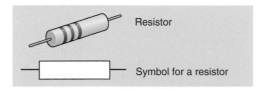

Resistor

Symbol for a resistor

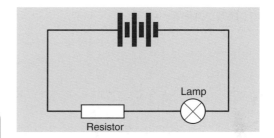

Lamp

Resistor

In this circuit a resistor is connected in series with the lamp. This protects the lamp, because extra resistance in the circuit means that the lamp won't blow.

You can change the flow of current through a circuit by using different resistors – high, medium and low, for example – but it is more accurate to use a **variable resistor**. A common kind of variable resistor has a very long coil of wire and a sliding contact. The sliding contact allows you to control the length of the wire that is included in the circuit and so control the amount of current that is able to flow.

Variable resistors can control current

A variable resistor with a sliding contact

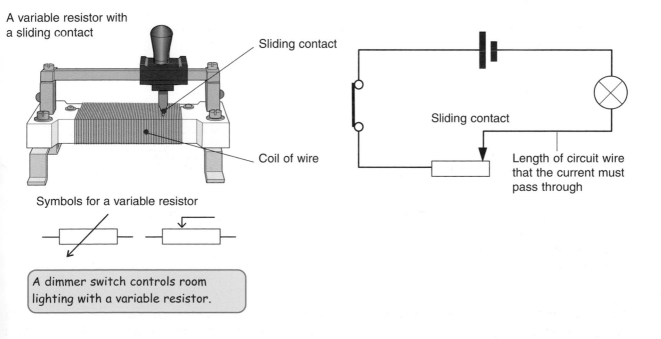

Sliding contact

Coil of wire

Sliding contact

Length of circuit wire that the current must pass through

Symbols for a variable resistor

A dimmer switch controls room lighting with a variable resistor.

Short circuits: Taking the easy route

Electricity takes the easiest route in a circuit. A **short circuit** occurs when the electric current is able to flow around the circuit without going through any components (i.e. without doing any work). This sometimes means that it is taking the **shortest** route (thus the name), but sometimes it will take a longer (but easier route) to avoid going through a component (which is hard work!). The diagram shows some problems due to short circuits.

Short circuits

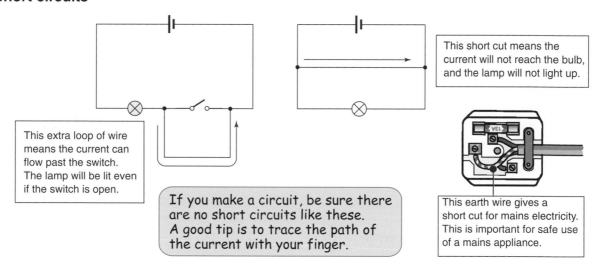

This short cut means the current will not reach the bulb, and the lamp will not light up.

This extra loop of wire means the current can flow past the switch. The lamp will be lit even if the switch is open.

If you make a circuit, be sure there are no short circuits like these. A good tip is to trace the path of the current with your finger.

This earth wire gives a short cut for mains electricity. This is important for safe use of a mains appliance.

You could be in danger if there is some faulty wiring in a mains appliance. The current might try to flow through you instead of through the circuit. This is why plugs have an **earth** wire. If there is some faulty wiring which causes a short circuit, the earth wire lets the current take a short cut to the ground instead of through your body.

Key words

Short circuit – the easiest route in an electrical circuit.

Resistance – a measure of how difficult it is for electrical current to flow through a component.

Resistor – a component with a known resistance.

Exercise 20.3: Problems with circuits

1. Look at these two circuits. Which part of each circuit will the current miss out?

(A)

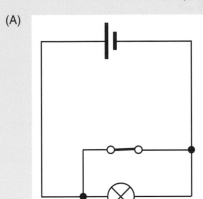

(B)

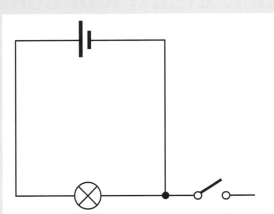

Extension questions

2. Draw a circuit diagram to show the possible faults you could find in a torch.

3. Bill and Jenny were interested in the factors that affected the resistance of a wire. They were given the following pieces of apparatus:

   Battery   Switch   Ammeter   Roll of thick copper wire   Roll of thin copper wire

   Roll of thin steel wire

   (a) Draw a circuit that they could use in their investigation.

   (b) Explain how they could carry out a fair test to see whether the thickness or length of wire is more important in affecting resistance.

Chapter 21
More electrical components

Starting points

● A complete electrical circuit has a power supply, a set of leads and one or more components.

● Components in an electrical circuit transform electrical energy into another useful form.

● Each electrical component can be recognised by a symbol that is used when drawing circuit diagrams.

We have already seen a number of components in electrical circuits (page 291). There are many other components that are useful in everyday life. Some of these are shown in this table.

Component and symbol	Uses	Example
Fuse	Breaks a circuit if the current becomes too great in the wire. Too much current can cause damage, or even fire.	Fuse in plug
LDR (light-dependent resistor)	These are components with a resistance that depends on light intensity. Usually the resistance is low in bright light and high in the dark. They are important in systems controlled by light intensity, such as automatic security lights and the driving lights on some cars.	Lights on a Volvo
Thermistor	Has a resistance that changes according to temperature, so its resistance is usually high when cold and lower when warm. Used in fire alarms or in frost-warning systems for greenhouses.	Fire alarm
LED (light-emitting diode)	These are small lamps used in electronic circuits, and give a very bright light when only a small current flows. They are used as indicator lamps in many electronic devices, such as 'on' signals for CD players. They are also used in flashing cycle lights.	Cycle light
Transistor (semiconductor diode)	A transistor is a small, electronically-controlled switch. These switches direct small currents into different circuits. Integrated circuits (ICs) contain many transistors in a single chip. These are important in computers and in the control systems for cars and motorbikes.	Motorbike

Fuses are particularly important components in electrical circuits because they play a part in the safe use of electrical appliances. There is a piece of wire inside a fuse. If the flow of current is too great, the wire becomes very hot and eventually melts. A high flow of current can be very dangerous. It could lead to electric shock or to a fire, but once the wire melts the circuit is broken and no current can flow.

How a fuse works

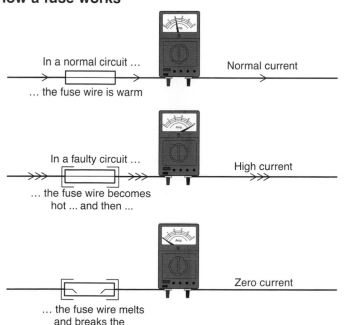

In a normal circuit ...

... the fuse wire is warm

Normal current

In a faulty circuit ...

... the fuse wire becomes hot ... and then ...

High current

... the fuse wire melts and breaks the circuit.

Zero current

> DANGER! Too much current could make an appliance live and give an electric shock. Many house fires are started by heated wires in appliances without the correct fuse.

Key words

Fuse – a component that breaks a circuit if the current in a wire becomes too great.

Exercise 21.1: Other components

1. Why is a fuse an important part of a plug that connects an appliance to the mains?

2. Sometimes a person replaces a fuse with a piece of metal foil. Why is this dangerous?

Project

3. Find out the current values for different household fuses. Make a table to show some examples of household appliances which should be protected by each type of fuse.

More about switches and control: Truth tables and logic gates

Remember

- Electric current can pass only through a complete circuit.

- Electric current is needed for a component of a circuit to work.

- Switches control electrical circuits.

Electricians can be given problems to solve. Often these problems involve providing an ideal circuit for the safe and efficient use of a machine. These circuits are likely to include switches. A set of switches connected together is called a **logic gate**. These logic gates make decisions and only allow information (electric current) through if the correct combination of switches is closed. Here are some examples of the sort of problem an electrician may have to solve:

Problem 1 : An electric grinding wheel must not be operated unless the safety screen is in position.

Solution : There are two switches arranged in series. One switch is the on/off switch for the grinding wheel. The other switch is on when the safety screen is in the correct position. The motor will only run if switch A *and* switch B are on. This arrangement is called an AND circuit, and is shown below:

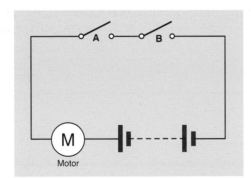

AND circuit: Both switch A **AND** switch B must be on before the motor will run.

Truth tables can be used to show the action of logic gates. A truth table shows what happens for all the possible positions of the switches. This is a truth table for an AND circuit:

Inputs		Output
Switch A	**Switch B**	**Motor**
Off	Off	Off
Off	On	Off
On	Off	Off
On	On	On

The switches can only be on or off. We can represent on with a 1 and off with a 0, and draw the table again.

Inputs		Output
A	**B**	**Q**
0	0	0
0	1	0
1	0	0
1	1	1

In this truth table, **Q** represents the output from the circuit (in case, the current to the motor). An output of 0 means 'no ac' and an output of 1 means 'action'.

Problem 2 : An alarm must go off if either the newsagent's door or the back window is opened.

Solution: To solve this problem two switches are arranged in parallel. The alarm will sound if either switch A or switch B is on. A circuit which makes this kind of decision is called an OR circuit.

The diagram below shows the operation of an OR circuit:

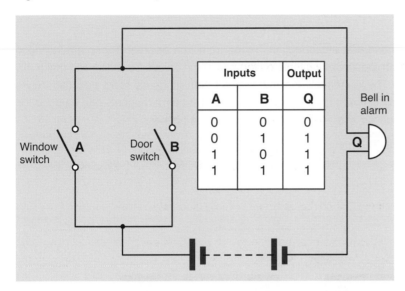

Inputs		Output
A	**B**	**Q**
0	0	0
0	1	1
1	0	1
1	1	1

OR circuit: If either switch A or switch B is on the alarm will sound.

AND and OR circuits can either allow current to pass (1) or not (0). These circuits are often called **gates**, for they open and close like gates in a field. We refer to these as an **AND gate** and an **OR gate**. Both AND and OR gates have symbols for use when drawing circuit diagrams. These are shown below.

Electronic equipment uses integrated circuits (chips) which have many logic gates packed together into one tiny component.

Key words

Logic gate – a set of connected switches that can make a decision about the flow of electric current.

AND gate – only allows current to flow if two switches are in the ON position.

OR gate – allows current to flow if either of two switches is in the ON position.

Chapter 22
Magnets and magnetic fields

Magnetic forces

We can sometimes find rocks in the ground that attract objects made from iron or steel. These naturally-occurring magnetic rocks are called **lodestones** and exert a pulling force on the iron in the object. Scientists can make **magnets** that work just like these magnetic rocks. These magnets are more useful than magnetic rocks because they can be made much stronger and made into many different shapes and sizes. These modern magnets can be used for many different jobs, e.g. fridge magnets, magnetised strips for closing doors and compasses.

Each magnet has two ends, called **poles**. The names of these poles come from the way in which a moving magnet points when it is affected by the magnetic rocks in the Earth. The poles of magnets exert forces on one another. These are shown in this diagram:

Magnets and poles

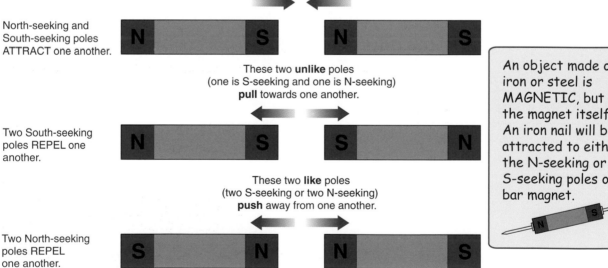

North-seeking and South-seeking poles ATTRACT one another.

These two **unlike** poles (one is S-seeking and one is N-seeking) **pull** towards one another.

Two South-seeking poles REPEL one another.

These two **like** poles (two S-seeking or two N-seeking) **push** away from one another.

Two North-seeking poles REPEL one another.

An object made of iron or steel is MAGNETIC, but not the magnet itself! An iron nail will be attracted to either the N-seeking or S-seeking poles of a bar magnet.

An object can be magnetic but *not* be a magnet. For example, a piece of iron is magnetic (it is attracted to a magnet) but does not act like a magnet itself. One piece of iron does not attract or repel another piece of iron. A magnetic object can be **magnetised** – this means that it is converted into a magnet!

An iron nail, for example, can be placed in a magnetic field and it will become a magnet itself. Here is an explanation of how this can happen:

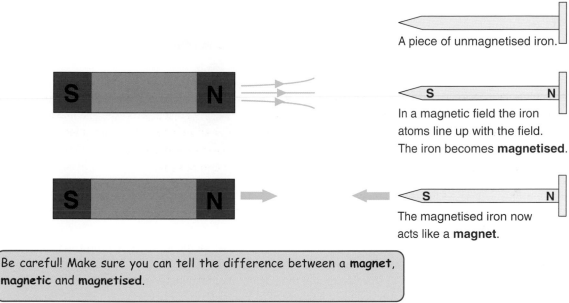

A piece of unmagnetised iron.

In a magnetic field the iron atoms line up with the field. The iron becomes **magnetised**.

The magnetised iron now acts like a **magnet**.

Be careful! Make sure you can tell the difference between a **magnet**, **magnetic** and **magnetised**.

Finding the poles of a magnet

Each magnet has a North-seeking and a South-seeking pole. You can find which pole is which by hanging the magnet up or floating it in liquid and seeing whether it points North or South. An easier way to do this is to use a **compass**.

Finding the poles of a magnet

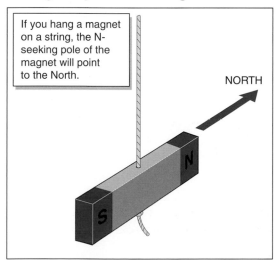

If you hang a magnet on a string, the N-seeking pole of the magnet will point to the North.

NORTH

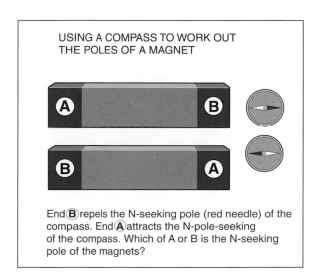

USING A COMPASS TO WORK OUT THE POLES OF A MAGNET

End Ⓑ repels the N-seeking pole (red needle) of the compass. End Ⓐ attracts the N-pole-seeking of the compass. Which of A or B is the N-seeking pole of the magnets?

A compass works in this way because the compass needle is itself a magnet. The needle points north-south because the Earth is also a magnet (a giant one!). The compass needle lines up with the Earth's **magnetic field**. If we know that the North-seeking pole of the compass needle always points towards the Earth's North Pole, we can work out the direction in which we are travelling. Hill walkers and explorers can use a compass and a map to find out where they are and to work out in which direction to walk to find a particular place and not get lost.

The Earth is just a giant magnet

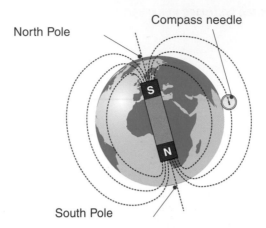

Magnetic materials can cause problems

Most substances are not magnetic. Iron is the most important magnetic element, but nickel and cobalt are also magnetic. Alloys – such as steel – that contain any of these elements are magnetic too. If you are trying to use a compass to find your way, it is important to make sure that there is no magnetic material nearby. These elements are found in rocks in the Earth's crust, and some electrical equipment is magnetic. In some parts of Scotland the rocks are so magnetic that a compass would just make you walk in circles!

Problems for hill-walkers

> A compass needle can be attracted to magnetic rocks instead of being lined up with the Earth's magnetic field.

Magnetic fields

If you bring a metal object towards a magnet, you will feel the pull of the magnet before the object and the magnet actually touch one another. This means that magnetism must be reaching out into the air around the magnet. Because magnetism is able to push or pull another object, we know that **magnetism is a force**. We can use a compass needle or iron filings to show the pattern of this magnetic force around a magnet:

The magnetic field of a magnet

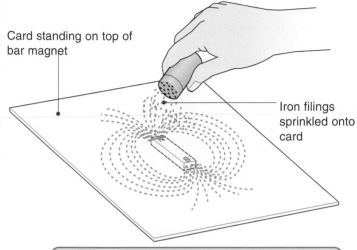

Card standing on top of bar magnet

Iron filings sprinkled onto card

To see the magnetic field of a magnet:

- Place a magnet onto some card.

- Sprinkle iron filings onto card.

- Each filing then becomes magnetised and lines up with the magnetic field of the magnet.

- The pattern of the filings shows us the **shape** of the magnetic field.

FACT: The field is actually in three dimensions around the magnet.

Note: look at these patterns and compare them with the Earth's magnetic field (see page 310).

Here's another way to see the magnetic field:

- Use a small compass (a *plotting compass*) to trace the lines of the magnetic field.

- The compass needle can rotate and so will show the **direction** of the magnetic field as well as its shape.

FACTS

- The field is strongest (lines closest together) near the poles.

- The field lines run from North to South.

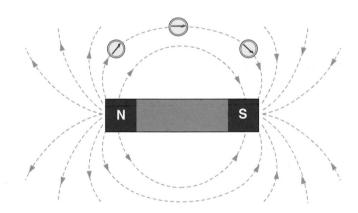

This pattern of magnetic force is called a **magnetic field**. Any object inside the magnetic field will be affected by the magnetic force. The magnetic field is strongest where the lines of magnetic force are closest together and weakest where the lines are far apart.

Key words

Magnet – a material that can put a pulling force on any object that contains iron.

Magnetism – the pulling force between a magnet and a magnetic object.

Magnetic – attracted by a magnet.

Compass – an instrument that can measure the direction of the Earth's magnetic field.

Pole – one end of a magnet.

Magnetic field – a region where there is a magnetic force.

Exercise 22.1: Magnets

1. Fill in the gaps to complete these sentences using words from the following list:

    poles   iron   repel   North   attract

    (a) A magnet can be hung up so that it can move easily. If this happens, one end will point .... and the other end will point South. The two different ends of a magnet are called the .... Magnets exert forces on materials that contain ....

    (b) Like poles of magnets .... one another, but unlike poles ....

2. Draw a diagram to explain how a compass works. Explain how magnetic objects can make a compass unreliable.

3. Make a copy of this table. Complete the table to show you understand the forces between magnets.

Pole of first magnet	Pole of second magnet	Do they attract or repel?	Is this a push or a pull?
N	S		
N	N		
S	S		

4. Complete this paragraph using words from the following list:

    repelled   North   magnetised

    When an unmagnetised nail is put into a magnetic field, it becomes .... The South-seeking pole of a magnetised nail will be attracted to the .... pole of a magnet, but will be .... by the South-seeking pole of a magnet.

Electricity and magnetism

Remember

●   Magnetism is a force.

●   A magnet has a magnetic field that exists in three dimensions all around it.

A piece of steel that has been magnetised so that it keeps its magnetic properties is called a **permanent magnet**. Scientists have discovered that an electric current also exerts a magnetic force. This means that we can use electricity to make magnets, called **electromagnets**. Electromagnets can be turned on and off. Much of our modern technology depends on this.

Linking electricity and magnetism

The circuit shown below shows that there is a magnetic field around a wire that is carrying an electric current. This link between electric current and magnetism is called **electromagnetism**.

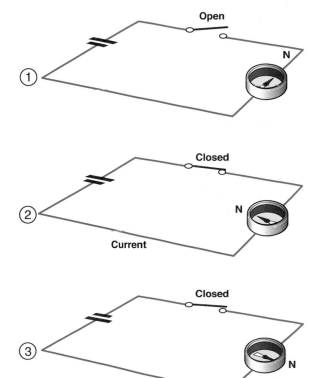

OERSTED'S EXPERIMENTS: The Danish scientist Oersted showed the effect of an electric current on a compass needle.

1. Switch open: There is no current flow. See how the compass needle lines up with the Earth's field.

2. Switch closed: The current flows. The compass needle is deflected and lines up with the magnetic field around the wire.

3. Switch closed but current reversed: The compass needle is deflected in the opposite direction because the lines of force in the magnetic field are now running in the opposite direction.

The magnetic field around an ordinary electric wire is not very strong, but its shape can be shown using plotting-compasses and the apparatus shown below:

A magnetic field around a wire

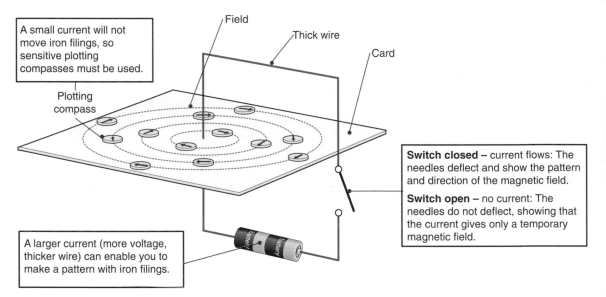

A small current will not move iron filings, so sensitive plotting compasses must be used.

Field

Thick wire

Card

Plotting compass

Switch closed – current flows: The needles deflect and show the pattern and direction of the magnetic field.

Switch open – no current: The needles do not deflect, showing that the current gives only a temporary magnetic field.

A larger current (more voltage, thicker wire) can enable you to make a pattern with iron filings.

Electromagnets

A coiled wire (called a **solenoid**) gives a stronger field than the straight wire shown above. The field becomes even stronger if the wire is coiled around a rod of iron. The rod of iron is called the **core**, and the coil and core together make up an electromagnet. The field pattern around an **electromagnet** is the same as that around a bar magnet, as shown:

The magnetic field around an electromagnet

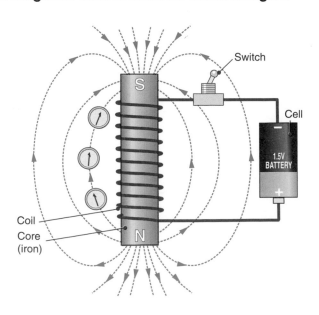

Switch

Cell

Coil

Core (iron)

The pattern and the direction of the magnetic field around an electromagnet are the same as the field around a bar magnet (see page 311).

Making the field stronger

It is very useful to have a magnet that can be switched on and off. The pulling force of the magnet can be used to lift a magnetic object. The current can then be switched off and the magnetic material can be dropped. An electromagnet like this can be used for separating magnetic materials from non-magnetic materials, for example in a scrapyard.

An electromagnet can be used to sort out materials in a scrapyard

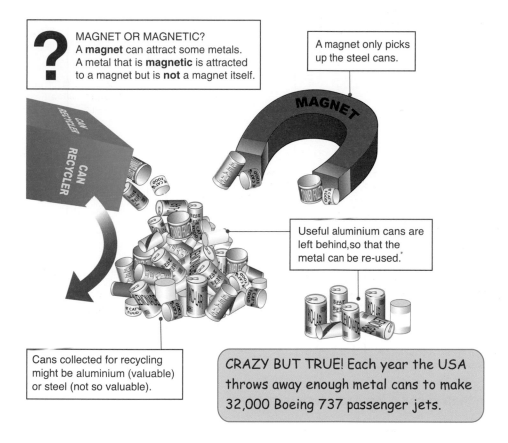

MAGNET OR MAGNETIC?
A **magnet** can attract some metals. A metal that is **magnetic** is attracted to a magnet but is **not** a magnet itself.

A magnet only picks up the steel cans.

Useful aluminium cans are left behind, so that the metal can be re-used.

Cans collected for recycling might be aluminium (valuable) or steel (not so valuable).

CRAZY BUT TRUE! Each year the USA throws away enough metal cans to make 32,000 Boeing 737 passenger jets.

As well as just switching an electromagnet on or off, it is also possible to control the strength of the magnetic field. There are three ways that this can be done:

● by increasing the electric current;

● by increasing the number of coils in the solenoid; or

● by changing the material in the core.

Investigating the strength of an electromagnetic field

A current flowing through
a coiled wire acts like a magnet.

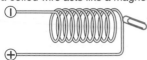

1. Use a bigger current.

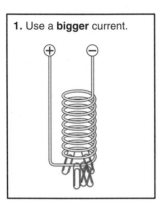

2. Put more turns of wire on the coil.

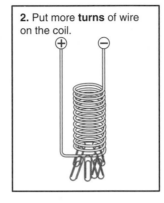

3. Use an Iron core inside the coil.

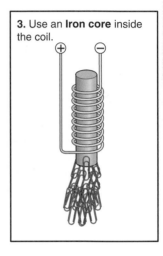

FAIR TEST?
If you are investigating the strength of an electromagnet, then keep:
● the number of coils; and
● current constant.
Can you think of any factor to keep constant?

You can then check if the core material matters.

Iron core

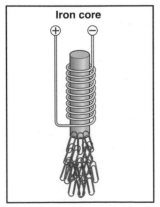

Steel core

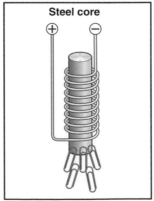

Glass core

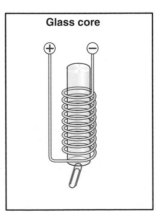

More uses for electromagnets

So we now know that electromagnets can be switched on and off. This makes them very useful in many ways:

Magnets and medicine

Electromagnets are used:

- to remove metal splinters from wounds;

- to look inside the body, using Magnetic Resonance Imaging (MRI) [see photograph].

An electric bell

- Switch (1) is closed, usually by pushing a button.

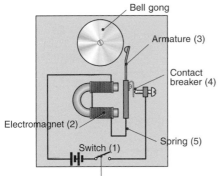

- The electromagnet (2) produces a pulling force.
- The armature (3) is pulled towards (2), so the gong strikes the bell.
- The contact breaker (4) breaks the circuit, so the pulling force stops.
- The spring (5) pushes the armature back, the circuit is complete again and the whole cycle is repeated... RRRIIIIIINNNGGG!

Magnetic Trains

Monorail train systems, like those at Disneyworld, use electromagnets to 'float' about 15 mm above the track. This gives a very smooth ride, and saves wear on the wheels and track.

ELECTRO-MAGNETS ARE USEFUL

A relay is an electrically-controlled switch.

This uses a **small** current to turn on another circuit. The second circuit may carry a **large** current, needed to turn a powerful motor.

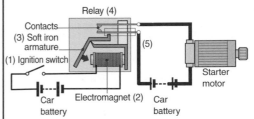

- The ignition switch (1) is closed and a small (safe!) current flows to the electromagnet (2).
- The armature (3) is pulled across to the electromagnet.
- A pivot in (3) means the contacts (4) are pushed together so that the second circuit (5) is completed.
- A large current flows in (5) to turn the starter motor (see p318 for circuit diagram).

A **reed switch** is a small relay used in electronic circuits.

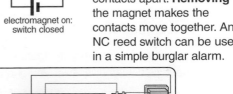

The reed switch has thin metal contacts inside a glass tube.

A magnet can bring the contacts together in a normally-open (NO) switch.

In a normally-closed (NC) switch the magnet keeps the contacts apart. **Removing** the magnet makes the contacts move together. An NC reed switch can be used in a simple burglar alarm.

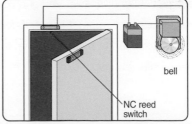

Key words

Electromagnet – a magnet formed when electric current passes through a wire.

Solenoid – a coil of wire that forms part of an electromagnet.

Core – an iron bar that may be placed inside a solenoid to form a powerful electromagnet.

Exercise 22.2: Electromagnetism

1. How would the pulling force of an electromagnet be affected by:

    (a) Changing the iron core for a copper core?

    (b) Increasing the current through the coils?

    (c) Using a coil with fewer turns?

    (d) Changing the iron core for a steel core?

2. What is the main reason for using a relay to switch on an electric motor?

3. Look at the diagram of the relay on page 317.

    (a) Copy out the diagram with the switch in the closed position. Use a red pencil or pen to trace the flow of current through this circuit.

    (b) Show in your diagram where the largest current would be measured.

4. Look at the circuit diagram below. Redraw it to show what happens when the driver of a car closes the ignition switch by using a key.

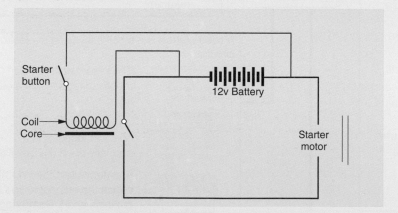

Extension question

5. Describe how you would investigate how the number of coils in an electromagnet affects the strength of the magnetic field. In your answer you should include:

    (a) Diagrams of the apparatus set up for use.

    (b) Any steps taken to make sure that this is a fair test.

    (c) The results you might expect to get.

Chapter 23
More about energy

Temperature and energy

Remember

- No action can take place without energy.
- There are different forms of energy.
- Energy can be changed from one form to another – these changes always involve internal/thermal energy.

Hot and cold: Measuring temperature

You should by now be familiar with the concept of measuring temperature. Dipping your finger in is not very reliable!

What do we mean by temperature?

Remember that internal/thermal energy is just one kind of energy. If a material has a lot of internal/thermal energy, we say it is **hot** and, if it has very little heat, we say it is **cold**. **Temperature** is a scale of numbers that we use to measure the amount of internal/thermal energy that a material has.

Look back to the section on dissolving solids (page 159). We saw that we can dissolve more sugar in hot water than we can in cold water. Rather than just saying 'hot' it would be better to give an actual number. What feels like hot to one person may not feel quite so hot to another person. For this reason, scientists measure the temperature of the water using a thermometer when they are doing an experiment such as this. So every person who measures the temperature of the same hot water, using a thermometer, should get exactly the same number.

Temperature scales

The **Fahrenheit** scale was invented in 1724. Gabriel Daniel Fahrenheit decided that the zero on his scale would be the lowest temperature he could reach; this was the temperature of the strongest salt solution he could make. He also decided that 100 °F would be the temperature of our bodies.

In 1742 Anders Celsius, a Swiss astronomer, invented a different scale. This was the **Celsius** (or Centigrade) scale. This scale was based around the freezing point and boiling point of pure water. In science, we use the Celsius scale.

There is also another scale used in science, called the **Kelvin** (K) scale. On this scale the zero is at minus 273 °C, the lowest temperature possible. 0 °C is the same as 273 K (note that we don't write in the ° sign on the Kelvin scale; we just use a K to show that the Kelvin scale is being used).

Here is a comparison of the three temperature scales:

Different temperature scales

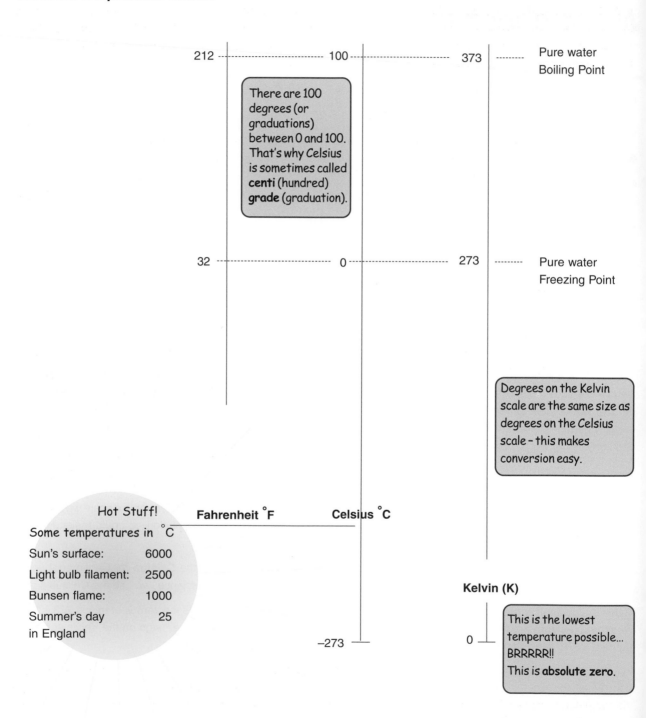

212 ---------------------------------- 100 ---------------------------------- 373 --------- Pure water
Boiling Point

There are 100 degrees (or graduations) between 0 and 100. That's why Celsius is sometimes called **centi** (hundred) **grade** (graduation).

32 ---------------------------------- 0 ---------------------------------- 273 --------- Pure water
Freezing Point

Degrees on the Kelvin scale are the same size as degrees on the Celsius scale – this makes conversion easy.

Fahrenheit °F   **Celsius °C**

Hot Stuff!

Some temperatures in °C

Sun's surface:	6000
Light bulb filament:	2500
Bunsen flame:	1000
Summer's day in England	25

Kelvin (K)

−273   0

This is the lowest temperature possible... BRRRRR!!
This is **absolute zero**.

Different thermometers

There are many different types of thermometer as well as the liquid-in-glass type you are already hopefully familiar with. **Thermocouples** have two different wires twisted together. Two sets of these junctions are connected to an instrument (a galvanometer) that measures voltage. The thermocouple produces a voltage when it is heated. One of the junctions is put into melting ice at 0 °C to provide a reference point and the other junction is used to measure the temperature you want to know. Thermocouples have several advantages:

● they can work at higher temperatures than many other types of thermometer; and

● they can be used to measure the temperature of very small objects.

Thermocouples can be built into **temperature probes**. These have a metal or glass casing outside the thermocouple which means that they can be pushed into quite hard objects. Temperature probes are very useful for measuring the temperature of foods (such as meat and fish) and soil. A cheap and convenient thermometer uses a **liquid crystal strip** which changes colour according to temperature. These strips are used as aquarium thermometers and can give a rapid indication of your skin temperature if placed against the forehead.

Different types of thermometer

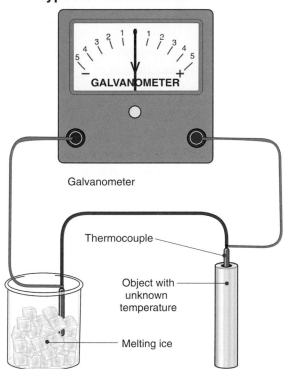

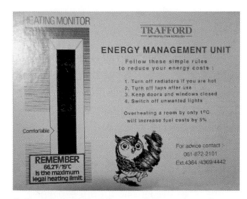

A liquid crystal strip used for measuring room temperature

Body temperature: How warm is warm blooded?

Humans, like other mammals, are **warm blooded**. This means that they can keep their body temperature constant even when the temperature of their surroundings is changing. We can check just how warm a human is by using a thermometer. Doctors can use a special thermometer with a very short scale that starts at the lowest possible body temperature someone can have and goes up to the highest. Many people have a thermometer like this at home. If you aren't feeling very well, your mother or father can check your temperature.

Measuring body temperature

The human body temperature can be measured with a thermometer, either:
• under the tongue; or
• in the armpit.
The thermometer should be left in place for the recommended time before reading it.

If microbes infect our body, the temperature may go up to 39-40 °C. This is called a FEVER. If the temperature gets higher than this, it can be very dangerous.

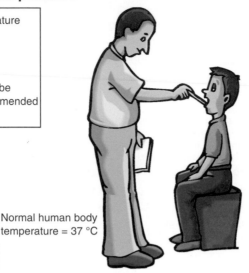

Normal human body temperature = 37 °C

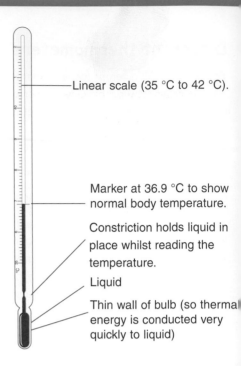

Linear scale (35 °C to 42 °C).

Marker at 36.9 °C to show normal body temperature.

Constriction holds liquid in place whilst reading the temperature.

Liquid

Thin wall of bulb (so thermal energy is conducted very quickly to liquid)

In summary: Energy and temperature

● **Temperature** is a way of describing how hot or cold an object is. It gives a measure of how concentrated the internal/thermal energy is in an object. The unit of temperature is the **degree Celsius** (°C), and temperature is measured using a **thermometer**.

● **Internal/thermal** is one form of energy. The unit of energy is called a **joule** (J).

An object can contain a great deal of internal/thermal energy without having a high temperature. For example, a warm bath contains a great deal of thermal energy, but it is not very hot. This is because the thermal energy is spread out between the many particles of water in the bath. An object may contain a lot of other types of energy without being warm. Foods and fuels contain a great deal of energy, but they don't become hot until the energy is released as thermal energy when the object burns.

Temperature and the kinetic theory

Remember that the kinetic theory explains the behaviour of solids, liquids and gases in terms of moving particles (see page 151). When the particles are close together, there are strong forces between them and they attract one another. When a substance is heated, the particles move more quickly. The source energy is transferred to the particles as increased **kinetic energy**. At the same time the substance's temperature goes up.

The **temperature** of a substance is a measure of the **average kinetic energy of its particles**.

Key words

Temperature – a measure of how concentrated an object's internal/thermal energy is.

Thermometer – an instrument for measuring temperature.

Internal/thermal energy – giving an object more of this makes it hotter.

Thermocouple – two wires twisted together that can be used as a very sensitive thermometer.

Kinetic energy – energy possessed by moving particles.

Exercise 23.1: Temperature

1. Explain how a thermometer works.

2. What is the melting point of pure water using the Celsius scale? What is the boiling point of pure water using the Celsius scale?

3. Sugar and fat contain a lot of energy. Ice cream contains a lot of sugar and fat. Why isn't ice cream hot?

4. What is the body temperature of a normal healthy human?

5. Which is hotter, a burning sparkler or the school swimming pool? Which one has the most internal/ thermal energy?

Extension question

6. Two liquids often used in thermometers are mercury and alcohol. Some of the properties of these two liquids are compared in this table:

	Mercury	Alcohol
Boiling Point	365 °C	78.5 °C
Freezing Point	-39 °C	-117 °C
Colour	Silver	Clear, but can be dyed
Cost	Expensive	Cheap
Conducts thermal energy	Well (heats up quickly)	Not so well (heats up slowly)
Toxicity	Poisonous	Not poisonous in small amounts
Metal or not	Metal	Non-metal
Conducts electricity	Well	An insulator
Flammability	Non-flammable	Flammable
Density	High	Low
Surface Tension	High	Not so high
Degree of expansion when heated	Average	Large

(a) Which property is most important if you want a very sensitive thermometer?

(b) Why is alcohol most common in school laboratory thermometers?

(c) Which type of thermometer would be most useful for measuring the temperature of a lamb stew?

(d) Which liquid would be best-suited in a thermometer used to measure the temperature in a freezer?

The passage of thermal energy: Insulators and conductors

Remember

● Temperature depends on the average kinetic energy of particles.

Before we start learning some new things, it is probably a good idea just to check that you have remembered exactly what thermal conduction and thermal insulation mean.

What is thermal conduction?

Thermal energy can pass from one place to another. This thermal energy can take place in three ways: **radiation** (e.g. thermal energy from the Sun), **convection** (e.g. when the liquid in a saucepan rises and begins to cook the food) and **conduction** (e.g. thermal energy reaching your hand when you touch a hot plate). We are now going to learn about all three.

Materials that allow thermal to pass through them are called **thermal conductors**. Some materials are better thermal conductors than others. A good thermal conductor often feels cold because it's so good at conducting thermal energy away from your hand (assuming its colder than your hand in the first place).

Thermal energy will always travel **from a warmer place to a cooler one**. This can be a problem for many reasons:

● Our bodies are usually warmer than our surroundings, so we would cool down by losing thermal energy. If we got too cold, it could easily affect our life processes (see page 8).

● Our houses are usually warmer than the surroundings, so they lose thermal energy. We can help stop this thermal energy loss by having good insulation in our homes. This is important because the thermal energy was produced in the first place by burning fuel. Fuel is expensive and there is only a limited amount of fuel available on this Earth.

● Freshly-cooked food and drinks can cool down once they are taken away from the place they were cooked.

● Frozen food is colder than its surroundings. It will tend to gain thermal energy, warm up and melt. This means we cannot store it for very long.

What is thermal insulation?

Some materials do not let thermal energy pass through them. These materials are called **thermal insulators**. Being a thermal insulator is very useful in helping to stop thermal energy moving from one place to another. For example, oven gloves, a wooden handle on a saucepan, a cork teapot stand, the plastic casing of a refrigerator, a tea cosy.

How does conduction happen?

We can use the idea of kinetic energy in particles to explain what happens when a hot object is placed in contact with a cold object. Metals are good conductors of thermal energy because of the way in which their atoms are packed together (see page 151). If one end of a bar of metal is heated, the atoms at that end will start to vibrate because of the thermal energy. These atoms will pass on their vibration to other atoms near them.

In this way thermal energy is passed along the metal, as shown below:

Thermal energy transfer by conduction

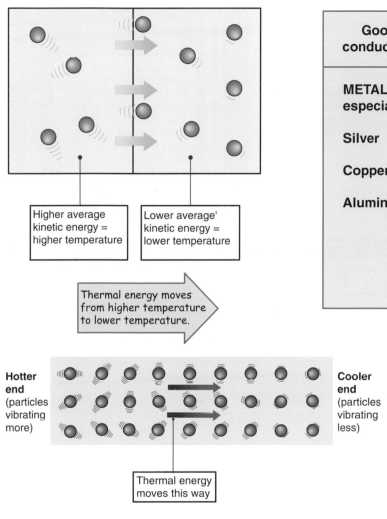

Good conductors	Poor conductors (insulators)	
METALS especially:	Glass	
	Water	
Silver	Plastic	
Copper	Wood	
Aluminum	Materials with air trapped in them	Wool Fibrewool Plastic foam Fur Feathers
	Air	

Higher average kinetic energy = higher temperature

Lower average' kinetic energy = lower temperature

Thermal energy moves from higher temperature to lower temperature.

Hotter end (particles vibrating more)

Cooler end (particles vibrating less)

Thermal energy moves this way

Fat is an excellent insulator:

Sea mammals, like whales and dolphins, have a thick layer of blubber (fat) beneath the skin. This reduces the loss of thermal energy from the body to the cold water

Insulators such as those shown in the diagram on page 275 do not have this kind of structure. The particles in glass, plastic, rubber and wood cannot pass on this kinetic energy from one to another. Air is an excellent insulator because the particles are so far apart that they cannot easily pass on energy.

Convection

Although air is an excellent insulator, it can pass on thermal energy *if it is free to circulate*. When air is heated, it expands because the air particles gain energy and move further apart. As it expands, it becomes less dense (see page 151), and it floats upwards because cooler, denser air sinks and pushes it out of the way. This circulating flow of air is called a **convection current**:

Thermal energy transfer by convection

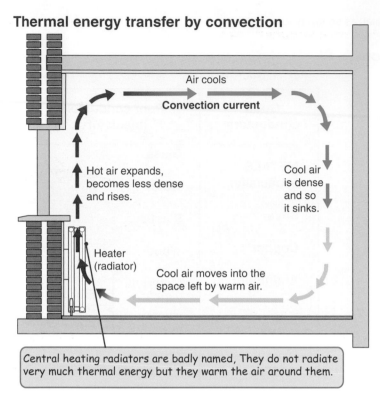

Air cools

Convection current

Hot air expands, becomes less dense and rises.

Cool air is dense and so it sinks.

Heater (radiator)

Cool air moves into the space left by warm air.

Central heating radiators are badly named, They do not radiate very much thermal energy but they warm the air around them.

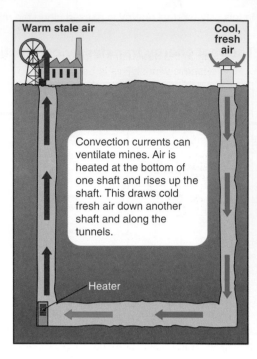

Warm stale air

Cool, fresh air

Convection currents can ventilate mines. Air is heated at the bottom of one shaft and rises up the shaft. This draws cold fresh air down another shaft and along the tunnels.

Heater

WInds are caused by convection currents. During the day the land warms up more quickly than the sea. The warm air over the land rises and cold air from the sea moves in to replace it. So, during the day, breezes blow from the sea towards the land. At night the land cools down faster than the sea. The warm air over the sea rises and cold air from the land moves in to replace it. So, during the night, breezes tend to blow from the land out towards the sea.

Convection currents cause winds

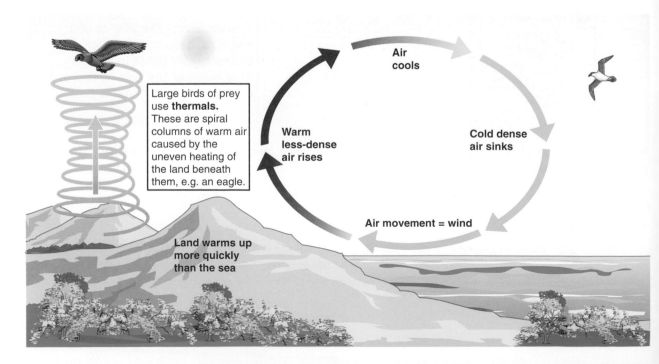

Air cools

Large birds of prey use **thermals.** These are spiral columns of warm air caused by the uneven heating of the land beneath them, e.g. an eagle.

Warm less-dense air rises

Cold dense air sinks

Air movement = wind

Land warms up more quickly than the sea

Hard work on a summer's day!

Cycling to the beach in the morning – against the onshore winds! This is because the land **warms** more quickly than the sea.

Cycling home in the evening against the offshore winds! This is because the land **cools** more quickly than the sea.

Convection also transfers thermal energy in liquids

Here's an experiment which shows how convection also transfers thermal energy in liquids. If you drop a crystal of potassium manganate (VII) into a beaker of water, a purple colour begins to spread out into the water as the crystal dissolves. If the water is gently heated, the colour rises through the water. This happens because the thermal energy transferred to the water raises the kinetic energy of the water and the potassium manganate (VII) particles. The particles move further apart and the water expands. The warmer water is now less dense than the colder water at the top of the beaker, so the warmer water rises upwards, carrying the coloured potassium manganate (VII).

Convection in liquids

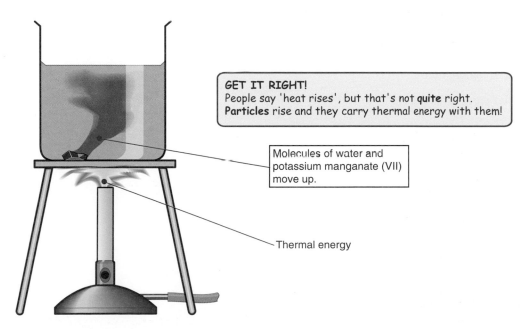

GET IT RIGHT!
People say 'heat rises', but that's not **quite** right.
Particles rise and they carry thermal energy with them!

Molecules of water and potassium manganate (VII) move up.

Thermal energy

Key words

Thermal conduction – movement of thermal energy through a medium.

Thermal insulation – prevention of the movement of thermal energy.

Convection – movement of thermal energy as a flow of a liquid or gas.

Exercise 23.2: Conduction and convection

1. Why do a knife and fork feel colder than the table they are lying on?

2. Why does glass in a window feel cooler than the wooden window frame around it?

3. Put these materials into order of thermal conduction with the best conductor first and the worst one last.

   steel   plastic   glass   air   wood   cloth

4. Explain each of the following:

   (a) In most saucepans the base is made of metal but the handle is plastic.

   (b) The best sleeping bags have pockets filled with feathers and air.

5. In this diagram thermal energy is flowing through a metal bar. Which end of the bar has:

   (a) The higher temperature?

   (b) The faster-moving particles?

More methods of thermal energy transfer

Starting point

●   Thermal energy can be transferred to the particles that make up all substances.

As we have learnt, thermal energy can be transferred by conduction and convection. These two processes transfer thermal energy to the particles of substances. Another way of transferring thermal energy is **evaporation**. To understand how this works, we must make sure we know how particles behave and understand kinetic theory (see page 152). In a liquid the molecules vibrate and move around, but they are still close enough for the forces of attraction to hold them together. Not all the molecules move at the same speed (i.e. they don't all have the same kinetic energy). Some molecules move more quickly than average and some move more slowly. A molecule can gain enough energy to overcome the forces of attraction and that's when a molecule can escape from other molecules. This is what happens during evaporation:

Thermal energy transfer by evaporation

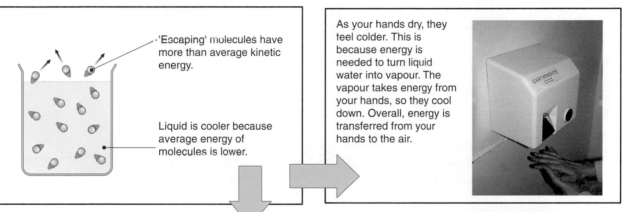

'Escaping' molecules have more than average kinetic energy.

Liquid is cooler because average energy of molecules is lower.

As your hands dry, they feel colder. This is because energy is needed to turn liquid water into vapour. The vapour takes energy from your hands, so they cool down. Overall, energy is transferred from your hands to the air.

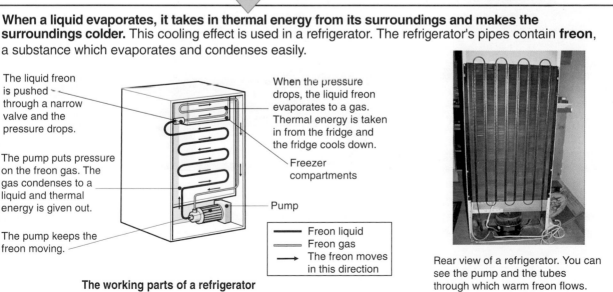

When a liquid evaporates, it takes in thermal energy from its surroundings and makes the surroundings colder. This cooling effect is used in a refrigerator. The refrigerator's pipes contain **freon**, a substance which evaporates and condenses easily.

The liquid freon is pushed through a narrow valve and the pressure drops.

The pump puts pressure on the freon gas. The gas condenses to a liquid and thermal energy is given out.

The pump keeps the freon moving.

When the pressure drops, the liquid freon evaporates to a gas. Thermal energy is taken in from the fridge and the fridge cools down.

Freezer compartments

Pump

—— Freon liquid
=== Freon gas
→ The freon moves in this direction

The working parts of a refrigerator

Rear view of a refrigerator. You can see the pump and the tubes through which warm freon flows.

Only the fastest molecules (the ones with the most energy) can break free from the liquid. This means that the average energy of the molecules left behind is lower, and so the temperature of the liquid falls slightly. In other words, *evaporation of a liquid causes cooling.*

Radiation

The Earth obtains an enormous amount of thermal energy from the Sun. The Sun's energy travels to all parts of the solar system as electromagnetic radiation. This includes:

- light rays (that we can see); and

- infrared rays (which are invisible).

All rays cause heating.

The Sun and radiation

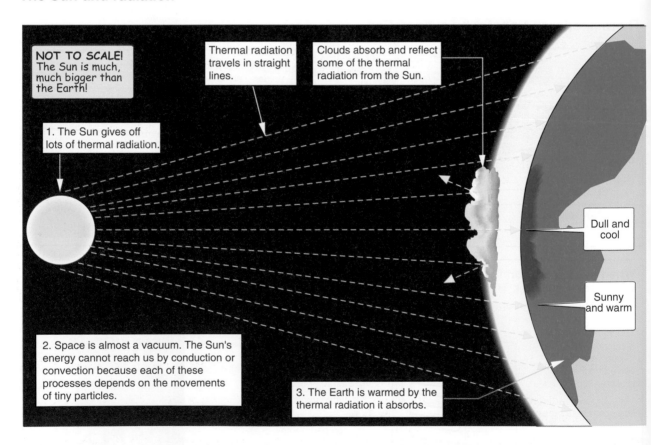

The radiation we absorb can heat us up and so is called **thermal radiation**. All warm or hot objects give off thermal radiation. Some examples are shown on the next page:

The grill's heating element gives off thermal radiation in all directions

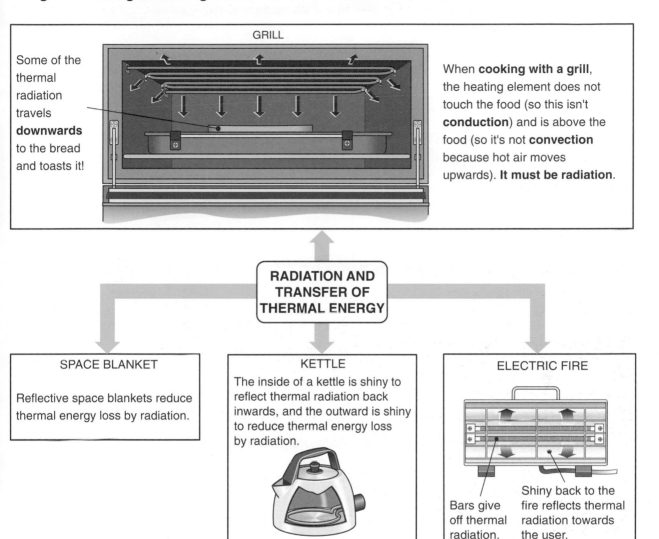

GRILL

Some of the thermal radiation travels **downwards** to the bread and toasts it!

When **cooking with a grill**, the heating element does not touch the food (so this isn't **conduction**) and is above the food (so it's not **convection** because hot air moves upwards). **It must be radiation**.

RADIATION AND TRANSFER OF THERMAL ENERGY

SPACE BLANKET

Reflective space blankets reduce thermal energy loss by radiation.

KETTLE

The inside of a kettle is shiny to reflect thermal radiation back inwards, and the outward is shiny to reduce thermal energy loss by radiation.

ELECTRIC FIRE

Bars give off thermal radiation.

Shiny back to the fire reflects thermal radiation towards the user.

Black surfaces are the best at giving off thermal radiation. A black surface looks black because it absorbs most of the light that falls on it (see page 419). A lot of this light energy is radiated as thermal radiation which cannot be seen. A good radiating surface also absorbs thermal radiation well; if you paint part of your hand black and hold it in front of a fire, the black part will feel hotter than the rest.

White or silvery surfaces are poor at absorbing radiation but good at reflecting radiation. In hot, sunny countries buildings are often painted white and light-coloured clothes are worn so that they absorb as little of the Sun's radiation as possible. These surfaces are also bad at releasing energy by radiation.

These rules of absorption and reflection are shown below:

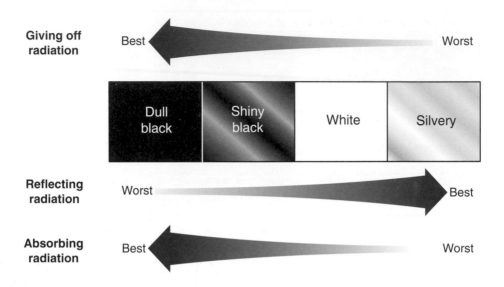

Radiation travels in straight lines. When you stand looking at a fire, the thermal radiation will warm your face but your back will feel cold. Radiation is not a good way of heating a room because it only heats the parts of the room that the radiation can reach in straight lines. An area behind your favourite armchair could be quite cold. Convection is a much better way of heating a space such as a room.

Reducing thermal energy flow: The vacuum flask

A vacuum flask is made of two containers inside one another and separated by a vacuum. The surfaces of both containers are silvery and so reduce energy transfer by radiation. The vacuum between the containers prevents thermal energy loss by conduction and convection. A vacuum flask can keep a hot liquid hot or a cold liquid cold (though not at the same time!).

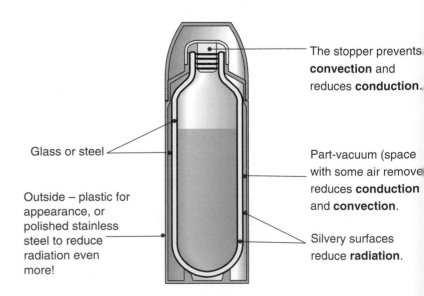

The stopper prevents **convection** and reduces **conduction.**

Glass or steel

Part-vacuum (space with some air remove reduces **conduction** and **convection.**

Outside – plastic for appearance, or polished stainless steel to reduce radiation even more!

Silvery surfaces reduce **radiation.**

Key words

Evaporation – transfer of thermal energy as a liquid changes to a vapour.

Radiation – transfer of thermal energy as electromagnetic waves.

Vacuum – a space that contains no particles.

Exercise 23.3: Radiation

1. If these cars are left standing in a sunny car park, which one would you expect to get hotter inside? Explain your answer.

2. An electric oven has heating elements in its walls. These walls release thermal energy as electricity flows through them.

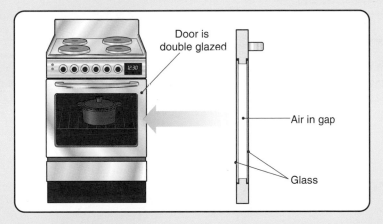

(a) Name the process that transfers thermal energy through the walls of the oven.

(b) The inside surfaces of the oven are usually painted black. Give a good reason for this.

(c) If you are cooking a pizza (which needs a high temperature), you are recommended to put it on the top shelf of the oven. Why should you do this?

(d) An oven door is double-glazed. Explain how the double-glazing cuts down the amount of thermal energy which is lost from the oven.

Extension question

3. Philip and Natasha wanted a cup of tea. They decide to investigate how quickly the tea cooled. They filled two mugs, made from different materials, with hot tea. The temperature of the tea was measured every five minutes for twenty minutes. Their results are shown in the table below:

Time in minutes	Temperature in mug A in °C	Temperature in mug B in °C
0	90	90
5	69	49
10	46	32
15	35	29
20	27	22

The room temperature stayed the same, at 20 °C.

(a) Plot the results on a line graph (you should have one line for each mug).

(b) What was the temperature in mug A after 4 minutes?

(c) How long did it take the tea in mug B to reach 30 °C?

(d) What was the difference in temperature between the tea in the two mugs after 15 minutes?

(e) Which mug was made from the better insulating material?

(f) If the two mugs were made from the same plastic material, but one was dark blue and the other was yellow, which colour was mug A and which was mug B? Explain your answer.

Chapter 24
Conservation of energy

Remember

- All energy chains end up as internal/thermal energy.
- Energy is not lost during an energy transfer.
- Energy can be changed from one form to another.

Power stations generate electricity by using some sort of fuel. Power stations are not 100% efficient. In fact, about half of the energy in the fuel does not end up as electricity that we can use. This energy is wasted as far as we are concerned, but it has not disappeared. We say that this energy has been **dissipated**.

Useful device

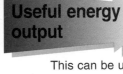

Wasted energy:

Thermal and sound

This energy is **dissipated**.

This can be used to carry out **work** that is useful to humans.

$$\text{Efficiency} = \frac{\text{Useful energy OUTPUT}}{\text{Energy INPUT}} \times 100$$

If we measure how much energy we put into a device and how much energy we get out of the device, we can work out how efficient the device is. **Efficiency** of a device or machine compares the energy used by the device with the useful energy given out by the device.

This diagram shows the efficiency of a common power tool, an electric drill:

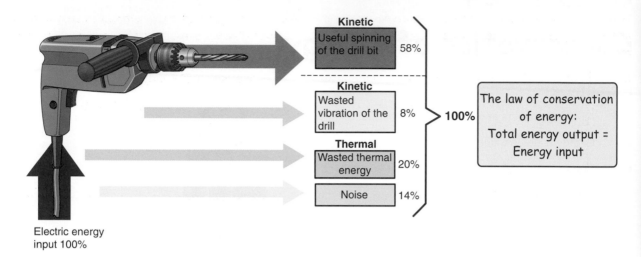

Kinetic
Useful spinning of the drill bit — 58%

Kinetic
Wasted vibration of the drill — 8%

Thermal
Wasted thermal energy — 20%

Noise — 14%

} 100%

The law of conservation of energy:
Total energy output = Energy input

Electric energy input 100%

We can use a special type of diagram to look at the energy transformations and losses when using a machine. This is called a **Sankey** diagram. A Sankey diagram for the electric drill is shown below:

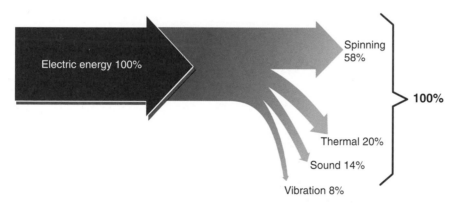

Electric energy 100%

Spinning 58%

} 100%

Thermal 20%

Sound 14%

Vibration 8%

An important example of energy transformation occurs in the engine of a car. We use cars a great deal in the U.K. and it is important to realise how much of the stored energy in a fossil fuel (petrol) is wasted.

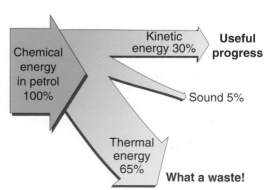

Chemical energy in petrol 100%

Kinetic energy 30% — **Useful progress**

Sound 5%

Thermal energy 65% — **What a waste!**

The Law of Conservation of Energy

Here is a reminder about the Law of Conservation of Energy. When energy is dissipated we can't use it any more but, as we have just learnt, it has not been lost. What in fact has happened is that the energy has been changed into some other form.

Energy can never be created nor destroyed – this is the **Law of Conservation of Energy**.

A final point to remember is that the conservation of energy is not the same as saving energy (see page 274).

Key words

Dissipated – spread out from the place of production.

Efficiency – a way of comparing the energy given out by a device with the energy it uses – high efficiency means very little energy is wasted.

Sankey diagram – a picture which shows what happens to the energy input to a machine.

Law of Conservation of Energy – energy can never be created or destroyed, but can be changed from one form into another.

Exercise 24.1: Energy conservation

1. What forms of energy does a TV set produce?

2. Give one reason why you should never put a piece of paper over a lamp to cut down the light it gives out.

3. Look at this diagram of a power station. Fill in the missing words in (a) – (e) to show how energy is lost as waste forms of energy.

Thermal energy losses at a power station

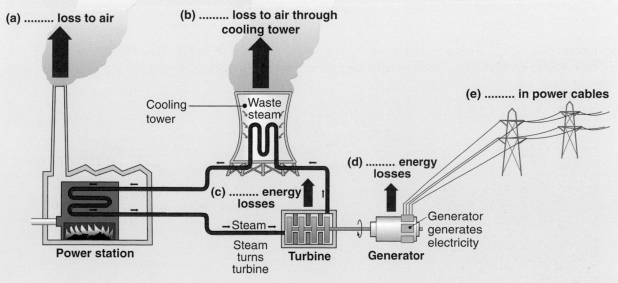

(a) .... loss to air

(b) .... loss to air through cooling tower

(e) .... in power cables

Cooling tower

Waste steam

(d) .... energy losses

(c) .... energy losses

Steam

Generator generates electricity

Power station

Steam turns turbine

Turbine

Generator

Now look at the Sankey diagram for the power station.

Coal in power station 200 J

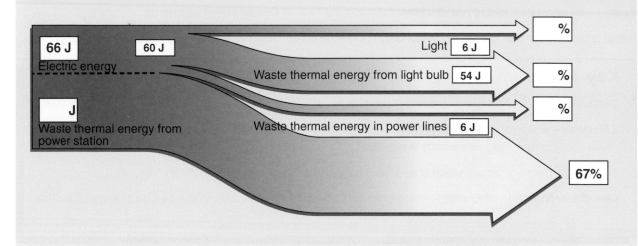

(f) What percentage of energy is wasted as thermal energy from light bulbs?

(g) What percentage of energy is lost as waste thermal energy in the power lines?

(h) How many joules of energy put into the power station end up as waste thermal enrgy from the power station itself?

(i) What is the overall efficiency of the power station in converting energy to light in light bulbs?

Energy and living things

You can tell that something is a living organism because it carries out certain life processes (see page 8). One of these life processes is **respiration**. Respiration releases the energy needed to carry out the other life processes (see page 46).

We obtain the energy needed to carry out these life processes from the stored chemical energy in food. Respiration releases the energy from food in small packets that can then be used to carry out the processes that keep a living organism alive. The link between food and life processes is shown here:

Energy is needed for work

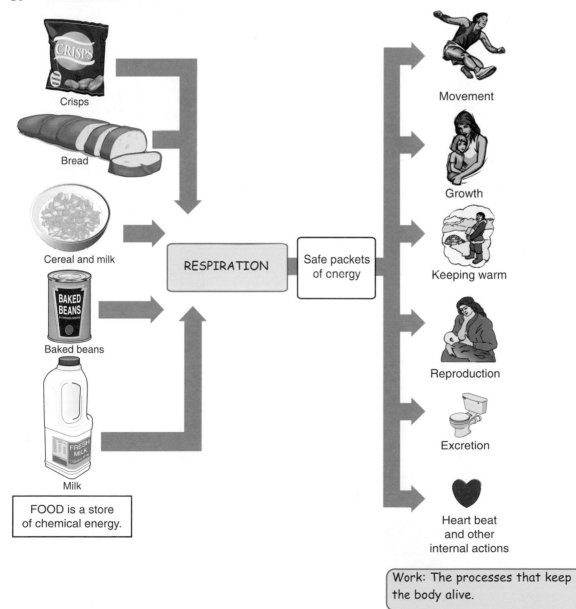

Crisps

Bread

Cereal and milk

Baked beans

Milk

FOOD is a store of chemical energy.

RESPIRATION

Safe packets of energy

Movement

Growth

Keeping warm

Reproduction

Excretion

Heart beat and other internal actions

Work: The processes that keep the body alive.

Where did the food energy come from?

Energy is transferred from one organism to another through **food chains** (see page 99). Plants are able to trap light energy and store it as food molecules. Different types of food molecules have different amounts of energy. It is important to balance the amount of food energy taken in with the amount of energy needed for keeping the body in good working order.

The energy balance

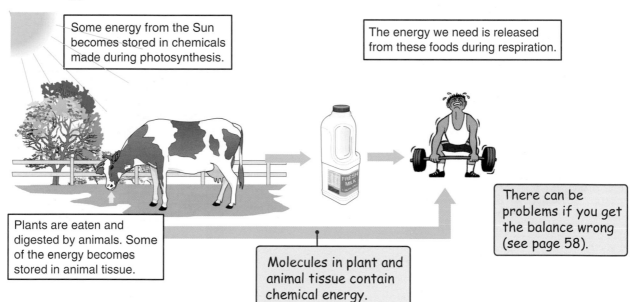

Some energy from the Sun becomes stored in chemicals made during photosynthesis.

The energy we need is released from these foods during respiration.

Plants are eaten and digested by animals. Some of the energy becomes stored in animal tissue.

Molecules in plant and animal tissue contain chemical energy.

There can be problems if you get the balance wrong (see page 58).

Energy intake from food ...		... energy needed for work.	
Energy drink 80 kJ	Cereal 1300 kJ	**Activity**	**Energy released by the body every ten minutes**
Crisps 550 kJ	Bread 300 kJ per slice	Lying in bed	60 000 J (60 kJ)
Chapatti 1500 kJ	Cream cake 1250 kJ	Walking slowly	135 000 J (135 kJ)
		Walking quickly	210 000 J (210 kJ)
		Running	250 000 J (250 kJ)
		Swimming	330 000 J (330 kJ)

... must be balanced with ...

Keeping warm on cold days increases the amount of energy you need.

Remember that energy is measured in **joules** (J) and that one thousand joules is called a **kilojoule** (kJ). You can find out the energy content of different foods by reading the information on the packet. It is a legal requirement to show how much energy is contained in a food.

Energy in foods

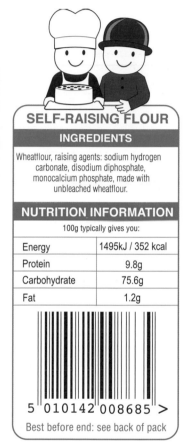

NUTRITION INFORMATION

100g typically gives you:

Energy	1495kJ / 352 kcal
Protein	9.8g
Carbohydrate	75.6g
Fat	1.2g

5 010142 008685 >

Best before end: see back of pack

Self-raising flour

NUTRITION INFORMATION

Typical values	per 100gm of Nestle Shreddies	per 45gm with 125ml Semi-skimmed milk
Energy	1485kJ 350kcal	922kJ 218kcal
Protein	9.9g	8.8g
Carbohydrate of which: sugars	73.4g 15.5g	39.2g 13.8g
Fat of which: saturated	1.9g 0.4g	2.9g 1.3g
Fibre	9.8g	4.4g
Sodium	0.4g	0.2g

Cereal

NUTRITION INFORMATION

Typical values	Per 100g	Per serving (207g)
Energy	306kJ/72kcal	633kJ/149kcal
Protein	4.6g	9.6g
Carbohydrate (of which sugars)	12.9g (4.8g)	26.8g (9.9g)
Fat (of which saturated)	0.2g (trace)	0.4g (trace)
Fibre	3.7g	7.6g
Sodium	0.3g	0.7g
Salt equivalent	0.9g	1.8g

Baked beans

NUTRITION INFORMATION

100g of uncooked pasta weighs approximately 190g when cooked

TYPICAL VALUES (dry weight)

	per 90g	per 100g
Energy	1403k J 330 k cal	1559 kJ 367 k cal
Protein	10.4g	11.5g
Carbohydrate of which sugars of which starch	71.2g 1.8g 69.4g	79.1g 2.0g 77.1g
Fat	0.5g	0.5g
Fibre	1.8g	2.0g
Sodium	less than 0.1g	less than 0.1g
per 90g	**330 calories**	**0.5g fat**

GUIDELINE DAILY AMOUNTS

EACH DAY	WOMEN	MEN
CALORIES	2000	2500
FAT	70g	95g

OFFICIAL GOVERMENT FIGURES FOR AVERAGE ADULTS

Pasta

Basmati Rice

NUTRITION INFORMATION

Healthy living, a low fat food
A 75g serving of rice weighs approx. 195g when cooked

TYPICAL COMPOSITION	Uncooked	
	A 75g (2.5 oz) serving provides	100g (3.5 oz) provide
Energy	1103kJ 260kcal	1470kJ 346kcal
Protein	6.3g	8.4g
Carbohydrate of which sugars	0.7g 0.2g	0.9g 0.2g
Fat of which saturates	57.1g trace	76.1g 0.1g
Fibre	trace	0.1g
Sodium	trace	trace

1 kg℮

The King of rices with fragrant flavour and aroma

Gluten free

See bottom of pack for best by date:

Rice

One joule is a very small amount of energy compared with the amount of energy that we use. You use up 1 joule of energy by lifting a mass of 100 g (such as an average-sized apple) through 1 metre. If you lift 1 kg through 1 metre, then you use up 10 J of energy. Don't forget that we use energy from food for many things and not just for movement.

A famous scientist called John Tyndall did not realise this and assumed that all the energy from his food could be used in moving. He calculated that he could climb to the top of the Matterhorn (a mountain in Switzerland) using just the energy from a ham sandwich. He tried to do this, and only took a ham sandwich to eat – he became very tired and did not complete the climb!

Key words

Respiration – the release of energy from food molecules.

Food chain – the transfer of energy from one organism to another.

Joule – the unit of energy. One **kilojoule** equals one thousand joules.

Exercise 24.2: Food and energy

1. Look at the food labels on page 341. Make a table with these headings for the different foods.

Food type	Energy

(a) Put in the correct units. Think carefully about this. The food label will give energy values per serving and per 100 g. Which one should you use if this is going to be a fair test?

(b) Make a bar chart to show the energy values for the different foods.

(c) Which food would be most useful if you were going on a long bike ride? Explain your answer.

(d) Running uses up about 250 kJ in ten minutes. How long would you need to run for to burn off the energy in a bar of chocolate?

2. Let us assume that if you lift 1 kg through 1 m, you will use 10 J of energy.

(a) Freddie weighs 100 kg, and has to climb steps to a total height of 12 m as he moves around the school one morning. How many kilojoules of energy will he use?

(b) Gena weighs 50 kg. She has to climb steps to a total height of 12 m as she moves around the school. How many kilojoules of energy of energy will she use.

(c) What advantage does Gena have over Freddie? What are the likely future health implications for Freddie?

Extension question

3. You can find out how much energy a food contains by burning it to release the stored energy. The thermal energy given off is then used to raise the temperature of a certain volume of water, as shown in the diagram.

Measuring the energy content of food

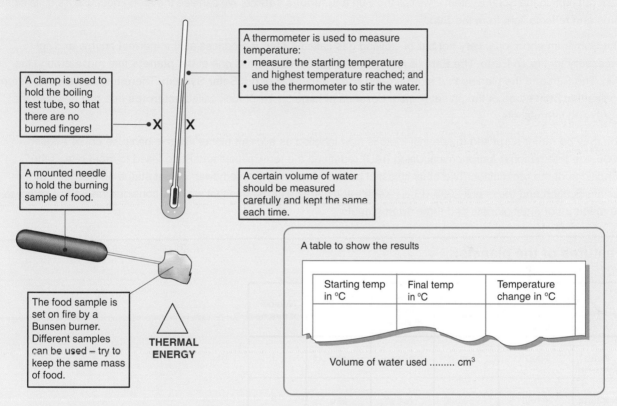

A clamp is used to hold the boiling test tube, so that there are no burned fingers!

A thermometer is used to measure temperature:
* measure the starting temperature and highest temperature reached; and
* use the thermometer to stir the water.

A mounted needle to hold the burning sample of food.

A certain volume of water should be measured carefully and kept the same each time.

The food sample is set on fire by a Bunsen burner. Different samples can be used – try to keep the same mass of food.

THERMAL ENERGY

A table to show the results

Starting temp in °C	Final temp in °C	Temperature change in °C

Volume of water used .... cm³

(a) What is the input (independent) variable in this experiment?

(b) What is the outcome (dependent) variable in this experiment?

(c) Which factors are kept constant to keep this a fair test?

(d) Scientists know that it takes 4.2 J to raise the temperature of 1 cm³ of water by 1 °C. In an experiment like this one, Freddie found that his food sample raised the temperature of 20 cm³ of water by 60 °C. Work out how much energy the food sample gave to the water.

Chapter 25
The Earth and the Solar System

We live on the Earth but we can see the Sun and the Moon quite clearly. We can see the Sun because it is the source of all our light in the Solar System – we call the Sun a **luminous source**. We can see the Moon because it's quite close to us and reflects light from the Sun.

The Sun is an enormous, very hot ball of glowing gas called a **star**. It produces all the thermal energy and light necessary for life on Earth. The Earth is much smaller and cooler, and is one of the **planets** that move around the Sun. The Sun and the planets that move around it make up most of our **Solar System**. There are also **moons** (large bodies that orbit some of the planets) and thousands of large lumps of rock called **asteroids** in a belt between the fourth and fifth planets.

You may be rather surprised to see that Pluto is now labelled as a 'dwarf planet'. This is because on 24 August 2006, the International Astronomical Union (IAU) redefined the term 'planet' and Pluto failed to meet one of the conditions of the redefinition. Two other celestial bodies have been granted dwarf planet status on the basis of the reclassification and these are 2003 UB_{313} ('Xena') and Ceres. This means that we now consider the Solar System to be made up of eight planets and three dwarf planets.

Features of the planets:

Planet	Average distance from Sun in million km	Diameter in km	Orbit time in years	Surface temperature in °C	Number of moons
Pluto Dwarf planet	5900	2300	247.00	-230	1
Neptune	4490	50 000	164.80	-220	8
Uranus	2870	51 000	84.01	-210	15
Saturn	1427	120 000	29.46	-180	23
Jupiter	778	143 000	11.86	-150	16
ASTEROID BELT					
Mars	228	6800	1.88	-23	2
Earth	150	12 800	1.00	20	1
Venus	108	12 100	0.62	480	0
Mercury	58	4900	0.24	350	0

Remember:
Water boils at 100 °C and freezes at 0 °C.

The Solar System is too big for sizes and distances to be shown on some diagrams. In this diagram, sizes are approximately to scale but distances from the Sun are not.

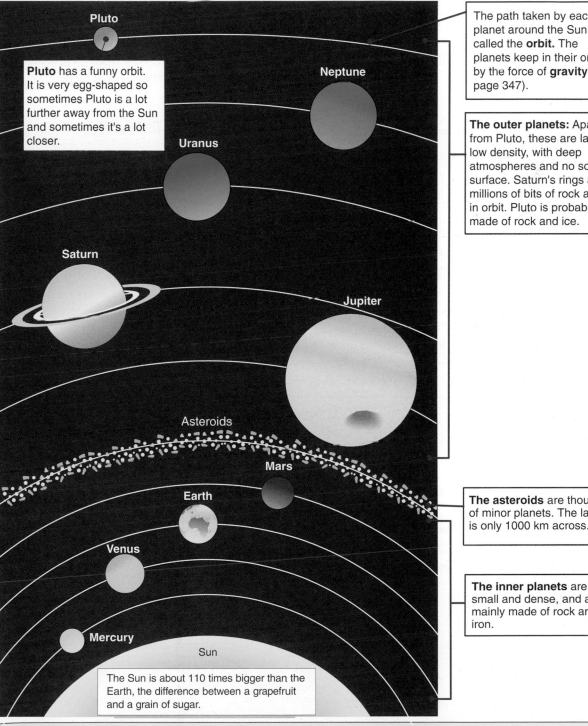

Pluto

Pluto has a funny orbit. It is very egg-shaped so sometimes Pluto is a lot further away from the Sun and sometimes it's a lot closer.

Neptune

The path taken by each planet around the Sun is called the **orbit.** The planets keep in their orbits by the force of **gravity** (see page 347).

Uranus

The outer planets: Apart from Pluto, these are large, low density, with deep atmospheres and no solid surface. Saturn's rings are millions of bits of rock and ice in orbit. Pluto is probably made of rock and ice.

Saturn

Jupiter

Asteroids

Mars

The asteroids are thousands of minor planets. The largest is only 1000 km across.

Earth

Venus

The inner planets are small and dense, and are mainly made of rock and iron.

Mercury

Sun

The Sun is about 110 times bigger than the Earth, the difference between a grapefruit and a grain of sugar.

Remembering names can be difficult! Make up a silly story to help you remember the order of the eight planets and the dwarf planet Pluto.
My Very Eccentric Mother Just Shot Uncle Norman's Pig

When we look at the Sun, it appears circular. It doesn't matter where we look from, or what time of the year it is, the Sun *always* looks round. This tells us that the Sun is a **sphere**. Astronauts travelling around the Earth have been able to take pictures that show us that the Earth and the Moon are also spheres.

Before we move on to learn some new things, it is worth just checking that you have remembered how we get night and day and how shadows are formed. Both of these can be explained by the way in which the Earth moves in relation to the Sun (see **Science** Book 1 page 210).

Day and night

The way in which the Earth moves in space gives us day and night. The reasons for this are as follows:

- The Earth slowly spins around the **axis** of the Earth (the line running fron the North pole to the South pole).

- It takes one **day** (24 hours) for the Earth to go through one complete turn.

- The side of the Earth facing the Sun is lit up and it's **daytime** on this side.

- The side of the Earth away from the Sun is in the dark and therefore it's **nighttime** on this side.

- The Earth is always travelling around the Sun in an elliptical path called an orbit.

- It takes 365¼ days (one year) for the Earth to go through one complete orbit.

Sun and shadow

The Sun always stays in the same place which is at the centre of our Solar System. The Sun *appears* to move across the sky as the day goes on because the Earth is moving. Any objects in the way of the Sun cast a **shadow**. The size and direction of the shadow depends on where the Sun is when it shines on an object.

Key words

Star – a large, hot ball of glowing gas.

Moon – a large body orbiting a planet.

Asteroid – a large lump of rock out in the solar system.

Axis – an imaginary line between the North and South poles of the Earth.

Exercise 25.1: The Sun and the Earth

1. Use a diagram to explain why it is midday in London at the same time that it's midnight in Australia.

2. Complete this paragraph:

    The Earth is a .... that moves around the .... The Sun is at the centre of the .... and is a very hot ball of glowing gas called a .... The .... travels around the Earth and we can see it because of light .... from the Sun.

3. What shape is the Sun? How do we know?

Extension question

4. Scientists are very interested in the possibility of life on other planets. Give two reasons why you think that it is very unlikely that we will find organisms similar to those on Earth on any other planet.

Keeping the planets in orbit: The force of gravity

Remember

- The Sun is at the centre of the Solar System.
- The planets move in orbit around the Sun.

Everyone knows that objects fall when they are dropped. If you throw a cricket ball or a rounders ball into the air, it will fall back towards the centre of the Earth. The force that pulls the object back towards the Earth is called **gravity** (see page 374). Sir Isaac Newton made some observations and concluded that:

- There are forces of gravity between **all** objects (not just between objects and the Earth).
- The size of the gravitational force depends on the **mass** of the objects pulling on each other. This means the bigger the masses, the greater the attraction due to gravity.
- The size of the gravitational force depends also on the **distance** between the two objects. As the distance increases, the force of gravity gets less (but gravity *can* work over enormous distances!).

Gravity and orbits

Most of the objects that we see are too small to create very large gravitational forces. Planets, however, are huge! They can create gravitational forces that hold objects close to the planet's surface – that's why we don't fall off the Earth! The Sun contains about 99% of all the matter in the Solar System. This huge mass creates a gravitational force that is enough to hold the planets in orbit. Each planet's orbit is a balance between the tendency of the planet to fly off into space and the pull on the planet due to the Sun's gravity.

The reason why planets orbit the Sun

> Planets orbit the Sun because of a balance between movement and the force of gravity

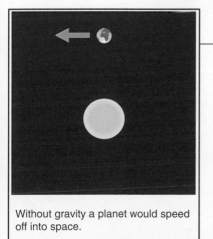

Without gravity a planet would speed off into space.

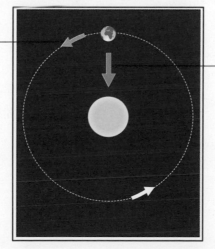

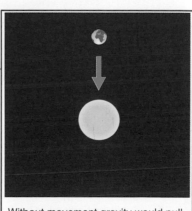

Without movement gravity would pull a planet into the Sun.

It's a bit like throwing a hammer!

The heavy ball tends to move away.

The wire acts like gravity and keeps the ball in orbit.

There are some important points to note:

- The orbits are not quite circular. They are elliptical, with the Sun very close to the centre.

- The planets all travel around the Sun in the same direction.

- The dwarf planet Pluto has a very elliptical orbit and sometimes cuts inside the orbit of Neptune.

The planets' orbits are shown below:

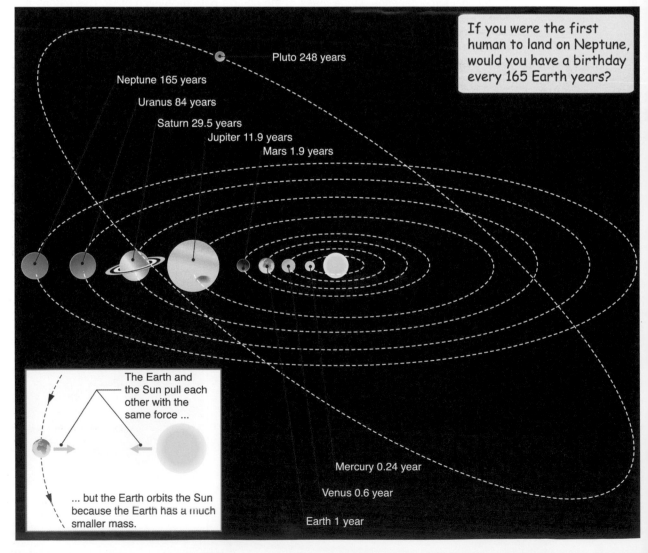

If you were the first human to land on Neptune, would you have a birthday every 165 Earth years?

Pluto 248 years

Neptune 165 years

Uranus 84 years

Saturn 29.5 years

Jupiter 11.9 years

Mars 1.9 years

The Earth and the Sun pull each other with the same force ...

... but the Earth orbits the Sun because the Earth has a much smaller mass.

Mercury 0.24 year

Venus 0.6 year

Earth 1 year

The rules of gravity mean that:

- An inner planet will be pulled towards the Sun more strongly than an outer planet.

- A massive planet, such as Saturn, will be pulled towards the Sun more strongly than a small planet such as Neptune.

You can see that the time taken for a planet to orbit the Sun depends on its distance from the Sun. The bigger the orbit, the longer the planet takes to complete the orbit. One complete orbit by Neptune takes 165 Earth years!

Remember that gravity works both ways. The Earth attracts the Sun with exactly the same size of force as the Sun attracts the Earth. The Earth goes around the Sun (rather than the Sun around the Earth) because the Sun is so much more massive than the Earth.

Any object that completes an orbit around another one is called a **satellite**. For example, the Moon is a satellite of the Earth, and the Earth is a satellite of the Sun.

What is a comet?

Comets are bodies of rock and ice that move in orbit around the Sun. The orbits of comets are not all in the same plane, so the comets don't keep a fixed distance from the Earth. The famous Halley's Comet comes close to the Earth and Sun every 76 years. It speeds up when it approaches the Sun and slows down as it moves away again.

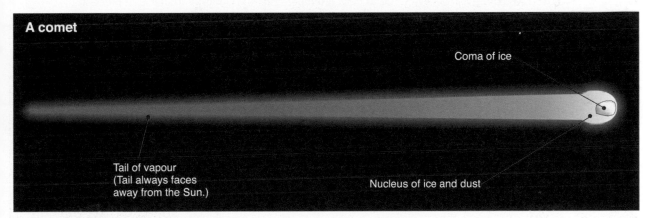

A comet

Coma of ice

Tail of vapour
(Tail always faces
away from the Sun.)

Nucleus of ice and dust

Key words

Orbit – the path followed by one object as it travels around another one in Space.

Satellite – any object completing an orbit around another object.

Comet – lumps or rock and ice in orbit around the Sun.

Exercise 25.2: Gravity and orbits

1. Complete these sentences, using words from the list below:

   orbit   less   smaller   moving   larger   same   gravity

   Planets stay in orbit because they are .... and because of the force of .... The force of gravity between two objects is exactly the .... on both objects, but the .... object orbits the .... one. A satellite has .... mass than a planet, so the satellite is in .... around the planet.

2. Halley's Comet was last seen in 1986. When will be able to see it again?

3. Why is a Neptunian year much longer than a year on Earth?

Extension question

4. Use the table on page 344 (features of the planets) to draw a graph of surface temperature against distance from the Sun.

   (a) What pattern does the graph show?

   (b) If the temperature of the Earth's surface were 40 °C higher, then life could not survive. How far away from the Sun would the Earth have to be to have a temperature 40 °C higher than it is at present?

   (c) Imagine that another planet had been discovered, 2000 million kilometres from the Sun. What do you think its surface temperature would be?

Artificial satellites help us to understand the solar system

Starting points

- A satellite is an object that moves in an orbit around a larger body in the Solar System.

- Movement in an orbit depends on a balance between the movement of the satellite and the gravity exerted by the larger body.

Some orbiting bodies are **natural satellites** which means they have not been put in orbit by humans. The Earth is a natural satellite of the Sun, and the Moon is a natural satellite of the Earth (see page 356). There are also hundreds of **artificial satellites**. These are man-made objects that have been put into orbit by rockets or by the American space shuttle.

Orbits for satellites

Satellites are held in orbit by the gravitational force of the Earth. The speed of the satellite depends on its height above the Earth. Satellites in low orbits travel faster than those in high orbits. These different orbits are described below:

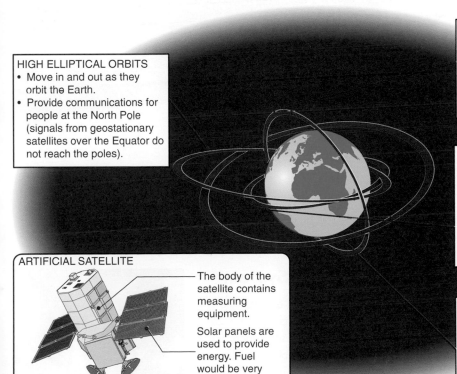

POLAR ORBITS
- Study weather and help to predict storms.
- Provide navigation signals.
- Are not much use for communication as they go out of sight very quickly.

HIGH ELLIPTICAL ORBITS
- Move in and out as they orbit the Earth.
- Provide communications for people at the North Pole (signals from geostationary satellites over the Equator do not reach the poles).

LOW EARTH ORBITS
- Have very short orbit times – 30 minutes or so.
- Used mainly for reconnaissance, they are close to the Earth's surface and so can provide very detailed photographs. They are widely used by the military to follow troop movements.

ARTIFICIAL SATELLITE
The body of the satellite contains measuring equipment.
Solar panels are used to provide energy. Fuel would be very heavy.

GEOSTATIONARY ORBIT
- Move at a speed and height which makes them appear stationary above the Earth.
- Widely used in communications and for navigation and weather forecasting.

Geostationary satellites

A satellite that is exactly 36 000 km above the Earth takes exactly 24 hours to complete one orbit. This is exactly the same time that the Earth takes to turn once on its axis and as a result, the satellite is always above the same place on the Earth's surface. This type of satellite behaves as though it is not moving, so it is very useful for sending information from one place to another. A **satellite dish** can be aimed at the satellite to receive signals and once it is correctly aimed, the dish never needs to be moved.

Communications are helped by geostationary satellites

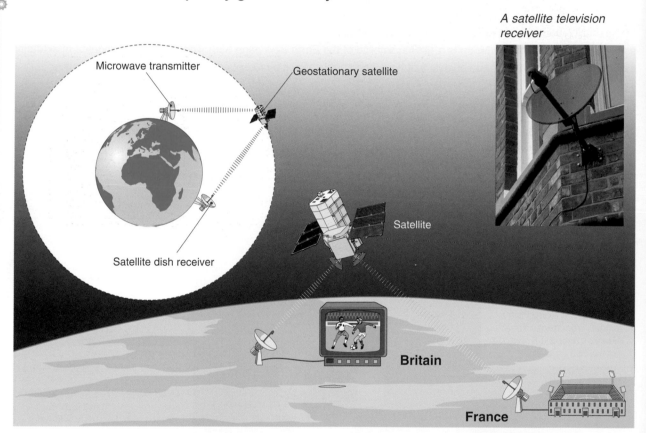

A satellite television receiver

Microwave transmitter

Geostationary satellite

Satellite

Satellite dish receiver

Britain

France

Satellites and exploration of the Solar System

Satellites can help us to look at other planets. Telescopes placed on satellites can give a much clearer view of stars than can be obtained from telescopes on Earth because the images are not spoiled by dust and dirt in the Earth's atmosphere. The Hubble telescope is an example of this kind of instrument. The Hubble telescope can allow us to see seven times as far as we could from the Earth's surface.

Deployment of the Hubble Space Telescope from the space shuttle Discovery on 24th April 1990

Satellites and the Global Positioning System

The **Global Positioning System (GPS)** uses 24 satellites orbiting the Earth in six different orbits. A receiver on the ground can receive signals from at least four of the satellites at any one time. A small computer then allows the receiver to work out exactly where it is, to within 10 square metres. GPS is very valuable to the military, to mountaineers, hill walkers and to drivers. Cars use the system to tell them the best route to take, as well as where they are.

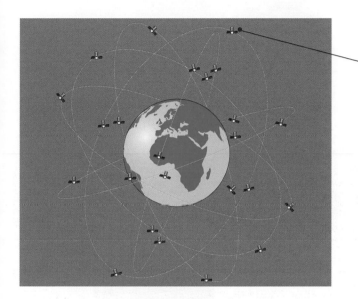

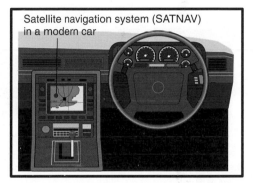

GPS uses 24 satellites in 6 orbits around the Earth

Satellite navigation system (SATNAV) in a modern car

Key words

Satellite – an object that moves around a larger mass in the Solar System.

Geostationary – an orbit that keeps a satellite in a fixed position above the Earth.

Elliptical – shaped like an oval.

Exercise 25.3: Satellites

1. Which type of satellite would be used by a satellite television network?

2. Give two uses for low Earth orbit satellites.

3. Why do you think that so many satellites are solar-powered?

Extension question

4. Use the Internet or textbooks to find out how satellites directly affect your life.

Exploration of space: A timeline

1966: The USA landed a robot spaceship, *Surveyor 1*, on the surface of the Moon. *Surveyor 1* had sophisticated cameras on board, and was able to transmit detailed photographs of the Moon's surface back to Earth. The analysis of these photographs helped scientists to work out how humans could land safely on the Moon.

1961: Yuri Gagarin, a Russian cosmonaut, became the first human in space. Gagarin orbited the Earth once – it took almost two hours – in the spacecraft *Vostok 1*. Gagarin had to bail out of *Vostok 1* using a parachute, as the spacecraft could not be designed to land softly!

The first woman in space was also Russian – Valentina Tereshkova. She orbited the Earth 48 times on board *Vostok 6*.

1959: Russia landed a space probe (*Luna 2*) on the Moon, although the landing impact was so great any human on board would have been killed!

1957: The real start of the Space Age – Russia launched the first satellite into space. *Sputnik* (which means 'satellite' in Russian) weighed about 83 kg and is believed to have orbited Earth at an altitude of about 250 km. It had two radio transmitters which emitted 'beeps' that could be heard by radios around the globe. *Sputnik* burned up upon re-entry on 3 January 1958. Also in 1957, the Russians launched a satellite carrying Laika, a dog (Laika means 'barker' in Russian), which therefore became the first living organism to orbit the Earth.

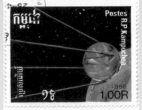

1950: The USA first launched a two-part rocket. The *Bumper* rocket could reach then-record altitudes of almost 400 km. This *Bumper* was used primarily for testing rocket systems and for research on the upper atmosphere: it carried instruments that allowed it to measure factors including air temperature and cosmic ray impacts.

1949: Albert II, a rhesus monkey, became the first monkey in space. He was launched on a modified V-2 rocket, and reached a height about 140 km above the Earth. Albert II did not complete an orbit of the Earth, so the information collected about the possibilities of animals surviving in space was quite limited.

1942: The German V-2 was the first rocket to reach the boundary of space (100 km above the Earth's surface). The rocket was designed by Wernher von Braun with the intention of sending explosive warheads to the UK: von Braun later worked with NASA as a co-designer of the rocket systems used to launch animals into space and to send robots to the Moon.

1969: Neil Armstrong and Buzz Aldrin, two American astronauts, became the first men on the Moon (or, indeed, on any other celestial body). The spaceship which carried them to the Moon, *Apollo 11*, travelled 250 000 miles to the Moon and back. As part of the Apollo series of Moon explorations, a total of 6 missions landed there with 12 astronauts walking (and, on the fourth, fifth and sixth missions, driving the Lunar Rover) on the Moon's surface.

1973: The Russian space probe *Mars 2* explored Mars. The probe had two parts: one stayed in orbit for a year and the other attempted to land on the surface of the planet. The landing attempt was not a success, and the lander was destroyed when its parachute failed.

1981: The Space Shuttle was launched for the first time. This 'space vehicle' was designed to be reused, in an attempt to reduce the enormous costs of space exploration. At launch, the Space Shuttle consists of the shuttle stack which includes a dark orange-coloured external fuel tank, two white, slender solid rocket boosters and the Orbiter Vehicle which contains the crew and payload. In 1986 Space Shuttle *Challenger* exploded shortly after launch, following a fuel leak. All seven astronauts on board were killed – a reminder of the dangers of space travel. In 2003, Space Shuttle *Columbia* burned up on re-entry to the Earth's atmosphere. The Space Shuttle will probably be retired in 2011 after a final mission to deliver parts to the International Space Station.

1986: Construction of the MIR space station began. MIR was built up in sections, carried into space, and then bolted together – construction was completed in 1996, and MIR continued to be inhabited until 2001. In 1991 Helen Sharman became the first British astronaut in space when she spent eight days on MIR.

1994/1995: The longest single human spaceflight is that of Valeriy Polyakov, who left Earth on 8 January **1994**, and didn't return until 22 March **1995** (a total of 437 days 17 hours 58 minutes 16 seconds aboard MIR).

2000: The first permanent crew moved into the ISS (International Space Station). This is so large that it can be seen from the Earth with the unaided eye! It contains several advanced laboratories,

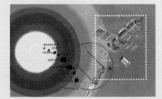

working, for example, on the effects of reduced gravity on animals and plants. The ISS has been built and is maintained by space agencies from the USA, Russia, Europe and Japan.

2001: The American millionaire Dennis Tito became the first space tourist when he paid for a visit to the ISS. He spent a week in orbit, and the trip cost him $20 000 000!

2003: After four unmanned tests, *Shenzhou 5* launched, carrying Chinese astronaut Yang Liwei and making the People's Republic of China the third country to put a human being into space through its own endeavours. In 2008, China successfully completed the *Shenzhou 7* mission, making it the third country to have the capability to conduct a spacewalk.

2004: US President George Bush announced that NASA would resume missions to the Moon, and begin construction of a permanent moon base. NASA also plans manned missions to Mars, although the difficulties of a two-year voyage and the harsh conditions on Mars make this a very tough proposition.

Exploration of space

During the past three or four centuries human scientists have investigated many of the problems which affect life on the planet Earth – in the last sixty years, however, scientists have extended their investigations to include the space beyond planet Earth.

Some of the methods which astronomers have used include:

● Observations made by telescopes from Earth's surface.

● A variety of space missions have sent satellites carrying instruments capable of making measurements in space (see page 353) and sending this information back to powerful computers on Earth.

● The design of robots and space vehicles, and rockets to carry them, allowing exploration of the surface of other planets.

● The construction of rockets and life-support systems which have allowed people to visit and explore other parts of the solar system.

A brief timeline of some of these investigations and discoveries is shown on the previous pages.

Since the successful 1957 launch of *Sputnik*, the first artificial satellite, into orbit around Earth, more and more countries have joined the space age. Currently, scientists believe that the USA, Russia, China, India (and even the Isle of Man!) might have the capability to send humans into space. What began as a 'space race' – in which the United States and the then Soviet Union raced each other to demonstrate superiority in space technology (possibly with military reasons) – has developed into a co-operative effort to find answers in space.

Because of the challenge and expense of space travel for humans, robotic exploration of space is much more practical. Robots are ideal for space research because they can be designed and built with one particular mission in mind. They are able to withstand the harsh conditions of space (no oxygen, for example) and to survive the extremely long missions.

There are different types of different specialised robotic missions:

● A **flyby** collects information as the spacecraft travels past the target object, possibly on a longer mission. For example, the Cassini-Huygens mission did a flyby of Venus and Jupiter while on its way to visit Saturn and its moons.

● An **orbiter** allows a longer period of study as the spacecraft travels in repeated orbit around the object under study.

● A **probe** passes down through a planet's atmosphere to study what it's made of. For example, the Huygens probe of the Cassini-Huygens mission studied the atmosphere of Saturn's moon Titan.

● **Landers** gather data about the surfaces of the celestial objects on which they land. **Rovers** also study the surfaces of objects, but they are mobile and thus can examine a greater area.

Each of these missions involves the efforts of many different scientists and engineers, often communicating with one another from different countries.

The year and the seasons

Remember

- The Sun is at the centre of the Solar System.
- The Earth is one of the planets that move around the Sun.
- The Earth rotates around a line called its axis.

What is a year?

The Earth moves around the Sun in an orbit. The Earth is kept in this orbit by the pull of the Sun's gravity. One **year** (actually 365¼ days) is the time taken for the Earth to complete one orbit.

The Earth rotates around its axis to give day and night (see page 346). The axis of the Earth is not exactly upright; it actually leans to one side, so that the North Pole and the South Pole don't get exactly the same amount of sunlight.

During the course of a year the North Pole is sometimes closer to the Sun and sometimes further away from the Sun. When the Earth is rotating with the North Pole nearer the Sun, it is summer in Britain and winter at the opposite end of the Earth. It is winter in Britain when the Earth is rotating with the North Pole *away from* the Sun.

The tilting of the Earth gives us the seasons

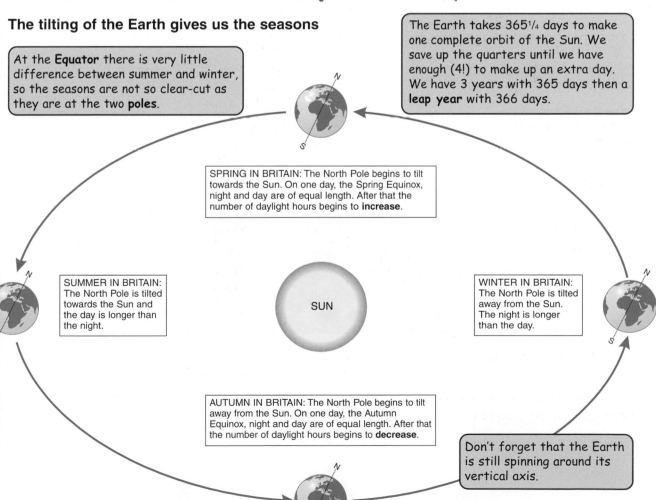

At the **Equator** there is very little difference between summer and winter, so the seasons are not so clear-cut as they are at the two **poles**.

The Earth takes 365¼ days to make one complete orbit of the Sun. We save up the quarters until we have enough (4!) to make up an extra day. We have 3 years with 365 days then a **leap year** with 366 days.

SPRING IN BRITAIN: The North Pole begins to tilt towards the Sun. On one day, the Spring Equinox, night and day are of equal length. After that the number of daylight hours begins to **increase**.

SUMMER IN BRITAIN: The North Pole is tilted towards the Sun and the day is longer than the night.

SUN

WINTER IN BRITAIN: The North Pole is tilted away from the Sun. The night is longer than the day.

AUTUMN IN BRITAIN: The North Pole begins to tilt away from the Sun. On one day, the Autumn Equinox, night and day are of equal length. After that the number of daylight hours begins to **decrease**.

Don't forget that the Earth is still spinning around its vertical axis.

The height of the Sun varies from season to season

The Sun is highest in the sky at midday (12 noon) on any given day. The Sun appears in Britain to be at its greatest height in the sky when the North Pole is tilted towards the Sun, i.e. in the summer.

Remember that the height of the Sun affects the length of shadows. The Sun is lowest during the winter, so the shadows on sunny days in winter are longer than those on sunny days in summer.

When the Sun is lower in the sky, it does not heat up the surface of the Earth as well as it does when it is high in the sky. Winter is colder because:

● the Sun is lower in the sky, so its energy does not fall so directly onto the Earth's surface.

● the Sun is not shining on the Earth so long, as the days are shorter.

What about the Moon?

The Moon is the natural **satellite** of the Earth. It orbits the Earth just as the Earth and the other planets orbit the Sun. It takes about 28 days for the Moon to complete one orbit of the Earth. This length of time is called a **lunar month** (the word 'lunar' means 'to do with the Moon'). The Moon is kept in this orbit by the pull of the Earth's gravity.

The Moon is our nearest neighbour in the Solar System and is close enough to have been visited by humans and to have been studied enough to let us produce a Moon map!

The Moon is the Earth's natural satellite

The Moon rotates once during one complete orbit of the Earth, so the same side always faces the Earth.

The **dark side of the Moon** can only be seen from space.

Gravity on the Moon is only 1/6th of that on Earth. A human could pole-vault 30 metres on the Moon!

The Moon's surface is dry and covered in dust.

Craters are caused by collision with meteorites.

Lunar surface, the Hadley-Apennine region of the Moon. Photographed during the Apollo 15 mission of 1971

Moon days and nights last for 14 Earth days!

Moon day: temperature = 120 ∞C

Moon night: temperature = −150 ∞C

Moon has no atmosphere to support life – astronauts need a space suit with oxygen cylinders.

The Moon is not **luminous,** which means it does not give out its own light but it does reflect light from the Sun. We see different amounts of reflected light at different times in the Moon's orbit around the Earth. The different views we get at different times of the month are called the **phases of the Moon**.

The Moon and its phases

Gravity on the Moon is less than on the Earth, because the Moon is smaller. Astronauts can jump higher and longer on the Moon than on Earth.

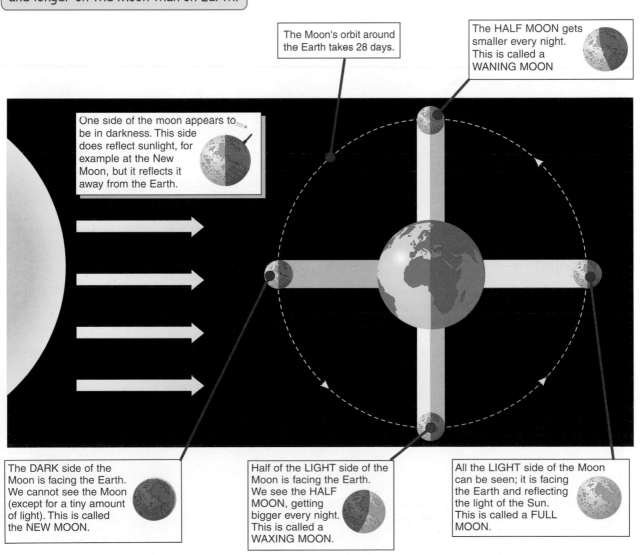

The Moon's orbit around the Earth takes 28 days.

The HALF MOON gets smaller every night. This is called a WANING MOON

One side of the moon appears to be in darkness. This side does reflect sunlight, for example at the New Moon, but it reflects it away from the Earth.

The DARK side of the Moon is facing the Earth. We cannot see the Moon (except for a tiny amount of light). This is called the NEW MOON.

Half of the LIGHT side of the Moon is facing the Earth. We see the HALF MOON, getting bigger every night. This is called a WAXING MOON.

All the LIGHT side of the Moon can be seen; it is facing the Earth and reflecting the light of the Sun. This is called a FULL MOON.

The Moon and eclipses

Lunar eclipse

A **lunar eclipse** or eclipse of the Moon happens when **the Earth comes between the Moon and the Sun.** As a lunar eclipse takes place, we can usually see the shadow of the Earth slowly moving across the face of the Moon.

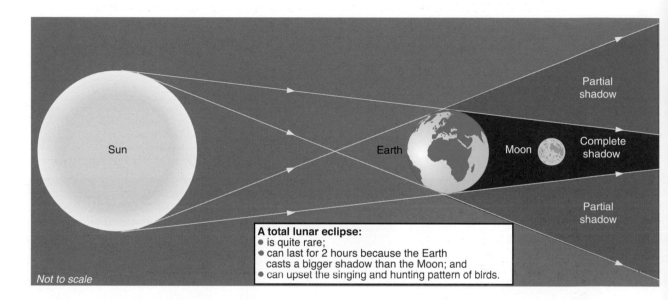

Partial shadow

Complete shadow

Partial shadow

A total lunar eclipse:
- is quite rare;
- can last for 2 hours because the Earth casts a bigger shadow than the Moon; and
- can upset the singing and hunting pattern of birds.

Not to scale

Solar eclipse

A **solar eclipse**, otherwise known as an eclipse of the Sun, happens when **the Moon comes between the Earth and the Sun**. Light from the Sun is hidden from us on Earth and the Moon looks like a black disc surrounded by a bright ring (the corona) of the Sun.

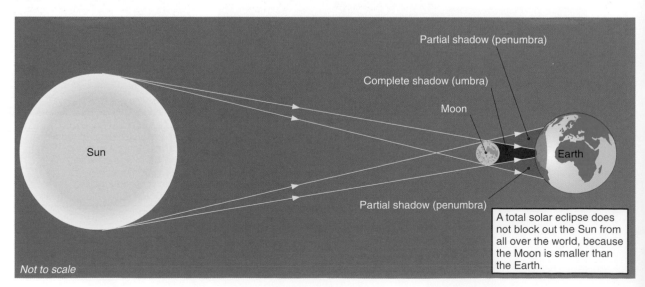

Partial shadow (penumbra)

Complete shadow (umbra)

Moon

Partial shadow (penumbra)

A total solar eclipse does not block out the Sun from all over the world, because the Moon is smaller than the Earth.

Not to scale

The Moon starts to cover the Sun.

The start of totality where the Moon first covers the Sun.

The end of totality where the Moon stops covering the Sun.

The eclipse finishes.

TAKE CARE!
You must **never** look directly at the Sun! This could damage the retina and blind you, so special filters are needed to view an eclipse.

Total solar eclipse of 11th July 1991, California, USA

Key words

Year – the time taken for the Earth to complete one orbit of the Sun.

Lunar month – the time taken for the Moon to complete one orbit of the Earth.

Phases of the moon – different views of the Moon at different times of the month.

Eclipse – when either the Moon or the Sun is hidden from viewers on the Earth.

One day and one night (24 hours) – the time taken for the Earth to spin once around its axis.

Exercise 25.4: Sun, Earth and Moon

1. How long does it take for:

   (a) The Earth to orbit the Sun?

   (b) The Moon to orbit the Earth?

   (c) The Earth to turn once on its axis?

2. Give two reasons why it is colder in winter than in summer.

3. Look at this diagram (not drawn to scale):

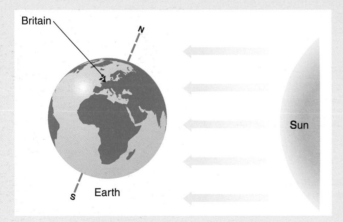

   (a) Copy it and shade in the part of the Earth that is in shadow.

   (b) Is it summer or winter in Britain?

   (c) Is it daytime or nighttime in Britain?

4. How does a solar eclipse give us evidence that light travels in straight lines?

5. Draw a diagram showing how a lunar eclipse happens.

Extension questions

6. Find out what is meant by 'midnight Sun'. Use a diagram to explain how it can happen.

7. How many times does the Moon orbit the Earth while the Earth completes one orbit of the Sun? Give a reason for your answer.

The Sun and other stars

Starting points

- The Sun is at the centre of the Solar System.

- We currently know of eight planets and three dwarf planets which orbit at great distances around the Sun.

- The Sun is luminous and provides light and thermal energy for the Earth.

The Universe contains everything that exists. The Solar System is just one part of the Universe; it is part of a galaxy called the **Milky Way.**

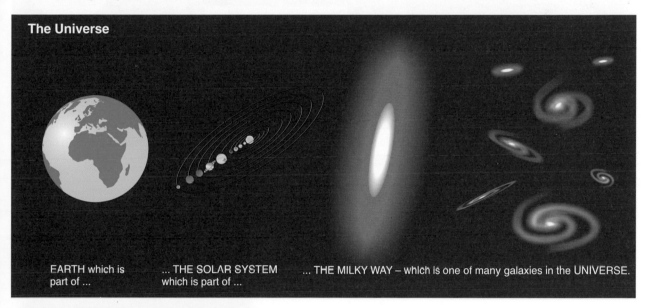

The Universe

EARTH which is part of ...

... THE SOLAR SYSTEM which is part of ...

... THE MILKY WAY – which is one of many galaxies in the UNIVERSE.

Milky Way galaxy seen in the night sky above a desert, Calfornia, USA.

The universe contains many galaxies and each galaxy contains millions of **stars** together with clouds of dust and gas. The stars can be very different from one another:

- Their **size** can vary, from supergiants that are very much bigger than the Sun, to neutron stars that are only the same size as the Earth.

- Their **brightness** can vary from 100 000 times brighter than the Sun to 100 000 times less bright than the Sun.

- The **distances** between them can vary, but in every case the distance is very large indeed.

Remember that stars can be seen because they are *luminous* (i.e. they give out their own light). Size, brightness and distance from the Earth all affect how easily we can see a star. This is different to planets and moons that are only seen because they *reflect* light from the Sun.

How we see stars and planets

Stars can be seen at night because they are luminous.

Clue: If it twinkles, it's a star, if it doesn't, it's a planet.

Planets do not give out their own light. We can see them because they **reflect** light from the Sun.

Stars are light years from Earth

Because the Universe is so large and the stars are so far away, it is not easy to measure distances in normal units, such as kilometres. It is easier to use a unit called a **light year**. A light year is the distance travelled by light in one year. Light moves very quickly and in one year it covers 9 461 000 000 000 km.

Light moving at 300 000 000 m/s
will travel around 9 461 000 000 000 km in a year

It takes light only 0.125 s to travel all the way around the Earth!

1 Light Year

A LIGHT YEAR IS A UNIT OF DISTANCE IN ASTRONOMY.

The closest star to the Earth, other than the Sun, is 4.2 light years away and astronomers have discovered some stars that are 10 000 000 light years away. These distances are very much greater than the distances between the planets in the Solar System.

The stars in the Milky Way form patterns, called **constellations**. People have studied these constellations for thousands of years and have given them names according to their appearance from the Earth.

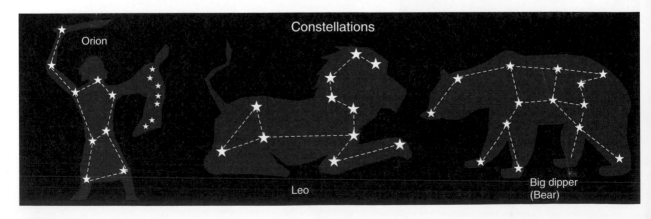

Constellations

Orion

Leo

Big dipper (Bear)

The nearest large galaxy to the Milky Way is called **Andromeda** and is 2 million light years away. When we see light from Andromeda we are actually looking at something that happened 2 million years ago, around the time when the first ape-like humans were appearing on the Earth.

The Sun is a star

Stars appear to us as tiny pinpricks of light because they are so far away. The exception is the Sun. The Sun looks very large to us because:

- It is more than a thousand times bigger than the Earth.

- It is very close – only 149 million kilometres away!

The Sun was formed from gas and dust over 5000 million years ago. The gases became squashed together and hydrogen atoms combined to form helium atoms. This is a **nuclear fusion** reaction, and releases enormous amounts of thermal and light energy. Scientists think that the temperature at the centre of the Sun is as high as 14 000 000 °C, with the surface being much cooler at only 6000 °C!

Only a very small amount of the energy released from the Sun ever reaches the Earth but it is enough to provide the energy for all of our food chains (see page 99). Scientists believe that the Sun has already used up about half of its hydrogen fuel. When the hydrogen runs out, the Sun will first collapse, then swell to form a huge **red giant**. The red giant will swallow up and burn Mercury and the Earth, then it will collapse again to end up as a tiny **white dwarf** star.

Death of the Sun

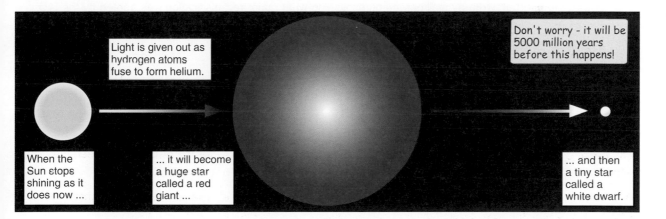

Key words

Milky Way – the galaxy that includes our Solar System.

Light year – a unit of distance in the Universe – the distance travelled by light in one year.

Galaxy – a collection of millions of stars.

Exercise 25.5: Sun and the stars

1. Choose words from this list to fill in the gaps in the following paragraphs.

   luminous   sun   star   light-years   reflection

   constellations   galaxy   universe   kilometres

   (a) We can see stars because they are .... The Moon and some planets are visible because of the .... of light from the .... Many stars seem to be arranged in patterns called ...., and there may be several of these in a single ....

   (b) Distances in space are so great that we need to measure them in .... All the planets, stars, gases and dust together make up the ....

2. Why are large telescopes for observing stars usually built on hills well away from large cities?

3. Light travels at 300 000 km per second. The Sun is 149 million kilometres from the Earth. How long does light take to reach the Earth from the Sun?

Extension question

4. Using the internet, write a small paragraph explaining what major reclassification was agreed by the IAU on 24 August 2006.

Chapter 26
Forces and linear motion

What is a force?

A force is either a **push** or a **pull**. You can't see a force, but you can see what a force does. Forces can:

- Change the **speed** of things. They can make things speed up or slow down.
- Change the **direction** that something is moving in.
- Change the **shape** of things.

Forces act in one direction

We need to know two things about a force to understand what it is doing. We need to know: the **size** of the force and the **direction** in which the force is acting in.

We use arrows to show the size and the direction of forces:

This arrow shows the force driving the motorbike forwards:
- the arrow is BIG because the force is big;
- the arrow is pointing in the direction in which the engine is pushing the motorbike.

This arrow shows th force of air through which the motorbike is being driven:
- the arrow Is SMALL because the force is small'
- the arrow is pointing at the motorbike because the force is AGAINST THE MOVEMENT of the motorbike.

This arrow shows the RESULTANT forcel This force is the difference between the bigger force and the smaller one. The size of the arrow tells you how big the force is and the direction tells you that the motorbike is moving forward.

WHICH ONE WINS?
When two different forces work on the same object, the **BIGGER ONE WINS.**

Forces and motion

Things are moving all around us:

- On a very small scale, the particles that make up atoms and molecules are always moving (we say that they are in motion).
- Movement (motion) is more obvious in animals (including humans) and machines than the movement of particles.
- On an enormous scale, the Earth is in motion around the Sun, and the stars move around in the different galaxies.

Sir Isaac Newton studied many of these moving objects and noticed certain patterns about the way in which they move. From these patterns, he formulated the **Laws of Motion** – there are three of them. These laws are used in many ways. For example:

● Car designers use them to improve the efficiency of new models.

● Aerospace engineers use them to improve the design of aircraft and to work out how to get rockets to carry satellites into orbit.

● Sports coaches use them to analyse the performance of all types of athletes.

Speed and movement

Speed tells us how fast an object is moving. The speed of any moving object is the distance it moves in a certain amount of time. The units we use for speed have to include **distance** and **time**. For example, we can describe speed in kilometres per hour (km/h), or in metres per second (m/s). The way that these units are written (i.e. a unit of distance divided by a unit of time) helps us with a definition of speed.

$$\text{Speed} = \frac{\text{Distance}}{\text{Time}}$$

We can write out this useful equation in symbols

$$s = \frac{d}{t}$$

where: s = speed
d = distance
t = time taken

A reminder about units (see also page 127)

Quantity	Unit
Mass	gram (g)
	kilogram (kg)
Length	millimetre (mm)
	centimetre (cm)
	metre (m)
	kilometre (km)
Area	square metres (m²)
	square centimetres (cm²)
Volume	cubic metres (m³)
	cubic centimetres (cm³)
	(one cm³ is the same volume as one ml – a millilitre)
Time	second (s)
	minute (min)
	hour (h)

The prefixes to the names of units help you to work out their relative sizes.

e.g. milli – means 'one thousandth': $\frac{1}{1000}$

centi – means 'one hundredth': $\frac{1}{100}$

kilo – means 'thousand': 1000 ×

so 1 centimetre contains 10 millimetres

1 metre contains 100 centimetres
or 1000 millimetres

Measuring speed

If we are going to make an accurate measurement of speed, we need to know:

● the exact distance travelled (including the correct units); and

● the exact length of time taken (including the correct units).

An example of a speed measurement that can be made in a school laboratory is shown below:

Measuring speed in a laboratory

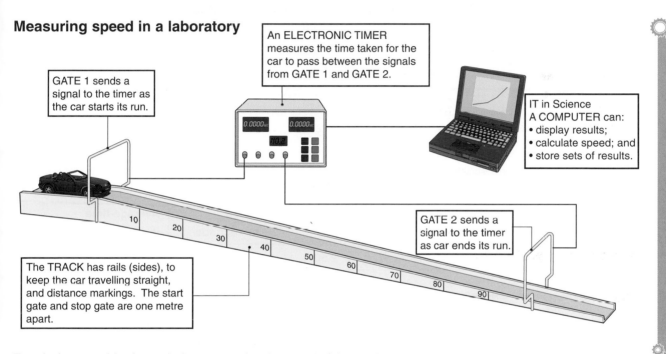

An ELECTRONIC TIMER measures the time taken for the car to pass between the signals from GATE 1 and GATE 2.

GATE 1 sends a signal to the timer as the car starts its run.

IT in Science
A COMPUTER can:
• display results;
• calculate speed; and
• store sets of results.

GATE 2 sends a signal to the timer as car ends its run.

The TRACK has rails (sides), to keep the car travelling straight, and distance markings. The start gate and stop gate are one metre apart.

Exactly the same idea is used when measuring the speed of drag-racing cars or human athletes running a 100 m race.

Key words

Force – a push or a pull – it has both size and direction.

Speed – how fast an object is moving – distance travelled divided by time taken.

Exercise 26.1: Forces

1. Choose words from this list to complete this paragraph about forces:

   speed   size   direction   forces   direction   shape

   .... are pushes or pulls, exerted by one thing on another. Forces can change the .... of things, change the .... and the .... of things. They have two important features: .... and .... These two features of a force can be shown by drawing an arrow.

2. (a) Name three things that a force can do.

   (b) Give an example of each of these things.

3. In the National Swimming Championships, the swimmers are timed electronically. A very accurate electronic clock is started as the starter's signal is given and stopped as the swimmers touch a pressure pad at the end of the pool. Work out the average speed for these race winners. Choose the correct units for your answers.

Event	Distance in m	Time taken in seconds	Speed in m/s
Freestyle	50	28	
Backstroke	100	60	
Butterfly	100	56	
Breaststroke	200	140	
Individual medley	400	275	

4. Anne wanted to investigate the speed of different model cars. She set up the same kind of apparatus as shown on page 367 and obtained the following results:

Car number	Run 1 in seconds	Run 2 in seconds	Run 3 in seconds	Average time in seconds
1	2.40	2.50	2.60	
2	2.90	2.75	2.78	
3	2.35	2.55	4.90	

   (a) Which one of the results seems to be unreliable?

   (b) Leaving out this result, work out the average speeds of the three cars.

   (c) What is the input variable in this experiment?

   (d) What is the outcome variable in this experiment?

   (e) How could Anne be sure that this was a fair test?

Extension question

5. Use the Internet or a textbook to find:

   (a) The fastest living organism.

   (b) The fastest mammal on land.

   (c) The world land speed record.

   (d) The world water speed record.

   In each case make sure that you include the correct units in your answer.

   (e) The fastest human has run at about 10.5 m/s. How many times faster than this does the fastest mammal move on land?

Distance and time

Remember

● Speed is the **distance** travelled in a certain amount of **time**.

Formula One racing teams need to travel around the world to take part in different Grand Prix. Many of these teams are based in England and need to take ferries to reach the European mainland. One team needed to be on a ferry by 10 o'clock in the morning and had to decide the best time to leave the factory base in Oxfordshire. Of course, a racing team would be well aware of the relationships between time, speed and distance. They could calculate how long their trip to the ferry terminal would take. This is how they worked things out:

Calculation of journey time

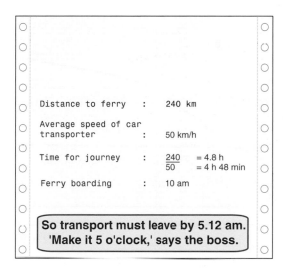

```
Distance to ferry    :    240 km

Average speed of car
transporter          :    50 km/h

Time for journey     :    240    = 4.8 h
                          50     = 4 h 48 min

Ferry boarding       :    10 am
```

So transport must leave by 5.12 am.
'Make it 5 o'clock,' says the boss.

Remember that there is an equation that relates speed, distance and time. If you know two of the things in the equation, you can always work the other one out. There is a **speed triangle** that can help you with this type of calculation:

Speed triangle

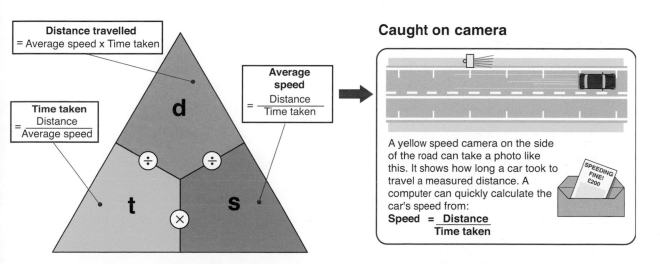

Distance travelled
= Average speed x Time taken

Time taken
= Distance / Average speed

Average speed
= Distance / Time taken

Caught on camera

A yellow speed camera on the side of the road can take a photo like this. It shows how long a car took to travel a measured distance. A computer can quickly calculate the car's speed from:

Speed = Distance / Time taken

SPEEDING FINE! £200

Distance/time graphs

A distance/time graph is obtained if we plot how much distance is covered during a certain part of a journey. Here's an example. Measure how far a boy travels in each minute during a cycle ride to school:

A distance/time graph

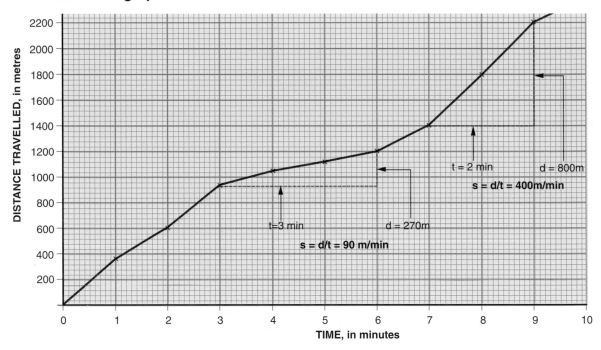

Exercise 26.2: Distance and time

1. How far would you travel:

    (a) In 90 minutes if you cycled at an average speed of 30 km/h?

    (b) In 20 seconds if you ran at 5 m/s?

    (c) In 50 seconds if you were in an aeroplane travelling at 50 m/s?

2. How long will the following journeys take:

    (a) A 400 m walk at 2 m/s?

    (b) A 2 km run at 4 m/s?

3. Find the speed of:

    (a) A dog that runs 300 m in 12 s.

    (b) A motorcycle that moves 1000 m in 45 s.

4. Look carefully at this graph:

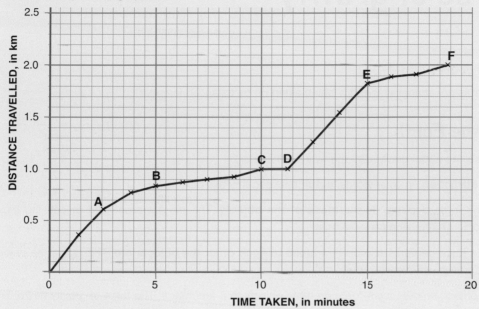

(a) How long did the total journey take?

(b) When did the boy stop to tie his shoe lace?

(c) Which part of the graph shows where he was walking up a steep hill?

(d) Which part of the graph shows where he was walking downhill?

(e) What was his average speed over the whole journey?

Extension question

5. David and Hannah were asked to observe a car moving along a marked track. They had an electronic timer and they were able to see exactly how far the car had travelled by looking at the markings on the track. They obtained these results:

Time in seconds	0	1	2	3	4	5	6	7	8
Distance travelled in metres	0	20	40	60	80	100	120	140	160

(a) Plot a line graph of these results.

(b) What is the car's speed in m/s?

(c) From the graph, work out how far the car would have travelled after 3.5 s.

(d) How far did the car travel between 4.0 s and 7.0 s?

(e) If the car continues at this speed, how far will it travel in 25 s?

(f) How long would it take for the car to cover 400 m?

(g) Was the car moving uphill, downhill, or along the level? Give a reason for your answer.

The force of gravity

Remember

- A force can be a push or a pull.

- Any object that is not changing speed is being acted on by balanced forces.

Gravity and the Earth

Let's just remind ourselves about gravity and the way it behaves:

Gravity is a **force of attraction**, in other words, a **pull** between any two objects.

- The size of the force depends on the **mass of the objects**. The *more massive* the object, the *bigger* the gravitational force of attraction between them.

- The size of the force depends also on how **close to each other the objects are**. The *closer* the objects, the *bigger* the force of gravity between them.

The Earth is a large object, so puts a pull force on other objects that are near it. The force of gravity has a direction, and this direction is towards the centre of the Earth.

The Earth and gravity

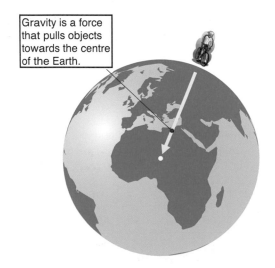

Gravity is a force that pulls objects towards the centre of the Earth.

GRAVITY EXISTS BETWEEN ALL OBJECTS

Even very small objects, like two tomatoes, are pulled towards each other. The force is very small, so it would be really difficult to measure it. The force of gravity only becomes noticeable when one (or both) of the objects has a huge mass.

The Earth's mass is about 6 000 000 000 000 000 000 000 000 kg so it has an enormous gravitational pull. Objects pull on each other equally. A bird in the air pulls as much on the Earth as the Earth pulls on the bird. **But this force won't move something as massive as the Earth!**

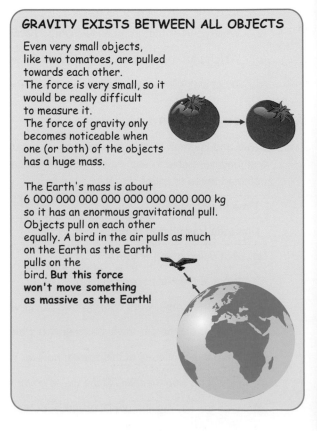

There are two important things to remember about gravity:

● Gravity will pull an object towards the centre of the Earth, whether the object is in the air, standing on the ground or in water.

● Most places on the surface of the Earth are approximately the same distance from the centre of the Earth. Because of this, the force of gravity is almost exactly the same all over the Earth. You need to get a long way away from the Earth before you notice any real reduction in the force of gravity.

Measuring gravity

The force of gravity acting on objects can make them feel very heavy. This heaviness as a result of gravity is the **weight** of an object. Because weight is a force, we can measure it using a **forcemeter**. The weight of an object should be measured in **newtons (N)**.

Gravity is different on other planets!
A bag of sugar has a **mass** of 1 kg, but a **weight** of 10 N on Earth.
On the Moon the force of gravity is only $\frac{1}{6}$ of that of Earth, so the sugar's **mass** is still 1 kg but its **weight** is now $\frac{1}{6}$ x 10 = 1.67 N.

Using a forcemeter to measure weight

We use a **forcemeter** (sometimes called a **newtonmeter**) to measure the size of a force. A forcemeter has a spring inside it and the larger the force, the more the spring will be stretched. The stretching of the spring changes the reading on the forcemeter. You can hang a weight on the hook at the bottom of a forcemeter. When the spring inside the forcemeter is stretched, it tries to pull back towards its normal length. The weight hangs in one position because this pull of the spring equals the downward pull of gravity on the weight. The two forces are **balanced.**

Measuring gravity with a forcemeter

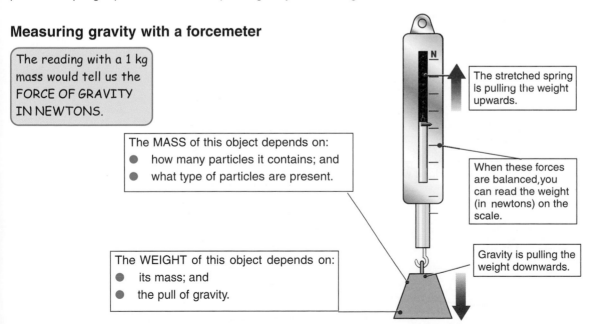

The reading with a 1 kg mass would tell us the FORCE OF GRAVITY IN NEWTONS.

The MASS of this object depends on:
● how many particles it contains; and
● what type of particles are present.

The WEIGHT of this object depends on:
● its mass; and
● the pull of gravity.

The stretched spring is pulling the weight upwards.

When these forces are balanced, you can read the weight (in newtons) on the scale.

Gravity is pulling the weight downwards.

Weight and mass

The two words weight and mass are often confused with one another. **Weight is the force of gravity pulling an object towards the centre of the Earth** (or some other body) and is measured in newtons (N). The **mass** of an object is **a measure of how much matter it contains** and is measured in grams or kilograms.

A kilogram mass is pulled towards the Earth by a force of 10 newtons; we say that the strength of gravity (on Earth) is 10 newtons per kilogram. If you know the mass of an object, you can calculate its weight by multiplying its mass in kilograms by the force of gravity. A two kilogram bag of flour has a weight of 2 x 10 = 20 N.

Stretching the limits

The spring in a forcemeter will stretch, depending on the mass added. The amount of stretch is *proportional* to the mass added. Usually the spring will stretch the same amount if identical masses are added, and will go back to its original position if the mass is taken off it. We say that the spring is **elastic** (the material we call elastic is called this because it returns to it original length after it has been stretched). Something unusual can happen if you keep on and on adding mass. The spring will suddenly stretch much more than expected and it won't go back to its original length once the mass is removed. Scientists say that we have exceeded the **elastic limits** of the material. This is shown below:

A spring has an elastic limit

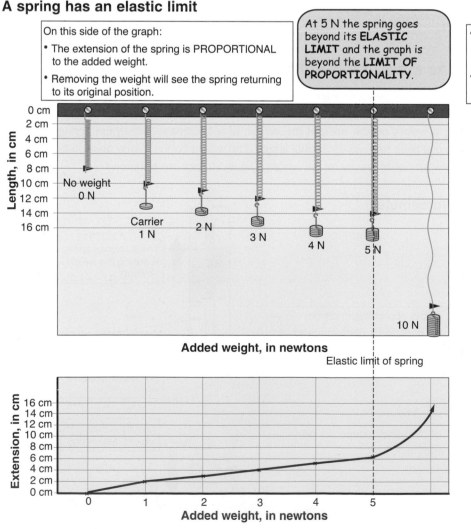

On this side of the graph:

- The extension of the spring is PROPORTIONAL to the added weight.
- Removing the weight will see the spring returning to its original position.

At 5 N the spring goes beyond its **ELASTIC LIMIT** and the graph is beyond the **LIMIT OF PROPORTIONALITY**.

- The extension of the spring is now **not** proportional to the added weight.
- The spring will not return to its original position.

When they are using materials, engineers must be very careful that they don't exceed the elastic limits for the materials they are using. It might have disastrous consequences.

Beating the force of gravity

The Earth is very tightly packed with materials such as rocks, so gravity can't pull us through to the centre of the Earth. Gravity does tend to pull us until we reach the Earth's surface, though. We can beat gravity in three ways:

1. By exerting a force in the opposite direction.
This could involve using a rocket motor which burns fuel to push it against the force of gravity.

2. Using an upward force to support you.
This is an example of a reaction force. This could involve something as simple as standing on a chair.

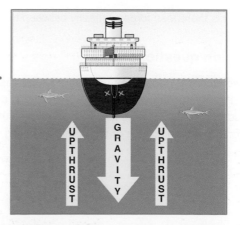

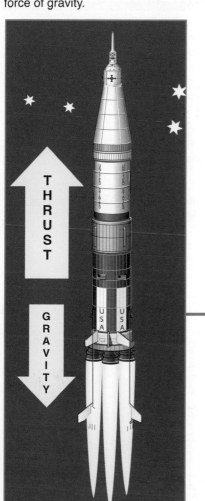

Beating gravity

3. Using the upthrust of water.
Water pushes up against objects that are floating in it. This cancels out some of the force of gravity pulling the object to the centre of the Earth. An object will float when the force of gravity is balanced by the upthrust of the water.

Key words

Mass – how much matter an object contains.

Gravity – a force of attraction between any two masses.

Weight – the force of gravity that pulls an object towards another object (usually towards the Earth).

Reaction force – an upward force that supports a body.

Upthrust – a push of water against an object floating in it.

Elastic – being able to return to its original length after it has been stretched.

Exercise 26.3: Gravity

1. Complete these sentences using words from the following list:

    grams or kg   newtons   size   mass   gravity

    Weight is a force and is measured in .... It is caused by .... acting on an object. .... is not a force; it depends on the number and .... of particles in an object. Mass is measured in ....

2. On Earth, the force of gravity is about 10 newtons per kg. Use this information to complete this table:

Mass in kg	Weight in newtons
2.0	
	15
3.7	
5.5	
	92

3. Why is there less force of gravity between two apples than between the Earth and one apple?

Extension questions

4. Two students hung a spring from a strong support alongside a long ruler. They measured where the bottom of the spring was when there was no metal disc added to the spring; this was the starting point. They then added different discs to the spring and measured where the bottom of the spring reached on the scale. They worked out the stretch of the spring by taking away the starting point from the finishing point each time.

Here are their results.

Mass of added discs in grams	Position of spring in millimetres	Amount of stretch in millimetres (extension)
0	12	0
10	22	
20	35	
30	48	
40	60	
50	73	
60	85	
70	97	85
80	110	
90	122	
100	136	
110	149	
120	160	

(a) Complete the table by working out the amount of stretch (extension) for each added disc.

(b) Plot a graph of the added mass against the stretch of the spring.

(c) What is the pattern in these results?

(d) What do you think would happen if the two students kept adding discs to the spring? Draw a simple diagram of the graph they might get if they added a 1000g (1 kg) disc. Explain this result.

5. The American space shuttle can be used to put satellites and measuring equipment into orbit. An empty shuttle vehicle has a mass of 70 tonnes and can carry a cargo of 28 tonnes.

(a) What is the total mass of the full shuttle, in kilograms?

(b) What is the weight of the shuttle as it sits on the launch pad?

(c) How much force (thrust) would the rockets have to produce just to balance this weight at take-off?

Balanced and unbalanced forces

Remember

- A force is a push or a pull.

- A force has both size and direction.

How to measure forces

As you learnt in the previous section (page 375), we use a **forcemeter** (sometimes called a **newtonmeter**) to measure the size of a force. Remember, if an object isn't moving, then the forces on it must be balanced. An object that is *moving at a constant speed* also has balanced forces acting on it.

Keeping still

Here is a jaguar lying on a branch.

The jaguar has mass, so there is a force acting downwards towards the centre of the Earth. The jaguar isn't moving, so the branch must be pushing back against the jaguar with a reaction force. This force must be equal in size to the jaguar's weight, but is acting in the opposite direction.

Moving at a constant speed

Balanced forces can still be acting on an object even if it is not still. A moving object with balanced forces acting on it will keep moving at exactly the same speed all the time. A sports car travelling along a straight road will move at a constant speed, so long as the force provided by the engine balances the air resistance and the friction from the road (see page 384).

FORCE PRODUCED BY ENGINE

AIR RESISTANCE

FRICTION

We can investigate the speed of an object moving with almost no friction with an air track. This is a metal tube which can act as a track for a trolley.

- Air is pushed up through the track to make a cushion for the trolley.

- Light gates are used to check the speed of the vehicle as it moves along the track.

Using an air track

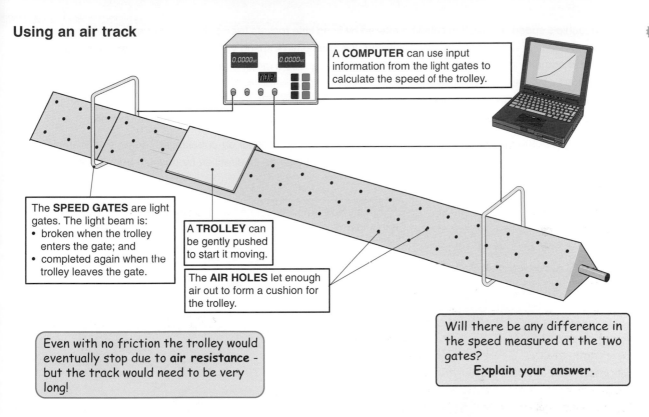

A **COMPUTER** can use input information from the light gates to calculate the speed of the trolley.

The **SPEED GATES** are light gates. The light beam is:
• broken when the trolley enters the gate; and
• completed again when the trolley leaves the gate.

A **TROLLEY** can be gently pushed to start it moving.

The **AIR HOLES** let enough air out to form a cushion for the trolley.

Even with no friction the trolley would eventually stop due to **air resistance** - but the track would need to be very long!

Will there be any difference in the speed measured at the two gates?
Explain your answer.

Engineers use air cushions like this to reduce the forces that slow down the movement of some machines, for example a hovercraft.

Changing speed and direction

Sometimes the forces acting on an object are **unbalanced**. Unbalanced forces can change the speed or direction of motion of an object. Let's think about what would happen to a spaceship travelling so far out into space that there is no longer any gravitational force (see page 377) acting on it. The spaceship has no engine to push it and no gravity or friction to slow it down. The space ship will just travel on and on at the same speed and in the same direction.

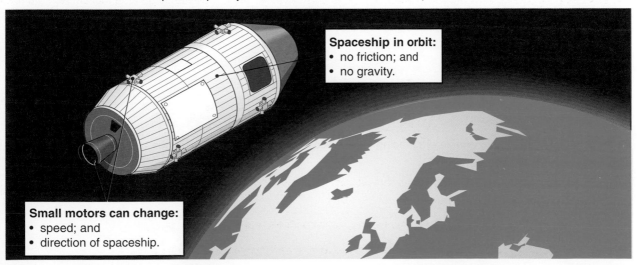

Spaceship in orbit:
• no friction; and
• no gravity.

Small motors can change:
• speed; and
• direction of spaceship.

The spaceship's speed or direction could be altered by firing little rockets fixed to it. If the rockets provide an extra force in the same direction as the spaceship is travelling, the spaceship's speed will change. **Acceleration** tells us how fast the speed of something is changing. A great acceleration requires a large, unbalanced force to be acting on an object. These rockets could also be used to manoeuvre a spaceship or satellite into the correct position for it to carry out its job. The rockets would now be providing an unbalanced force in a different *direction* from the travel of the spaceship. Unbalanced forces can change the speed or the direction of an object, or even both at the same time.

Many of you will probably already have carried out your own experiments on unbalanced forces. For example, when your Mum or Dad tries to push a supermarket trolley, you can change its direction by pushing from the side.

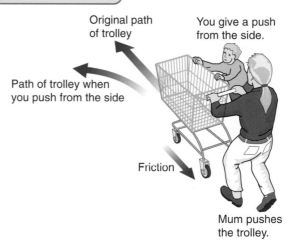

A simple supermarket experiment.

Original path of trolley

You give a push from the side.

Path of trolley when you push from the side

Friction

Mum pushes the trolley.

The risk of dangerously unbalanced forces!

How does mass affect acceleration?

The acceleration of an object depends on the size of the force acting on it and on the mass of the object. The best acceleration is obtained by either reducing the mass of the object or by increasing the force used to move it. Designers of racing cars and motorbikes understand this and they try to get the lightest vehicle and the most powerful engine.

Drag racers, for example, have:

● large powerful engines;

● very light bodies; and

● very light alloy wheels.

All these factors combine to enable drag-racing cars to accelerate to 60 m/s in 5 seconds.

Key words

Acceleration – how fast the speed of something is changing.

Forcemeter (newtonmeter) – an instrument used to measure the size of a force.

Exercise 26.4: Balanced and unbalanced forces

1. Make a drawing of a car accelerating away from traffic lights. Draw the force arrows to show the forces acting on the car.

2. A large lorry may have a more powerful engine than a racing car but cannot accelerate as quickly. Explain why this is the case.

Extension question

3. This equation can be used to calculate the rate of change of speed (acceleration).

$$\text{Acceleration} = \frac{\text{Change in speed}}{\text{time taken}}$$

This table shows how the speed of a motorcycle changes over a 5-second period.

Time in seconds	0	1	2	3	4	5
Speed in metres per second	0	4	8	12	16	20

(a) What is the acceleration of the motorbike?

(b) If the motorbike keeps on accelerating at this rate, how fast will it be going after:

   (i) 9 seconds?

   (ii) 20 seconds?

(c) Why would it be difficult to predict how fast the motorbike would be going after 50 seconds?

Chapter 27
Friction and motion

Remember

- Moving objects often slow down because there is a force acting on them.

- The force is acting in the opposite direction to the way the objects are moving. This force is called **friction**.

Friction is a force that tends to stop two things from sliding over each other. Sometimes friction is **useful**:

- Car tyres can push against the surface of the road, so the car can move forward.

- Brake blocks can squeeze against a bicycle wheel rim, so that the bike slows down.

- Shoes can grip the floor, so that you don't slip when you try to walk.

However, sometimes it is a **nuisance**:

- It slows moving things down, and extra force is needed to keep them moving.

- It can heat things up and can damage the moving surfaces.

FRICTION CAN BE A NUISANCE!

FRICTION CAN BE USEFUL!

ENGINE: Friction generates thermal energy and wears engine parts out.

STEERING WHEEL AND DRIVING GLOVES: These make it easier to hold on and steer the car.

BRAKE PADS AND DISCS: Friction between them will slow the car down.

TYRES AND GROUND: Friction means:
- the engine can push car forward;
- grip means the car will stick to the ground and will stop the car when braking; and
- the car can be made to change direction.

Brakes, tyres, roads and friction

Driving a motor car or motorbike safely would be impossible without friction. Especially important is the friction between the tyres and the road. When the driver or rider puts on the brakes, the wheels stop turning and the vehicle will slow down as long as the tyres can grip the road. The grip between the tyre and the road depends on friction. This friction can be affected by:

- **The type of road surface.** Some surfaces are specially roughened to provide good friction and safe braking.

- **Whether the road is wet or not.** Water acts as a lubricant between the tyre and the road and makes braking more difficult.

- **The state of the tyres.** Worn tyres are smooth and so friction with the road is reduced, especially in wet conditions.

This diagram shows how braking is affected by the condition of the road

Assume a driver of a car travelling at 80 km per hour (50 mph) wants to stop his car.

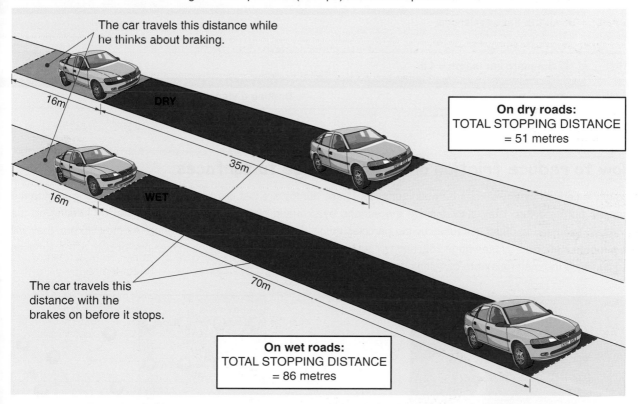

The car travels this distance while he thinks about braking.

16m DRY

On dry roads:
TOTAL STOPPING DISTANCE
= 51 metres

16m WET

35m

The car travels this distance with the brakes on before it stops.

70m

On wet roads:
TOTAL STOPPING DISTANCE
= 86 metres

Speed and braking

Even when a car has perfect tyres and brakes and the road is dry, stopping a car can be very difficult. The faster a car is travelling, the longer it will take for it to stop. This is because the car will travel further while the driver reacts to the situation and also because the friction must act for longer to stop the car moving forward. The Highway Code shows the distances required for braking at different speeds. At 60 mph under perfect conditions, stopping the car still takes nearly twenty times the length of the car.

Speed affects braking distance

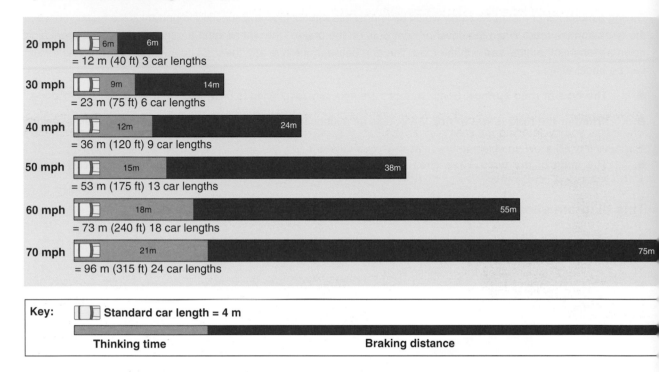

20 mph 6m 6m
= 12 m (40 ft) 3 car lengths

30 mph 9m 14m
= 23 m (75 ft) 6 car lengths

40 mph 12m 24m
= 36 m (120 ft) 9 car lengths

50 mph 15m 38m
= 53 m (175 ft) 13 car lengths

60 mph 18m 55m
= 73 m (240 ft) 18 car lengths

70 mph 21m 75m
= 96 m (315 ft) 24 car lengths

Key: Standard car length = 4 m

Thinking time   Braking distance

How to reduce friction and stop damage to surfaces

Friction is caused by tiny bumps between surfaces. These bumps are just like tiny pieces of sandpaper and stop the surfaces from moving. They also damage the surface by scraping pieces of material away and by heating up the surfaces. The heating effect is caused by the particles in the surface being forced to vibrate. As they vibrate, they will have more kinetic energy (see page 252) and will get hotter. The heat can be enough to melt one or both of the surfaces and can stop the materials from carrying out their job properly.

Space shuttle re-entry. The space shuttle is covered in thermal-resistant tiles made of silica. These protect it from the thermal energy generated by friction as it enters the atmosphere at high speed. The glow is due to the tiles being heated until they are white hot (see at the nose at upper right).

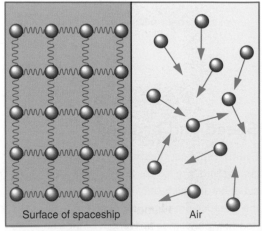

Surface of spaceship   Air

Vibrating particles generate thermal energy.

The friction, and the damage it can cause, can be reduced by:

● Smoothing off the surfaces. A smooth surface has less friction than a rough one.

● Adding a substance that keeps the surfaces slightly apart. This kind of substance is called a **lubricant**. Good examples are grease or oil. (See **Science** Book 1 page 183.)

Air resistance is a kind of friction

Air resistance (sometimes called **drag**) is a kind of friction between a moving object and the air. This kind of drag acts on you as you cycle along the road. The amount of drag can be reduced by making the object more **streamlined**. Streamlining will allow an object to travel faster through the air.

These motorbikes would meet a lot of air resistance.

This motorbike is streamlined to reduce wind resistance. The same amount of force will make this one go faster than the ones in the first photograph.

Streamlining works in other situations too

The streamlined shape that helps to reduce air resistance also helps in movement through water. The evolution of living organisms that live in water has provided many excellent examples of streamlining. Some of these are so effective that humans have copied them.

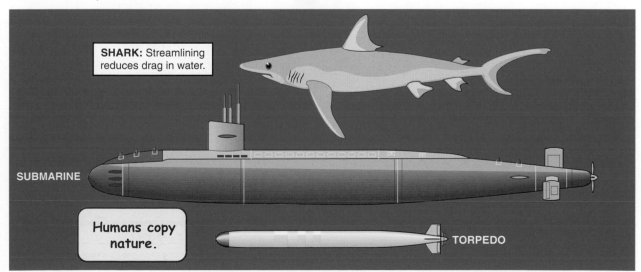

SHARK: Streamlining reduces drag in water.

SUBMARINE

Humans copy nature.

TORPEDO

Air resistance and thermal energy

When an object moves through the air, it will make the particles of the air move about. This can be very serious. The space shuttle, for example, generates an enormous amount of thermal energy when it re-enters the Earth's atmosphere. Some of this thermal energy is transferred back to the spacecraft which makes it glow 'white hot'. The shuttle would be severely damaged by this massive amount of thermal energy if it did not have protection from the special tiles that cover it. This heating effect, together with damage to the tile covering (that happened on take-off), caused the disastrous break-up of the space shuttle Columbia in 2003.

Measuring friction

Because friction is a force, it too can be measured using a forcemeter. The way that this is done is shown in the diagram. Measurements of friction between different kinds of surface must be done as a **fair test**.

Measuring friction

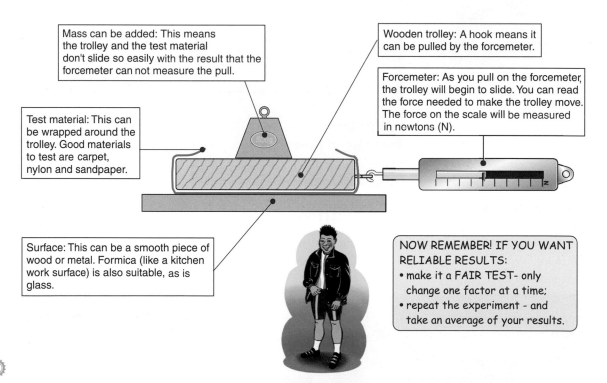

Mass can be added: This means the trolley and the test material don't slide so easily with the result that the forcemeter can not measure the pull.

Wooden trolley: A hook means it can be pulled by the forcemeter.

Forcemeter: As you pull on the forcemeter, the trolley will begin to slide. You can read the force needed to make the trolley move. The force on the scale will be measured in newtons (N).

Test material: This can be wrapped around the trolley. Good materials to test are carpet, nylon and sandpaper.

Surface: This can be a smooth piece of wood or metal. Formica (like a kitchen work surface) is also suitable, as is glass.

NOW REMEMBER! IF YOU WANT RELIABLE RESULTS:
• make it a FAIR TEST- only change one factor at a time;
• repeat the experiment - and take an average of your results.

Key words

Friction – a force that tries to stop two things sliding over one another.

Lubricant – a substance that reduces friction between two objects.

Air resistance – friction between the air and a moving object (sometimes called **drag**).

Exercise 27.1: Friction

1. Write down two friction forces that would slow down a bicycle.

2. This diagram shows two of the forces acting on a remote-controlled model car when it is moving.

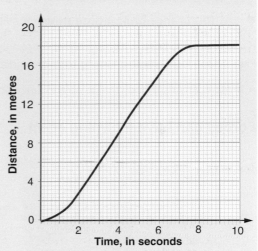

(a) When the motor was switched off, the car slowed down and then stopped. While the car was slowing down, which of these statements (i) – (iv) was true?

(i) Forward force and friction were both greater than zero.

(ii) Friction was zero and the forward force was zero.

(iii) The forward force was zero and the friction was greater than zero.

(iv) Friction was zero and the forward force was zero.

(b) Look at the distance time graph. What was the time when the car started to slow down?

3. Give two things that always happen when friction takes place.

4. What is air resistance?

Extension questions

5. Look at the diagram on page 388 showing how to measure friction. Imagine that you are a scientist studying friction between wood and other materials. Describe:

(a) What you would be changing.

(b) What you would be measuring.

(c) What you would need to keep constant.

6. A motorcyclist is travelling at 25 m/s (nearly 60 mph) on a dual carriageway when he notices that there has been an accident 70 metres in front of him. He takes 0.5 s to react before squeezing the brakes. The brakes take 3 s to stop the motorbike.

(a) Draw a speed-time graph from the time he notices the accident to the time the motorbike stops.

(b) What was his total stopping distance? (Hint: to find the stopping distance you will need to calculate the area under the speed-time graph.)

(c) What do you think happened?

Forces and rotation

- A force can cause an object to change its speed or direction of movement.

- This change could include making a stationary object move.

Forces can also have a **turning effect**; for example, a spanner can be used to turn a bolt, or a lever can be used to lift a load. These tools create a turning effect around a **pivot**. Spanners and levers can be used to increase turning effects.

A **lever** is any rigid body that is able to turn about a pivot.

Forces can have a turning effect

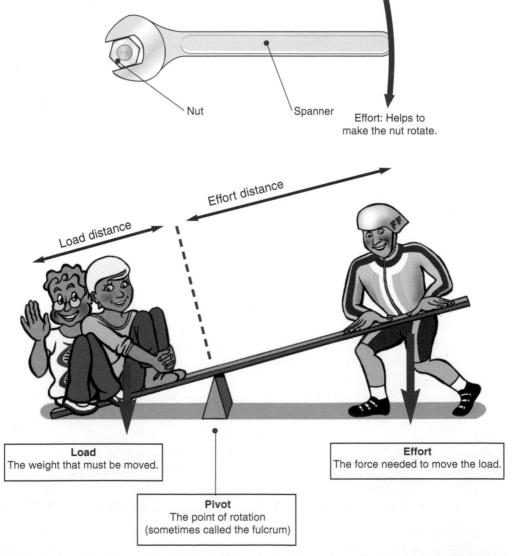

Nut

Spanner

Effort: Helps to make the nut rotate.

Effort distance

Load distance

Load
The weight that must be moved.

Effort
The force needed to move the load.

Pivot
The point of rotation
(sometimes called the fulcrum)

The strength of a turning effect is called a **moment**. The moment depends on the **amount of effort used** and on the **distance between the effort and the pivot**.

The size of the turning effect

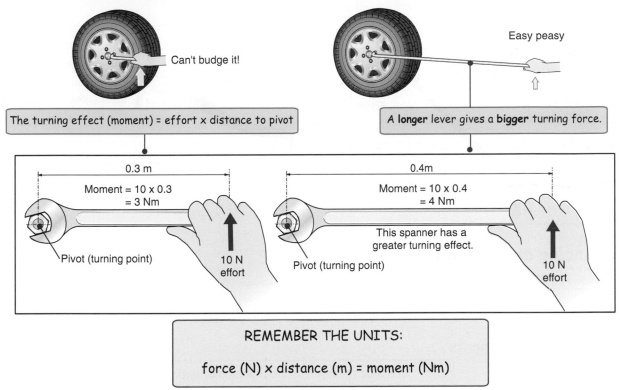

Can't budge it!

Easy peasy

The turning effect (moment) = effort x distance to pivot

A **longer** lever gives a **bigger** turning force.

0.3 m

Moment = 10 x 0.3
= 3 Nm

Pivot (turning point)

10 N
effort

0.4m

Moment = 10 x 0.4
= 4 Nm

This spanner has a
greater turning effect.

Pivot (turning point)

10 N
effort

REMEMBER THE UNITS:

force (N) x distance (m) = moment (Nm)

The units for moments (turning forces) are called **newton-metres (Nm)**.

Everyday levers

Humans use this lever effect in many ways. Some everyday levers are shown here:

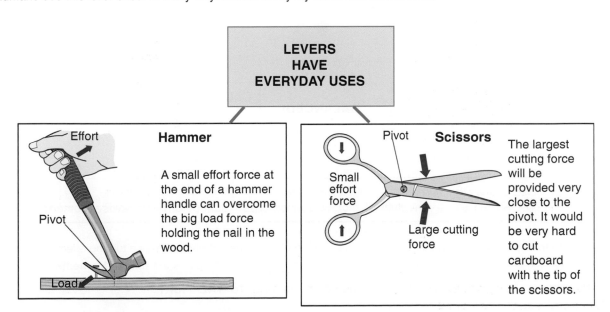

LEVERS
HAVE
EVERYDAY USES

Effort

Hammer

A small effort force at
the end of a hammer
handle can overcome
the big load force
holding the nail in the
wood.

Pivot

Load

Pivot

Scissors

Small
effort
force

Large cutting
force

The largest
cutting force
will be
provided very
close to the
pivot. It would
be very hard
to cut
cardboard
with the tip of
the scissors.

Here are some more everyday levers:

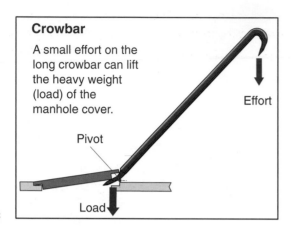

Crowbar

A small effort on the long crowbar can lift the heavy weight (load) of the manhole cover.

Effort

Pivot

Load

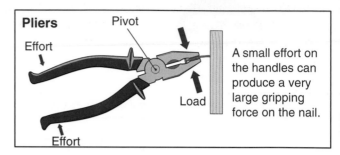

Pliers

Pivot

Effort

A small effort on the handles can produce a very large gripping force on the nail.

Load

Effort

Balancing and moments

Sometimes it is important that turning forces are **balanced**. For example, two people sitting on a see-saw might want to make it possible for both of them to move equally easily. This will only be possible if the moment in one direction is balanced by the moment in the other direction, as explained below:

Balancing and moments

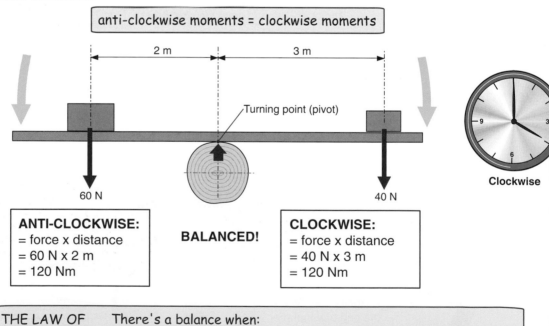

anti-clockwise moments = clockwise moments

2 m

3 m

Turning point (pivot)

60 N

40 N

Clockwise

ANTI-CLOCKWISE:
= force x distance
= 60 N x 2 m
= 120 Nm

BALANCED!

CLOCKWISE:
= force x distance
= 40 N x 3 m
= 120 Nm

THE LAW OF MOMENTS — There's a balance when:
the sum of clockwise moments = sum of anti-clockwise moments

You can see from this example that one weight has a turning effect to the left and one has a turning effect to the right. If the two turning effects are equal, the ruler will be balanced. This is an example of the **Law of Moments:**

moment turning to the left = moment turning to the right

Centre of gravity and stability

A ruler will balance without any additional weights if it is supported at its mid-point. This is because the weights of all the particles on one side of the pivot are balanced by the weights of all the particles on the other side of the pivot. It seems as if all of the weight of the ruler is acting through just one point. This point is called the **centre of gravity** (or the centre of mass).

Centre of gravity

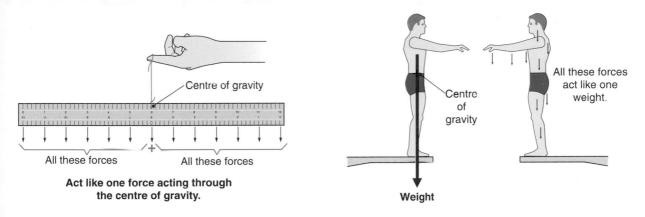

Centre of gravity

All these forces

All these forces

Act like one force acting through the centre of gravity.

Centre of gravity

Weight

All these forces act like one weight.

Some objects fall over very easily when they are pushed. This is because they are unstable. A stable object is much more difficult to topple. How stable an object is depends on how far we can tip it **before its centre of gravity is moved outside its base.**

Centre of gravity and stability

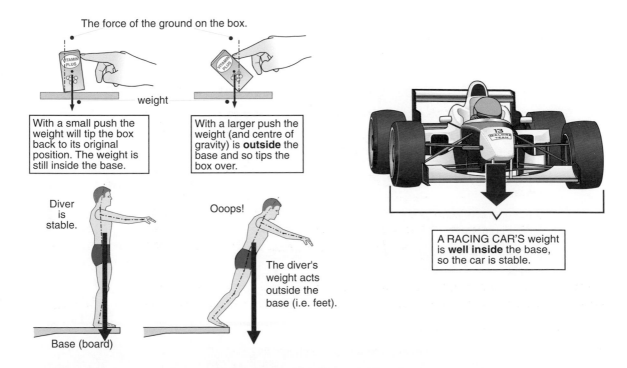

The force of the ground on the box.

weight

With a small push the weight will tip the box back to its original position. The weight is still inside the base.

With a larger push the weight (and centre of gravity) is **outside** the base and so tips the box over.

Diver is stable.

Ooops!

The diver's weight acts outside the base (i.e. feet).

Base (board)

A RACING CAR'S weight is **well inside** the base, so the car is stable.

Key words

Pivot – the point around which something turns.

Moment – the strength of a turning effect of a force – it equals the force x the distance to the pivot.

Law of moments – a situation where moments are balanced.

Centre of gravity – the point that the weight of an object seems to pass through.

Exercise 27.2: Forces and rotation

1. Look at this diagram:

    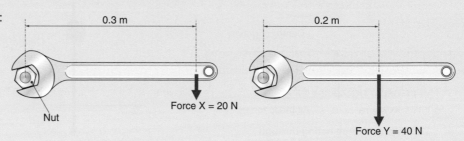

    (a) Which of the forces, X or Y, has the greater turning effect? Explain your answer.

    (b) How could you increase the turning effect of Y?

2. Make a drawing to explain the meaning of each of these words.

    (i)   Lever   (ii)   Load   (iii)   Moment
    (iv) Effort   (v)   Load distance (vi)   Effort distance

3. Write down the formula for calculating a moment. Show how the formula can be extended to describe the Law of Moments.

Extension questions

4. Look at the diagram of a skeleton (page 27). Show where the levers are in this diagram.

5. The diagram below shows a crane. The crane has a movable counter-balance.

    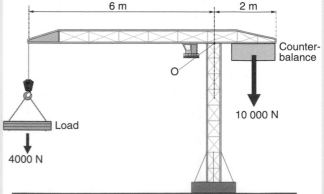

    (a) Why does the crane need a counterbalance?

    (b) Why must the counterbalance be movable?

    (c) What is the moment of the 4000 N force (about point O)?

    (d) If the crane is balanced when the 4000 N load is being lifted, what moment must the 10 000 N force have?

    (e) How far from O should the counterbalance be placed?

    (f) What is the maximum load (in N) the crane should lift?

Force and pressure

You will have heard the word pressure earlier in connection with the force exerted by gas particles on the walls of a container (see page 150). Pressure can also be used to describe the force exerted by a solid or by a liquid.

Pressure is a way of describing how concentrated a force is. Pressure therefore depends on two things:

- how **big** the force is; and
- how **large an area** the force is working on.

The diagram below shows a drawing pin being pushed into a noticeboard. Although the pushing force generated by the muscles in the thumb does not change, there are other pressures that exist:

- The pressure on the head of the drawing pin and on the tip of the thumb. This pressure is *low* because the force is spread out over a large area.
- The pressure on the tip of the pin and on the noticeboard. This pressure **is high.** This is because the force has been concentrated over a small area.

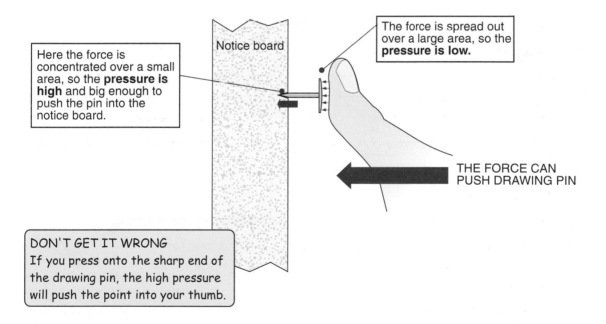

Here the force is concentrated over a small area, so the **pressure is high** and big enough to push the pin into the notice board.

The force is spread out over a large area, so the **pressure is low.**

Notice board

THE FORCE CAN PUSH DRAWING PIN

DON'T GET IT WRONG
If you press onto the sharp end of the drawing pin, the high pressure will push the point into your thumb.

If we use the same amount of force; the **force concentrated on a small area** gives a **higher pressure** than the **force spread out over a large area**, which gives a **lower pressure**.

Pressure in everyday situations

There are many occasions when an understanding of force, area and pressure can be useful. Some of these are shown below:

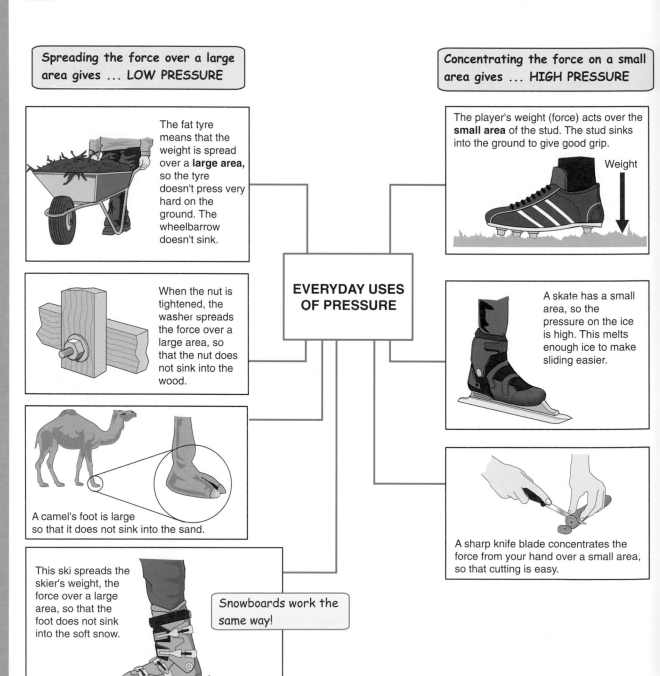

Spreading the force over a large area gives ... LOW PRESSURE

The fat tyre means that the weight is spread over a **large area,** so the tyre doesn't press very hard on the ground. The wheelbarrow doesn't sink.

When the nut is tightened, the washer spreads the force over a large area, so that the nut does not sink into the wood.

A camel's foot is large so that it does not sink into the sand.

This ski spreads the skier's weight, the force over a large area, so that the foot does not sink into the soft snow.

Snowboards work the same way!

EVERYDAY USES OF PRESSURE

Concentrating the force on a small area gives ... HIGH PRESSURE

The player's weight (force) acts over the **small area** of the stud. The stud sinks into the ground to give good grip.

Weight

A skate has a small area, so the pressure on the ice is high. This melts enough ice to make sliding easier.

A sharp knife blade concentrates the force from your hand over a small area, so that cutting is easy.

Calculating pressure

The pressure caused by a force is calculated using the formula:

$$\text{pressure} = \frac{\text{force}}{\text{area}}$$

Force is measured in newtons (N) and area is measured in square metres (m²); so the units for pressure will be newtons per square metre (N/m²). However, this unit is given the name **pascal (Pa)**, so when 1 newton acts on an area of 1 square metre, the pressure is 1 pascal or 1 Pa.

Here are some examples of calculating pressure:

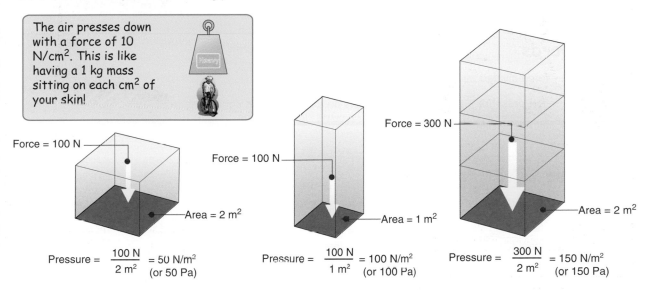

The air presses down with a force of 10 N/cm². This is like having a 1 kg mass sitting on each cm² of your skin!

Force = 100 N

Area = 2 m²

$$\text{Pressure} = \frac{100 \text{ N}}{2 \text{ m}^2} = 50 \text{ N/m}^2 \text{ (or 50 Pa)}$$

This block exerts a pressure of 50 Pa.

Force = 100 N

Area = 1 m²

$$\text{Pressure} = \frac{100 \text{ N}}{1 \text{ m}^2} = 100 \text{ N/m}^2 \text{ (or 100 Pa)}$$

The pressure is now 100 Pa because the same force is pressing on a

Force = 300 N

Area = 2 m²

$$\text{Pressure} = \frac{300 \text{ N}}{2 \text{ m}^2} = 150 \text{ N/m}^2 \text{ (or 150 Pa)}$$

The pressure here is 150 Pa. The force is three times bigger than just

Small areas can cause problems. Many calculations involve areas much less than 1m². Units are sometimes given as N/cm². **Watch out for this.**

An elephant weighs 60,000 N and each foot has an area of 0.25 m². How much pressure in total does it apply?

Calculating force or area

Sometimes you might need to calculate the force or the area when you are given a value for the pressure. You can rearrange the formula above to give these two formulae:

$$\text{force} = \text{pressure} \times \text{area} \quad \text{and} \quad \text{area} = \frac{\text{force}}{\text{pressure}}$$

You might find it easier to use a pressure triangle in calculations like this. One of these is shown here:

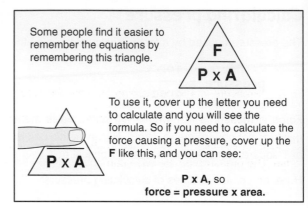

Some people find it easier to remember the equations by remembering this triangle.

To use it, cover up the letter you need to calculate and you will see the formula. So if you need to calculate the force causing a pressure, cover up the **F** like this, and you can see:

P x A, so
force = pressure x area.

Key words

Pressure – force divided by the area that the force is acting on.

Pascal – unit of pressure – when one newton acts on an area of one square metre.

Exercise 27.3: Pressure

1. What are the units for pressure? Write down a simple formula that will let you calculate a pressure.

2. A woman is wearing stiletto heels. If she stands on one heel, she puts a pressure of 1200 N/cm² on the ground and each heel has a surface area of 0.5 cm². What is her weight in newtons?

3. Use your ideas about pressure to explain why:

   (a) It is easier to walk on soft snow if you have snow shoes rather than ice skates.

   (b) It is easier to pick up food with the prongs of a fork than with the handle.

4. The block in this diagram weighs 18 000 N.

   (a) What is the area under the block?

   (b) What is the pressure under the block?

   (c) If the block is tipped onto its side, what will the new pressure be?

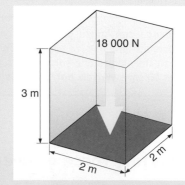

18 000 N

3 m

2 m

2 m

Extension question

5. (a) What pressure do you put onto the surface of the Earth? You can calculate this by firstly working out the area of your feet by standing on some squared graph paper. You then draw around the outline of your feet and count the number of centimetre squares you cover. Then work out your weight in newtons by measuring your mass (in kg) and multiplying by 10. You should now be able to calculate the pressure you exert in N/cm².

   (b) There are 10 000 cm² in 1 m². Calculate the pressure you exert in pascals.

Pressure in liquids: Hydraulics

Starting points

● Pressure is a force pushing on a certain area.

● Pressure is high when the force presses onto a small area and low when the force presses onto a large area.

If you pour a liquid into a container, such as a bottle or jug, the weight of the liquid pushes down on the container's base. The pressure on the base can be calculated from knowing the force (weight) and the area it is acting on:

$$\text{pressure} = \frac{\text{force}}{\text{area}}$$

There are three important points to remember about pressure in liquids:

● Pressure in a liquid increases with depth.

● Pressure at any point in a liquid acts equally in all directions.

● The shape of the container does not affect the pressure in a liquid.

These concepts are explained below:

Pressure

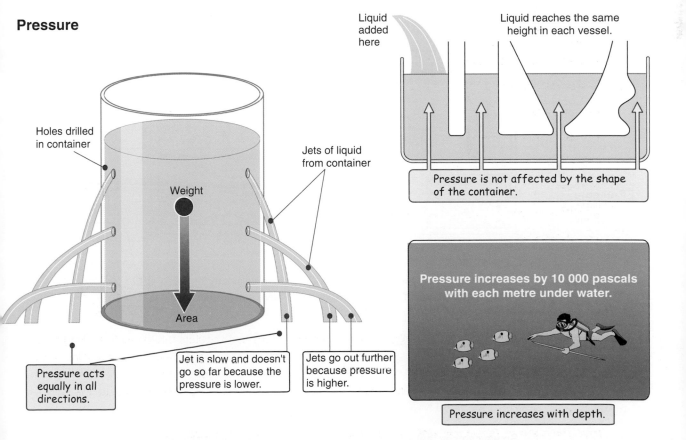

Liquid added here

Liquid reaches the same height in each vessel.

Holes drilled in container

Jets of liquid from container

Weight

Area

Pressure is not affected by the shape of the container.

Pressure acts equally in all directions.

Jet is slow and doesn't go so far because the pressure is lower.

Jets go out further because pressure is higher.

Pressure increases by 10 000 pascals with each metre under water.

Pressure increases with depth.

Hydraulics

Liquids are very difficult to compress (squeeze). This is because their particles are very close together and there is no space between them for them to move around. This means that if you apply a force to the surface of a liquid in a container, the force will be transmitted through the liquid, as this diagram explains:

Pressure is transmitted through a liquid

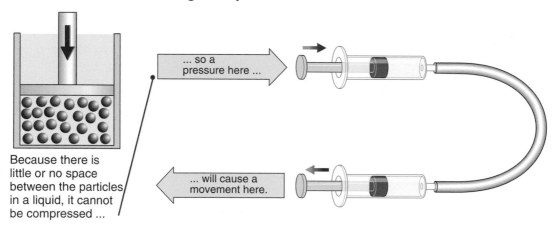

... so a pressure here ...

Because there is little or no space between the particles in a liquid, it cannot be compressed ...

... will cause a movement here.

Humans use some of these rules about pressure in liquids to build machines which use **hydraulic pressure**. The hydraulic pressure is used to move pistons inside cylinders. The engineers who design the machines can use pistons of different sizes to change forces in hydraulic systems, as explained below.

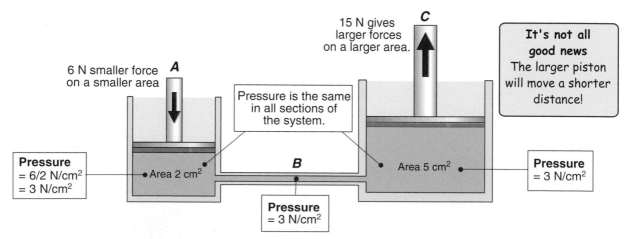

15 N gives larger forces on a larger area.

C

It's not all good news
The larger piston will move a shorter distance!

6 N smaller force on a smaller area   *A*

Pressure is the same in all sections of the system.

Pressure = 6/2 N/cm² = 3 N/cm²

Area 2 cm²

B

Area 5 cm²

Pressure = 3 N/cm²

Pressure = 3 N/cm²

If you know the pressure and area at *C*, you can calculate the force at *C*, by using the equation for pressure, that you have just learned:

At *C* we know that: P = 3 N/cm² and A = 5 cm²

If $P = \dfrac{F}{A}$

Then   F = P x A
              = 3 N/cm² x 5 cm²
              = 15 N

So we can say that a force of 6 N at *A* causes a force of 15 N at *C*.

Hydraulics and braking

Hydraulic forces are used to operate the braking systems of cars and motorbikes. A small piston is pressed with a small force at one end of a tube, either by the brake pedal of a car or the brake lever of a motorbike. The tube which has thick, strong walls, that won't bulge under pressure, is filled with a special hydraulic fluid. The pressure in the fluid is transmitted to a larger piston which forces brake pads onto the disc. The wheel is slowed down by the friction of the brake pads on the disc (see page 384).

Hydraulic braking system

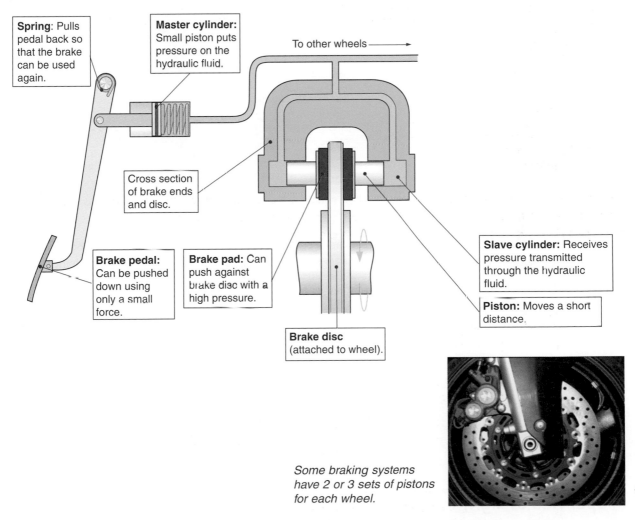

Spring: Pulls pedal back so that the brake can be used again.

Master cylinder: Small piston puts pressure on the hydraulic fluid.

To other wheels

Cross section of brake ends and disc.

Brake pedal: Can be pushed down using only a small force.

Brake pad: Can push against brake disc with a high pressure.

Slave cylinder: Receives pressure transmitted through the hydraulic fluid.

Piston: Moves a short distance.

Brake disc (attached to wheel).

Some braking systems have 2 or 3 sets of pistons for each wheel.

Key words

Hydraulic pressure – pressure transmitted through a liquid.

Chapter 28
Light and light sources

Light is a sort of energy that your eyes can detect. If there is no light, in other words, when it is completely dark, you cannot see at all. The light we need in order to see objects comes from **light sources** including the Sun, stars, light bulbs and burning objects. These objects or light sources are able to produce light energy, for example by burning, or by the conversion of electrical energy. Anything which can produce and give off its own light energy is called a **luminous source**.

Luminous sources give out light

Sun

Car headlamps

Some other objects look as though they are light sources because they are so bright. These objects look bright to us because they reflect light into our eyes from another light source. These **reflectors** include the Moon, mirrors and even this page.

These objects are not luminous even though we can see them

The Moon reflects light from the Sun.

THIS WRITING

You can read this because light is reflected off the paper.

Properties of light

Let us just for a moment check we know the very important properties of light:

- **Light is made of rays that always travel in straight lines**. This means that we can't see an object if there is anything in the way of these straight lines. When we try to draw the way light is travelling, we always use straight lines.

Light travels in straight lines

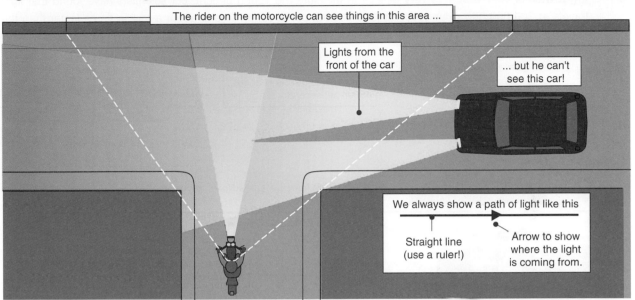

The rider on the motorcycle can see things in this area ...

Lights from the front of the car

... but he can't see this car!

We always show a path of light like this

Straight line (use a ruler!)

Arrow to show where the light is coming from.

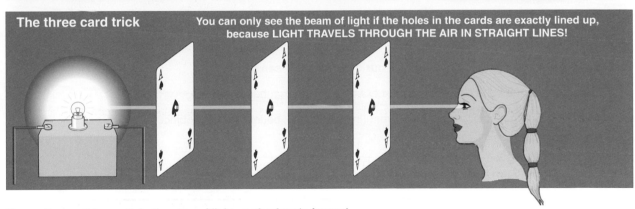

The three card trick   You can only see the beam of light if the holes in the cards are exactly lined up, because LIGHT TRAVELS THROUGH THE AIR IN STRAIGHT LINES!

● If something gets in the way of light, a **shadow** is formed.

Light rays can pass through a **transparent** material without being distorted.

Light rays cannot pass through an **opaque** material.

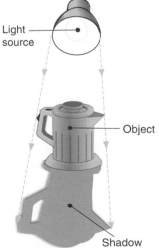

Light cannot get around an object, so it produces a **shadow.**

Light source

Object

Shadow

- **Light travels very fast**. It is very difficult to measure the speed of light, but scientists have found that light travels at 300 000 000 m per second (300 000 km per second). This is about a million times faster than the speed of an aeroplane.

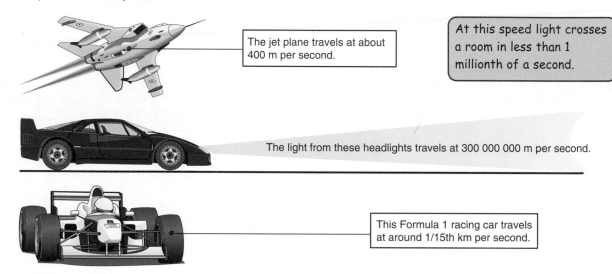

The jet plane travels at about 400 m per second.

At this speed light crosses a room in less than 1 millionth of a second.

The light from these headlights travels at 300 000 000 m per second.

This Formula 1 racing car travels at around 1/15th km per second.

Using our eyes – how we see things

Remember, we see things when **light enters our eyes**. The light can come:

- directly from the source to our eyes, for example light from a burning match;

- when light from a source is reflected from (in other words, bounces off) an object.

How we see things

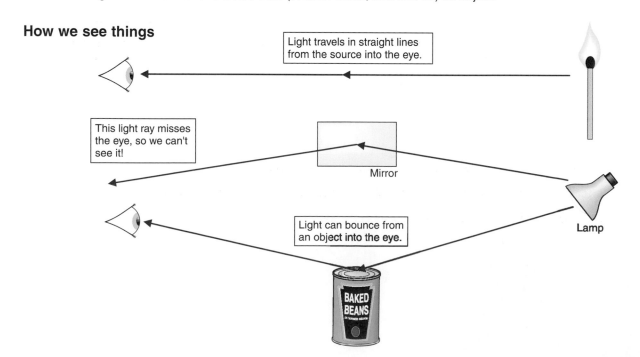

Light travels in straight lines from the source into the eye.

This light ray misses the eye, so we can't see it!

Mirror

Light can bounce from an object into the eye.

Lamp

BAKED BEANS

No matter where the light comes from, we just won't see an object unless:

● the light can reach the eye in a straight line from the object;

● the light rays can actually enter the eye.

The pinhole camera

A **pinhole camera** is a very simple device that can show how light travels in straight lines and can form an image on a screen. The image that is formed is *inverted* (upside down). This is how an image is formed on the back of a human eye. Our brain has learned that the image needs to be corrected, so that we actually see things the right way up.

Pinhole camera

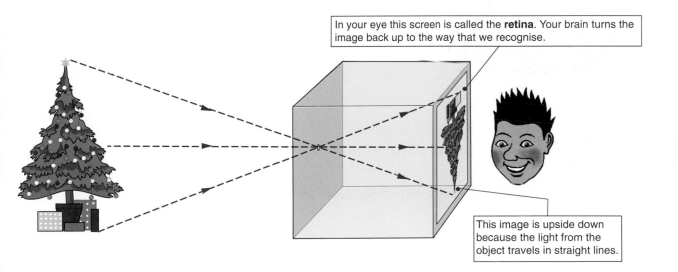

In your eye this screen is called the **retina**. Your brain turns the image back up to the way that we recognise.

This image is upside down because the light from the object travels in straight lines.

Key words

Luminous – a light source that produces and gives off its own light.

Reflector – an object that is bright because light from another source can bounce off it.

Shadow – an area formed when an object gets in the way of rays of light.

Exercise 28.1: Light

1. Complete this paragraph using the words from the list below:

    light   shadows   reflect   energy   light source   energy   straight lines

    You can't see an object unless there is some .... The objects you can see are either .... (give out light) or .... light into your eyes. Light is made up of .... and always travels in .... A .... is formed because light cannot pass through solid objects.

2. Which of these objects is a light source?

    Moon   Sun   a torch   burning candle
    the silver paper wrapper from a chocolate bar   the chrome radiator grille on a sports car

3. Draw an accurate diagram to show how a shadow forms behind a house on a sunny day. Use a ruler to draw the straight lines.

4. During a power cut, electric lights go off. Write down three different things you could use to provide you with light during a power cut.

Extension questions

5. Draw a diagram to explain why you can see your watch by moonlight. It isn't a luminous watch!

6. Use straight lines to explain why you can still see a cat in the shadow behind a house. This is definitely not a luminous cat!

7. Use the Internet or your library to find out how scientists are able to measure the speed of light.

Mirrors and the reflection of light

Remember

- Some objects are luminous – we can see them because they give out their own light.

- We can see other objects because they reflect the light that shines on them.

- Light rays travel in straight lines.

Mirrors reflect light

You should already know quite a lot about mirrors, but here is a little revision before we look at them in more detail. When light hits a shiny surface, the light rays bounce off the surface. We say that the light rays are **reflected**. If the reflection gives a perfect image, the surface is acting as a mirror.

We can use almost any shiny surface to act like a mirror. Dull or rough surfaces are no use as mirrors because they don't let the light bounce back without mixing up the light rays. There are many other surfaces that do reflect light but don't act as mirrors. Paper is a very good example of this kind of material.

Reflection from different surfaces

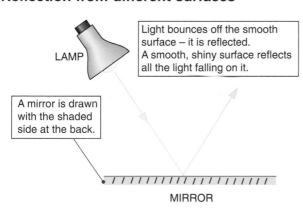

LAMP

Light bounces off the smooth surface – it is reflected.
A smooth, shiny surface reflects all the light falling on it.

A mirror is drawn with the shaded side at the back.

MIRROR

A smooth sea looks bright and the colour of the sky. The small waves act like moving mirrors and the Sun's reflections seem to sparkle. Bigger broken waves make the sea look darker and duller.

LAMP

Very small bumps mean the light rays are reflected in many different directions. This means we can see what's written on the paper from more than one direction.

We can see words on the paper from anywhere over here.

PAPER

LAMP

Light rays get so mixed up that we don't get a clear reflection from a very rough surface.

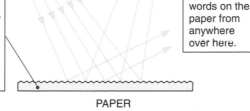

CLOTH

Looking in a mirror

A mirror that is flat is called a **plane mirror**. When you look into a plane mirror, you see that:

● the image you see is *the same size* as the object that is reflected;

● the image is the *right way up* (**upright**);

● the image seems to be *behind* the mirror; and

● the images are *back-to-front* (**laterally inverted**).

How do mirrors reflect light

We can study reflection using this apparatus:

Rules of reflection

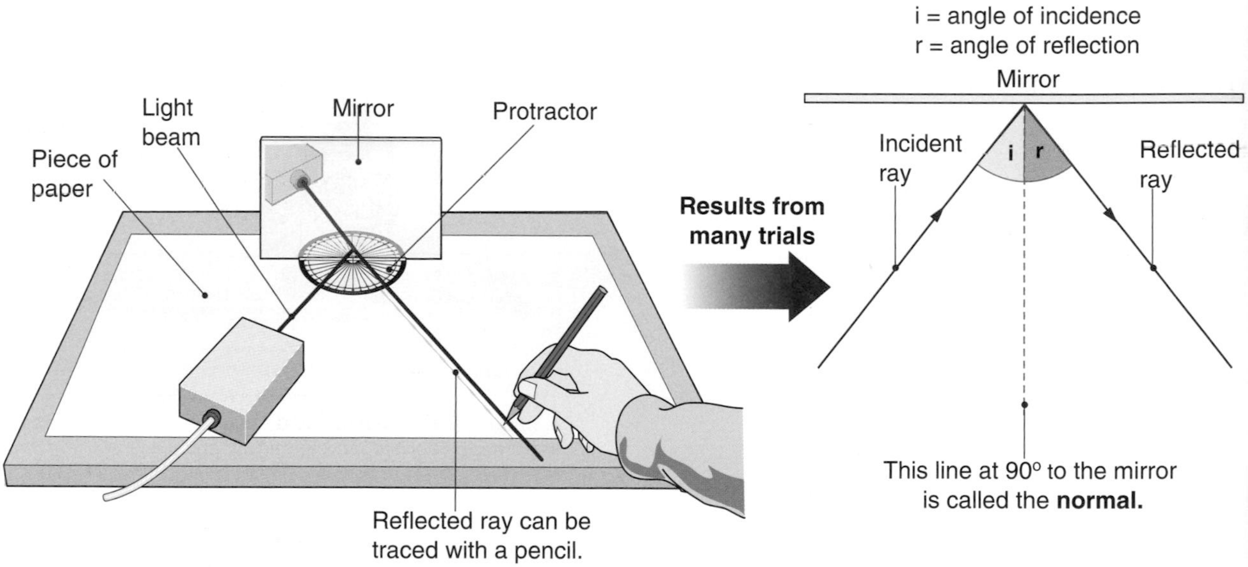

i = angle of incidence
r = angle of reflection

Light beam
Mirror
Protractor
Piece of paper

Incident ray
Reflected ray

Results from many trials

Mirror

This line at 90° to the mirror is called the **normal.**

Reflected ray can be traced with a pencil.

> angle of incidence (i) = angle of reflection (r)

The rays of light that hit the mirror from the ray box are called **incident rays**. These rays hit the mirror at an angle called the **angle of incidence**. If we trace the **reflected rays** of light from a plane mirror, we can measure the **angle of reflection**. No matter where we move the ray box to, the angle of reflection and the angle of incidence are always the same, so remember:

angle of incidence = angle of reflection

Virtual images

When you look at an image in a mirror, the image seems to be the same distance behind the mirror as the object is in front of it. This image is called a virtual image because, even though it appears to be behind the mirror, there is really nothing there! The formation of a virtual image can be explained by drawing a ray diagram, as shown:

Forming a virtual image

Tricks of a magician's trade

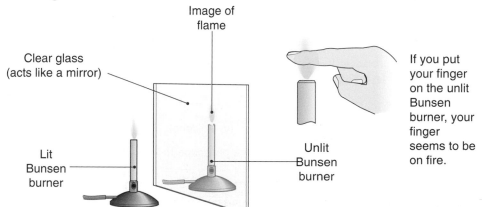

Using a periscope

The direction of light rays can be changed more than once by using more than one mirror. A periscope uses two mirrors to let you see round or over an object. Periscopes were first used by soldiers in the First World War. They let the soldiers see out of their trenches without taking the risk of being shot. They also let the commander of a submarine see what is going on up on the surface of the water, or allow the driver of a school bus to see what's going on upstairs.

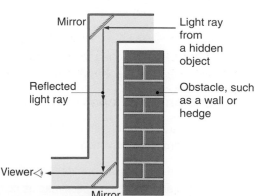

Seeing around awkward corners: Optical fibres

Optical fibres are made from materials which let light pass along them. They work because light is reflected inside them until it reaches the other end. Optical fibres have many uses:

Reflection in an optical fibre

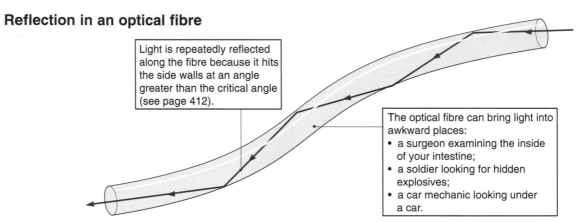

Light is repeatedly reflected along the fibre because it hits the side walls at an angle greater than the critical angle (see page 412).

The optical fibre can bring light into awkward places:
- a surgeon examining the inside of your intestine;
- a soldier looking for hidden explosives;
- a car mechanic looking under a car.

Key words

Angle of incidence – the angle between the normal and the incident ray.

Angle of reflection – the angle between the normal and the reflected ray.

Reflection – the bouncing of light from a surface.

Plane mirror – a reflecting surface that is flat.

Virtual image – an image that appears to be behind a mirror.

Exercise 28.2: Reflection

1. What does each of these words mean?

   (i) image   (ii) virtual   (iii) inverted   (iv) plane   (v) incidence

2. Draw a diagram to show how a shopkeeper could use a periscope to keep watch on the goods in another aisle.

3. (a) Look at this clock. It is viewed in a mirror. What time is it?

   (b) Write out the same time as it would appear on a *digital* watch viewed in a mirror.

4. Write your name and address (include the postcode) on a piece of paper so that it will be the right way round when viewed in a mirror.

Extension questions

5. Make a list of five reflecting surfaces in your home. Choose one surface that is normally transparent but can sometimes be reflecting (think carefully).

6. Use the Internet or your library to find out how optical cables are used in communications. Try to find out the advantages of using optical cables compared with copper cables.

Refraction of light

Refraction occurs whenever light passes from one substance to another. It happens because of the different speeds at which light is able to pass through different substances. Light passes easily through gases, such as the air, but travels more slowly through materials, such as glass, perspex or water. It is rather like a car moving at different speeds on different surfaces. The process of refraction is explained below:

Light and refraction

Refraction is like the movement of a racing car from tarmac through gravel back to tarmac.

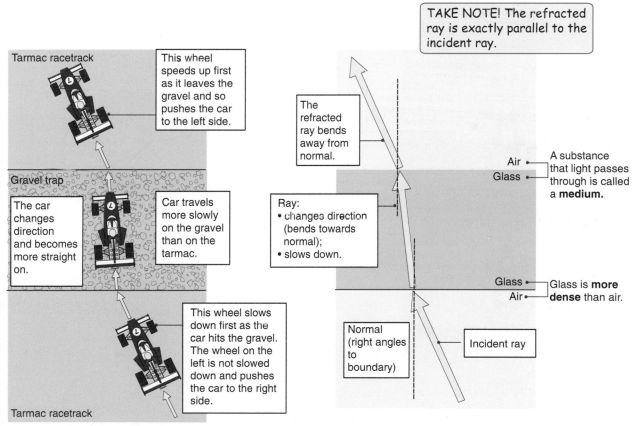

Tarmac racetrack

This wheel speeds up first as it leaves the gravel and so pushes the car to the left side.

Gravel trap

The car changes direction and becomes more straight on.

Car travels more slowly on the gravel than on the tarmac.

This wheel slows down first as the car hits the gravel. The wheel on the left is not slowed down and pushes the car to the right side.

Tarmac racetrack

TAKE NOTE! The refracted ray is exactly parallel to the incident ray.

The refracted ray bends away from normal.

Ray:
• changes direction (bends towards normal);
• slows down.

Air
Glass

A substance that light passes through is called a **medium.**

Glass
Air

Glass is **more dense** than air.

Normal (right angles to boundary)

Incident ray

There are two important rules to remember:

● Light rays passing from a **less** dense medium to a **more** dense medium always **bend towards the normal.** The normal is at right angles to the boundary between the two media.

● Light rays passing from a **more** dense to a **less** dense medium always **bend away from the normal.**

Straight on

If both wheels of a racing car hit a sand trap at exactly the same time, they slow down together. The car then continues to go through the sand trap without turning, but it now travels more slowly than it did on the tarmac. Light rays do exactly the same if they pass from one medium to another at right angles.

Light can travel straight through a boundary

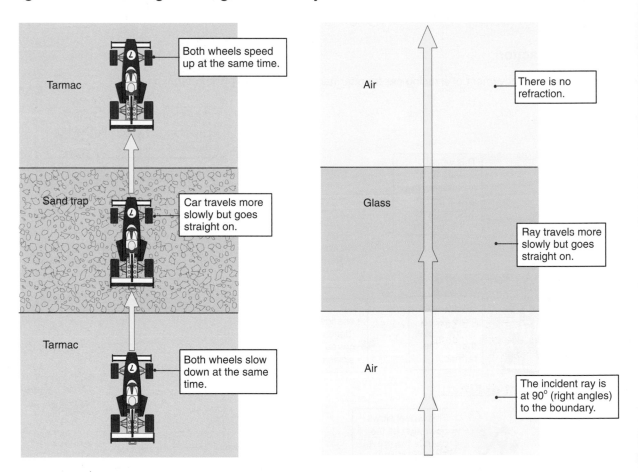

Reflection and refraction

Some reflection occurs during the refraction process! When light reaches a boundary between the more dense and the less dense material, some of the light is reflected back into the denser medium. The amount that is reflected compared with the amount that passes through depends on the angle at which the light meets the boundary. The larger this angle, the more light is reflected and the less light passes through. Eventually an angle is reached where *all* the light is reflected back into the denser medium. This is called the **critical angle** and is important in understanding how optical fibres work (see page 410).

Critical angle and total internal reflection

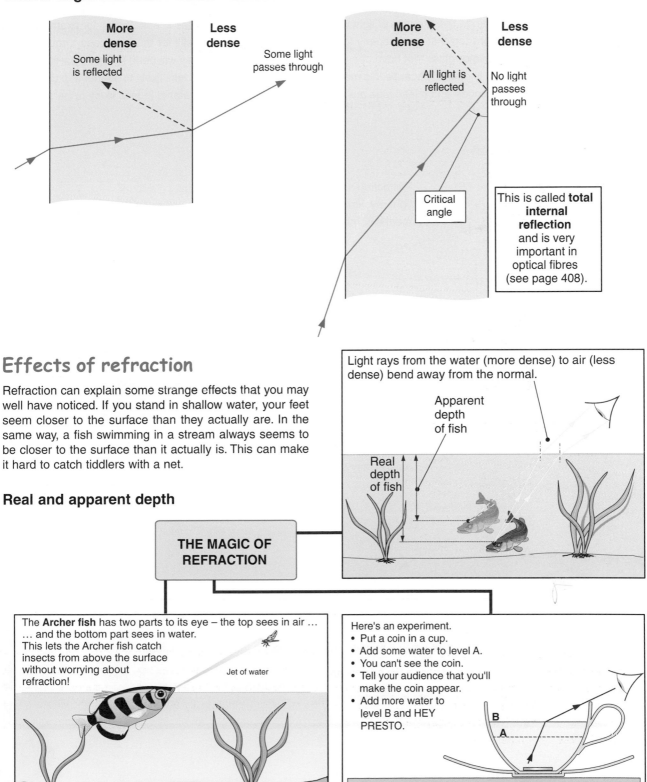

More dense | **Less dense**

Some light is reflected

Some light passes through

More dense | **Less dense**

All light is reflected

No light passes through

Critical angle

This is called **total internal reflection** and is very important in optical fibres (see page 408).

Effects of refraction

Refraction can explain some strange effects that you may well have noticed. If you stand in shallow water, your feet seem closer to the surface than they actually are. In the same way, a fish swimming in a stream always seems to be closer to the surface than it actually is. This can make it hard to catch tiddlers with a net.

Real and apparent depth

THE MAGIC OF REFRACTION

Light rays from the water (more dense) to air (less dense) bend away from the normal.

Apparent depth of fish

Real depth of fish

The **Archer fish** has two parts to its eye – the top sees in air ...
... and the bottom part sees in water.
This lets the Archer fish catch insects from above the surface without worrying about refraction!

Jet of water

Here's an experiment.
• Put a coin in a cup.
• Add some water to level A.
• You can't see the coin.
• Tell your audience that you'll make the coin appear.
• Add more water to level B and HEY PRESTO.

B

A

Using refraction

We sometimes need to change the direction of light without using mirrors. The lenses in spectacles, for example, must change the direction of light (so that it is properly focused in the eye) but must still let the light pass through them. **Lenses** are pieces of plastic or glass that have been ground into shape so that they will bend light in a particular way. Spectacle lenses are usually plastic, because this material is lighter than glass and less likely to shatter in a dangerous way. The lenses in microscopes and telescopes are usually glass because this material is less likely to be scratched than plastic.

Lenses and refraction

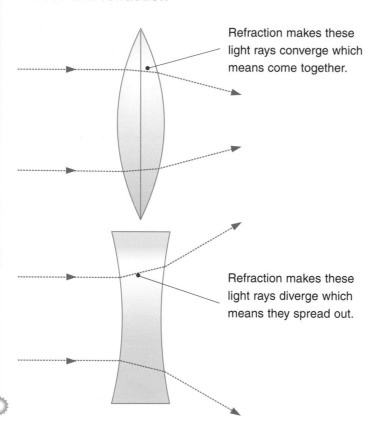

Refraction makes these light rays converge which means come together.

Refraction makes these light rays diverge which means they spread out.

Which lenses you need depends on what's wrong with your eyes.

Key words

Refraction – the bending of light when it moves from one medium to another of different density.

Angle of refraction – angle between the normal and the refracted ray.

Lens – an object that can bend light in a particular way.

Exercise 28.3: Refraction

1. Complete this paragraph, using words from the list below:

   less   away from   medium   refracted

   Light is .... when it reaches a boundary between two different substances. Each of the substances that light can pass through is called a .... Light passing from a more dense to a .... dense medium always bends .... the normal.

2. Use your knowledge of refraction to explain:

   (a) Why it is difficult to pick up a coin from the bottom of a swimming pool.

   (b) Why it is hard to spear a fish if you are standing on the seashore.

   Use diagrams to help your explanation.

Extension question

3. Use a textbook or the Internet to find a diagram of a microscope. Make a simple copy of the diagram to show how lenses direct a beam of light through the instrument.

Light and colour

Seeing the point

● Light travels, as light rays, in straight lines.

● We can see objects because light from the objects enters our eyes.

Sound waves can only travel through a definite medium (see page 427) but there is a group of waves that can travel through a vacuum. These are called **electromagnetic waves** and are produced when molecules, atoms or electrons vibrate when they absorb energy. There are different types of electromagnetic wave. The type of wave depends on the frequency and on the wavelength. All types of wave travel at the same speed, about 300 000 km per second. This is usually called the **speed of light** because light is a type of electromagnetic wave. The complete range of electromagnetic waves is called the **electromagnetic spectrum**, and an example is shown here.

Electromagnetic spectrum

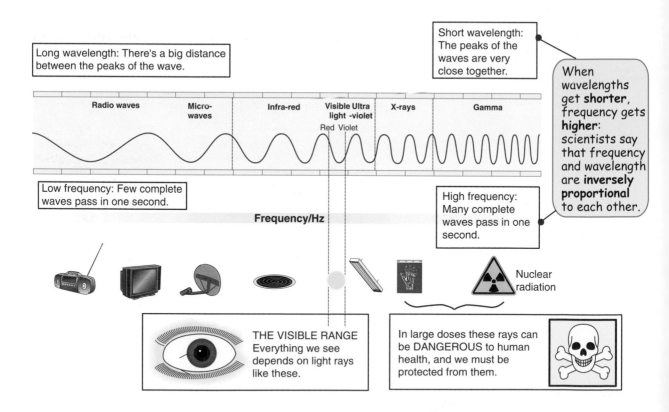

The light that we see is only a small part of the entire electromagnetic spectrum. It is called **visible light** because it can be detected by our eyes (see page 405). It is also called **white light** because it looks white to our eyes. White light is made up of several different colours. This range of colours is called the **visible spectrum**. We see the visible spectrum when white light from the Sun hits drops of water. The colours are separated out to produce a rainbow.

Colours of the rainbow

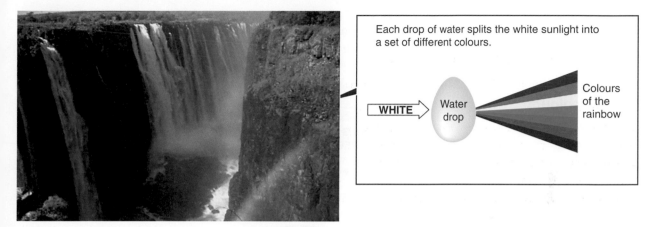

Each drop of water splits the white sunlight into a set of different colours.

Newton's prism

Sir Isaac Newton created a spectrum in his laboratory by using a triangular glass **prism**. The angle of the glass in a prism is ideal for splitting white light into its seven different colours:

Newton's prism

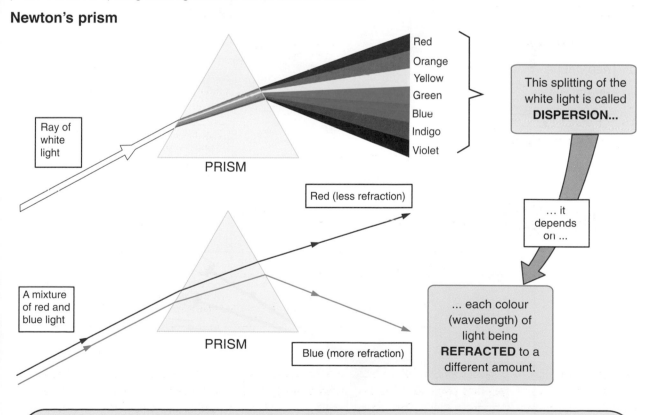

This splitting of the white light is called **DISPERSION...**

... it depends on ...

... each colour (wavelength) of light being **REFRACTED** to a different amount.

You can make up a rhyme to help you remember the seven colours of the rainbow:

Richard of York gave battle in vain

The eye and colour vision

Although light is split up into seven different colours by a prism, the eye actually only has three different types of sensor for colour. One type responds to red, one to blue and one to green. These are called the **primary colours**; if our eyes receive the three colours at the same time we see white light. This can be shown by shining three coloured lights onto a screen and where they overlap white is seen.

Primary colours

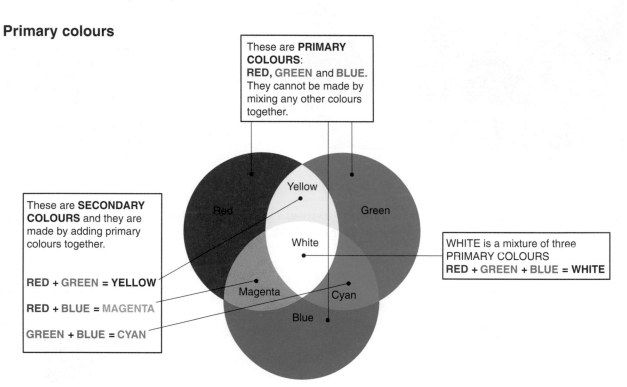

These are **PRIMARY COLOURS**:
RED, GREEN and **BLUE**.
They cannot be made by mixing any other colours together.

These are **SECONDARY COLOURS** and they are made by adding primary colours together.

RED + GREEN = YELLOW

RED + BLUE = MAGENTA

GREEN + BLUE = CYAN

WHITE is a mixture of three PRIMARY COLOURS
RED + GREEN + BLUE = WHITE

Red   Yellow   Green

White

Magenta   Cyan

Blue

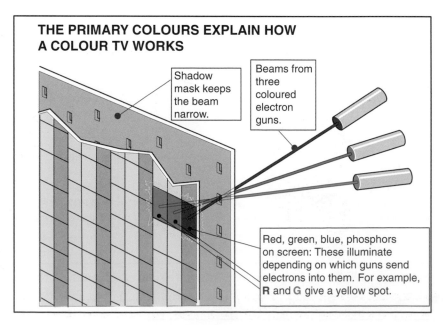

THE PRIMARY COLOURS EXPLAIN HOW A COLOUR TV WORKS

Shadow mask keeps the beam narrow.

Beams from three coloured electron guns.

Red, green, blue, phosphors on screen: These illuminate depending on which guns send electrons into them. For example, **R** and **G** give a yellow spot.

Colours can be combined using a spinning coloured disc.

Newton's disc

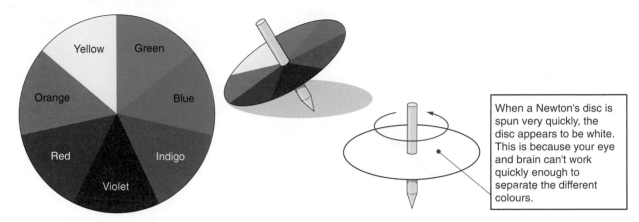

When a Newton's disc is spun very quickly, the disc appears to be white. This is because your eye and brain can't work quickly enough to separate the different colours.

Looking at coloured objects

Why do objects look coloured? They are coloured because the materials they are made of *absorb* some of the visible spectrum and *reflect* the rest. We only see the reflected light.

Reflection causes colour

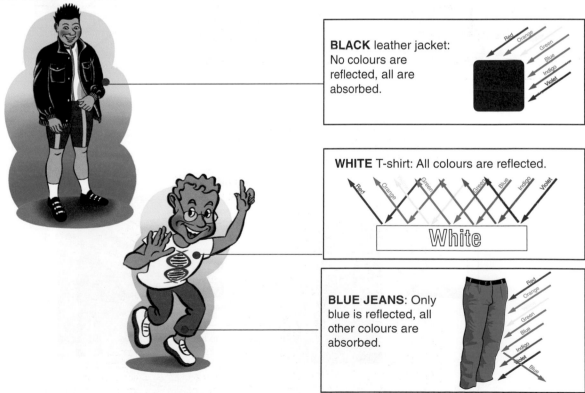

BLACK leather jacket: No colours are reflected, all are absorbed.

WHITE T-shirt: All colours are reflected.

White

BLUE JEANS: Only blue is reflected, all other colours are absorbed.

Chemicals that absorb some colours and reflect others are called **pigments**. An important pigment is chlorophyll. This is the green colour in plant chloroplasts (see page 68) and appears green because it *absorbs* red and blue light and *reflects* green light.

There are three important rules for understanding the colour of objects:

● **Coloured** objects reflect **some of the light** that shines on them. These objects are the colour of the reflected light.

● **White** objects reflect **all the light** that shines on them.

● **Black** objects reflect **none of the light** that shines on them; they **absorb** all the colours.

Coloured light and changing colours

Coloured objects only reflect some of the light that falls on them. They reflect the colour that they are, but only if the light falling on them included that colour. White light contains all the colours, so coloured objects will look the right colour in white light. If the light falling on an object doesn't include the light that the object reflects, the object will appear to be the wrong colour. This principle is described below:

Change of colour

| In white light | In red light | In green light |

White light

Red light

Green light

Boots: Red because they reflect **RED** from **WHITE LIGHT.**

Laces: Green because they reflect GREEN from **WHITE LIGHT.**

Boots: Red because they reflect **RED** from **RED LIGHT.**

Laces: Black because there is no GREEN to reflect from **RED LIGHT.**

Boots: Black because there is no **RED** to reflect from GREEN LIGHT.

Laces: GREEN because there is GREEN to reflect from GREEN LIGHT.

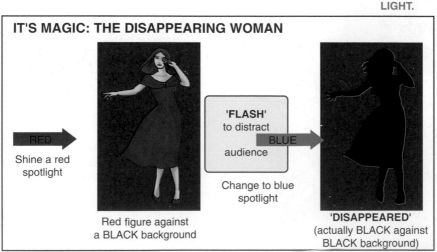

IT'S MAGIC: THE DISAPPEARING WOMAN

RED

Shine a red spotlight

'FLASH'
to distract
audience

BLUE

Change to blue spotlight

Red figure against a BLACK background

'DISAPPEARED'
(actually BLACK against BLACK background)

Some of you will have experienced this if you have been to a disco or to a party with coloured lights. Some clothes can look very strange under coloured lighting.

Coloured filters work by letting only some light through

Filters are transparent pieces of glass, plastic or celluloid. The colour of the filter is the same as the colour of the light that passes through it, but only if the light arriving at the filter contained this colour in the first place. White light contains all the colours. A filter *does not* add colour to white light, but t*akes colours away*. A blue filter looks blue because it absorbs all the colours except blue.

Colour filters absorb light

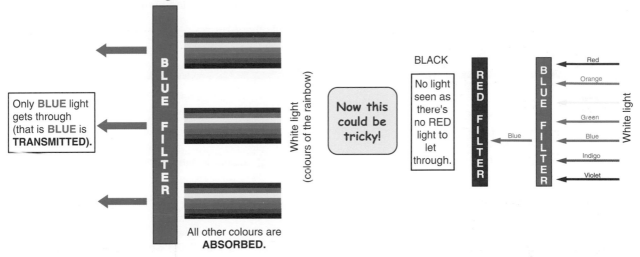

Only **BLUE** light gets through (that is **BLUE** is **TRANSMITTED**).

White light (colours of the rainbow)

All other colours are **ABSORBED.**

Now this could be tricky!

BLACK

No light seen as there's no RED light to let through.

Water acts like a filter, and absorbs most of the red and some of the yellow and green light passing through it. Because of this, deep water looks blue. The water acts like a blue filter.

Underwater

Colours as seen underwater

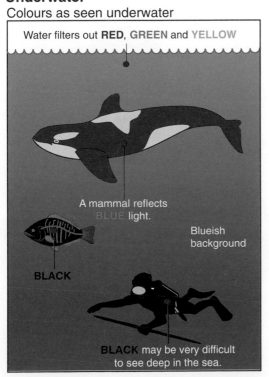

Water filters out **RED**, **GREEN** and **YELLOW**

A mammal reflects BLUE light.

Blueish background

BLACK

BLACK may be very difficult to see deep in the sea.

WHITE LIGHT

Actual colours

These can now reflect colours from white light.

Key words

Spectrum – a range of colours of light.

Prism – a glass triangle that can split white light into its seven different colours.

Electromagnetic spectrum – the complete range of electromagnetic waves.

Primary colours – three colours that combine to give all other colours seen by the human eye.

Pigment – a substance that absorbs some colours and reflects others.

Filter – a transparent object that only allows some colours to pass through it.

Exercise 28.4: Colour

1. Make up your own rhyme to help you remember the order of colours in the visible spectrum – make this different from the one on page 417.

2. Snooker is played on a green table with red, blue, brown, green, yellow, black and white balls. Explain why it would be very difficult to play snooker under a blue light.

3. A dancer wears a red jacket. What colour would it appear to the audience if she were lit by a:

   (a) red spotlight?   (b) green spotlight?   (c) magenta spotlight?

4. Why is it a good idea for scuba divers to have white markings on their equipment, and not to wear red wetsuits?

5. Misha has a pair of special glasses with coloured filters in place of normal lenses.

   (a) Misha closes her left eye and looks at a lamp. The lamp gives out white light but Misha sees it as green. Explain how this is possible.

   (b) Misha looks at a red lamp.

       (i) What colour will the lamp appear if she closes her right eye? Explain your answer.

       (ii) What colour will the lamp appear if she closes her left eye? Explain your answer.

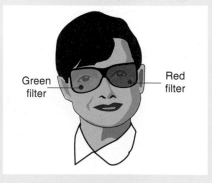

Green filter   Red filter

Chapter 29
Vibration and sound

Making sound

There are many different sounds but, as you know, they all have one thing in common. Sounds only happen when something **vibrates**. When something vibrates to make a sound, it moves backwards and forwards. Sometimes it is really easy to see a **vibration**, but at other times we can *hear* a sound without *seeing* a vibration. Even if we can't see a vibration, one *must* be happening if we hear a sound. We can sometimes demonstrate a vibration even if we can't see one.

Sound depends on vibrations

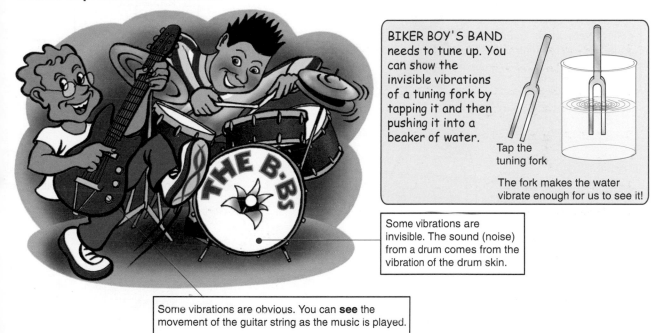

BIKER BOY'S BAND needs to tune up. You can show the invisible vibrations of a tuning fork by tapping it and then pushing it into a beaker of water.

Tap the tuning fork

The fork makes the water vibrate enough for us to see it!

Some vibrations are invisible. The sound (noise) from a drum comes from the vibration of the drum skin.

Some vibrations are obvious. You can **see** the movement of the guitar string as the music is played.

Many of the sounds we hear every day come from radios, minidisk players or television sets. These work by making a **loudspeaker** vibrate.

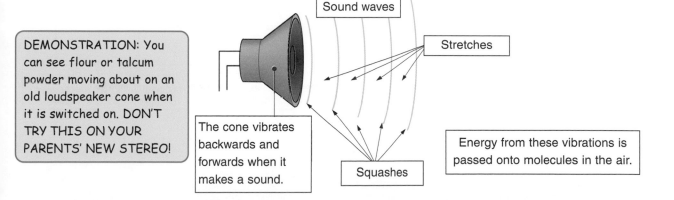

DEMONSTRATION: You can see flour or talcum powder moving about on an old loudspeaker cone when it is switched on. DON'T TRY THIS ON YOUR PARENTS' NEW STEREO!

Sound waves

Stretches

The cone vibrates backwards and forwards when it makes a sound.

Squashes

Energy from these vibrations is passed onto molecules in the air.

How sounds reach our ears

When the cone of a loudspeaker is vibrating, it makes the air next to it vibrate as well. The air is squashed and stretched to make **sound waves**. These sound waves travel through the air until they reach our ears. When the vibrations reach our ears, they make our **eardrums** vibrate. These tiny pieces of skin pass on their vibrations through a series of bones to a structure called the **cochlea**. This structure can change vibrations into electrical messages. These messages are then sent to the brain. When these messages reach the brain, we finally hear a sound.

The ear and hearing

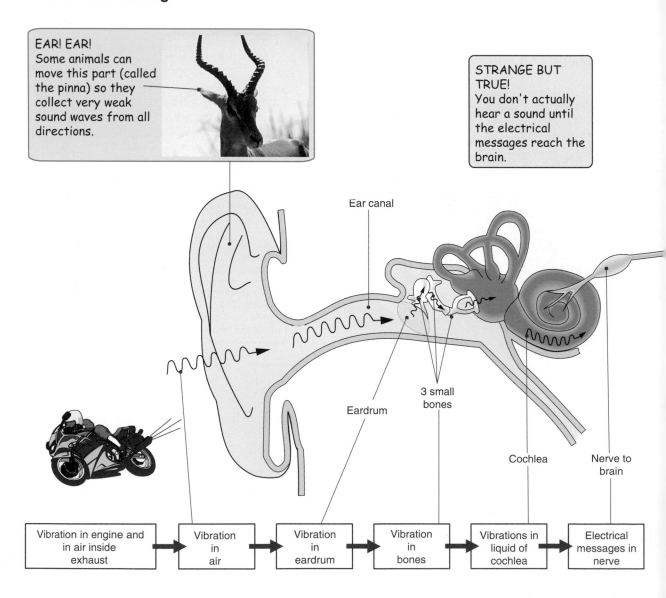

EAR! EAR!
Some animals can move this part (called the pinna) so they collect very weak sound waves from all directions.

STRANGE BUT TRUE!
You don't actually hear a sound until the electrical messages reach the brain.

Ear canal

3 small bones

Eardrum

Cochlea

Nerve to brain

| Vibration in engine and in air inside exhaust | Vibration in air | Vibration in eardrum | Vibration in bones | Vibrations in liquid of cochlea | Electrical messages in nerve |

Sound travels as waves

Sound energy travels because it is passed on from molecule to molecule in the air, between the source of sound and our ears. The molecules move backwards and forwards in a pattern we call a **sound wave**. The pattern looks as if some molecules are pushed together: these parts of the wave are called **compressions**; others are more spread out: these parts are **rarefactions**. Here is a diagram showing this pattern:

A sound wave involves movement of air particles

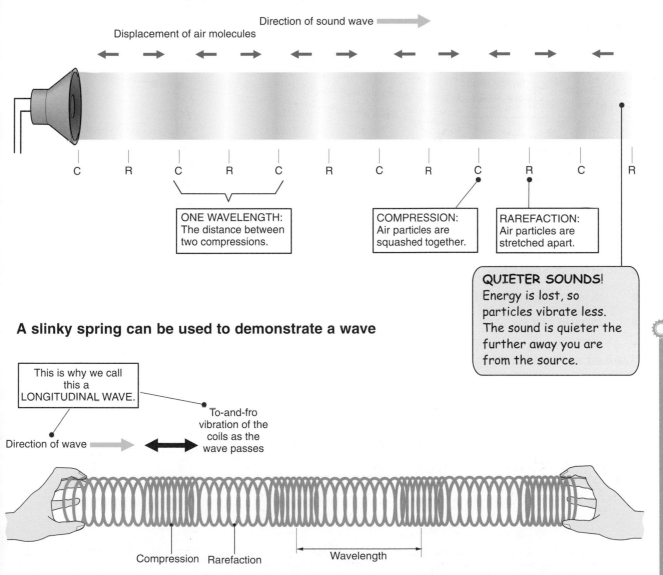

Direction of sound wave

Displacement of air molecules

C R C R C R C R C R C R

ONE WAVELENGTH:
The distance between two compressions.

COMPRESSION:
Air particles are squashed together.

RAREFACTION:
Air particles are stretched apart.

QUIETER SOUNDS!
Energy is lost, so particles vibrate less. The sound is quieter the further away you are from the source.

A slinky spring can be used to demonstrate a wave

This is why we call this a LONGITUDINAL WAVE.

To-and-fro vibration of the coils as the wave passes

Direction of wave

Compression Rarefaction

Wavelength

The vibrations that make up a sound wave travel along in the same direction as the wave is travelling. This is why we call it a **longitudinal wave**. All sound waves are longitudinal waves.

Sound and echoes

Sound waves can be reflected in the same way as light rays. Sound travels much more slowly than light, so it takes some time to travel through the air. If you make a sound such as a shout or a bang near a cliff or a big building, you may hear an **echo**. This is caused by the sound waves bouncing back to you.

Echoes

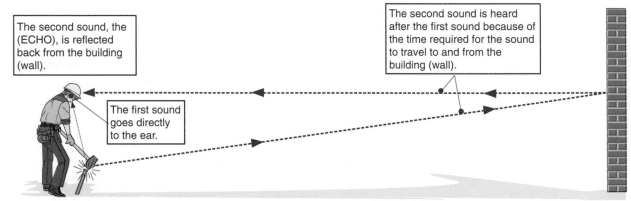

The second sound, the (ECHO), is reflected back from the building (wall).

The second sound is heard after the first sound because of the time required for the sound to travel to and from the building (wall).

The first sound goes directly to the ear.

Sound waves and echoes can be used to locate underwater objects. A ship on the surface sends out a sound wave and then picks up the echo from anything beneath the ship. This technique, shown below, is called **echo-sounding** or **sonar**. Echo sounding can be used:

- to locate sunken ships;

- to detect submarines;

- to search for shoals of fish;

- to check that the water is deep enough for a ship to move safely in shallow water.

Uses of echo-sounding

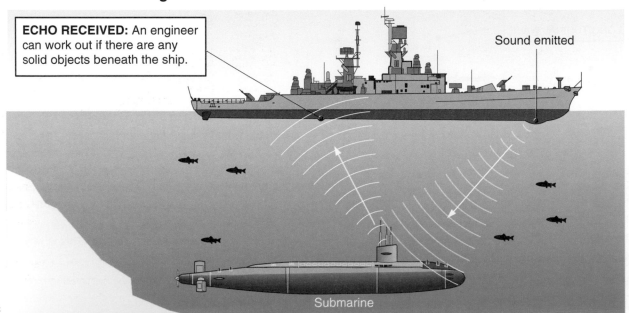

ECHO RECEIVED: An engineer can work out if there are any solid objects beneath the ship.

Sound emitted

Submarine

Sound needs a material to travel through

Sound waves must have something to pass through, or they can't travel from one place to another. Most of the sounds we hear travel through the air, but sound can also travel through other materials. These materials include liquids, such as water, and solids, such as brick, wood and glass.

Sounds are transmitted through solid, liquid and gas

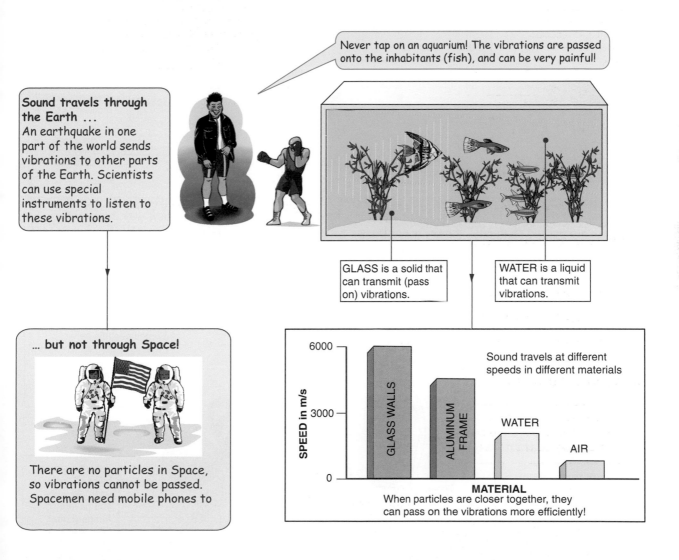

Never tap on an aquarium! The vibrations are passed onto the inhabitants (fish), and can be very painful!

Sound travels through the Earth ...
An earthquake in one part of the world sends vibrations to other parts of the Earth. Scientists can use special instruments to listen to these vibrations.

GLASS is a solid that can transmit (pass on) vibrations.

WATER is a liquid that can transmit vibrations.

... but not through Space!

There are no particles in Space, so vibrations cannot be passed. Spacemen need mobile phones to

Sound travels at different speeds in different materials

SPEED in m/s — GLASS WALLS — ALUMINUM FRAME — WATER — AIR

MATERIAL
When particles are closer together, they can pass on the vibrations more efficiently!

Sound waves travel much more efficiently through solids and liquids than through the air. You can check this by listening to a gentle tap on a laboratory bench – try it. You can hear it if your ear is pressed close to the bench but you may not hear it at all if you rely on it travelling through the air. Anything that the sound energy can travel through is called a **medium**.

Sound cannot travel through a **vacuum**. A vacuum is an empty space where there is no air, water or other molecules to be compressed and rarified. Light can travel through a vacuum because light rays do not need particles to pass on their energy.

The need for a medium can be shown using a vacuum bell:

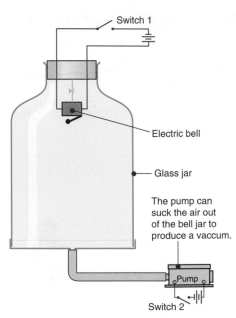

As air is drawn out, the ringing sound becomes quieter and quieter – but you can still see the clanger moving!

Switch 1

Electric bell

Glass jar

The pump can suck the air out of the bell jar to produce a vaccum.

Pump

Switch 2

Problems with hearing

Different people can hear different sounds. The **audible range** for a person tells us the upper and lower frequencies of sound that the person can detect (see page 425). The audible range depends on how well the vibrations in the eardrum are passed on through the tiny bones. As we get older, these bones wear out and we find it especially difficult to hear high-frequency (high-pitched – see page 432) sounds. The audible range is reduced as our ears get older!

The ears can suffer more serious damage than this general wear-and-tear and we can become deaf. This deafness can be **temporary** or **permanent,** depending on what causes it. These are some of the problems associated with hearing:

Causes of deafness

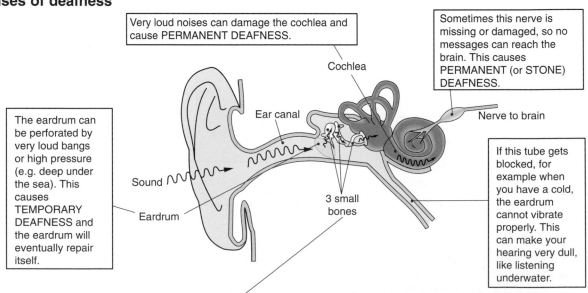

Very loud noises can damage the cochlea and cause PERMANENT DEAFNESS.

Sometimes this nerve is missing or damaged, so no messages can reach the brain. This causes PERMANENT (or STONE) DEAFNESS.

Cochlea

Nerve to brain

The eardrum can be perforated by very loud bangs or high pressure (e.g. deep under the sea). This causes TEMPORARY DEAFNESS and the eardrum will eventually repair itself.

Ear canal

Sound

Eardrum

3 small bones

If this tube gets blocked, for example when you have a cold, the eardrum cannot vibrate properly. This can make your hearing very dull, like listening underwater.

The three small bones can become worn, so that they cannot pass on all vibrations. This reduces the audible range. This can happen more quickly if you listen to too much loud music.

AUDIBLE RANGE:
A young person has a range from 20 Hz (20 cycles per second) to 20 000 Hz.
This range is reduced to about 30 - 16 000 Hz as you get older.

The speed of sound

Sound travels much more slowly than light. This makes it much easier to measure the speed of sound than the speed of light. These measurements can be made outdoors using echo timing, or indoors using time switches and an electronic timer.

Measuring the speed of sound

Outside

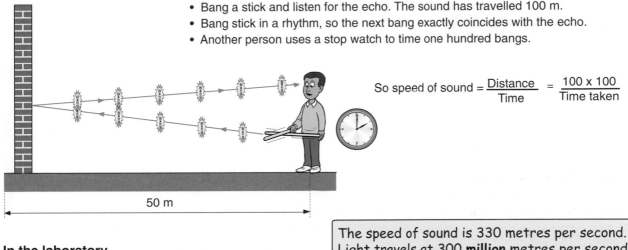

- Bang a stick and listen for the echo. The sound has travelled 100 m.
- Bang stick in a rhythm, so the next bang exactly coincides with the echo.
- Another person uses a stop watch to time one hundred bangs.

So speed of sound = $\dfrac{\text{Distance}}{\text{Time}}$ = $\dfrac{100 \times 100}{\text{Time taken}}$

50 m

In the laboratory

The speed of sound is 330 metres per second. Light travels at 300 **million** metres per second.

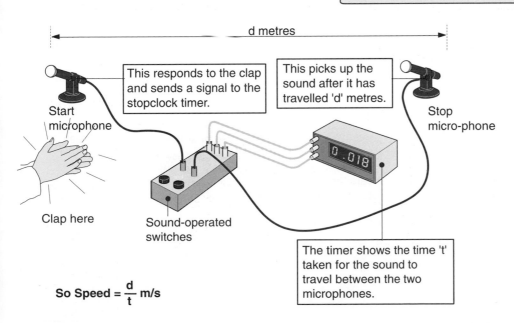

d metres

This responds to the clap and sends a signal to the stopclock timer.

This picks up the sound after it has travelled 'd' metres.

Start microphone

Stop micro-phone

Clap here

Sound-operated switches

0.018

The timer shows the time 't' taken for the sound to travel between the two microphones.

So Speed = $\dfrac{d}{t}$ m/s

Because light travels so much more quickly than sound, we can see an event happen before we hear it. A well-known example of this difference concerns thunder and lightning. During a thunderstorm you usually see the lightning before you hear the thunder. In fact, the light travels so quickly that you see the lightning almost as soon as it happens. The differences between the speed of sound and light means that you can work out how far away the thunderstorm actually is.

Light travels faster than sound

Thunder (sound) travels 1 km in 3 seconds

Lightning (light) travels 1 000 000 times faster (we see it instantly!)

Distance from storm = $\dfrac{\text{Time between lightning and thunder}}{3}$

For example, if you **hear** thunder 9 seconds **after** you **see** lightning, the storm is $^9/_3$ = 3 kilometres away.

Another example which illustrates the difference between the speeds of sound and light is when you see the smoke from an explosion before you hear the bang.

Key words

Vibration – a pattern of movement, up-and-down or side-to-side.

Sound wave – a pattern of vibrations carrying sound energy through the air.

Medium – the material that a sound wave travels through.

Vacuum – a space containing no air particles.

Eardrum – a membrane that vibrates when sound waves reach it.

Exercise 29.1: Sound

1. Complete these sentences.

    Sounds are made when something .... Vibrations then travel through the .... to our ears. Vibrations can also travel through .... (such as water) and .... (such as brick). Animals such as .... are very good at hearing sounds underwater.

2. Look at the diagram of the vacuum bell (page 428). Say what you would hear when switch 1 is closed. What would you hear when the pump is switched on? Give reasons for your answers.

3. (a) Jack throws a stone into a pond. He hears the plop sound and watches ripples spreading out across the surface of the pond. Which travels fastest – **sound, ripples on water** or **light**?

    (b) Which of these sentences about sound is correct?

    (i)   Sound cannot travel through air.

    (ii) Sound only travels through air.

    (iii) Sound cannot travel through a vacuum.

    (iv) Sound cannot travel through water.

    (v)   Sound travels well through space.

Extension questions

4. Design an experiment to find out who has the most sensitive hearing in your group.

    Say exactly what you would measure and explain how you would make certain that your experiment was a fair test.

5. Use a library book or the Internet to explain how a hearing-aid works.

Different sounds

Remember

- Sounds can only happen if an object vibrates.

- We can only hear sounds if the vibration reaches our ears.

- Sound travels as waves.

Not all sounds are the same. Some sounds are **louder** than others, and some sounds are **higher** (squeakier) than others. It would be useful to be able to look at the pattern of vibrations in a particular sound to try to understand why sounds are so different.

Looking at sound

A microphone is able to change the vibrations in the air into electrical signals. These signals can be seen as a wave pattern if the microphone is connected to an **oscilloscope**. This wave pattern is called a **trace**. The trace shows the changes in pressure of the air as it hits the microphone.

Looking at sound waves

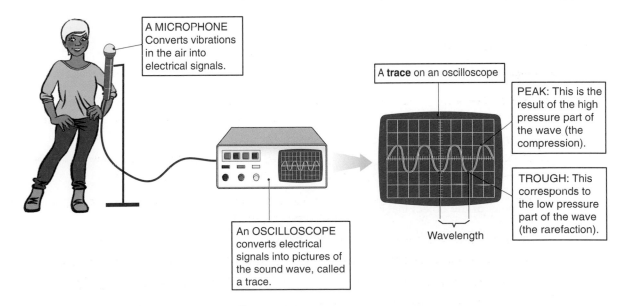

A MICROPHONE
Converts vibrations in the air into electrical signals.

An OSCILLOSCOPE converts electrical signals into pictures of the sound wave, called a trace.

A **trace** on an oscilloscope

PEAK: This is the result of the high pressure part of the wave (the compression).

TROUGH: This corresponds to the low pressure part of the wave (the rarefaction).

Wavelength

Amplitude and the loudness of sounds

All sounds are caused by vibrations. Sometimes these vibrations are too small to see (see page 423), but sometimes they can be seen quite easily. If you started to play a guitar, you would be able to see the string vibrate as it makes a sound. You could make the sound **louder** if the string were plucked so hard that the vibrations were very large. The sound would be **quieter** (softer) if the string were plucked gently and the vibrations were quite small.

Large vibrations in an object make bigger sound waves. A big sound wave has **more energy** than a small one and this is why its sounds louder. In other words, the harder you hit or pluck something, the more energy there will be in a vibration from this object, and the louder the sound will be.

Loudness will depend on energy

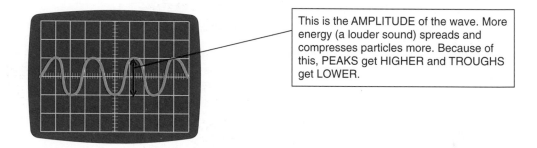

This is the AMPLITUDE of the wave. More energy (a louder sound) spreads and compresses particles more. Because of this, PEAKS get HIGHER and TROUGHS get LOWER.

- A **quiet** noise means there are **small vibrations**, a **small amplitude** and **very little energy**.

- A **loud** noise creates **big vibrations**, **big amplitude** and a **lot of energy**.

The size of the vibrations is called the **amplitude** of the wave. The more energy a wave has, the greater the amplitude.

Pitch is another difference between sounds

Remember that the **pitch** of a sound is how high or low the sound is. There are several things that affect the pitch of a sound:

- The **size of the object** that is vibrating:

  – **long** and **thick** gives a **low-pitched** sound; and

  – **short** and **thin** gives a **high-pitched** sound.

- The **tightness of the object** that is vibrating:

  – a **tight** string vibrates and makes a **high note**; and

  – a **loose** string vibrates and makes a **low note**.

The pitch of the sound depends on how many vibrations (how many compressions and rarefactions) are fitted into the same amount of time. Scientists can measure how many vibrations take place in a time as short as one second. This is called the **frequency** of the sound. If there is a high frequency, i.e. many vibrations per second, the sound will be very high (squeaky) and if there is a low frequency, i.e only a few vibrations per second, the sound will be very low (deep).

Pitch and frequency

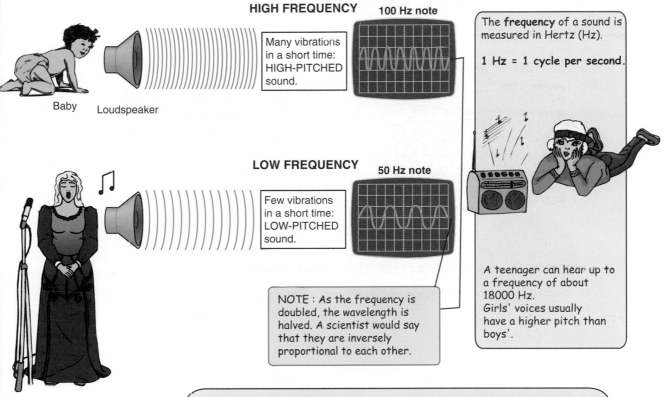

HIGH FREQUENCY 100 Hz note

Many vibrations in a short time: HIGH-PITCHED sound.

Baby — Loudspeaker

LOW FREQUENCY 50 Hz note

Few vibrations in a short time: LOW-PITCHED sound.

Opera singer

NOTE : As the frequency is doubled, the wavelength is halved. A scientist would say that they are inversely proportional to each other.

The **frequency** of a sound is measured in Hertz (Hz).

1 Hz = 1 cycle per second.

A teenager can hear up to a frequency of about 18000 Hz. Girls' voices usually have a higher pitch than boys'.

SQUEAKY McSQUEAK!
The squeaky voice of Donald Duck could be due to breathing helium! Helium gas is much less dense than air. If you have breathed helium, your voice travels more quickly (with a higher frequency). The sound travels normally as it passes through the air, but the higher frequencies are heard more than normal.
The result is a squeaky voice!

Key words

Pitch – how high or low a sound is – affected by the frequency of the sound.

Amplitude – the size of a vibration, determines how loud or soft a sound will be.

Frequency – the number of vibrations in a certain time determines the pitch of a sound.

Wavelength – the distance between two successive peaks of a wave.

Hertz – the units of frequency – number of cycles per second.

Exercise 29.2: Pitch and loudness

1. Complete the following paragraph, using the words in the list below.

   hertz   frequency   wavelength   pitch

   The distance between the tops of the waves on an oscilloscope trace is called the .... The number of these that pass per second is called the .... of the sound – it is measured in units called .... and directly affects the .... of a sound.

2. Imagine you were playing a guitar. How could you alter the instrument so that it made lower-pitched sounds?

3. Freddie can change the ring-tone on his mobile phone. These diagrams show the patterns made by four sound waves on an oscilloscope screen.

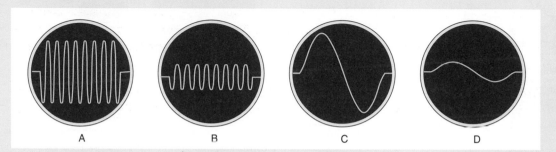

A   B   C   D

   Which trace matches each of these descriptions:

   (a)   A loud sound with a high pitch.

   (b)   A loud sound with a low pitch.

   (c)   A quiet sound with a high pitch.

   (d)   Two sounds with the same frequency.

   (e)   Two sounds with the same amplitude.

Extension questions

4. Describe a fair test you could carry out to check if the length of a string affects the pitch of the sound that is made when the string is plucked. Describe how you could use an oscilloscope to check your results.

5. Freddie wanted to check something about the loudness of sounds. He dropped a number of weights onto the floor, and used a sound-meter to find out the loudness of the sound. Here are the results of his experiment.

Number of weights	1	5	6	10	15	20	22
Loudness of sound (units on sound-meter)	3	14	18	29	43	59	65

(a) Plot a graph of his results.

(b) What is the pattern of his results?

(c) Use the graph to work out the loudness of dropping 12 weights.

(d) Draw the oscilloscope traces he would have seen if he had compared the effects of five weights and ten weights.

(e) Give two things he had to do if this were a fair test.

(f) Give one way in which he could have improved the experiment.

Life cannot continue without energy. Now that you have completed this section of your science course, you will have a good idea of where we obtain our energy from. You will be able to explain how one kind of energy is converted into another (often more useful) form and how humans need to be careful in the way in which we release energy from fuels and use it.

You will also be able to explain how forces are able to bring about movements and be able to describe the force of gravity. This section will also have described our Solar System and explained how planets and other bodies move within the Solar System.

We hope that you will be able to see how quite simple physical processes can help to explain everything that is happening in our environment. You should certainly see that these three sections of your course – Life and living processes, Materials and their properties and Physical processes are all closely linked to one another.

Now you are a scientist!

Index